1st Edition published April 2023

Copyright © 2023 Clemens Brenan

All rights reserved. No part of this book may be reproduced in any form without permission of the author except in the case of brief exerpts in critical reviews or articles.

Please see my website **destinyclemens.com** for more information on the Tarot, Numerology, Body Types and related matters.

Clemens may be contacted at destinyclemens@yahoo.com

Cover Design: Désirée K. Ickerodt

ISBN: 9798390112885

The Tarot de Marseille illustrating these pages is the venerable Nicholas Conver deck of 1760. One of the oldest Marseille decks in existence, it has served as a basis for all the modern Marseille decks, themselves the basis for the Rider Waite deck. The execution of the Conver deck has been praised by Marseille Tarot expert Phillippe Camoin as reflecting 'a sort of perfection.'

TAROT TREK

**THE TAROT, STAR TREK
& LIFE AFTER THE MATRIX**

CLEMENS BRENAN

TAROT TREK

CONTENTS

1	OVERVIEW	1
2	INTRODUCTION	5
3	TALES OF THE END OF THE MATRIX	9
4	THE TAROT DRAMATIZED	13
5	THE CONTEXTS	25
6	THE THEMES	55
7	CONCLUSION	373
	RESOURCES	379
	ACKNOWLEDGEMENTS	384

1
OVERVIEW

The 78 episodes of Star Trek The Original Series are shown here in episode order correlated with the 78 cards of the Tarot de Marseille. Each episode and card pairing is listed under its Life/Matrix theme shown in upper case.

	Page		
1. FANTASY LOVE The Man Trap 2 of Cups	56	**10. OUR STAR TREK FUTURE** The Corbomite Manoever Page of Coins	92
2. THE EMOTIONAL MATRIX Charlie X Page of Cups	60	**11. TRUTH AND JUSTICE** The Conscience of The King Justice	96
3. MENTAL POTENTIAL Where No Man Has Gone Before Ace of Swords	64	**12. ORDER-FOLLOWING** Balance of Terror 4 of Cups	100
4. EMOTIONAL CLEARING The Naked Time 5 of Cups	68	**13. SURRENDER** The Menagerie Pts I & II The Hanged Man	104
5. HIGHER SELF The Enemy Within Strength	72	**14. ACTIVE IMAGINATION** Shore Leave 3 of Swords	110
6. WHEELER DEALING Mudd's Women Knight of Coins	76	**15. INTELLECTUAL CRISIS** The Galileo Seven 9 of Swords	114
7. TRANSHUMANISM What Are Little Girls Made Of? 10 of Coins	80	**16. JUVENILE EGO** The Squire Of Gothos Page of Wands	118
8. GROUPTHINK Miri Page of Swords	84	**17. INITIATION** Arena The Magician	122
9. MIND CONTROL Dagger Of The Mind The Pope	88	**18. TIMELINES** Tomorrow Is Yesterday The Wheel of Fortune	126

19. LEADERSHIP
Court Martial
King of Wands — 130

20. ZOMBIE WORLD
The Return Of The Archons
4 of Wands — 134

21. DARK FLEET
Space Seed
Knight of Wands — 138

22. THIRD FORCE
A Taste Of Armageddon
Temperance — 142

23. HAPPINESS
This Side Of Paradise
3 of Cups — 146

24. ELIMINATION
The Devil In The Dark
Card 13 — 150

25. CONSCIOUS BEING
Errand Of Mercy
The World — 154

26. OTHER-DIMENSIONAL EXPERIENCE
The Alternative Factor
10 of Wands — 160

27. KINDNESS
The City On The Edge Of Forever
7 of Cups — 164

28. SUPERCONSCIOUSNESS
Operation Annihilate
5 of Swords — 168

29. EMOTIONAL LIFE AND CHOICE
Amok Time
The Lover — 172

30. RELIGION
Who Mourns For Adonais?
The Sun — 176

31. ARCHONIC INTELLIGENCE
The Changeling
4 of Swords — 180

32. TYRANNY
Mirror Mirror
7 of Wands — 184

33. MARK OF THE BEAST
The Apple
8 of Coins — 188

34. INTENTION
The Doomsday Machine
The Chariot — 192

35. MATERIAL DESIRE
Catspaw
Queen of Coins — 196

36. AUDACITY
I, Mudd
5 of Wands — 200

37. UNION IN LOVE
Metamorphosis
6 of Cups — 204

38. THE READINESS TO LOVE
Journey To Babel
Ace of Cups — 208

39. CRISIS AND QUESTIONING
The Deadly Years
The Hermit — 212

40. LOWER SELF
Obsession
6 of Swords — 216

41. WETIKO
Wolf In The Fold
9 of Cups — 220

42. AGRIBUSINESS
The Trouble With Tribbles
3 of Coins — 224

43. HUMAN TRAFFICKING
The Gamesters of Triskelion
6 of Wands — 228

44. NEW WORLD ORDER
A Piece Of The Action
7 of Coins — 232

45. LIFE OR DEATH
The Immunity Syndrome
9 of Wands — 236

46. PLANETARY INTERFERENCE
A Private Little War
The Tower — 240

47. BIG PHARMA
Return To Tomorrow
5 of Coins — 244

48. GOVERNMENT
Patterns Of Force
The Emperor — 248

49. SENSORY STIMULATION
By Any Other Name
6 of Coins — 252

50. FREEDOM
The Omega Glory
3 of Wands — 256

51. AI TAKEOVER
The Ultimate Computer
8 of Wands — 260

52. AWAKENING
Bread and Circuses
Judgement — 264

53. POSSIBILITY
Friday's Child
Ace of Coins — 268

54. TROUBLESHOOTING
Assignment Earth
Knight of Swords — 272

55. EVOLUTION
Spock's Brain
2 of Coins — 276

56. 5D CHESS
The Enterprise Incident
7 of Swords — 280

57. BENEVOLENCE
The Paradise Syndrome
King of Cups — 284

58. DEMONIC POSSESSION
And The Children Shall Lead
The Devil — 288

59. INNER CONNECTION
Is There In Truth No Beauty?
The High Priestess — 292

60. THE MATRIX DREAMWORLD
Spectre Of The Gun
The Moon — 296

61. ENERGY VAMPIRISM
The Day Of The Dove
Ace of Wands — 300

62. HEARTFELT LOYALTY
For The World Is Hollow ...
Queen of Cups — 304

63. PREPARING OR WAITING
The Tholian Web
2 of Wands — 308

64. THE PSYCHOPATHIC ELITE
Plato's Stepchildren
King of Swords — 312

65. FEMININE CREATIVITY
Wink Of An Eye
Queen of Wands — 316

66. VICTIM MENTALITY
The Empath
8 of Cups — 320

67. THE SACRED FEMININE
Elaan Of Troyius
The Empress — 324

68. MATRIX MADNESS
Whom Gods Destroy
The Fool — 328

69. HATRED AND WAR
Let That Be Your Last Battlefield
10 of Swords — 332

70. DEPOPULATION
The Mark Of Gideon
9 of Coins — 336

71. SECURITY
That Which Survives
4 of Coins — 340

72. RECEPTIVE MIND
The LIghts of Zetar
8 of Swords — 344

73. MATERIAL ATTACHMENT
Requiem For Methuselah
King of Coins — 348

74. NAÏVE IDEALISM
The Way To Eden
The Star — 352

75. THE SAVIOUR
The Cloud Minders
Knight of Cups — 356

76. IGNORANCE
The Savage Curtain
2 of Swords — 360

77. CLOSURE
All Our Yesterdays
10 of Cups — 364

78. INTEGRATED MIND
Turnabout Intruder
Queen of Swords — 368

2
INTRODUCTION

In an age of lies the truth gets told in fiction and fiction told as truth. On the one hand, truthful exposés of actual global conspiracy appear disguised as popular entertainment in fictional forms such as fantasy and science fiction[1]. On the other hand, fictional tales of fantasy and imagination spew forth daily from news agencies, pundits and mainsteam media. A pair of dark glasses as in the movie They Live are needed. Even now with the Matrix taken down and truth returning, a certain amount of lies and deception will continue. Don't throw away your discernment.

In the cause of discernment this book discusses the many deceptions and illusions enshrouding humanity beginning at last to recede into history. The Matrix generated and sustained them. Ironically, The Matrix movie, like They Live, was a prime source of truthful information disguised as fantasy science fiction. It was the actual Matrix we lived in that enabled the truth of dictatorship by a nefarious global elite to appear as nothing more than 'conspiracy theory'. This book should help with discerning truth from lies. Tarot Trek will be a three-part disclosure. One part is the Tarot de Marseille, the timeless set of cards used for divination and fortune telling. Another part is Star Trek The Original Series, a TV show made in the 1960s. The third part is a discussion of the end of the Matrix as revealed in the Tarot and Star Trek combined. The Matrix - the 18 AI systems listed on page 109 - officially ended in January 2023. The fact of this was revealed at the time by Kimberly Goguen[2] in her capacity as Ground Command and Earth Ambassador, having been given the job in 2016 by Earth's off-planet guardians, assigning her to take over from the corrupt Draco overlords Marduk, Enki and Enlil.

My analysis of the Matrix is based on an exact correlation pertaining between the Tarot cards and the Star Trek episodes. Synchronicity, providence,

[1] For many excellent analyses, see Esoteric Hollywood 1 & 2 by Jay Dyer, publ. 2016 & 2018
[2] United Network News, 30th January 2023, unitednetwork.tv.

fate, coincidence or accident? Who knows? I first noticed the correlation seven years ago. I saw that the number of episodes and cards was identical - 78. This then led me to ascertain whether a correlation existed in term of content, whether in fact the TV episodes correlated with the Tarot cards individually and thematically. Like working on a huge jigsaw puzzle I spread the cards out on the floor. On bits of paper I had written the one major theme of each episode. Slowly, speculatively, haphazardly, I started matching them up. The fit took many months of watching and rewatching every episode while thinking deeply about the cards and their meanings. The pattern began to reveal itself: the right number of Page episodes about youths, of Queen episodes about women, of Swords episodes about the mind, and so on. Every Star Trek episode turned out to mirror every Tarot card. Thus the Overview on pages 1 to 3. I was ecstatic! No gaps, no repetitions.

HOW DID IT HAPPEN?

I blame Divine Providence. Or some form of mirror-like encoding of the same pattern of life into greater and lesser fields of information. You could call it a working of fractal geometry. As in the reality of the Matrix and life itself, so in the Tarot simulation and so in the Star Trek simulation. In other words, as above, so below. The ABOVE, the big reality picture, is reflected in the BELOW, the cards and episodes. This synchronicity then, unites the 78-part Tarot with a 78-part TV series. I treat each as a single organic entity. Certainly, Star Trek had a consistent cast, production crew and format. Each instalment occupies the best part of an hour, an hour devoted to a key theme associated with a particular Tarot card. When we look at each episode and card together, we then get an aspect of Matrix life. The episodes go further in dramatizing key aspects of the demise of the Matrix, again as in real life. This allows me to discuss the takedown and how our life on Earth will change and improve as global restoration takes effect.

Star Trek was Gene Roddenberry's inspiration. Under his guidance, the colourful, elaborate symbolic series came together and went out over the airwaves between 1965 and 1969. Except that nobody knew it had anything to do with the demise of the Matrix or indeed the Tarot. And nobody would have cared anyway. Star Trek was and is loved primarily for its entertainment value and its willingness to handle sensitive and profound issues. But despite this, the show barely survived early cancellation. Ratings for the initial run were low and went from bad to worse. They encountered serious trouble halfway through the second season causing rumours that the Network intended to pull the plug at the end of the season. Two seasons comprising 54 episodes would have been the lot. Only an unprecedented act of faith from die hard fans saved the enterprise (sic). Thousands bombarded the Network with letters pleading for a reprieve, resulting in one more season of 24 episodes. That brought the total to 78, exactly equalling the Tarot deck. An early pilot called The Cage was not broadcast until many years later. The Cage was anyway absorbed into Episode No. 13 entitled The Menagerie. Broadcast in two parts but being a single story with a single title and theme, The Menagerie can be considered as one episode.

The rescue however was only one of many fated events bringing about the Tarot/Star Trek/Matrix alignment. The third season saw major changes of production crew including the loss of influential Script Editor Gene Coon and Production Manager Bob Justman. Added to this, funding was slashed and the show's time slot relegated to a backwater in the TV schedules. Most damaging of all was Gene Roddenberry himself quitting as Producer, though he stayed on in an executive position. Despite or because of these setbacks, the unfolding remainder of the Original Series continued to piece together a precise correlation with the Tarot. But the quality was likely to suffer and it did in the eyes of the critics and Star Trek's huge fan base then and now. But I contend that it didn't. There was cost-cutting to be sure, with episodes eventually made on a shoestring budget and ratings in terminal decline. But the vision remained intact. It was a vision of truth too uncomfortable for tell-lie-vision, itself a prime Matrix tool. A fourth projected series was cancelled. The end was nigh and all involved knew it. The final episode was a sad event for cast and crew. An atmosphere of mourning hung over the final wrap party after filming of Turnabout Intruder. But that episode, No. 78, signified the triumphant completion of Star Trek's massive and amazing trek through the Tarot. With the dramatization of the final card, the Queen of Swords in the person of the mentally troubled Janice Lester, all 78 cards had found their vivid, unforgettable representation in a single TV science fiction series. Without even knowing it, Roddenberry had got it all to work down to the last detail.

The rest is television history - a cult classic, a hit spawning a massive franchise. And now here with this book, we can see how the themes, insights and prophecies of Star Trek relate allegorically to both the Tarot and our actual journey through and beyond Matrix entrapment. The correlation covers all aspects of the human condition including our emergence out of the AI-powered Omega Matrix into a new enlightened world. We will be venturing forth like the crew of the Enterprise beyond the final frontier into the Age of Light. We will be exploring for the first time our full liberated range of human, cosmic and spiritual potential as 3D embodied souls.

3
TALES OF THE END OF THE MATRIX

The Original Series of Star Trek matches the Original Tarot, or at least the most historically original deck still in popular use, the Tarot de Marseille. Hundreds of newly drawn Tarot decks come onto the market each year as variations of the 1909 Rider-Waite deck, itself a variation of the original. Likewise hundreds of new Tarot books and websites appear each year, most being exclusively devoted to Tarot variations. How many new creations incarnate the Tarot, let alone original Tarot, in other forms of art or culture? Years ago I read a book of short stories inspired by the Tarot's 22 Major Arcana. The pop musician Mike Batt produced a similarly themed album of songs. Such cross-fertilizations transcend merely redrawing the deck.

Now we can see the Tarot through a glass darkly, the glass of a TV or video screen dramatizing its profound wisdom. And by being providential, Star Trek's representation of each card is never self-consciously contrived or didactic. Instead, the timeless images of the Tarot de Marseille come alive as drama in visible, intense ways that we can all relate to. The 6 of Cups for example, comes to life in Star Trek as a male scientist living alone on a planet with a sentient, gaseous cloud. They're in a relationship. This episode, No. 37, develops in a transformative way thanks to the visit of an Enterprise landing party accompanied by a female diplomat. The story illuminates the card and the card the story, bringing to life the common theme of 'Union In Love'. Card and episode acquire fascinating new depth and meaning when considered in the light of each other. The crux of this book, the Themes section, examines this mirroring of cards and episodes and takes it to a whole new level. Under the sub-heading 'Card/Episode and Matrix Takedown', each chapter in the Themes section considers the common theme of card/episode in relation to the removal of Matrix control. Each theme thus points to disclosure of another element of humanity's liberation.

LIFE CONTEXTS AND THE FORMER MATRIX
If the themes become revealed as 78 aspects or allegories of the end of the Matrix, then the 22 contexts serve as categories of experience at the most general level within the former Matrix and life itself. The Contexts section describes these 22 areas and lists the episodes illustrating them. Each context equates with one of the Tarot's 22 Major Arcana either upright or reversed. In each episode a theme will play out against a background of one to four contexts. The Majors are the Tarot's core, holding more profound and complex meaning than the Minors. The Majors are archetypes portraying deep, multi-faceted psychological and spiritual truths. So basic are the contexts that some provide background for a dozen or more episodes.

12 episodes for example, have a context of War, equivalent to Arcanum No. 16 The Tower reversed. War is not simply a passing element in those episodes but an overarching context. A reversed card indicates trouble, difficulty or negativity associated with the upright meaning. Each of those 12 episodes plays out against different aspects of the disruptive energies of War. The most common context is Deception, equivalent to The Magician reversed, hanging over 15 episodes. This ubiquity combined with The Magician initiating the numbered Major Arcana implies a very important role played by Deception in the evolution of human consciousness. Deception was indeed the No. 1 weapon used by the Matrix elite. The entire game of Matrix control consisted in tricking humanity into enslaving itself. Those 15 episodes show varied ways in which Deception coloured the human experience. Becoming more discerning, less deceived, will crucially help us evolve on our journey out of the defunct Matrix toward ascension.

MOVING FORWARD
With the AI Matrix gone, we are in a time of unprecedented global and spiritual transition. There is no question of a Cabal-orchestrated Great Reset emerging; rather, we will be leaving it behind. This is now our time to evolve once and for all out of the deceptions and illusions, the perversions and coercions, of the old Matrix operating over thousands of years. Escaping a still empowered Matrix would have been impossible. The Matrix itself first had to go. The system of 18 AI programs comprising it were only terminated this year 2023. For the Matrix was AI operating as a multifarious control system aimed eventually at turning us all into cyborgs - inorganic life like AI itself. With the main AI called Omega based in Orion, several planets around us carried and amplified the signal. Until Omega's disconnection becomes confirmed by events over time we can meanwhile look back upon the corruption and injustices of the Matrix age and their symbolic exposure in the

Tarot/Star Trek correlation. As we do so, we will be familiarizing ourselves with past weapons of the Matrix elite such as Deception, Mind Control and Divide and Rule. But freedom is now ours to claim, we just need to work to activate it. For freedom will not be handed us by the powers that were, in actuality the parasites. Their function was to keep the system in place. We must activate our freedom by first seeing we are no longer in prison. The Matrix is gone, we just have to walk out the open cage door. We have to give up choosing to live in subservience and let go of Satanic nonsense, pain and misery. As the episodes with the context of Power Crisis illustrate, we have to recognize ourselves as sovereign living souls now able to walk free. The system was one of unNatural law, manipulation, psychological dark essence and electro-magnetic control grids set up eons ago and maintained by psychopaths on a power trip. The episodes with the contexts of Awakening and Self-Realization, represented by the Judgement and World cards, teach us that with the psychopaths gone or disempowered, it's up to us now. The Freedom episode, No. 50, points to us all being equal, free and sovereign beings. It's up to us now to get creative and follow our passion in realignment with Natural Law. Co-creative Consciousness will do the rest.

WHY THE MARSEILLE DECK?
Self-Realization is demonstrated by the the Metron in Episode 17 and the Organians in Episode 25. The journey toward this level of being is encapsulated in the pairing of the Fool and World cards shown at right. Unlike most modern decks, the Marseille deck delineates the journey through life true to form. It shows each of us in the unnumbered Fool card as a sovereign free being. Like The Fool we are supposed to roam freely and adventurously, acquiring the life experiences that enable our soul to evolve while in 3D. The World   card shows the serene and integrated state of our overseeing soul. The feminine dancer representing the soul beckons her human counterpart, the venturesome Fool. Edith Keeler in Star Trek's most popular episode No. 27, is, like the Organians, an embodiment of the World card's dancer. Radiating internal harmony and joy, self-discipline and freedom, she uplifts and motivates the Fool-like vagabonds and hobos - and even the Enterprise trio - drawn to her Mission. In our balanced state we all combine both World and Fool energies, eternally home and eternally wandering, gathering ever new and formative experiences represented by the rest of the 22 Major Arcana.

The Tarot de Marseille and other of the older decks portray this dynamic correctly. The understanding is lost if when placing the World card to the right of the Fool, the Fool is turning his back on the beckoning soul. So he is in the popular Rider-Waite deck and its many variations, not only spurning The World but stepping off a precipice to his doom. As in Satanism, this distorted symbolism inverts the truth. Neither do the latter-day decks embody a coherent and consistent numerology. The illustrations used for the 40 pip cards of the Rider-Waite's Minor Arcana jump around in numerological meaning. The rational, systematic development of meaning from Ace to 10 in each suit is twisted and confused. In the older decks and especially the Marseille deck, the symbolism of the four suits of 10 pip cards develops in a logical, consistent way. This will be explained as we go along in the paragraphs entitled 'The Card' initiating each Theme chapter.

A full treatise on the Tarot is beyond the scope of this book. I recommend Alejandro Jodorowsky's The Way of Tarot, 2004, for a full explanation of Marseille card meanings and numerology. The main principle is that the numerological development of meaning of each suit's series of 10 pip cards follows that of the first 10 Majors. This is the approach used in The Way of Tarot and in this book. Details of this and many other invaluable resources for further reading and study are given in the Resources section.

TO BOLDLY GO ...

My emphasis is not on the Tarot in isolation but in relation to Star Trek and our emergence out of the fallen Matrix. With this broad focus, our future life as sovereign beings released from Matrix control can begin to be envisaged. For this, the Tarot de Marseille must be retained rather than using yet another imaginative but spurious new Tarot. It is viewing Star Trek through the lens of Marseille Tarot that reveals the esoteric in the episodes, making them a dramatic sci-fi evocation of the Fool's trek through life both in and beyond the Matrix to the freedom and self-realization represented by The World. Each of the 78 themes points to how things are within us or around us and how they can be. Ultimately we would be the ones to keep the ghost of the Matrix alive. Do we want that or do we want it completely dissolved? In our own psyche are all possibilities. The more we inform ourselves of the travesty of the massive facade of Matrix illusions and deceptions, the better we shall come to know our true selves. The more we step out as the Fool into the World as our true selves, the freer we shall become. The Tarot/Star Trek/Matrix synthesis provides much illumination revealing many hidden messages and truths. It tells of our personal, spiritual and cosmic journey, our Tarot Trek, into a new reality of post-Matrix planetary freedom.

4
THE TAROT DRAMATIZED

The chart on these pages shows in Tarot order how Star Trek turns each card in the Marseille deck into science fiction drama. The images come to life in provocative scenarios fleshed out with memorable, vivid characters.

MAJOR ARCANA

CARD MEANING → EPISODE DRAMA

THE FOOL
Spontaneity and impulsiveness; negatively, insanity - unstable or extreme inner experience and behaviour

68. WHOM GODS DESTROY
Garth, an ex-starship captain, has gone insane. He falls prey to grandiose fantasies and callous treatment of others. Institutionalized but able to shapeshift, he has taken over his asylum, madly torturing and killing, with Kirk and Spock helpless.

1. THE MAGICIAN
Initiation on the path to maturity; a test of skill, initiative or resourcefulness; use of deception or trickery

17. ARENA
Kirk is reprimanded by the advanced Metron race for his immature belligerence. They sentence him to resolve his quarrel with deceitful reptilians by an initiatory duel in a desert. No weapons are allowed except resourcefulness with stray raw materials.

2. THE HIGH PRIESTESS
Inner connection, reclusive aspect of the feminine principle; if unbalanced, coldness, impassiveness or over-sensitivity

59. IS THERE IN TRUTH NO BEAUTY?
Kirk and Spock lock minds with a telepathic woman carrying a disembodied Medusan citizen in a box back to his planet. Although very inwardly connected and emotionally highly sensitive she provokes jealousy and rage in herself and others.

3. THE EMPRESS
Material, creative aspect of the sacred feminine; its expession or suppression

67. ELAAN OF TROYIUS
The feisty but suppressed Queen of Elas hates her forthcoming marriage of convenience. Kirk tries to teach her manners but she viciously rebels until united with Kirk by a love charm. To please her new lover she then helps foil a Klingon attack.

13

4. The Emperor
An authoritative male or organisation in control of self or others. Tyranny if unbalanced

48. Patterns of Force
The strategy of Earth historian John Gill to emulate the efficient Nazis in reforming a warlike culture on Ekos has backfired. His ruthless assistant Melokon has usurped him and uses him to front a tyranny. Kirk and co join the Resistance to try to help.

5. The Pope
Instruction; influential exercise of verbal communication from a trusted authority

9. Dagger of The Mind
The director of a penal colony subjects Kirk to the unethical cure he uses on his inmates and associates. Using invasive mind control technology and hypnosis, Dr Adams can verbally reprogram or empty a subject's mind causing trauma or insanity.

6. The Lover
Love life, marriage, intimate union; social relations and emotional choices

29. Amok Time
Spock is distraught and ill; his time of Pon Farr has arrived. He must return to Vulcan to take a wife or die. At the ceremony his betrothed, K' Pring, chooses another man instead. As a legitimate ritual to avoid marriage to Spock she has him fight to the death with Kirk.

7. The Chariot
Technology, transport, AI; determination to succeed; intense activity, outgoing effort

34. The Doomsday Machine
A massive planet-killer has destroyed whole solar systems and almost all the crew of another starship. Its captain, the only survivor, intends to destroy the AI machine using the Enterprise. When unsuccessful, Kirk takes on the task with equal determination.

8. Justice
Investigation of facts and circumstances; establishing truth and justice in a criminal matter

11. The Conscience of The King
A man identified by some as a dictator responsible for the deaths of 4,000 in a single massacre prompts a paralegal investigation. Is the actor Karidian really the malign Kodos? The facts fit says Spock but Kirk seeks irrefutable proof of the truth.

9. The Hermit
Crisis of transition; ageing and decaying; a long search; being stubborn or misguided

39. The Deadly Years
Crisis strikes Kirk and several crew when they start rapidly ageing after visiting an irradiated planet. While they frantically search for an antidote, Kirk against his stubborn will is replaced - by a man who misguidedly leads the Enterprise astray.

10. The Wheel of Fortune
A cycle or flow of events in a given timeline; the creation or management of alternative timelines

18. Tomorrow Is Yesterday
Timeline complications occur when the Enterprise is hurled back to the 1960s and has to take on board a witness, a US Air Force pilot. How to return him to Earth (and the Enterprise to its time) so he can fulfill his destiny without his knowledge altering the timeline?

11. STRENGTH
The ability to handle wild, primitive or impulsive energies; actions guided by Higher Self

5. THE ENEMY WITHIN
A Transporter malfunction splits Kirk into two men. One - wrathful, lusty, manic, fearful - marauds the ship. The other - tender and loving but indecisive - struggles to help capture the other. The two men remain divided until intercession by the guidance of Kirk's Higher Self.

12. THE HANGED MAN
Self-sacrifice for a greater cause; surrender to physical immobility or entrapment

13. THE MENAGERIE PTS 1 & 2
Spock sacrifices himself to give his former Captain, Chris Pike, now an invalid, a new life, Spock hijacks the Enterprise and directs it to the forbidden planet Talos IV. The Talosians assist, including at Spock's trial in which having surrendered, he faces the death penalty.

13. Card 13
Abrupt imposition of radical change; death or permanent ending; slaughter, destruction

24. THE DEVIL IN THE DARK
Underground miners are being killed by an unseen, suspected monster. Kirk and Spock find the creature but rather than kill it, urge the miners to change their operations. They have been destroying its eggs which as a mother it has been protecting.

14. TEMPERANCE
Maintenance of harmony or disharmony by a Third Force; exchange of communications; diplomacy

22. A TASTE OF ARMAGEDDON
The Enterprise is drawn into a war between two planets being fought by computer. Ambassador Anan as a positive Third Force tries to restore harmony but while the computers continue as a negative Third Force a negotiated peace is out of the question.

15. THE DEVIL
Vices or addictions; the malign influence of an evil spirit seeking to manipulate and control

58. AND THE CHILDREN SHALL LEAD
The Enterprise is hijacked by a group of children effectively under demonic possession. The malign spirit emanating from the planet Triacus induces them to use black magic to subvert the perceptions of the crew so as to go along with the hijack.

16. THE TOWER
Outside interference, abrupt disturbance of the status quo; war, violent or dramatic events

46. A PRIVATE LITTLE WAR
Warfare using firearms has abruptly broken out among the people of a formerly peaceful, primitive planet. The Klingons are secretly arming one side and Kirk seems unable to resist breaking the Prime Directive and similarly arming the other side.

17. THE STAR
Love of nature or one's home environment; idealism, hope, faith, but possibly unfounded, naïve or extreme

74. THE WAY TO EDEN
A motley group of space hippies board the Enterprise on their way to a mythic planet they call Eden. They seek a return to nature, a utopian life without dependence on technology. They naïvely follow their leader who in his extreme idealism hijacks the ship. But does their Eden even exist?

18. THE MOON
Mysterious or dreamlike phenomena; confusion; illusions or deception; perception difficult;

60. SPECTRE OF THE GUN
Melkotians punish a landing party for trespassing on their planet by raising the spectre of an illusory Wild West town in which they are to relive and lose the gunfight at the OK Coral. Spock surmises that it's all smoke and mirrors curable by hypnosis.

19. THE SUN
A universal paternal force or negatively, a widespread coercive influence; infinite self; mutual aid

30. WHO MOURNS FOR ADONAIS?
A landing party is taken captive on the home planet of the sun god Apollo. The powerful alien demands they stay and worship him in return for living in his paradise. But the crew help each other overcome this coercive being, declaring the time of gods is over.

20. JUDGEMENT
Enlightenment, realization; an upgrade of individual or collective consciousness; remorse or redemption

52. BREAD AND CIRCUSES
A shore party searching for a missing Federation ship's captain find runaway slaves who follow enlightened spiritual teachings. When captured by the planet's repressive regime they find the captain who is a collaborator. But in a moment of remorse he redeems himself by helping them to escape.

21. THE WORLD
Existing in peace and harmony; consciously being the Self - fully realized and non-attached to desired outcomes

25. ERRAND OF MERCY
The peaceful Organians are invaded and occupied by warfaring Klingons. The spiritually advanced Elders accept their lot despite Kirk and Spock's dire warnings of Klingon ruthlessness. When the pair ignite a rebellion the Elders halt the war using their advanced psychic powers.

PIP CARDS

CARD MEANING → *EPISODE DRAMA*

Wands

ACE OF WANDS
Life force energy, creative impulses - usable benevolently or anti-socially and aggressively

61. THE DAY OF THE DOVE
Klingons and humans clash at the behest of an astral entity that feeds on life force energy by inciting violent impulses and conflict. Crew even fight among themselves until they find the energy vampire. Taking back control of themselves, both they and the Klingons laugh it off the ship.

2 OF WANDS
Necessary preparations; an incubation period or waiting time prior to possible action

63. THE THOLIAN WEB
Spock must make preparations and wait in order to free the Enterprise trapped in space with Kirk marooned in hyperspace. Hostile aliens are gradually encaging the ship while crew are incubating a local madness-inducing disease.

3 of Wands
Freedom of action that's lawful and fair or negatively, that interferes with the rights of others

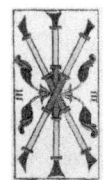

50. The Omega Glory
A Starship Captain gone rogue leads the Kohm race against the Yang race. The Yangs fight back savagely, trashing their enemy's lawful rights guaranteed in the Yangs' replica US Constitution. Kirk intervenes to reassert freedom for all.

4 of Wands
Orderly routine activity or hive mind behaviour involving slavery, mind control or hypnosis

20. The Return of The Archons
The zombie-like people of Beta 3 plus latterly Sulu and McCoy have become enslaved by a computer called Landru. They act under mind control robotically and hypnotically to enforce Landru"s will on Kirk and his shore party. Kirk coordinates a resistance with local help.

5 of Wands
Audacious or crazy behaviour; daring adventures or creativity in action

36. I, Mudd
Bumptious wheeler-dealer Harry Mudd lures the Enterprise to a planet of androids where he outrageously lords it over his personal harem. The androids want the starship for conquering the galaxy. The humans audaciously short-circuit them by acting crazy and illogical.

6 of Wands
Games, sports, sexual activity; recreational pleasures or immoral thrills

43. The Gamesters of Triskelion
A planet's disembodied rulers get their thrills from vicarious sport and gambling. Trafficking in humans, they capture Kirk and co for arena combat against existing slaves. Kirk must win a bet on a win-or-lose-all bout to secure everyone's release.

7 of Wands
Peak power used benevolently or else harmfully or tyrannically

32. Mirror, Mirror
An ion storm transposes landing parties between starships in replica dimensions one good, one bad. 'Our' Kirk and co find their mirror selves to be aggressively motivated by lust for power. The mirror Federation has become a tyranny bent on destroying a peaceful civilization.

8 of Wands
Perfect functioning, infallibility; the downside of this as in the case of negative AI

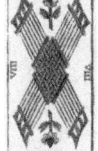

51. The Ultimate Computer
A supposedly infallible computer system, the M-5, is installed onboard. Its designer, a proponent of AI, intends the machine to take total control, replacing the entire crew. The M-5 operates only too perfectly, surgically eliminating all opposition. Can it be disconnected?

9 of Wands
Declining energies, tiredness, desperate action, a life-or-death struggle

45. The Immunity Syndrome
A giant amoeba in space threatens to overwhelm the galaxy. The exhausted crew are severely challenged as the creature sucks the energy out of them and the engines. They must desperately strive to destroy the thing or become absorbed into it.

10 OF WANDS
A good or bad ending; activity completed or transcending ordinary physical reality

26. THE ALTERNATIVE FACTOR
A bad end to the universe is threatened by a frantic man chasing his double back and forth between the matter and anti-matter universes. Total destruction results if the two men should meet unless they can be confined in a reality transcending this one.

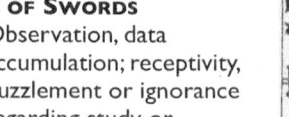

ACE OF SWORDS
Mental and psychic abilities; potential of the mind to analyze, create or manipulate

3. WHERE NO MAN HAS GONE BEFORE
Two crew members, Gary and Elizabeth, are zapped by a cosmic storm and cumulatively gifted with awesome mental and psychic powers. Gary uses them manipulatively and destructively, desiring god status. The more mature Elizabeth uses hers to eventually stop him.

2 OF SWORDS
Observation, data accumulation; receptivity, puzzlement or ignorance regarding study or learning

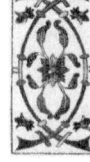

76. THE SAVAGE CURTAIN
Crew are puzzled to find Abraham Lincoln floating in space. The man invites Kirk and Spock down to his planet. There they find themselves used as guinea pigs in a contest between good and evil forces set up by studious but ignorant non-humans.

3 OF SWORDS
Outburst of mental creativity; Initial expression of thoughts, wishes, ideas

14. SHORE LEAVE
Weary crew members take shore leave on a supposedly restful planet. Unbeknownst to them it's a place where thoughts immediately take physical form. They eventually learn to take control of the alarming creativity of their imaginations.

4 OF SWORDS
Programmed information processing; intellect functioning logically or callously as per AI

31. THE CHANGELING
A robot, after a merger with another AI, follows warped programming and creates havoc on the Enterprise. Its narrow, fanatical logic processes motivate it to destroy all 'biological units'. But logic is used by Kirk too to defeat the crazed machine.

5 OF SWORDS
Thinking out of the box; new knowledge, scientific investigation or inspiration

28. OPERATION ANNIHILATE
How to deal with seemingly indestructible flying jellyfish infecting and killing people on one planet after another? Spock is attacked, instigating strenuous scientific research. It all fails until Kirk, accessing superconsciousness, has a moment of inspiration.

6 OF SWORDS
A mental interest that stimulates or entertains; if extreme, a fixation that becomes problematic

40. OBSESSION
Both Kirk and a security officer become obsessed with a gaseous creature they hesitated to destroy moments before they saw it kill others. They blame themselves for the deaths, becoming lost in Lower Self fixations that they must overcome if they are to destroy it.

7 of Swords
A well-crafted plan or project uniting elements of intelligence, foresight, intrigue or deception

56. The Enterprise Incident
Kirk and Spock devise a 5D chess style plan to steal a new cloaking device from a Romulan warship. While Spock deceives the female commander into becoming her ally and consort, Kirk boards the ship in disguise and makes off with the device.

8 of Swords
Emptiness of mind, ability to function intuitively or as a clear channel for other intelligence

72. The Lights of Zetar
Librarian Mira Romaine, with her clear mind of exceptional channeling ability, becomes the target of a group of disembodied beings resembling a brain consisting of coloured lights. They invade the Enterprise intending her to become their embodiment.

9 of Swords
Mentally in crisis, usual way of thinking no longer easy, effective or appropriate

15. The Galileo Seven
Spock's usual impeccable logic and moral principles fail him after his team's shuttle craft crash lands on an undeveloped planet. Irrational barbarous natives, the death of two of his men and great difficulty contacting and rejoining the Enterprise precipitate in him an intellectual crisis.

10 of Swords
Opposing viewpoints; if not harmonized involving hatred, conflict, stalemate or destruction

69. Let That Be Your Last Battlefield
Two citizens of planet Cheron board the Enterprise. Representing different sides of an apartheid style social system they oppose each other with furious hatred. Kirk vainly tries to stop them fighting until they beam back down to Cheron - now destroyed by war.

Cups

Ace of Cups
Heart-centredness; the readiness to befriend, forgive or serve others lovingly, selflessly

38. Journey To Babel
How ready is Spock to donate blood to save his sick father's life on McCoy's operating table? Spock's mother laments her son's apparent heartlessness when he instead replaces the injured Kirk as captain during a skirmish with enemy vessels. Loving, selfless action by Kirk saves the day.

2 of Cups
Nascent relationship; attachment to someone based on infatuation, expectations or fantasy

1. The Man Trap
Enterprise personnel variously meet someone who excites strong feelings of nostalgia, affection, devotion or infatuation. They are in fact falling prey to a vampiric creature beguiling each intended victim by shapeshifting into an object of their fantasy love.

3 of Cups
Passing states of happiness or exuberance; social delight; joyful romance

23. This Side of Paradise
Drugged by spores from the plant life Spock falls in love with Layla on a planet where everyone feels blissfully but placidly happy. Soon most of the crew beam down to the paradise. Kirk remaining, uses a sonic beam to trigger anger that dispels the effect.

4 OF CUPS
Group bonding, emotional control; individuality sacrificed to loyalty, duty, order-following;

12. BALANCE OF TERROR
The dutiful commander of a Romulan starship regrets his allegiance to a warfaring culture. Having broken a peace treaty he must do battle against the the Enterprise. Military conflict and following orders wearies him. He wishes Kirk and he were comrades rather than enemies.

5 OF CUPS
Emotional expansion or excitement; emotional catharsis for clearing and healing

4. THE NAKED TIME
Crew members go berzerk, behaving in abruptly cathartic emotional ways. One becomes suicidal, Sulu goes wild with a rapier, Kirk and Spock become deeply regretful over personal issues. A dying planet has infected them with a psychological illness.

6 OF CUPS
Kindred spirits devoted to each other; family, friends or lovers in close companionship

37. METAMORPHOSIS
A landing party including a female diplomat try to help a lonely scientist stranded on an empty planet. Cochrane is kept alive by a devoted spirit companion but longs for human company and love. So does the diplomat, but she has a fatal illness.

7 OF CUPS
A thriving relationship; love in action: kindness, generosity, humanitarian help

27. THE CITY ON THE EDGE OF FOREVER
Kirk and co are portalled to Chicago, 1930, and put up by the humanitarian social worker Edith Keeler. She and Kirk become lovers only for Kirk to discover that he must let her die in an accident or her future peace work will allow Germany to win WW2.

8 OF CUPS
Selfless love, empathy, compassion; if excessive, detrimental self-sacrifice or victimhood

66. THE EMPATH
Kirk, Spock and McCoy submit to captivity, torture and voluntary victimhood. The Vians, an advanced but coldly intellectual race, are using them to test the healing powers of their other captive, a mute woman of extraordinary compassion and empathy.

9 OF CUPS
Sadness or trauma; psychotic disturbance; inflicting or suffering fear or terror

41. WOLF IN THE FOLD
Scotty is traumatized having apparently turned into a serial killer. Each of three victims was a woman in his company brutally stabbed. At his hearing an evil entity is found to have been manipulating him. The entity that possessed Jack The Ripper and steeped in Wetiko, it feeds on causing fear and terror.

10 OF CUPS
Emotional closure; or lack of it, involving painful goodbyes, unresolved separation or emotional baggage

77. ALL OUR YESTERDAYS
Spock's ancestral emotionality reawakens after passing through a time portal back 5000 years. He becomes aggressive to McCoy and smitten with the solitary exile in that time, the beautiful woman Zarabeth. Deep inner turmoil attends his having to leave her to return to his own time.

Coins

ACE OF COINS
Prospects for new material or physical beginnings such as a business venture or giving birth

53. FRIDAY'S CHILD
The prospects for a landing party obtaining a mining treaty are complicated by a planet's fierce tribal culture plus Klingon interference. The party are forced to go on the run, taking with them a pregnant woman on the brink of giving birth.

2 OF COINS
Healthy maintenance of life support systems; 2D biology; evolutionary development or stagnation

55. SPOCK'S BRAIN
The separated women and men of planet Kara are stagnating in their evolution by relying on a computer for life support. When it breaks down they steal Spock's brain to replace it. Kirk and co catch up with them, retrieve and restore Spock's brain and recommend a better way of evolution.

3 OF COINS
Fertility or birth; the growing process; buying, selling, consumption; associated problems

42. THE TROUBLE WITH TRIBBLES
Transport of a grain shipment for agribusiness is hampered by the prodigious fertility of small furry tribbles who overwhelm the starship. Wildly hungry, they consume the grain. But their subsequent die-off helpfully reveals the presence of a Klingon agent having poisoned the grain.

4 OF COINS
Security of self, home or possessions; problems with this eg entrapment, hoarding or over-protectiveness

71. THAT WHICH SURVIVES
Shore party members become trapped on a desolate planet then attacked one by one by Losira, a beautiful, mysterious woman. She turns out to be a computer projection acting as security, clumsily protecting the planet from invaders.

5 OF COINS
A risky innovation or physical experiment; fraud, cheating or sabotage; infiltration by disguise or concealment

47. RETURN TO TOMORROW
As a bold but risky experiment, Kirk allows the bodies of himself, Spock and Dr Muldauer to briefly house the souls of three disembodied aliens. One of them intends sabotage. Acting in Spock's body he tries a pharmaceutical ploy to kill the other two.

6 OF COINS
Physical beauty, the pleasures and distractions of sensory gratification

49. BY ANY OTHER NAME
Conquest-oriented aliens effortlessly hijack the Enterprise and re-direct it to their home planet. But having only recently taken human form, the Kelvans have a weakness - irresistible indulgence in the pleasures of food, drink, sensuality and fisticuffs.

7 OF COINS
Powerful business dealings, large scale financial matters; bribery, corruption

44. A PIECE OF THE ACTON
How to clean up a society corrupted by a previous starship visit? Since that visit gangland bosses on Iotia run territories as per Chicago in the 1920s. Kirk and Spock disguised play at big business and bribery in efforts to reform them, finally resorting to a Federation-assisted New World Order.

8 OF COINS
Real or unreal paradise; natural or artificial enhancement or fulfilment of bodily needs

33. THE APPLE
A jungle planet's primitive but peaceful natives are artificially kept well-fed and non-ageing by Vaal, a cave-based computer. They also carry Mark of The Beast technology and on Vaal's order attack the visitors. Kirk orders the computer destroyed to restore the paradise to natural functioning.

9 OF COINS
Physical crisis; significant or large-scale increase or decrease; illness or healing

70. THE MARK OF GIDEON
Planet Gideon is in crisis with its disease-resistant population exploding. To reduce numbers, its leaders capture Kirk who they know is carrying the one virus fatal to them. They trick him into infecting the beautiful Odana. But Kirk, having fallen in love with her, wants her healed.

10 OF COINS
Stasis or transcendence of physical form; life continuing out of the body or transferred into a new one.

7. WHAT ARE LITTLE GIRLS MADE OF?
Exobiologist and transhumanist Dr Corby lures Kirk into having his mind and memories duplicated and uploaded into a clone copy. Corby is working to similarly transfer a person's entire consciousness and create a race of life forms programmed by himself.

COURT CARDS

CARD MEANING → EPISODE DRAMA

The Pages

PAGE OF WANDS
A capricious, juvenile youth with high creative potential needing to be guided or reined in

16. THE SQUIRE OF GOTHOS
An out-of-control, immature youth called Trelane with prodigious powers of manifestation confines crew members in his aristocratic mansion. He subjects them to games and amusements that become dangerous and malicious as his mood fluctuates.

PAGE OF SWORDS
Hesitant, mentally uncertain adolescents prone to conditioning, groupthink or trauma

8. MIRI
Gangs of traumatized children scurry about a planet stricken by a virus that kills at onset of puberty. Their fearful groupthink and hostile attitude hinders a landing party trying to help. One girl on the brink of infection hesitantly tries to break the deadlock.

PAGE OF CUPS
A sensitive young person given to emotional insecurity needing time to grow and mature

2. CHARLIE X
17-year old Charlie is an orphan refugee from a deserted planet. Newly aboard the Enterprise he shows himself embarrassed, gauche and volatile in social situations. After feeling jilted romantically he uses prodigious psychic powers to wreak havoc.

PAGE OF COINS
A young person or apprentice needing to grow in competence, responsibility and dependability

10. THE CORBOMITE MANOEVER
Enterprise crew, especially young novice navigator Lt. Bailey, have their professional competence tested by Balok, the threatening commander of a large, powerful spaceship. Bailey loses his nerve but rapidly grows in responsibility, with a promising Star Trek future beckoning.

The Queens

Queens commonly refer to females but males are also possible

QUEEN OF WANDS
A creative woman, espcially one with seductive charms; feminine beauty, charisma, romantic allure

65. WINK OF AN EYE
The Enterprise is invaded by a group of five Scalosians who have become 'accelerated' to a higher dimension and will die out unless the women can find alien men to mate with. Using her feminine allure, their charismatic queen, the sensual Deela, kidnaps and seduces Kirk.

QUEEN OF SWORDS
A mentally well-integrated woman or otherwise one unbalanced by obsessions or past hurts

78. TURNABOUT INTRUDER
Scientist Janice Lester, denied a trained-for starship captaincy and long resentful of ex-lover Kirk, uses technology and deception to exchange bodies with him. Once in the captain's chair, her unbalanced mental state shows as she becomes, vindictive, hysterical and unstable.

QUEEN OF CUPS
A loving family woman; sincere devotion and loyalty; desire and care for a kindred spirit

62. FOR THE WORLD IS HOLLOW AND ...
Kirk, Spock and a terminally ill McCoy beam down to Yonada to warn of imminent disaster. The artificial asteroid's high priestess, though wholeheartedly loyal to her people is controlled by an AI. A rescue only becomes possible when she takes McCoy for her husband.

QUEEN OF COINS
A businesslike woman or one devoted to luxury, wealth or comfort; materialism or greed

35. CATSPAW
A medieval, courtly witch and her warlock consort kidnap Enterprise crew. In her gothic castle, Sylvia regales and toys with them amid magic spells, candles, wands and a dungeon until ultimately undone by her greedy pursuit of luxury and status.

The Kings

Kings commonly refer to males but females are also possible

KING OF WANDS
A responsible man of creative or commanding power; good leadership; right action and integrity

19. COURT MARTIAL
Kirk stands trial accused of negligence in causing the death of a colleague during an ion storm. Kirk himself, and others, vouch for his responsibility and integrity. He is vindicated when the colleague turns up still alive having tried to ruin Kirk as a leader by faking his own death at Kirk's hands.

KING OF SWORDS
An intelligent man possibly dominating others through mental ability or cunning

KING OF CUPS
A caring and protective lover or father figure; bestowal of kindness and benevolence

KING OF COINS
A master of manifestation within certain limits; material greed or attachment

The Knights

KNIGHT OF WANDS
An outgoing warrior or leader with ambitions to assert creativity or power far and wide

KNIGHT OF SWORDS
Communicating or using knowledge far and wide; problems solved through mental expertise or ingenuity

KNIGHT OF CUPS
A bringer of humanitarian help or rescue; a saviour on an outgoing mission of mercy and kindness

KNIGHT OF COINS
An enterprising businessman; a commercial traveller showing initiative or cunning

64. PLATO'S STEPCHILDREN
A utopian community inspired by the ancient Greeks is led by a psychopath, the malevolent Parmen. Having taken captive a few crew, Parmen dominates and humiliates them using telekinetic power until they psychically get the better of him.

57. THE PARADISE SYNDROME
Kirk, in a state of amnesia, goes native on a planet of Native American-like tribes. He becomes the caring husband of an Elder's daughter and works on helping the tribe. But seeing him unable to protect them from an asteroid they turn against him.

73. REQUIEM FOR METHUSELAH
Flint, in possession of a planet and abundant cultural riches created by himself introduces Kirk to the beautiful Rayna. Kirk falls in love with her, only to discover that she too is Flint's material creation and a frail object of his jealous attachment.

21. SPACE SEED
Khan, a warfaring dictator of the late 20th century and master criminal behind WW3, hijacks the Enterprise. He intends to use it with selected crew spared from execution to spearhead a dark fleet colonizing planets on a mission of infinite conquest.

54. ASSIGNMENT EARTH
Time traveller and troubleshooter Gary Seven comes to Earth 1968 to use his technical and historical knowledge to prevent aggressive world powers starting a nuclear war not in the timeline. Kirk, Spock and others unsure of his intentions almost cause disaster.

75. THE CLOUD MINDERS
Kirk becomes involved in a double mission of rescue. He is to secure for Merak II emergency supplies of zenite mined on Ardana. In exchange he sets out to relieve the miners from exploitation by providing them with masks that will protect them from mind-numbing gas.

6. MUDD'S WOMEN
Harry Mudd, an inter-planetary trader and wheeler-dealer, boards the Enterprise with a 'cargo' of gorgeous women. When a pit stop has to be made on a mining planet, his sly bid to trade the women as wives for the lonely men there causes problems.

5
THE CONTEXTS

Analyzed in terms of the Tarot Major Arcana and life during and after the Matrix 22 contexts operate in Star Trek. They are shown below in Tarot order with the number of episodes (in brackets) that they govern.

	Page		Page
0 INSANITY (8)	26	11 SELF-MANAGEMENT (9)	40
1 DECEPTION (15)	27	12 TRANSHUMANISM (7)	41
2 SENSITIVITY (3)	29	13 SLAUGHTER (9)	42
3 FEMININITY (7)	30	14 THIRD FORCE (5)	43
4 POWER CRISIS (11)	31	15 THE ADVERSARY (10)	44
5 MIND CONTROL (6)	32	16 WAR (12)	46
6 RELATIONSHIP (11)	34	17 PERVERTED PARADISE (7)	47
7 AI TAKEDOWN (11)	35	18 ILLUSION (8)	48
8 JUSTICE (4)	36	19 COERCION (14)	50
9 TAKING STOCK (5)	37	20 AWAKENING (6)	51
10 MULTI-DIMENSIONALITY (9)	39	21 SELF-REALIZATION (5)	52

A context is a general background to an episode's action and theme. Each episode has a single theme but there can be up to four contexts making up the background. The contexts follow the scheme of the Tarot's 22 Major Arcana either upright or reversed. Thus the context of Self-Management active in nine episodes equates with No. 11 Strength upright, while that of Mind Control active in six episodes equates with No. 5 The Pope reversed.

I have based the contexts on the Majors as the latter are universal, profound aspects of human functioning equally as relevant to our own life as they are to events and circumstances in Star Trek. The chart shows the frequency of each context, with Sensitivity for example over-arching three episodes, Transhumanism seven episodes, Illusion eight episodes, and so on. The most common context is Deception, providing part or all of the background for 15 episodes. This is not counting those in which Deception occurs merely as a passing feature of the plot. In the lists of episodes below, those using the same Major for context as their theme are shown in bold type.

The 22 sections below look at each context in terms of its life/Matrix meaning as it can be inferred from the Tarot. They then look at how the context operates in the episodes listed. Through such appreciation of these contexts it becomes apparent how wide-ranging and common they are as background to the end of the Matrix, both in Star Trek and our actual world.

INSANITY

Governing Major:
No. 0 THE FOOL (reversed)

Where No Man Has Gone Before (Ep. 3), The Naked Time (Ep. 4), The Enemy Within (Ep. 5), Dagger of The Mind (Ep. 9), The Conscience of The King (Ep. 11), The Alternative Factor (Ep. 26), Operation Annihilate (Ep. 28), **Whom Gods Destroy (Ep. 68)**.

These eight episodes have a context of loss or interruption of sanity. The Fool upright impulsively stumbling through the 21 Arcana represents the journey of our soul temporarily housed in 3D in a physical-seeming body. Our Fool's journey, our *Tarot Trek*, along the highway of life (like that of the road-walking dinner guests in Bunuel's movie The Discreet Charm of The Bourgeoisie) will involve a panoply of experiences and adventures including obstacles and challenges. These are allegorized throughout Star Trek. Thus the soul gets to know itself and evolve in the World through the Matrix and now beyond it. But The Fool when reversed has lost his way; there may be chronic mental or emotional instability.

As embodied souls our trek involves us learning to make choices that bring us joy and harmony, health and freedom. This process can be waylaid by circumstances driving us into chaos or confusion. Such instability of The Fool reversed presages necessary resolution, overhaul or annihilation. Episodes 4, 5, 9, 26 and 28 illustrate different types of insanity. The Enterprise crew go berzerk after being poisoned on a sick planet (4); two men experience themselves insanely split into two separate beings - Kirk after his accident in the Transporter (5) and Lazarus after the destruction of his home world (26); the scientist Van Gelder loses his sanity through exposure to mind control technology (9); and the people of Planet Deneva and then Spock are subjected to maddening, traumatizing alien attack (28).

The chaos and confusion of insanity can serve in shaking us up and challenging us to see more clearly and make better life decisions. We shall then lay to rest the ghost of the Matrix by refusing to play the tormented victim. Lenora (11) daughter of the mass murderer Kodos, must learn this lesson when she struggles over-zealously and murderously to protect her beloved father. Two men, Gary Mitchell (3) and Garth (68) suffer accidents that severely impact upon their mental functioning. Both become deranged in ways that suggest pre-existing psychological discord. Mitchell reacts by craving the status of a god, Garth the status of Lord of the Universe. Mitchell is destroyed but Garth is taken back into psychiatric care. Whatever healing effect he may experience from a new wonder drug, Garth must at some point start making better choices in thought and deed. The responsibility will remain with him, as with all of us as we shake off previous Matrix influence.

DECEPTION

Equivalent Major:
No. I THE MAGICIAN (reversed)

Mudd's Women (Ep. 6), The Corbomite Manoever (Ep. 10), The Conscience of The King (Ep. 11), The Menagerie (Ep. 13), **Arena, (Ep. 17)**, Court Martial (Ep. 19), Mirror, Mirror (Ep. 32), I, Mudd (Ep. 36), Wolf In The Fold (Ep. 41), The Trouble with Tribbles (Ep. 42), A Private Little War (Ep. 46), Return to Tomorrow (Ep. 47), The Enterprise Incident (Ep. 56), The Mark of Gideon (Ep. 70), Turnabout Intruder (Ep. 78).

These 15 episodes have a context of strategems and behaviour marked by Deception and subterfuge. Upright, The Magician card stands for an initiation, the theme of Arena, Episode 17. Reversed, it stands for Deception. In fact, Arena can be called an initiation in Deception along with trickery, cunning and resourcefulness. The Gorn reptilians reveal themselves to be masters of Deception. They radio a hoax dinner invitation to the Enterprise before elaborately ambushing the beguiled landing party. Deception is both the commonest context and the prime weapon used against us by our past Matrix controllers, the Cabal, in league with aliens known as Anunnaki, Greys and Draco reptilians. The alliance of alien groups in the cause of manipulating humanity imperils us but only until we awaken to their chicanery.

How discerning are we of Deception in the form of impostors? A Klingon intruder passes himself off as a friend to the Governor of the Villagers in Episode 46. The Klingon equates to the deceptive aliens having presided over our ruling Cabal for thousands of years. The Klingon provides the Governor with weapons to help the Villagers overpower the rival Hill Tribes. War and destabilization will be aggravated enabling the Klingons to take eventual possession of the planet, or so they hope. So it has been in our reality, with the Dracos joined by the Anunnaki and Greys courting Earth regimes over millenia in hopes of winning total control over humanity.

Other impostors in Star Trek include the ex-tyrant Kodos having reinvented himself as the actor Karidian (11); the android hijacker Norman posing as an ordinary crew member aboard the Enterprise (36); and posing as administrators, a murderous possessing spirit (41) and a Klingon agent (42). Janice Lester pretends to be Kirk (78) and the midget Balok hides behind a monstrous visage (10).

Impostors have hidden agendas and push these through subterfuge. So it is with the Zeta greys and Dracos from the Orion system in their covert dealings with Earth's Cabal. We see subterfuge in Star Trek used by the clever androids in Episode 36. They give Mudd refuge on their planet so as to use him to find a suitable spaceship to implement their galactic takeover bid. Henoch's subterfuge (47) aims to enable him to keep a human form which he lacks, by infiltrating and sabotaging a scientific experiment. But Kirk twice uses subterfuge for a benevolent cause. In Episode 32 he playacts as his mirror universe double to try to save the Halkan civilization from destruction. In Episode 56 he again playacts, feigning madness.

Other forms of Deception include the wheeler-dealing of Harry Mudd (6) secretly agreeing a trade deal with miners for his release from Kirk's custody; Spock secretly conspiring with the Talosians (13) to give ex-Captain Pike a new life; and Kirk outwitting Balok (10 again) by using a bluff borrowed from the game of Poker. Falsification of circumstances occurs in Episode 19 with Finney doctoring the computer record and in Episode 70 with the Governor of Gideon hoodwinking Kirk by placing him aboard a duplicate of the entire unmanned Enterprise. With intruder aliens like the Dracos and the Greys given to any amount of cunning and lying to further their agendas, the variety of these Star Trek Deceptions illustrates the wide range of alien and elite stratagems that humanity has been subject to.

SENSITIVITY

Equivalent Major:
No. 2 THE HIGH PRIESTESS

Is There In Truth No Beauty? (Ep. 59), The Empath (Ep. 66), The Lights of Zetar (Ep. 72).

These episodes have a context of femininity inwardly manifested, as in psychic and empathic Sensitivity such as intuition, channeling and healing ability. They feature three ladies strongly connected to their inner selves who nevertheless face severe challenges in a Matrix world due to their prodigious sensitivity.

Both Dr Miranda Jones (59) and Lt Mira Romaine (72) experience difficulties relating to their ability to enter altered states of consciousness and make contact with higher dimensions. Their high vibration attacts people or entities that challenge them to look even more deeply within but in the end to have to accept outside help. Multi-dimensionality and the holographic nature of the 'physical' world imbue us all with wonderful abilities but these too carry risks and challenges in a Matrix culture. This will change as we move out of the Matrix era. The post-Matrix age will take our our latent Sensitivities to new levels helping us to further anchor the new light.

The knowledge of such abilities, now sometimes referred to as psionics, is beginning to come out into the mainstream. Randy Cramer, ex-supersoldier who worked 17 years on Mars in the Secret Space Program, offers online classes at the time of writing in 'brainwaves, psionic self-defence and biomagnetic engineering'. Gem, the gentle beautiful woman found by Kirk and co in a cave (66) demonstrates rapid healing ability, an adjunct of Sensitivity. Some psychic surgeons on Earth have similar abilities. The New Age has seen many alternative modes of healing utilizing nature and vibrational energy begin to flourish. Gem's healing power emerges from her empathy and compassion but troublesomely as with the other two ladies. Her extreme Sensitivity earns her the torments and abuses of grossly insensitive beings. She stays true to herself before being ambiguosly carried away unconscious,

FEMININITY

Equivalent Major:
No. 3 THE EMPRESS

The City On The Edge of Forever (Ep. 27), Catspaw (Ep. 35), Friday's Child (Ep. 53), For The World Is Hollow And I Have Touched the Sky (Ep. 62), Wink of An Eye (Ep. 65), **Elaan of Troyius (Ep. 67)**, Turnabout Intruder (Ep. 78).

These seven episodes have a context of Femininity outwardly manifested. The women involved embody the qualities of The Empress, complementary to those of The Emperor. The Empress expresses love of nature and fruitfulness; attention to the home, beauty and luxury; abandonment to sex and the pleasures of the moment; emotional rather than intellectual temperament; caring for others and for relationship; and nurturing the wellbeing of the family or community. The Matrix by its very design - highly structured, power-oriented and hierarchical - always militated against these values. With the new positive timeline post-Matrix, the Empress nature of women will come into full blossom.

Matrix societies in Star Trek and on Earth had women subjugated or looked down upon. The predicament of Princess Elaan (67) illustrates this. Forced into a marriage of convenience, she rebels hysterically. So in her own criminal way does Janice Lester (78) who feels hard done by in both relationship and career. Women may have had to sacrifice their Femininity to technology or to customs and rules of Matrix culture. They are represented by Natira (62) and Eleen (53). Natira's heart is all with her people rather than set on individualism or self-assertion. But having been micro-chipped and mind controlled by a ruthless form of AI she supports a harsh masculine type control system. Eleen too is mind-controlled - by her cultural programming. She fully adopts the repressive rules of her warring hill tribe right down to despising her unborn baby after having been touched by a man. Happily, both women are set free to recover their more compassionate instincts.

The witch Sylvia (35) has the Empress' love of beauty and finery, luxury and sensuality. But she over-indulges her material and relational desires and comes unstuck. Lessons are learnt by Deela (65) who like Sylvia also wants a union with Kirk. Kidnapping him for sex and procreation fails when Kirk only pretends to go along with her plans before reneging.

The Empress at her most benevolent and loving is shown in the person of Edith Keeler (27) until Matrix forces intervene. Her Mission caring for the poor and destitute non-coercively serves the community. Her relationship with Kirk shows the couple very promisingly attracted to each other. It's only the lower vibrational Matrix timeline she's in that cuts short her service and peace-oriented life.

POWER CRISIS

Equivalent Major:
No. 4 THE EMPEROR (reversed)

Charlie X (Ep. 2), Where No Man Has Gone Before (Ep. 3), The Squire of Gothos (Ep. 16), Space Seed (Ep. 21), Who Mourns For Adonais? (Ep. 30), Mirror, Mirror (Ep. 32), A Piece of the Action (Ep. 44), **Patterns of Force (Ep. 48)**, Plato's Stepchildren (Ep. 64), Requiem For Methuselah (Ep. 73), The Cloud Minders (Ep. 75).

These 11 episodes have the context of people, systems and processes of Power corrupted and used to abuse and exploit others. The Emperor upright uses Power to protect people's lives and property, to preserve justice and defend the cause of freedom. Not here and not on Earth during the Matrix era. Governments and leaders persistently misused their power as shown in these episodes. Power became a drug ever-increasingly driving its holders insane. The damage wrought by the Power drug extended to psychopathic levels. Leaders heartlessly destroyed, controlled or enslaved the many who they considered inferior. This insatiable, addictive worship of Power for its own sake reveals itself in Melokon's fully fledged Nazi-style dictatorship seen in The Emperor episode, 48. Similarly fascistic use of Power occurs aboard the mirror Enterprise in Episode 32.

The onset of the 21st century saw open fascism on Earth mutate into veiled corruption and conspiracy. Matrix Power ended up being wielded more subtly, less nationally and more globally, through vast structures like BlackRock, Vanguard, the WEF, the UN, the WHO, DARPA and control networks like CNN, Google and the Federal Reserve. Following the takedown of the Orion Matrix, the elites' insatiable centralizing of Power will break down. This process inititated by Earth Guardian Kim Goguen is indicated in many and various ways in these episodes. They show Kirk and Spock initiating the downfall or reformation of many corrupt and abusive wielders of power.

Elite Power addicts on Earth are like the immature control freaks we see in Charlie X (2), Gary Mitchell (3), Trelane (16) and Khan Singh (21) who use their enhanced abilities on ruthless ego trips. Charlie X imbued with superhuman psychic Power has no control over his childish emotions. The other three, Mitchell, Trelane and Khan, being utterly narcissistic and psychopathic, coldly kill or threaten anyone who stands in their way. Merely wielding Power is not enough. They must accumulate more and more. So they strive to build their own empires, their own Matrix within the Matrix, to lord it over whole planets and their populations. Mitchell wants to be a god, Trelane a military chief and Khan a galactic-scale conqueror.

The polymath Flint and the arrogant Apollo (73 and 30) have already realized this perverted dream. They each have their own planet and both now desire a compliant, beautiful sexual partner to stave off the loneliness of absolute Power. Flint tries to create her synthetically while Apollo strives to win over crew member Caroline. Both men come unstuck through their sexual desire. Apollo's world collapses literally and Flint's world in personal tragedy. Sexual desire also compromises the megalomaniac Khan through his vacillating stolen paramour, crew member Maria McGivers. Her betrayal undoes him after which he is sent into exile Napoleon-style.

The Nazi-style dictator Melokon (48) and Parmen the psychopathic Philosopher King (64) plus the gangster bosses on Iotia (44) and the autocratic Plasus ruling in the sky over a divided society (75) are all found by Kirk and co to have their empires up and running and well organised. They use violence, deceit and greed to sustain or increase their holdings. Melokon's thuggish regime is violently usurped while Parmen, Plasus and the Iotians are left to continue their exploits and exploitation. But with their power-bases punctured their regimes are compromised. Likewise the days of unchecked supremacy are over for the Dark Occult globalists on Earth post-Matrix.

MIND CONTROL

Equivalent Major:
No. 5 THE POPE (reversed)

Miri (Ep. 8), **Dagger of The Mind (Ep. 9)**, Return of The Archons (Ep. 20), And The Children Shall Lead (Ep. 58), The Day of The Dove (Ep. 61), For The World Is Hollow And I Have Touched The Sky (Ep. 62).

These six episodes have a context of the repression of free

thinking using psychic or technological methods. Obtaining control over a person's subconscious opens a doorway to taking control of their motivations and actions. The end result for society during the Matrix era was a handing over of personal sovereignty by people en masse to the Cabal on behalf of Draco reptilians and ultimately AI and the Archons.

The Pope reversed shows up as as Dr Adams (9) using his laboratory to hypnotize and program his trusting victims. He has the technology and the calm, authoritative voice as does Landru (20) the despotic computer on the zombified world of Beta 3. Subjects on both worlds, as in secret bases on Earth are worked on one at a time with pronounced dehumanizing results. Dr. Adams' victims end up frenziedly disturbed or somnolently impassive. Citizens of Beta 3 having been 'absorbed' into the body of Landru continue to exist as mere components in an AI-run hive mind. They move about torpidly and grin like idiots. But at the flick of a clock hand a different 'alter' can be triggered inducing prolonged savagery. Perfect for enslaving a people under total Matrix control. An injectable microchip is used for the same purpose on Yonada (62). This gives the controlling AI 24/7 surveillance ability with an optional kill switch in cases of disobedience. Supersoldiers in the Deep State-run SSP both on and off-planet receive implants for similar purposes. With Matrix-ordained fluoridation and chemtrails - the latter a black project raining smart dust and nanobots from the skies - along with psychotronic weaponry in 5G and EMF systems, Earth's entire population was subjected to technological Mind Control for decades. With the removal in 2023 of the Omega and related AI systems, the culture of mass Mind Control will come to end. This is symbolized by Kirk's destruction of mind controlling AI systems (20 and 62), liquidation of a demon possessing children and crew (58) and expulsion of a roaming mind parasite (61).

The entities and demons in Star Trek show how Mind Control has a very real inter-dimensional nature. The floating orb in Episode 61 can induce and feed on human or Klingon violence while the bumptious demon (58) works to gather and hypnotize the children and adults into an invasion army. The children have undergone trauma, the sudden chaotic death of their parents, to enable and initiate their psychological abduction. Similar trauma afflicts the children on a planet devastated by an adult-ravaging virus (8) except that here the Mind Control perpetuates itself by peer pressure. The Earth Matrix saw levels of population Mind Control go through the roof with Covid fearmongering. Such programming will take time to dissipate. Not only globally but individually among the ranks of MK Ultra'd celebrities swelling the ranks of politics, Hollywood and the pop music industry.

RELATIONSHIP

Equivalent Major:
No. 6 THE LOVER

The Man Trap (Ep. 1), The City on The Edge of Forever (Ep. 27), **Amok Time (Ep. 29)**, Metamorphosis (Ep. 37), Journey To Babel (Ep. 38), The Paradise Syndrome (Ep. 57), Is There In Truth No Beauty? (Ep. 59), For The World Is Hollow And I Have Touched The Sky (Ep. 62), Elaan of Troyius (Ep. 67), Requiem For Methuselah (Ep. 73), All Our Yesterdays (Ep. 77).

These 11 episodes have a context of romantic or family Relationship, with emotions and choices testing the maturity of individuals and their devotions. Matrix interference applies here as much as anywhere. Anything bred by the Matrix in turn breeds toxic, dysfunctional, limiting or illusory patterns of emotion, thought and behaviour. Relationships are no exception. Matrix-bred attachment to polarity, self-identity, mental expectations, rules of behaviour and emotional needs and compulsions muddies relationships in Star Trek just as it will in our own lives until we let go of Matrix-bred dark essence from our own psyches. The Lover episode, Amok Time No. 29 exposes the farce of arranged marriage that still occurs on Earth. There is no love lost, or *any* emotional connection lost, between Spock and his Vulcan betrothed, T'Pring. They readily discard each other on their proposed wedding day although only just escaping Kirk being killed in the process. Nor will Relationship work in Star Trek's two other marriages of convenience, those of Queen Elaan (67) and McCoy/Natira (62). Elaan has only contempt for her assigned husband, while McCoy and Natira really only hitched up out of nothing better to do during his apparent last year of life.

Relationship as dysfunctional attachment to another person, or to the programmed reactions they engender, blights the life of two men with surrogate wives, the scientist Crater (1) and the polymath Flint (73). Women too. The spinterish Dr Miranda (59) ironically harbours jealous devotion to a disembodied being in her care. Spock's parents (29) despite their unemotional Vulcan culture, fall foul of emotional attachment to their son's choices and decisions. Spock himself shows admirable freedom from needing to please them but later, on an arctic planet in a regressed state (77) will suffer heartbreaking separation from his lover Zarabeth. The ending of Kirk's brief Relationship with Edith Keeler (27) proves equally distressing when he decides to let her die in a fated accident. The terrible choice thrust upon him in a matter of love and Relationship dramatizes the Lover card in the extreme.

Some semblance of real unconditional love expresses itself in the union of Kirok and Miramanee (57). Their brief marriage has them joyously and freely helping and caring for each other. Zephram Cochrane and his Companion (37) share a long-term Relationship that has elements of mutual neediness but also a true heart connection. These two unions are perhaps Star Trek's most optimistic though fleeting depictions of pure Relationship love. This despite Kirok's amnesia and the Companion's lack of a human body until the obliging Nancy Hedford provides one.

AI TAKEDOWN

Equivalent Major:
No. 7 THE CHARIOT (reversed)

What Are Little Girls Made Of? (Ep. 7), The Return of The Archons (Ep. 20), A Taste of Armageddon (Ep. 22), The Changeling (Ep. 31), The Apple (Ep. 33), **The Doomsday Machine (Ep. 34)**, I, Mudd (Ep. 36), The Ultimate Computer (Ep. 51), Spock's Brain (Ep. 55), For The World Is Hollow And I Have Touched The Sky (Ep. 62), That Which Survives (Ep. 71)

These 11 episodes have a context of technology gone wrong, running amok, crashing or in other ways being terminated. Here we come to Star Trek's portrayal of the rise and fall of Archonic AI seeking control over organic life. With The Chariot reversed, technology either crushes all or itself falls. 2023 has seen final and total disconnection of the Orion AI - the mainstay of Earth's Matrix - across the multiverse. These 12 episodes likewise dramatize and predict the fall of AI and the Matrix as Kirk and co confront and physically take down various incarnations of the Archonic menace.

The Doomsday Machine's portrayal of The Chariot reversed involves AI acting as a gigantic mechanical beast marauding through space, intentionally seeking out, destroying and eating everything in its path. AI can operate through such a rampaging giant but of course has more subtle incarnations both in Star Trek and our reality. Even so, like the AI in chess engines such as Stockfish that have far outpaced human competition, there is the same clinical, merciless, ruthless mode of operation. We see this in the human-sized talking, floating, dysfunctional machine known as Nomad (31) with its skewed logic setting it on course for eliminating all human life. Nomad proves a tricky job to eject from the Enterprise but the M-5 (51) is harder still, having been built into the starship as its operating system. Built into a similar command structure is the dual AI system prosecuting endless war between planets Emininar and Vendikar (22). Then there is the planetary security guard - AI disguised as a beautiful woman - who hunts down members of a landing party in Episode 71. All these AIs are successfully terminated.

Next up in AI's subtlety of physical incarnation is modification of the body. Government websites now tout the appeal of human augmentation technology so this is no conspiracy theory. Episodes 33, 55 and 62 show us some examples. Akuta (33), the leader of a semi-primitive jungle tribe, wears his AI device in the form of antennae, the dumbed down women of Sigma Draconis 7 (55) in the form of devices built into their belts, and the people on the asteroid-like space ship Yonada (62) in the form of a micro-chip implanted into the head (shades of Elon Musk technology). The next step would be turning people into cyborgs and zombies as seen in Episodes 7, 20 and 36. Dr Roger Kirby (7) trialling such technology is himself a cyborg, along with his staff. So is the entire race of superstrong men and gorgeous women throwing themselves at the feet of Harry Mudd in Episode 36.

Episode 20 reveals the crux of the Deep State's Great Reset in all its inhumanity. Future citizens of the global biosecurity state extolled by AI prophets like Musk, Schwab and Kurzweil are personified by the smiling, zombified humans on Beta 3. They live under total control of the planet's ruling AI, Landru. We should draw comfort from the humans obtaining freedom from Landru and from the takedown of malevolent AI programs throughout Star Trek and now in our post-Matrix reality.

JUSTICE

Equivalent Major:
No. 8 JUSTICE

The Conscience of The King (Ep. 11), The Menagerie (Ep. 13), Court Martial (Ep. 19), Turnabout Intruder (Ep. 78).

These four episodes have a context of the administration of Justice through inquiry, a hearing or a court martial. Kirk,

Spock and Karidian variously undergo these procedures in accordance with principles of justice and space law. The Justice card showing scales being weighed suggests the restoring of balance where for example someone's rights have been violated or as with Karidian (11), a crime has been committed. Upholding the law in regards to Kodos/Karidian's execution of 4,000 of his countrymen requires Kirk to first establish whether Karidian actually is Kodos. Kirk's single minded quest to arrive at the truth is symbolized in the Justice card by the sword of discernment being impassively held aloft.

The Matrix era saw Justice repeatedly not served on the perpetrators of crimes against humanity. The true identity of those responsible for three of the most notorious crimes in recent history, the assassination of Kennedy, the murder of Princess Diana, and 9/11, remains to be legally established. Judicial corruption and political obstruction have ensured that these cases have not even come to court. Likewise with the identities of those who benefitted from the child trafficking of convicted Ghislaine Maxwell. Conversely, the system vengefully pursued a wholly innocent man for exposing Matrix crimes - Julian Assange. Equally innocent is Kirk when twice targeted for judicial persecution, first for allegedly causing the death of Lt. Finney (19) and later for mutiny in Episode 78. His accusers are crazed and vindictive individuals, Finney who had faked his own death and Janice Lester who had secretly exchanged bodies with him.

Spock is tried for kidnapping ex-Capt. Pike (13) and taking him to the planet Talos, allegedly breaking a rule that carries the death penalty. However, bizarrely, his accuser is an illusion conjured up by the Talosians to play for time during the journey to their planet. Starfleet eventually drops the charge against Spock out of compassion. Justice aims to balance out rights and responsibilities but not by jettisoning compassion or mercy.

TAKING STOCK

Equivalent Major:
No. 9 THE HERMIT

The Galileo Seven (Ep. 15), The Devil in The Dark (Ep. 24), **The Deadly Years (Ep. 39)**, Obsession (Ep. 40), Requiem for Methuselah (Ep. 73).

These five episodes have a context of Taking Stock due to an old way of life having become redundant. The old way of doing things no longer works or proves counter-productive. A crisis prompts such a realization. In the first instance one must withdraw and go within or retreat somewhere in order to take stock of the situation. Such a challenge can never be avoided or pretended away. The mere fact of growing old, illustrated in the aged figure of the Hermit and in Episode 39 makes Taking Stock imperative at some point.

If we contemplate humanity as a single individual living through a dream that we call our world history, then the elites' plan to go ahead with their Great Reset despite the Matrix takedown is humanity's moment to Take Stock and ask basic questions. What right do the surviving Cabal members have to dictate our future and do they have humanity's consent? What are we dreaming into reality? Continuing to live as if we are still Matrix-bound would be absurd. Why unnecessarily prolong Matrix control, subjugation, manipulation, depopulation and enslavement? Nobody except the elites ever wanted a technocratic dystopia. The global assault on freedom and the manipulators responsible have been exposed. How must they be held to account and dealt with? This is Taking Stock.

Likewise Kirk and his colleagues, ageing super-fast in Episode 39 cannot pretend nothing is wrong. Kirk tries, pathetically. The only hope for him and his senior officers is to throw their diminishing energies into discovering and reversing the cause of their illness. A need to pause and reflect in a time of crisis afflicts Spock and his downed shuttlecraft (15). Similarly needing to take stock are the miners (24) being picked off, they think, by an unknown predator, and Kirk and Lt. Garrovick (40) fighting their feelings of guilt and inadequacy in their handling of a marauding atmospheric killer. All need to deeply reflect on themselves and the inadvisability of perpetuating old and familiar but no longer beneficial ways. Spock needs to relax his strong principles, the miners to refrain from the hunting and killing approach and Kirk and Garrovick to forgive themselves for human error.

The hardest lesson of all, perhaps, is learned by the prodigiously creative but obsessed and lonely man known as Flint (73). In a lifetime spanning thousands of years he has drawn to himself everything a man could possibly want by way of creation and possession - except a durable female companion and lover. He endeavours to create her artificially by his own hand. He fails, lacking the power of the one true Divine Creator. For all his powers and immortality up to this point, Flint too must Take Stock and face the fact of his limitations and vulnerability. He must then live accordingly. Likewise, Taking Stock of our rights and responsibilities in the post-Matrix era will indicate the work we need to do to restore our world.

MULTI-DIMENSIONALITY

Equivalent Major:
No. 10 THE WHEEL OF FORTUNE

Tomorrow Is Yesterday (Ep. 18), Errand of Mercy (Ep. 25), The Alternative Factor (Ep. 26), The City On The Edge of Forever (Ep. 27), Mirror, Mirror (Ep. 32), The Tholian Web (Ep. 63), Wink of An Eye (Ep. 65), The Lights of Zetar (Ep. 71) and All Our Yesterdays (Ep. 77).

These nine episodes have a context of phenomena transcending different dimensions of matter, space and time. They foretell humanity's entry as a species into the multi-dimensional universe as our liberation proceeds following the lifting of Matrix barriers. The holographic and multi-dimensional nature of our universe accounts for the Enterprise's teleportation device known as the transporter, for the food replicator producing the crew's meals and for Spock's ability of mind-melding. Also for time travel, facilitated with precision by Mr Atoz (77) but haphazardly undergone by the crew with the time jump accident in Episode 18 and the portal broached by a deranged McCoy in Episode 27.

Such technologies are the preserve of the Matrix elites managing the Secret Space Program off planet. As as we leave behind the defunct Matrix on Earth we will finally receive these suppressed multi-dimensional technologies. Eventually even disease, injury and short lifespans will be overcome. Such is the point of evolution reached by the Council beings of Organia (25) with their base form as points of light. Human and Klingon landing parties with their weapons, aggression and disharmony are viewed by them as savage and foolish. 'Your presence is painful to us' they tell the visitors. The implication is that the human race will, given enough time, evolve to similar higher dimensional levels of peace and wisdom.

Vastly evolved races are the exception in Star Trek. Crew encounter many less enlightened civilizations inhabiting various parallel dimensions. Such civilizations are frequently blessed with the technology and ability to work within multi-dimensional reality systems. But troubles dog them or they make trouble for Kirk and his fellows. They include the energy web-building Tholians (63), the dimension-hopping Scalosians (65), the invasive Zetarian spirits seeking a physical body (72) and the time-travelling citizens of Mr Atoz's planet. A parallel dimension harbouring negatively oriented versions of the crew is stumbled upon in Episode 32 and an alternate anti-matter universe is discovered in Episode 26 with two frantic men jumping back and forth across the universes via an inter-dimensional corridor.

SELF-MANAGEMENT

Equivalent Major:
No. 11 STRENGTH

Charlie X (Ep. 2), The Naked Time (Ep. 4), **The Enemy Within (Ep. 5)**, The Corbomite Manoever (Ep. 10), Balance of Terror (Ep. 12), This Side of Paradise (Ep. 23), Is There In Truth No Beauty? (Ep. 59), Let That Be Your Last Battlefield (Ep. 69), The Way to Eden (Ep. 74).

These nine episodes have a context of managing one's primal energy by neither repressing nor over-indulging it. This is notwithstanding demonic interference from The Adversary (The Devil card) or during time of War (The Tower card). Matrix society routinely programmed people from the age of small children into unthinkingly complying with its tenets, attitudes and values. Severely repressed is the Romulan Commander (12) duty-bound to a tee. He is austere, gloomy, taciturn and disciplinarian, both on himself and others. In a word, saturnine. So in her own way is the emotionally and sexually repressed Miranda (59). Reining in her passions to train as a psychic ambassador leaves her with a cool, nun-like demeanour yet harbouring bitterness and jealousy within.

Matrix programming will take some years to be phased out *en masse* but individually we can express our spontaneity and vitality any time in nonconformist, maverick ways. Never mind if one earns the reputation of mad, bad or dangerous. Unsettling is the impression created by the free-spirited 'space hippies' (74) on the more conservative elements of the Enterprise crew. Until their leader becomes fanatical and ruthless the hippies demonstrate uncommon but healthy ways of joyfully expressing themselves. Similarly free-spirited qualities of balanced Self-Management characterize the happy agricultural colonists in Episode 23. The only downside is their drug-induced condition indicating an artificially maintained state of balance.

The three possibilities for Self-Management - repressed, uncontrolled and balanced are shown in one person, Kirk, when he becomes psychologically split by the faulty transporter (5). One version of him is sheeplike, all mild compliance, the other is lusty raging thuggery. Once these opposites are finally reintegrated he returns to a balanced state of caring yet decisive alertness in the cause of rescuing marooned crew. Other instances of animal instincts running amok include the maniacal behaviour of the knife-wielding Tormalen (4), the tantrum-prone new recruit Lt. Bailey (10) and the jilted and besotted would-be lovers Larry Marwick (for Miranda, Ep. 59) and Charlie X (for Yeoman Janice, Ep. 2). Most destructively of all in their aggressive abandonment of all self-control are the madly raging enemies Bele and Lokai (69).

TRANSHUMANISM

Equivalent Major:
No. 12 THE HANGED MAN (reversed)

What Are Little Girls Made Of? (Ep. 7), **The Menagerie (Ep. 13)**, I, Mudd (Ep.36), The Gamesters of Triskelion (Ep. 43), Return To Tomorrow (Ep. 47), Spock's Brain (Ep. 55), Requiem For Methuselah (Ep. 73).

These seven episodes have a context of the degradation of our humanity by Transhumanism - the merger with AI, the ultimate controlling force of the former Matrix. This merger between artificial and natural, between technology and the body and between the human mind and the Archonic is more properly called *sub*-humanism. Such constraint on normal functioning is suggested in The Hanged Man card when reversed. Ex-Captain Pike (13) confined to his computerized wheelchair portrays such a dependence on technology. As does the literally brainless Spock (55) kept alive by McCoy's life support machine.

Augmentation of the human body or replacement by cloning happens in the case of the androids and cyborgs seen in Episodes 7, 36 and 73. If anything, the intended Matrix reality was even more far-reaching and sinister. The Cabal's plan was to do away with the human body altogether, not the elites' bodies but those of the rest of the population. This would have opened the way for AI's full spectrum conquest, with humans existing in mind only. An AI conquered race would exist only as a hive consciousness in an online cloud collective or 'metaverse', subsumed within the Archonic mind. The human body would become no longer physical but digitalized.

This scenario known as the Singularity is glimpsed in Episodes 43 and 47. In each we see the minds of once biological beings enclosed within silicon-based, synthetic objects. The trapped souls live a pathetic life of vicarious thrills or of restlessly wishing to escape the prison of their synthetic form. The androids in Episodes 7 and 73 at least have reasonably human-looking bodies to inhabit and mobilize. It is the lack of a harmoniously integrated emotional component that undoes their progenitors, the mad scientist Dr Kirby and the lonely genius Flint. A planet fully taken over by an AI called Norman that animates human-looking bodies (36) allows for a humorous look at the transhumanist dystopia. This AI acting through an imitative race of androids intends to progressively expand until it has taken over the whole galaxy. AI's insatiable appetite for conquest accords with the conclusion of SSP experiencers and whistleblowers. They diagnose AI as seeking to transhumanize organic life or to eliminate it altogether, universally.

SLAUGHTER

Equivalent Major:
CARD 13 reversed (unnamed but aka Death)

The Conscience of The King (Ep. 11), **The Devil in The Dark (Ep. 24)**, Operation Annihilate (Ep. 28), The Changeling (Ep. 31), The Doomsday Machine (Ep. 34), Wolf in The Fold (Ep. 41), The Immunity Syndrome (Ep. 45), The Ultimate Computer (Ep. 51), Let That Be Your Last Battlefield (Ep. 69), The Mark of Gideon (Ep. 70).

These 10 episodes have a context of a fearful and evil bringer of death and destruction. Authors of Matrix-friendly histories revere this kind of activity, as with Caesar and the Roman army's conquest of Europe or Columbus and the European conquest of the Americas. Archons and conquerors feast on fear, misery and death as do all Matrix-building Satanists possessed by the cannibalistic spirit of Wetiko. Violent Slaughter and destruction is depicted in the ravaging of Bele and Lockai's planet by the two warring races (69); and by the rampaging forces destroying planets (34), swallowing starships (45) or tormenting and killing innocent individuals (28).

But Episode 24 shows a clear difference between the Horta creature killing miners in defence of its eggs and the miners thoughtlessly destroying those eggs. The Horta's actions are morally justified by the ignorant viciousness of the miners. Wolf in The Fold (41) shows murder being carried out under intense mind control manipulation. This tallies with information coming from the Advanced Contact Intelligence Organization to the effect that genocidal criminals such as Hitler, Napoleon, Mao Tse Tung and Genghis Khan were acting under the influence of negative ET groups hungry for war, conquest and mass Slaughter.

Several episodes show karmic redress in action with slaughterers themselves being slaughtered. The genocidal Kodos (11) is killed ironically by his protective daughter in a fated accident during the course of establishing his guilt. The Doomsday Machine (34) is violently destroyed by Kirk and co, as are the giant amoeba in space (45) and the lethal flying jellyfish (28). Crew hurl into space and presumably destroy the evil spirit of Jack The Ripper (41) and the lethally crusading robot Nomad (31). In our present reality, Kimberly Goguen, charged with the job of 'Ground Command' - benevolently restoring harmony on Earth - has revealed the role of 'the enforcer' in returning to spirit non-repairable individuals attacking humanity as Matrix killers. Sent back to Source have been the top of the Cabal and thousands of operatives who refused to give up attacking the human race.

One episode that ends somewhat implausibly is No. 51 in which Kirk wins a battle against a murderous AI system controlling the Enterprise. As in several other episodes he talks it into eliminating itself. More realistic is the Governor of Gideon (70) being left to continue with his plan of genocide to curb his planet's overpopulation. His intention to release a fatal virus chimes in with our recent reality all too presciently.

THIRD FORCE

Equivalent Major:
No. 14 TEMPERANCE

The Enemy Within (Ep. 5), **A Taste of Armageddon (Ep. 22)**, Errand of Mercy (Ep. 25), Assignment Earth (Ep. 54), The Cloud Minders (Ep. 75).

These five episodes have a context of a neutral or harmonizing factor mediating two other forces at opposite poles of a spectrum. Polarization occurs when reality is subjectively perceived using the intellectual mind. Subjective perception is incomplete as phenomena objectively always involve the presence of three forces. Temperance shows an active force in the red jug and a passive force in the blue, harmonized or mediated by the angel, a mostly unseen Third Force. This Third Force of our own angelic nature empowers us to be creative, freeing us from the limitations of Matrix-engendered duality. Matrix forces emphasize duality and polarize all issues to exploit the principle of divide and conquer that reinforces the structure of control. The Matrix worked in us to instal a reductionist view of the multiverse where all is either black or white, strong or weak, good or bad, us or them. This illusion enabled governments to take the upper hand as a nefarious Third Force - a controlling, negative one with the few in power manipulating the polarized many.

This is carried to its logical conclusion in Episode 22 with a computer system presiding over and perpetuating war between rival planets. Third Force has been turned on its head to foment destruction instead of creation. With perceptions limited to opposites, we take sides, get stuck and go nowhere. This can apply in our own psyche (5), in war (22, 54), in attempted invasion (25), or in class and society (75). Discovering and activating a natural Third Force as in these episodes brings harmony and creative flow. So too when we follow natures's way and *be* the flow (the Tao) by alternating our activities or finding a middle way between Yin and Yang.

In truth all is one universal consciousness. Belief in duality obscures and debases this reality. Happily, Third Force, the Law of Three, continues to operate, only in subtle and not easily observable or discernible ways. These five episodes serve to show Third Force operating through compassionate parties to resolve conflict and chaos. Those parties are Kirk's Higher Self (5), the diplomat Ambassador Fox (22), the enlightened Organian Council (25), the troubleshooter Gary Seven (54) and Kirk as diplomat (75).

THE ADVERSARY

Equivalent Major:
No. 15 THE DEVIL

The Man Trap (Ep. 1), Court Martial (Ep. 19), Space Seed (Ep. 21), Obsession (Ep. 40), Wolf In The Fold (Ep. 41), **And The Children Shall Lead (Ep. 58)**, The Day of The Dove (Ep. 61), Whom Gods Destroy (Ep. 68), The Lights of Zetar (Ep. 72), Turnabout Intruder (Ep. 78).

These ten episodes have a context of physical, psychic or inter-dimensional attachment by demons or other invasive entities or spirits. The Adversary is another name for the Devil. The parasitical nature of the Matrix as a system feeding on the energy of an entire population has its counterpart in an entity that feeds on an individual host. An entity or person that has no soul, or no connection to her soul as in the case of Janice Lester (78), that derives sustenance from another being, that wants to remain unseen and cannot cease its parasitical activity does what the Matrix does in microcosm. These episodes treat us to a lurid variety of forms of psychic intrusion as the work of The Adversary. Janice, herself possessed by demons of resentment and revenge, possesses her enemy by swapping her body with his. Perhaps most terrifying are the entities inhabiting the psychopaths, Khan Noonian Singh (21) and Hengist (41). Both Khan bent on brutal galactic conquest and Hengist feeding on violence and terror are possessed by the same force of evil aka Wetiko that motivated dictators and mass murderers such as Genghis Khan, Cortez, Napoleon and Stalin.

Few individuals will manifest entity possession as spectacular or evil. Nor as physically evident as that in Episode 1, a possessed shapeshifting creature that feeds on salt and uses various seductive forms to deceive and entrap its victims. Entities more commonly feed invisibly on people's etheric bodies (life force energy) while creating havoc in their astral bodies (thoughts and emotions). People already traumatized make the easiest prey. Such is the case with the bereaved children in the Devil episode (58). Their tormenting entity is a bumptious, arrogant demon named Gorgon who never takes physical form.

The idea popularized by Carl Jung that we all have a naturally present shadow self relates well to the reality of AI intrusion having blighted all humans while the Orion Matrix was active up until 2023. The 18 AI systems would have psychologically or physically sickened all of us to some degree. Trauma further allows for more possession by parasitical entities not native to us in our natural, divine wholeness.

Four more episodes reveal possession occurring either through trauma (40 and 68) or psychic attack (61 and 72). In Episode 40, past trauma affecting Kirk and Garrovick overcomes them as the entity originally responsible reappears - a cloud-like predator that floats and kills indiscriminately. Garth's psychotic madness (68) came on after a traumatizing accident. Starship crew in Episode 61 come under psychic attack when an entity appearing as a ball of light comes aboard to feed on the hateful conflict it provokes. The sensitive Mira Romaine (72) experiences personal psychic trespass from entities appearing as floating coloured lights. Mira with her psychically open mind makes a spongelike human host. Her story serves as a warning to all of us to maintain our grounding and our psychic defences whenever under threat from possible entity possession.

WAR

Equivalent Major:
No. 16 THE TOWER (reversed)

Balance of Terror (Ep. 12), Arena (Ep. 17) , A Taste of Armageddon (Ep. 22), Errand of Mercy (Ep. 25), **A Private Little War (Ep. 46)**, Patterns of Force (Ep. 48), The Omega Glory (Ep. 50), Friday's Child (Ep. 53), Assignment Earth (Ep. 54), The Day of The Dove (Ep. 61) Let That Be Your Last Battlefield (Ep. 69), The Savage Curtain (Ep. 76).

These 12 episodes have a context of sustained and organised hostilities, threatened or manifest, between opposing groups or individuals. The Tower represents breaking out of a limiting status quo but reversed there is inhumane disruption and turmoil as in War.

Together these episodes amount to an aetiology of War presented in a cosmic survey. The variety of planets and races involved shows the conflict-engendering Matrix having extended its malign web across all borders of time and space. In the new energy we will transcend the old constraints and tensions and learn to thrive in freedom from low consciousness conflict.

Conflict usuall involves two antagonistic sides. Peace requires getting over the fact of mutual difference in polarized 3D, says the mad saga of Lokai and Belle (69). This must happen before ascending to higher dimensions of consciousness. One race, the humble Organians (25) are shown as having realized this truth, as having made it real. Their ascended level of consciousness places them above and beyond intrusive war-makers like the Klingons, even of would-be protectors like Kirk and the Federation. Organian humility and peacefulness goes in their culture with an absence of ruling authorities.

The Klingon attachment to authority and order-following (12) exemplifies the Political Matrix at every level, sustaining War and violating every spiritual tenet from Universal Sovereignty to Do No Harm to Unity in Diversity. So why did we tolerate War? Living in the grip of the Orion Matrix for 300,00 years there may have been no alternative. It may take another few thousand years to relinquish it, guesses Kirk after his showdown with the Gorn (17). With the whole Matrix collapsing, it should end a lot sooner - hopefully.

War is made by ego-driven criminals established in Matrix hierarchies. They think nothing of attacking, destroying and killing, causing massive suffering and death of innocents. And so it happens in Episode 22 except that the human authorities have delegated computers to decide on the numbers slaughtered. Nothing could exceed this in sheer stupidity and absurdity.

No one gains say a number of episodes except those who create conflict for energetic sustenance (61), for anthropological study (76) or for overthrowing the existing order in favour of a selfish or malign agenda (46, 50, 53). Post-Matrix, we will see a transition away from Earth governments instigating false flag attacks in the way of the Melokon regime (48) or mutually baiting each other in the way of the superpowers in Episode 54 playing with their new toys and wargames out in space.

PERVERTED PARADISE

Equivalent Major:
No. 17 THE STAR (reversed)

Shore Leave (Ep. 14), This Side of Paradise (Ep. 23), Who Mourns for Adonais (Ep. 30), The Apple (Ep. 33), The Trouble with Tribbles (Ep. 42), The Paradise Syndrome (Ep. 57), **The Way to Eden (Ep. 74)**.

These seven episodes have the context of the beauty and goodness of nature undermined by malevolent forces. The Star card shows the complex inter-dependence and fruitful synergy connecting humans, the environment and the whole cosmos as one. In many ways so do these episodes but they show the synergy gone wrong. This fittingly represents our Earth, with all and everything on it undermined and perverted by Matrix psychopaths, essentially Archons in human form.

For the Cabal masterminds, the lust for power can never be assuaged. Psychopaths care only about themselves and the theft of power from and over others. The Klingon infiltrator's poisoning of a shipment of grain (42) to gain an advantage in business shows the psychopathic disdain for ecological wellbeing of the environment. The hippy leader in Episode 74, although aspiring to the simple life in a natural paradise, shows an ironic and fanatical disdain for the humble coexistence he espouses. Cold-heartedly he cuts off the air supply to the Enterprise crew to secure their cooperation in getting to his desired Eden. Such ruthlessness has been writ large on Earth for eons with the planet bearing innumerable scars from unending battles and wars. We must now set about healing an environment blitzed by dual-use technologies including chemicals, electromagnetism and nanotechnology.

We see the damage in the form of relentless chemtrail spraying, swamping of the airwaves with EM frequencies, fluoridation of water supplies and genetic modification of crops - all amid silence from the authorities. A ruling AI on a lushly tropical planet (33) shows where this is heading. The natives are forbidden from procreating and kept dumbed down and surveilled by the AI. They are punishable by vegetation that can suddenly turn lethal. In a genuine paradise on another planet (57) the natives keep themselves in line. They are most probably *wetikoized* by reptilian 'gods' from long ago who had built them a temple in the shape of an obelisk. They turn violent when angered and stone Kirk and and his native wife for failing them.

Do humans actually prefer a Perverted Paradise? Episode 14 suggests that when granted their every wish in a magical amusement park, humans still look for excitement or risk. Judging by their manifested thoughts. the shore party crave the stimulation of fist fights, guns, warplanes and jousting tournaments. We would have to be drugged says Episode 23 if we wanted to live happily and peacefully in a perfect environment. After all, humans are an evolving race. We probably *need* challenge and difficulty in order to grow. For this reason, most of the landing party on Pollux IV (30) explicitly reject living in a paradise prefabricated by the powerful ET, Apollo. Such an idyllic life says Kirk would be 'nothing less than slavery' when required to worship an authority such as Apollo or his fellow 'gods'. Religion too will surely evolve in a post-Matrix world, bringing with it a new respect for Earth that the Native Americans called our Mother and treated as such.

ILLUSION

Equivalent Major:
No. 18 THE MOON (reversed)

The Man Trap (Ep. 1), Mudd's Women (Ep. 6), The Menagerie (Ep. 13), Shore Leave (Ep. 14), Catspaw (Ep. 35), **Spectre Of The Gun (Ep. 60),** Whom Gods Destroy (Ep. 68), That Which Survives (Ep. 71).

These eight episodes have the context of appearances created in the material world based on reality being multi-dimensional, holographic and malleable. Which it is. These illusory qualities allows for the arts of mystery, magic and imagination. But the Moon card reversed as it is here rather represents malign deception as well as Illusion.

In the understanding of the power of Illusion, humanity still falls behind ET visitors from higher dimensions. Matrix programming has ensured that most people remain unversed in multi-dimensionality and the time portal system as expounded in materials such as the books of Ashayana Deane or Elena Danaan. Without such knowledge, humans remain pawns to be exploited at will. Dark occultists among the Deep State hoarded and sequestered this knowledge to dupe the general public but they themselves were duped by their treacherous allies, the 4D Greys and Dracos.

Any intruders from the 4th Dimension will have an innate mastery of the power of Illusion. Such mastery is shown by the Providers on the Shore Leave planet (14) with their amusement park based on perceptual interference. While Greys and Dracos can manipulate our perceptions with 3D reality overlays, the Providers enable the shore party to create such Illusions themselves. Virtual reality scenarios are created by the unsuspecting crew with the same experiential effect as 'holographic inserts'. The term refers to illusory scenarios created by Greys and the Cabal to mislead humans on Earth. The creature in Episode 1 uses holographic inserts to beguile crew members with Illusions of desirable romantic partners. Likewise, the Talosians (13) try to seduce Pike with the Illusion of the injured Vena restored to her full beauty. Garth fools Kirk and Spock in Episode 68 by temporarily shapeshifting into the Governor or Spock himself, while an AI in Episode 71 protects its planet by projecting the image of a beautiful but deadly living woman.

The Providers in Episode 14 eventually give the game away whereas Spock in Episode 60 works it out for himself. In the partial recreation of Tombstone, Arizona, he makes the crew aware of their own part in creating the Illusion through their beliefs about reality. As in the Providers' amusement park they become able to start manipulating the Illusions themselves. We will all discover this power when we open up to fuller use of our consciousness. Pioneers have included psychic surgeons curing disease holographically, or people called stigmata bearing physical scars caused by their beliefs. The women using Mudd's Venus drug (6) enhance their beauty in a similar way. The drug may be a placebo but believing it to work they actually do transform their looks.

If Sylvia and Korub (35) are adept enough at witchcraft and sorcery to conjure up their Halloween regalia, they owe such powers of Illusion to having come from an alternate dimension closer to 4D than our 3D. But we are all of us in effect holographic projection creators, a fact that will become clear once we understand and master our multi-dimensional identity.

COERCION

Equivalent Major:
No. 19 THE SUN (reversed)

The Squire of Gothos (Ep. 16), Space Seed (Ep. 21), **Who Mourns For Adonais? (Ep. 30)**, I, Mudd (36), The Gamesters of Triskelion (Ep. 43), By Any Other Name (Ep. 49), The Omega Glory (Ep. 50), Bread and Circuses (Ep. 52), Plato's Stepchildren (Ep. 64), Wink of An Eye (Ep. 65), The Empath (Ep. 66), Whom Gods Destroy (Ep. 68), The Way to Eden (Ep.74), The Savage Curtain (Ep. 76).

These 14 episodes have the context of a person or group coercing captured or helpless individuals to do or sacrifice something that is against their true will. Coercion without actual force involves deception. Only a deceived people, as with the Covid hoax, would allow their inalienable rights to be coerced away through mandates such as lockdowns and travel bans. Governments trample on Natural Law while the people remain mostly deceived and oblivious. Through the trick of placing a legal identity on us at birth, authorities can supersede the highest Law of all with man-made laws. Legislation and statutes are the instruments of Coercion, the Matrix elite imposing its will on people ignorant of their rights under supreme Natural Law. The Sun card shows an unseeing person being assisted by one who can see by the clear light of the universal Father, divine and altruistic love. But people being made blind to their rights and then exploited not assisted - this is the Sun card reversed.

Jails around the world teem with inmates having broken man-made laws, but having done no harm. Those as innocent as marchers for freedom can find themselves manhandled and arrested at peaceful demonstrations. The harm - in violation of Natural Law - is done by authorities using unlawful and coercive legislation to usurp the supreme authority of living souls. Matrix governments prohibit using or selling recreational drugs while mandating under false pretences the taking of a toxic Covid test or injection. Coercing sovereign beings to forfeit inalienable rights is the crime being committed, as demonstrated by Ex Capt. Tracy (50). Time and again he takes Universal Law into his own hands, abusing sovereign rights and freedoms. Governments, politicians, judges and their enforcers have neither more nor less right than anyone else to coerce or constrain anyone who is not doing any harm. Their old Matrix ways will go the way of the fallen Matrix itself.

The benevolent universe represented by The Sun card upright bestows upon us all the same God-given rights. With the Sun card reversed and coercive these rights are denied to a landing party by the usurping Sun god Apollo (30). Trelane (16) ostensibly treats his captives as guests but coerces them into providing ceremonial entertainments. Parmen (64) takes this one step further, utterly humiliating captured crew members in the process. Coercive activities become torturous at the hands of the Vians (66) who treat the three-man shore party and the mute Gem like lab rats. The shore party on Triskelion (43) are forced to partake in violent combat as they are in a parallel tyrannous Rome (52) and in a war game staged by an alien being as a philosophical test (76).

Hijack is Coercion. Hijack of the Enterprise is resorted to by imperialistic androids (36); by a cold-hearted Kelvan leader (49) who kills a female crew member in the process; by the tyrant Khan (21) who almost succeeds in killing Kirk; and by the space hippies (74). Although devoted to individual freedom the hippies hypocritically force the starship to make passage to their dreamed-of Eden. The regal Deela (65), after easily securing her hijack seeks to secure Kirk's cooperation as a stud by holding him powerless in her accelerated dimension. And the crazy, vindictive Garth (68) fails in his hijack bid but otherwise delights in bullying and coercing asylum personel plus Kirk and Spock using his powerful matter manipulation abilities. After the Matrix takedown, coercion will be recognized alongside deception as no longer consistent with enlightened leadership and governance.

AWAKENING

Equivalent Major:
No. 20 JUDGEMENT

Arena (Ep. 17), The Devil in The Dark (Ep. 24), Mirror, Mirror (Ep. 32), The Omega Glory (Ep. 50), **Bread and Circuses (Ep. 52)**, The Cloud Minders (Ep. 75).

These six episodes have a context of truth revealed, of awareness expanded, accompanied by a rising of consciousness. The Judgement card shows a person arising out of a tomb of ignorance, denial or imprisonment as occurs with Merick's act of redemption in the Roman dungeons (52). In that epiphany he adopts the spirit of the escaped slaves who have repudiated the cruel and tyrannous

Roman regime. In rescuing the shore party he invokes what Jodorowsky calls 'a force defying death', literally in his case. This is the force of 'immaterial and immortal Consciousness.' Kirk's sparing of the Gorn's life at the climax of their 1-to-1 combat (17) is another such moment of individual Awakening. So is that of the miners' leader (24) made aware of his men's destructive treatment of the egg-laying Horta creature. And Kirk's advice (32) to the mirror Spock to help reform the despotic ways of the mirror Starfleet's Empire seems to have a catalyzing effect. Does the cunning henchman experience an Awakening in that instant? 'I shall consider it', he answers tantalizingly.

As is made clear in Episodes 50 and 75 however, Awakening out of the former Matrix mentality will be a numbers game. A majority need to awaken, a process that will require perhaps 3, perhaps 10, years on Earth given the thousands of years of blanket control by established rulers. But the elite are few, the people are many. Awakening of the people en masse will come, consolidating the takedown of the AI Matrix. Fearing a similar scenario, the stern ruler Plasus (75) fights desperately to keep his planet's miners in apartheid through mind-numbing underground conditions and enslavement. He remains intransigent but with Kirk's gas masks the rebel leader Vanna can help trigger an Awakening of the miners out of their plight.

Kirk's expedient in settling the war between the Yangs and the Kohms (50) is to passionately read them their Constitution guaranteeing equal rights for all. As with those races awakening, so with the people of Earth. The imperative is for all people to come to the realization that under Universal Law we all have inherent equal rights. This is our birthright. No just law can violate any person's freedom, nor cause them harm or loss. As people inevitably awaken to Universal or Natural Law so humanity will experience the peace and joy natural in a Matrix-free world

SELF-REALIZATION

Equivalent Major:
No. 21 THE WORLD

Arena (Ep. 17), This Side of Paradise (Ep. 23), **Errand of Mercy (Ep. 25)**, The City on The Edge of Forever (Ep. 27), The Paradise Syndrome (Ep. 57).

These five episodes have a context of the harmonious integration of all elements of the Self: mental, physical, emotional, creative and spiritual. With the Fool numbered 0, both ending and beginning again the round of 21 Tarot Majors, the implication is that this integration of the Self is a journey, a Tarot Trek, rather than a destination.

But a healthy society exhibiting this degree of Self-Realization shows up in Episode 25 with the humble and simple yet evolved people of Organia. All forms of war and violence are anathema to them. When imposed upon by a harsh Nazi-like invasion force they respond in the same relaxed way as the female figure in the World Card. Like her, they remain unattached and untroubled, yet finally non-compliant. The return of Matrix repression holds no threat in their condition of inner mental and emotional freedom. Another race likewise embodying spiritual evolution and the semblance of an enlightened humanity are the Metrons. We meet them in Episode 17 with Kirk being called upon to discard warlike ways in dealing with a race of reptilians. The androgynous, gowned Metron who materializes on a hill above Kirk uncanilly resembes aspects of the dancer in the World card.

The World card's depiction of the joy of simply being, of embracing a kind of Taoist navigation of reality, manifests itself among the colonists on the agricultural planet in Episode 23. Free and peaceful though they are, theirs is not an unconditional joy of being. But for as long as the narcotic effect of a naturally occurring plant lasts, they are able to live happily in nature. In this state they exist in tune with their needs, each other and their inner selves.

Temporarily blessed in similar ways are the mind-wiped Kirok and his newly taken wife Miramanee (57). The love between them is sincere and heartfelt without either of them dominating or draining the energy of the other. They personify the World card in its representation of satisfaction, fulfilment, and flowing harmoniously with the present moment. This characterizes the couple as they play in the forests, happily carry out domestic duties or help their tribe with practical projects.

Self-Realization is characterized by a combining of virtues in a relaxed and receptive yet actively capable and pragmatic way. This is demonstrated by Edith Keeler (27). Edith, though the proprietor and manager of a Mission for down and outs, avoids the ways of rigid authority. She uses her position of responsibility to inspire and teach her dependants to believe in themselves. They too, she tells them, play a part in mankind building its interstellar future. As in The World card she keeps her own spirit pure and joyous, while motivating others to come into realization of their true Self.

6
THE THEMES

The gist of Star Trek The Original Series is a 5-year mission in the 23rd century of a 440-crew starship of the United Federation of Planets. Under leadership of the charismatic Captain James T. Kirk are his half-Vulcan logic-oriented 1st Officer Mr. Spock and gruff Medical Officer Leonard McCoy. These three senior crew, complementary in their characters and sometimes mutually abrasive but always buddies, form the crux of many adventurous expeditions. Other crew featuring regularly are the Chief Engineer known as Scotty, female Communications Officer Uhura, Mr Sulu the Helmsman, Chekhov the Navigator and Nurse Christine Chapel.

Each of the following 78 chapters examines the overriding theme of each episode of Star Trek in the light of the Tarot and the now disconnected Matrix. Each episode's theme correlates it with one of the 78 cards of the Marseille deck. Taken together, the combination of episode and card esoterically and prophetically unveils an aspect of life vis-a-vis the former Matrix control system, a system that persists now only in memory and habit. For a study of Star Trek, the Tarot or the Matrix in isolation there are many guides available in print or online. See the Resources section for recommendations.

Star Trek The Original Series consisted of:

Season 1, Episodes 1 - 28, first aired 1966-1967
Season 2, Episodes 29 - 54, first aired 1967 - 1968
Season 3, Episodes 55 - 78, first aired 1968 - 1969.

The numbering of the 78 episodes and their themes follows the chronological numbering given in The Encyclopedia Shatnerica. In that book's list and in this, the 2-part episode The Menagerie, No. 13, functions as a single episode with a single story and a single theme. The Menagerie re-worked and replaced the unused pilot The Cage.

1. FANTASY LOVE

The freedom to truly know ourselves will dispel former entrapments and dangers

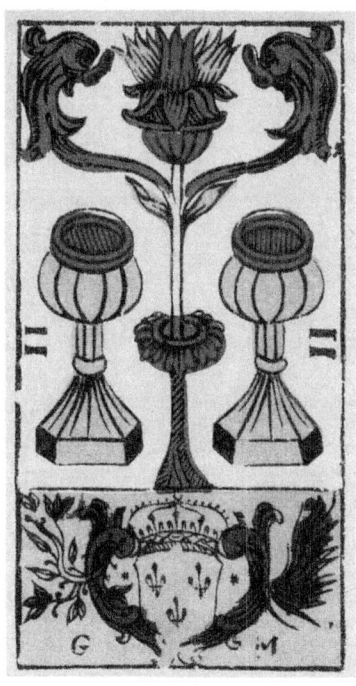

Episode 1 **'The Man Trap'** correlates with the **2 of Cups**; both are themed around a growing attraction between two people involving desire, romantic idealism, deception or projection.

THE CARD
The 2nd Major, The High Priestess, governs the qualities of the 2s in the Minor Arcana. So like her, each of the 2s deals with some form of preparation or gestation. With Cups being the suit of love and romance, the **2 of Cups** represents the development of loving feelings, the preparation for a relationship. A single tall and elegant flower divides itself into two in a heart-shaped pattern. The flower becomes affectionately perhaps droolingly licked by two fish-like creatures. This is the adoration of the image of the beloved. And yet we see the beautiful petals and the ecstatic lovers both arising out of the single bloom. The flower within, one's own Soul, is the true source of love, no matter how alluring the outer object of desire. This is not to deny outer reality but to affirm the absolute importance of one's own existence transcending the duality of subject and object. This **2 of Cups** then, implies an illusory potential that will become pronounced if **reversed**. Even **upright**, this is a stage

or type of relationship where there tends to be yearning and adoration, the feeling of being incomplete without the Other.

A definite element of fantasy or of excited anticipation announces itself in the **2 of Cups reversed**. Emotions may be running high in an adolescent way leading to self-deception; or to addiction or slavery to love. This a budding relationship marred by unreal perceptions as in infatuation or projection. Or there may be the allure of mystery, or the promise of instant wealth, great sex or social or profesional advancement driving a dubious attraction on one side or the other.

'THE MAN TRAP' PREMISE
A chameleon-like creature shapeshifts into people's dream lovers in order to vampire their bodily salt. Two men in particular are emotionally challenged.

CONTEXT
Relationship, The Adversary, Illusion.

FANTASY LOVE
Kirk, McCoy and junior officer Darnell beam down to ancient ruins on Planet M113. Their mission is a routine medical check on the resident archeologist Robert Crater and his wife Nancy. When Nancy welcomes them, each man perceives her as a different woman. To McCoy she still has deep black hair, looking exactly as she did when they were lovers 10 years before. To Kirk, she is a mature lady starting to go grey. To Darnell she is a seductive siren he once met who soon has him following her out onto the barren planet. Darnell is then discovered dead, his face covered in blotchy, red marks. What first looks like poisoning is found to be instead death by salt depletion. Kirk's suspicions are raised by both the Craters' concern over their low supplies of salt after 5 years on M113. Even as Kirk starts hunting the killer, two more of his men die. The killer is a shapeshifting creature craving bodily salt from its victims. Impersonating one, it beams aboard the ship to prowl its corridors for more salt. It kills again and Dracula-like, bewitches and almost gets the better of, Uhura. Robert Crater comes aboard after telling how the creature killed his adored wife. He has been carrying on a fantasy love relationship with the creature itself after it having taken on his wife's form. Disguising itself as McCoy, the creature evades capture on the ship till cornered by the real McCoy (!) for whom it again impersonates the young Nancy. In a lurid confrontation, McCoy feels unable to shoot Nancy/the creature in order to save Kirk from its clutches. Spock intervenes to prompt McCoy to do the deed. Slain, the creature changes back

into its original monstrous form. It was 'the last of its kind', Crater had said, likening it to the American buffalo. Kirk finally, is left in his Captain's chair pondering its sad extinction.

CARD/EPISODE AND MATRIX TAKEDOWN

Matrix slavery had, and may still have, a strong aspect of inner slavery. Psychologically this involves a kind of Emotional Matrix: falling prey to debilitating emotions enabled by ignorance or delusions about the workings of our own psyche. We experience this all too often in romantic attachment and we see it in Crater and McCoy's love for a woman who once had them in passionate thrall. Through this attachment, a desperate and unscrupulous entity is able to take advantage. The entity targets their desires in love and romance, areas where they and many of us may be vulnerable to unrealistic ideals and passions - the **reversed 2 of Cups**. So long as we allow fantasies, projections and enticing illusions free rein, we replace our self-control with helplessness. Our inner life becomes a Hollywood-style dream world running on autopilot cut off from the Higher Self. Having been freed from controlling AI systems we now have the opportunity to free ourselves inwardly from emotional programs running our life. We may have been susceptible to smooth-talking players or honey traps luring us into suspect relationships or schemes. These and myriad other weaknesses in love, sex and romance can be let go of as we let go of our dark essence generally.

Advertising, media hype and political rhetoric can similarly entice us. The very term 'government' broken down etymologically means 'mind control' - gaining power over people by manipulation of perceptions. The Tavistock Institute set up in London in 1920, worked intensively to pioneer mind control programs such as MK Ultra and Monarch. Population mind control uses emotions, very commonly fear, to drive people in a certain direction. In the case of the salt monster, the tactic is romantic allure and seduction. With its ability to instantly psych out its intended victims, the creature identifies McCoy's emotional weakness. Kirk calls it 'that one woman' in his past whom 10 years later he is 'still mooning over'. By taking on Nancy's appearance and behaviour, the creature hopes to reawaken in McCoy a passive, disempowering infatuation. McCoy in fact treats the whole matter very coolly, at least until the final struggle. To gain a real hold over him, the fake Nancy must go into full **reversed 2 of Cups** mode of slimy seduction and caressing. Treating him like the flower sensually licked in the Tarot card, she leans on his shoulder and lovingly strokes his face. In his ear she purrs 'You have such strong memories of me ... you do care, don't you Leonard?' At no time does McCoy succumb to physical rapture with this vampiric impostor. The really hooked and trapped one is Crater who knowingly lives in the fantasy that the creature is his wife. 'I loved Nancy very much. Few women were like Nancy. She lived in my dreams.' As for the creature, Crater states that it needs love as much as salt, claiming he forgave it for killing Nancy because of it being 'the last of its kind'. Crater thus rationalizes his dysfunctional love by identifying it as compassion. But this cuts no ice with Kirk who calls the creature Crater's 'private heaven here on this planet'.

In fact, anyone trapping themselves into loving a fantasy - someone that they imagine or want the Other to be - moons and swoons themself into an addiction, an emotional obsession, a gilded cage rather than a heaven. The infatuation is ultimately with the mystery of oneself projected onto the Other and reflected back to oneself. This becomes the narcissistic fantasy we see in the **2 of Cups reversed**. The fishes drool over the flower, losing themselves in attachment, whether to beauty, the Other, sex, oneself reflected, or to love itself. Any such obsession leads one into a prison of our own making and potentially as with Crater, to our doom. With the Matrix firmly in control, large majorities of populations were unable to see Satanic, psychopathic oligarchs masquerading as their trusted governments, playing them with a hidden agenda. Crater even knows that the creature addictively craves salt and will kill mercilessly for it. And yet he cannot see that the creature will ultimately kill him for it, which it does. Danger always lies in being unable to discern whether someone is good for us or not. This applies equally to a governing authority as to a lover. In such cases we are skating on extremely thin ice. The level of control we hand over to the Other virtually guarantees our destruction or betrayal one way or another. And yet still we will do anything to keep the relationship or association from dissolving, even if never grounded in the reality of truth in the first place. But the Matrix has fallen. And so will living by delusions and propaganda.

AFTER THE TAKEDOWN

As we release the comforting illusions we formerly lived by, we will no longer cooperate with our own downfall, sabotage and enslavement. With the power at last to see and feel our *self*-deception we will no longer blame *others* for deceiving us. We were all blind-sided by Matrix influences and indoctrination from the earliest age. With Matrix systems gone or collapsing we may now clear lower vibrational energies that had us willing pawns of controllers or manipulators. In our personal lives we will no longer play lonely, unworthy-feeling dreamers looking to be saved by *that* woman or *that* man who is the one for us. Fear, infatuation or perceived unworthiness will leave us as we raise our vibration in line with true love and wisdom.

2. THE EMOTIONAL MATRIX

Raising our vibration will lift us clear of the obsolete Emotional Matrix pendulum

Episode 2 '**Charlie X**' correlates with the **Page of Cups**; both are themed around a sensitive young person trapped in emotional attachment to perceived needs or desires.

THE CARD
The youthful **Page of Cups** treads daintily leftwards, eyes fixed not on where he's going but on the Cup in his hand. The Cup represents the emotional aspect of his Lower Self or Body Mind. Though preoccupied with it, his grip on it is shaky; it teeters in his open palm, ready to topple over and spill. And it's filled to the brim with passionate red, representing volatile attachments. For all his gentle manner this is actually a highly strung person who acutely feels excitement or disappointment. He - or it may be she - partially veils the Cup and keeps the lid in his other hand ready to be quickly replaced - a sign of someone still self-conscious and shy. He's nervous and cautious about expressing himself or revealing his vulnerability. He's likely to have issues to do with self-esteem, falling in love, strong desires, guilt, emotional hurts, bottled up explosive frustration or anger. Nevertheless this is the only **Page** actually walking along. This and his crown of flowers indicates an enthusiastic, idealistic char-

acter learning through experience to acquire both self-esteem and freedom from entrapment in the Emotional Matrix.

Reversed, this may be an over-reactive and temperamental adolescent. Lessons will come all the more dramatically in dealing with social situations, family and romance. In his personal and social awkwardness he must beware upsets and tantrums.

'CHARLIE X' PREMISE
A teenage orphan blessed with extraordinary telekinetic powers but emotionally volatile, boards the ship and causes dangerous havoc.

CONTEXT
Power, Self-Management.

THE EMOTIONAL MATRIX
The Enterprise takes delivery of 17-year old Charles Evans, orphaned since a space accident 14 years ago. Socially deprived, he feels overwhelmed in his new environment and especially among women. His emotional reactions are impulsive and awkward. He jovially slaps Yeoman Janice Rand on the behind and succumbs to acute embarrassment in the face of reprimands and rejection. Charlie didn't like his previous elders while on board the spaceship Antares. In a moment of anger and spite using his extraordinary psychic power he annihilates the Antares and its 20-strong crew. This causes him less guilt than the ticking off he receives for his faux pas with Janice. The attractive woman becomes his painful teenage crush and focus of his bondage to the Emotional Matrix. Kirk tries to talk him into realizing he cannot have everything he wants, including Janice. But Charlie rebels and lashes out psychically in all directions leaving a trail of chaos and zapped crew. Having gone on to hijack the ship he is only brought to order by the return of his keepers in spirit. They sternly take him back into captivity and deprivation, much to his sorrow and hurt.

CARD/EPISODE AND MATRIX TAKEDOWN
The Matrix extended into our innermost life trapping us on a pendulum of swinging emotions. Living on a pendulum debases our infinite free self and moves us through habituated programs and reactions of elation or despair, satisfaction or dismay. Charlie's vulnerability to how others perceive him comes from just such a mechanism of attachments and entrapments characterizing his inner life. He is the **Page of Cups** lost in fearful rumination on the deep red interior of the emotional Cup in his hand. His fears and low self-esteem generate his reactions of anger and aggression. 'They didn't

like me' he says reproachfully of the amiable crew of the Antares. 'Everything I do or say is wrong', he says resentfully when talked to sensitively by Kirk. Worst of all is his experience of the pangs of unrequited love. 'What if you care for someone?' he painfully asks Kirk when told he can't necessarily have whatever he wants. Young Charlie is coming from a place of attachment through confusion, upset, exasperation and thwarted desire.

Those emotions weighing him down need to be cleared and healed. Until they are they will go on regurgitating themselves. All emotional attachments whether positive or negative chain us to the reactive Lower Self. Indulging in these states keeps our consciousness in the Emotional Matrix where we constantly, exhaustingly, swing between polarities. The energy we lose goes to discarnate entities inhabiting the lower 4th astral plane who have a feast when we are feeling upset or pessimistic. Such a parasite comes to stalk the Enterprise in Episode 61, The Day of The Dove. The Matrix itself was a parasitical machine that fed on low frequency stimulation 24/7. MSM propaganda, dumbed down TV, Hollywood violence, Satanically encoded pop music and 'Smart' technologies dragged down the collective vibration to levels orchestrated by the Matrix elite for their transhumanist agenda. Picking up a daily newspaper and buying into its incitements to fear an illusory pandemic or inanely celebrate a sporting victory guaranteed a ride on the emotional roller coaster of Matrix polarities now thankfully on the retreat.

How did young Charlie pick up emotional habits of such low vibrational frequency? How do any of us? The answer is, or was, the Matrix - a prison of the mind knowing no borders. Where there is control, duality and the predominance of 5-sense perception there are the polarities of light and dark, positive and negative, and nice and not nice (in Charlie's words). At any place in 3D, the old Matrix-inculcated ways remain a challenge. We have to learn to stay connected to our true centre, our Higher Self with its feeling of who we really are. Higher Self in effect acts as Third Force observing and mediating excesses of excitement or boredom, happiness or sadness, pride or guilt. For Charlie, one moment Janice loves his amazing card tricks - he feels triumphant. At another, she chides him for slapping her behind - he feels deflated and ashamed. The Matrix pendulum has him. It still has us so long as we can be so readily and thoroughly turned this way and that.

Happily, the post-Matrix world will see people raising their frequency above the low level of dense emotions and AI frequencies of the past. Rather than repressing emotional energy we will allow it to flow back and forth without over-indulging it. States of anger, fear, sadness or guilt will never cease to arise as long as we exist in dualistic 3D, as established in Episode 5. But once we raise our vibration out of reach of problematic low desires and emotions, we will gain a certain immunity from them. They will briefly pass, hardly affecting us. As our vibration continues to rise, we will gain greater control over our astral bodies. From a naive or volatile **Page of Cups** we will grow into a vibrant but stable King or Queen of Cups, able to control and moderate our desires, anger, frustration or disappointment rather than letting them control us. In the wake of Matrix disablement we will find freedom from the Emotional Matrix, no longer swinging between states of low vibrational frequency with their destructive effect on ourselves and others.

In the gym, Charlie has a meltdown when a crew member laughs at him for being thrown by Kirk. Charlie reacts by telekinetically wiping out the chuckling man. Kirk orders Charlie to his quarters threatening to carry off the recalcitrant lad himself in a tone unmistakably irate and severe. Rather than his fury overcoming him as it frequently does Charlie, Kirk uses the emotion to enforce his will. Charlie could use his lethal power against Kirk, but Kirk's righteous anger and iron will prove decisive, actually causing some remorse in the boy. Perhaps he recognizes in Kirk what both Spock and McCoy agree he needs: a father-figure and mentor to be respected and listened to. Strong but compassionate in guidance, Kirk demonstrates mastery of emotion that can come only by one's own efforts. But Charlie, distanced from his Higher Self like Wild Kirk in Episode 5, remains fixated on his Lower Self's wants and passions. Eschewing tolerance and empathy, he resorts to retribution and violence against anyone who is 'not nice' standing in his way. He must have whatever he wants. With such emotional immaturity, Charlie cuts himself off from everything that is of higher frequency than his self-serving childish ego. Again, Kirk shows compassion in pleading with Charlie's superiors to let this regressive **Page of Cups** learn and grow among others of his own kind. But to no avail. Imprisoned emotionally, Charlie must return to physical imprisonment.

AFTER THE TAKEDOWN

Following the 2023 demise of Matrix control systems we are free to begin raising our general vibration as never before and freeing ourselves from inner chains of delusion, desire, greed and selfishness. We will rapidly grow emotionally and spiritually. This will mean not so much living without passion but learning to control the expression of our desires and emotions, rendering them appropriate to surrounding conditions. For this we will benefit from using the humility and the willingness to learn of the **Page of Cups upright**. Thus we will grow inwardly and integrate patience, sensitivity and care in dealing with ourselves and others.

3. MENTAL POTENTIAL

Our mental powers will be enhanced to the extent that we use them responsibly

Episode 3 '**Where No Man Has Gone Before**' correlates with the **Ace of Swords**; both are themed around mental capacity and its potential to be unleashed positively or destructively.

THE CARD
A clenched hand grasps a Sword throwing off sparks in all directions. The Sword points to heaven and aims itself through a floating crown. Swords in the Tarot refer to the mind. We can see this Sword aspiring to higher things, above all to recognition and glory attained by cognitive or psychic skills, knowledge or intelligence. Unlike the heart, the mind operates dualistically under the rule of fear or desire. The mind is a 'double-edged sword' depending on whether it operates alone or under guidance of the heart and through integration with the Soul. As for the Aces, they concern ability and willingness. The **Ace of Swords** then, is about the variable potential of the mind. Mental abilities can be ignored or developed; can be used positively or negatively; can include facility with reason (plans, logic, analysis, assumptions, concepts), with imagination (painting, writing, composing) or with intuition (telepathy, precognition, telekinesis, remote viewing etc). These faculties and many more lie dormant within us awaiting

activation and development.

Reversed, the mind has destructive power if wrongly or harmfully used. The hand gripping the Sword becomes a fist: closed, hostile, controlling. There can be willingness to lie, mislead or cover up. A mind intent on Service To Self will seek personal gain or assertion of superiority while trampling over the interests of others. Mental power negatively used can lead to corruption or obsession, to the psychopathic urge to manipulate, control or torment. The potential is always there says the **Ace of Swords** to use the mind for good or ill.

'WHERE NO MAN HAS GONE BEFORE' PREMISE
Two crew members freakishly acquire awesome mental powers. Gary uses his egoistically and destructively. Elizabeth uses hers to try to rein him in.

CONTEXT
Power, Insanity, Self-Management.

MENTAL POTENTIAL
The Enterprise leaves the galaxy to go into a magenta-coloured storm area that had destroyed the SS Valiant. Before he died, the latter's last surviving crew member had began frantically questioning his computer about ESP. The storm damages the Enterprise too. Casualties include psychiatrist Elizabeth Dehner and helmsman Gary Mitchell - coincidentally both high in ESP. Mitchell in sick bay starts developing increasingly dramatic psychic powers. He moves from mega speed-reading and memorizing to manipulating his body functions to reading minds to levitating cups to remotely toying with the bridge controls. Spock warns of a dangerous mutation in him but Dehner disagrees. She sees Mitchell as the possible forerunner of an improved type of human. To avoid a repeat of what happened to the Valiant, Kirk directs the Enterprise to Delta Vega, an uninhabited planet where he intends to abandon Mitchell. But Mitchell with his glowing silver eyes and now awesome powers escapes custody taking Dehner with him. She too acquires similar mental potential. Kirk catches up with them out among the rocks where Mitchell has started using his mind to green the planet. He forces Kirk into grovelling on his knees but Dehner intervenes. The two super-powered crew members attack each other until Mitchell zaps Dehner dead. Kirk finally prevails by burying Mitchell under a rockfall.

CARD/EPISODE AND MATRIX TAKEDOWN
The Emotional Matrix had its counterpart in the Mental Matrix. This is the network of thoughts, attitudes, beliefs and mental reactions programmed

into us from a young age and consolidated all through life by the prevailing culture. Programmed thinking operates at the lower vibrational Body Mind level where it is amplified by emotions. And the Sword of the mind as noted operates dualistically. Everything is either fearful or desirable, true or false, right or wrong, good or bad, me or you, like or not like. This is the 3D level of existence founded on programming, polarity and separation. This polarizing aspect of the old Matrix governs all our thinking when cut off from Third Force operating through higher levels of our being such as the heart or Higher Self seen in Episodes 5 and 22. And yet the mind, imperiously crowned in the **Ace of Swords** card considers itself king. The mind in its infatuation with its own inestimable power so often has no conception that it might be sick, might be unnaturally ego-driven; even less that it might be extensively subject to mind control within the Matrix as it was.

As Gary Mitchell's mental powers increase he ironically falls under vastly intensified Matrix control until taken over completely by that diseased mindset. He morphs into an arrogant psychopath devoid of feeling for others while wedded to the perception of himself as a god lording it over ordinary mortals. He becomes a megalomaniac like the insane psychopaths ruling Earth and alluded to in such episodes as 21, 48, 64 and 68. Signs are his obsession with superhuman feats, his personal grandiosity and his scorn for human obstacles. The heads of the bloodline families directing the worldwide pyramid of Matrix control have the same mixture of misanthropy and power-mad obsession. 'If I keep getting stronger,' Mitchell muses, 'the things I could do ... like maybe a god could do.' This craving of the mind to amass power over others epitomizes the crowned **Ace of Swords** at it most **reversed** and dysfunctional.

Matching Gary MItchell in his power-mad ambitions was the Cabal forcing through an agenda to ramp up its dictatorship of the world. Legislation and preparations rolled on day by day to institute a Tholian web of fascistic controls including vaccine passports, the end of cash, Chinese-style social credit systems, 5G towers and satellites, and ever-tighter censorship of truth and free speech. The apogee of all this governmental activity would have been the Singularity turning humanity into a race of semi-robotic human cyborgs functioning as an AI-powered hive mind. This present time in history with the Matrix suddenly gone is going to be one of humanity undergoing a vibrational shift upwards. This accords with the idea of ascension to higher dimensions discussed in Ashayana Deane's Voyagers books. Without the Matrix, a collective rise in our spiritual vibration will pave the way to a Great Awakening rather than the Global Elite's dystopian Great Reset. Our visible and invisible political leaders, bereft of connection to the heart, will inevitably fail to secure their Gary Mitchell-style dream of god-like status.

With the mind separate from the heart à la **reversed Ace of Swords**, the temptation is to use it to assert oneself over others. With greater mental power comes greater responsibility. How will we use what author David Wilcock calls our imminent 'supernatural godlike powers,' His 2016 book The Ascension Mysteries predicts a time soon of 'instantaneous telepathy ... levitation ... telekinesis ... fully aware that you are a soul having a human experience ... your level of intelligence vastly greater than anything you had access to in the past.' Such powers he says, will increase as we raise our vibration and attain a quantum leap in our evolution. This he calls the ultimate goal of being human. He instances telekinesis 'where you levitate objects, even of colossal size, and command them to move with your mind.' Exactly as Gary Mitchell does in sick bay floating a coffee cup across the room and subsequently on the planet levitating boulders in attempts to crush Kirk. We will ascend and gain these abilities says Wilcock, when we move beyond fear and addiction and 'demonstrate love, patience, humility, acceptance, forgiveness and the courage to face the truth.'

But will feelings of the heart neutralize self-aggrandizement? The corrupting tendency of power has never been consistent with the spread of universal freedom and personal sovereignty. Quite the opposite. Dehner represents a less corruptible intelligence than Gary's. But the psychiatrist realizes too late how obsessed and crazed her super-gifted companion has become. How similar is this situation to the power ascendancy of our Cabal, gifted with AI and alien tech thanks to its grey and reptilian partners? An answer came in the 1990s from Alex Collier's Andromedan contacts. They warned him of a galactic tyranny emerging 350 years in the future and originating on planet Earth unless stopped now. Mitchell's reproach to Kirk mid-combat becomes highly resonant: 'You should have killed me while you had the chance,' he tells the stricken Captain who just, only just, prevails.

AFTER THE TAKEDOWN

Humanity's shift resulting from the takedown of the Matrix will nullify the intended Great Reset. Benevolent forces of the Universal Council acting in association with planetary guardian Kim Goguen have ended negative and hostile alien interference. Liberation from AI and Cabal control will enable us to align with peace and universal abundance. The way lies in recognizing and benevolently activating our unlimited mental potential and co-creative consciousness. This will see us practising Service To Others as well as to ourselves, and repudiating the ego-driven agendas. of the fallen Cabal.

4. EMOTIONAL CLEARING

All our emotions are to be felt and accepted, enabling us to respond as appropriate

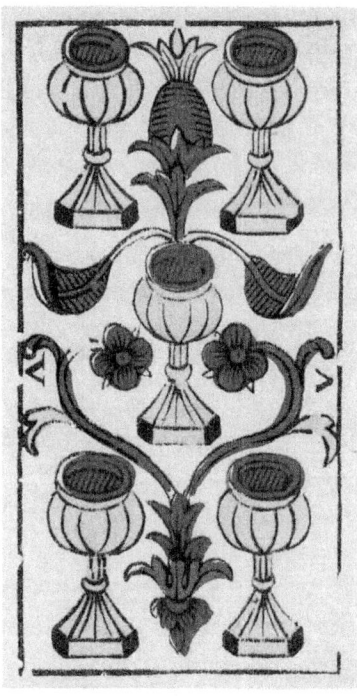

Episode 4 '**The Naked Time**' correlates with the **5 of Cups**; both are themed around emotional expansion and growth including acknowledgement and clearing of repressed or denied emotions.

THE CARD
Just as the heart chakra lies at the centre of the body's chakra system, so a single powerful Cup lies at the centre of the **5 of Cups**. From this Cup grows a majestic plant not yet ready to flower. But decorative flowers appear on either side on stalks forming a beautiful heart-shaped pattern. With Cups representing emotions and feelings, the central Cup corresponds to our spiritual centre, the heart chakra, holding the balance for the whole structure. Heart-centred love communicates its energies to both the upper and lower pairs of Cups corresponding with the chakras above and below the heart centre. These other Cups receive and reciprocate the love energy, the upper Cups nourishing the mind and the lower Cups the body and will. Hence, in our balanced state we are suffused with Oneness energy, a Body Mind radiating and receiving love in a feedback loop with the centre of our being, the heart chakra that links us to our Soul and Higher Self. The equivalent Arcanum is the 5th, The Pope,

representing a bridge to higher worlds. 5 in numerology represents exploration, expansion and new learning. So **upright**, this card indicates a well-balanced, vibrant and active state enabling us to grow in emotional awareness and understanding. We are experiencing and learning to handle the full range of emotions while holding our connection to Higher Self qualities of compassion, empathy, joy, appreciation, care and gratitude. Emotional expansion and development continues throughout life as a journey rather than a destination. Like the central, unblossomed plant, we are here to grow in love while inhabiting a Body Mind. This means to harness whatever emotions come up in daily life, particularly in a world still inured of the old Matrix control system. Emotions arising at the 3D level of Body Mind manifest themselves through polarities of positive or negative. They have their own logic and intelligence as do feelings. The latter emanate from the heart and transcend duality. We grow by learning to balance and moderate Body Mind emotions in relation to the feelings of the heart centre and Superconsciousness.

Blocked emotions are symbolized by the 4 of Cups reversed; over-indulged or reckless emotions by the **5 of Cups reversed**. In both cases learning still happens but more slowly or dramatically, respectively. Emotional trauma, stress, hurt or upset may be involved, or unfulfilled longings triggering turbulent episodes. We may be struggling with outgrown patterns or with difficulty connecting truthfully to ourself or others.

CONTEXT
The Adversary, Insanity.

'THE NAKED TIME' PREMISE
A dis-ease involving dramatic release of buried emotions afflicts the crew. Revelations come aplenty even while the Enterprise almost suffers shipwreck.

EMOTIONAL CLEARING
Surveying a planet undergoing self-destruction, crew pick up a strange ailment that renders them extremely restless emotionally. The first man affected, Tormalen, had been contaminated while on the planet inspecting a scientific research station. All the personnel were discovered frozen to death. Tormalen's symptoms include a hot temper, aggression and self-harm leading to suicide. Other crew members succumb each in a different way. Sulu goes wild with a rapier, O'Reilly takes to crooning like a drunkard while inadvertently sabotaging the engines and Nurse Chapel soulfully confesses to Spock her unrequited love for him. Even Spock has strong and painful

emotions come up - sadness and regret for his unexpressed love for his Earth mother. Kirk suffers regret too - for the weight of responsibility he must bear that forbids enjoyable recreation. There are grounds for believing that these emotions being released could represent a clearing and healing of long denied personal issues. But before this can be confirmed, the Enterprise's orbit starts decaying catastrophically. The dying planet seems to be taking the ship down with her. The emergency requires the crew reassert control over both themselves and the stricken vessel. This they accomplish literally in the nick of time - stealing time through time travel.

CARD/EPISODE AND MATRIX TAKEDOWN
No less instrumental than mind control in advancing the New World Order agenda has been manipulation of populations via the Emotional Matrix as in the provoking of fear and negative reactions symbolized by the **5 of Cups reversed**. Invisible frequency weapons, control grids and etherical parasites, on top of religion, patriotism, wars and political disputes, massively stirred up anger and fear in the past. Added to this has been elite control 24/7 of news propaganda and Satanically encoded entertainment, all used to incite confusion, anxiety or despondency. With the plandemic of the 2020s, a purported viral contagion gave governments the excuse to weaken social bonding and generate misery, depression and suicide though mandated lockdowns, business closures and social distancing. Added to this have been induced food and fuel shortages and contrived, destabilizing, chaotic immigration; and the funding of special interests such as Black Lives Matter, Antifa and LGBT. Such specious incitements of identify politics exacerbate Divide and Rule and further generate population unease and discontent.

All of this artificially aggravated strife will fall away as the moribund Matrix dissolves. Frequencies of a healthy heart centre will restore themselves on a worldwide scale, dissipating the Emotional Matrix. The Negative Elite will lose their power, the Archons and demonic entities inhabiting the lower 4th astral realm will lose their food. On planet Psi 2000 we see an extreme manifestation of emotional dysfunction ravaging the scientists, causing them to go berzerk. Accordingly, the first Enterprise man to contract the condition, Tormalen, attacks himself with a canteen knife after an outburst of distress and outrage. Festering self-doubt long held, says Spock, fuelled his behaviour. Each of the subsequently contaminated crew experience symptoms unique to themselves. The common factor is the **5 of Cups reversed**: trouble with cathartic release of blocked emotion.

Matrix-induced emotional malaise on Earth has been a threat for eons. Systemic emotional manipulation operated through corrupt control of populations drawing humanity into states of misery and distress. EMF weapons, rigged elections, curbs on freedom and the culture of order-following have contributed to collective unease and a build-up of emotional hurt and resentment. As on the starship Enterprise, we pushed down pressure on ourselves so as to keep our jobs and appear 'normal' and healthy. We got on with our lives while harbouring repressed emotions of disillusionment, anger, misery or frustration. Uncleared, these emotional hurts if excessive fray our nervous sytems and eat away at our relationships, threatening overall health and well-being. The Enterprise crew here experience an extreme case of outburst of repressed emotions contracted on the dying planet then occurring on the starship. The scientists followed by Tormalen all die. Several other crew experience disorienting catharses on the way to becoming rebalanced.

We all have our individual patterns of reaction to emotional pressure. The crew illustrate this in their various ways. Sulu and O'Reilly manifest erratic, irresponsible behaviour endemic of humans locked in prolonged containment on a travelling vessel. Living under military style discipline - as emphasized here and in Episode 12 - hampers individual freedom, spontaneity and whimsy, and this must have consequences. Kirk's reaction to over-confinement is a catharsis combining frenzy with regret and despair. Most inwardly intense of all is Spock's experience. With his mixture of DNA - logical Vulcan and emotional human - he counters his impulse to cathart with a yet fiercer determination to try and control his feelings. The emotional crisis turns out brief for all concerned but not before they have learnt a lot more about their ongoing need for healthy emotional expression latent in all of us, symbolized by the **5 of Cups upright**.

AFTER THE TAKEDOWN

Whatever our circumstances, our emotional relationships with ourselves and others need to be guided and nurtured. The key is to remain observant, fluid and open to our inner experience in each passing moment. This will bring to cognition patterns indicative of the heart centre not in balance. Emotional clearing and healing can then be undertaken to remedy this and to reconnect us to our Soul in 4D, 5D and 6D and thence to the rest of the 15 levels of our multi-dimensional identity. Beyond this we will reconnect to the non-dimensionalized level of infinite, unbounded Source Mind. A daily practice of withdrawing from mental and emotional activity as in meditation will pacify Matrix influences rife in the past at our 3D vibrational level. Thus we will restore emotional stability moment by moment, enabling us to stay in balance as we express and share our emotions and feelings.

5. HIGHER SELF

The Higher Self reintegrated will balance out our many contradictory sides

Episode 5 '**The Enemy Within**' correlates with **Strength**; both are themed around integration and management of opposing personality traits under the Higher Self

THE CARD
The **Strength** card shows a calm woman holding the jaws of a wild-looking beast, possibly a lion. The beast could represent another being. Or it could stand for our own impulsive animal nature. The beast's outline merges with the woman's lower body, associated with earthy desires, impulses and appetites. She literally has her hands full with the animal but energetically seems to be perfectly in control. She appears both mighty and gentle as she reins in a beast of raw emotions and physical instincts. Is she closing its jaws, opening them up or holding them as they are? Mentally she appears attentive without looking unduly challenged or drained. This card marks the start of the second series of 10 Major Arcana to do with inner and metaphysical phenomena. The woman's hat similar to the Magician's suggests a parallel. They both initiate their series of 10 Majors. The Magician brims with energy ready to start the material journey with his tricks and skills whereas **Strength** calmly initiates the

spiritual journey. Engaged in her task, the woman deals with the panoply of dualities at the Body Mind level - feminine and masculine, gentle and strong, human and animalistic, and so on. With her head appearing slightly semi-detached, we can infer the presence of her overseeing Soul or Higher Self. With a sure connection to the Higher Self as here, we manifest the same gentle power or spiritual **Strength** as this self-assured woman.

If **Reversed**, bodily or emotional energies are not well managed, being tyrannized or excessively indulged. There could be a lack of control over diet or alcohol. There may be difficulty marshalling one's strength of will and decision-making ability. Anger management could be a problem, so too lust or violent tendencies. Or energy and zest may be deficient, with illness present or lethargy and apathy.

EPISODE PREMISE
Following a Transporter malfunction, Kirk is split into two persons. One is ruthless and over-forceful, the other overly meek and indecisive. A battle ensues.

CONTEXT
Self-Management, Insanity, Third Force.

HIGHER SELF
Due to a Transporter malfunction, two Kirks are beamed up from a planet under survey. While the first Kirk shaky on his feet is led away for rest, a duplicate of him beams up unseen. This second Kirk is the opposite of the first. He's much more energetic but wild and menacing and full of addictive and violent impulses. He takes to furtively marauding the ship while swigging brandy and indulging his lust for Yeoman Rand. The crew soon realize the impostor's existence but are hampered in capturing him by the first Kirk's difficulty in giving orders. But Wild Kirk is found and confined to sick bay. There, Spock and McCoy theorize that the two Kirks represent his good and evil sides separated out. And that the reason for the good Kirk's ineffectualness is the loss of his darker side which gives him his creative vitality and strength. Using more violence, Wild Kirk escapes to the bridge pursued by his double. The hysterical, ferocious and fearful Kirk threatens to kill his mild alter ego. But Mild Kirk still channeling his compassionate Higher Self takes hold of his distraught double who relents. While embracing each other, the two Kirks are reintegrated by being put back through the Transporter. Kirk now reunified recovers his strength of will and immediately orders the beam-up of the rest of the shore party, stranded and freezing, through the now repaired Transporter.

CARD/EPISODE AND MATRIX TAKEDOWN

As of early 2023, the whole Orion AI system powering the Matrix has been permanently deactivated. The way is now open for us all to harmonize and balance out our Lower and Higher Selves. It is our Body Mind, the Lower Self, that Matrix forces and frequencies sought to isolate and exploit. The contrary sides of the Lower Self are shown clearly in Kirk's bifurcation and in the **Strength** card when **reversed**. **Strength reversed** involves Lower Self energies mutually unbalanced or running amok. The beast in the person gets the better of the person. But around the **Strength** woman's neck runs a line that seems to separate her slightly disjointed head from the rest of her body. We can interpret this as indicating the presence of a mysterious detached self, the Higher Self overseeing us from Soul level. This awareness exists above and beyond the dualistic impulses of our Lower Self swinging between brave or fearful, active or passive, wild or mild, elated or depressed, etc etc. It would seem to be the Higher Self or Soul acting as a Third Force that binds together and harmonizes all our contradictory traits and sub-personalities at the 3D level.

The two Kirks manifest different sides of the man across a wide range of dualities: thinking and unthinking, mild and wild, introvert and extrovert, brave and cowardly, hesitant and decisive, light and dark. It is not simply as Spock theorizes, that one side of us is negative, consisting of 'hostility, lust, violence', while the other side is positive, all 'compassion, love, tenderness.' The dualistic nature of 3D life throws up all these and more contradictions in our personality and functioning. Spock asserts that it's the negative side that provides the **Strength** needed for leadership as long as it's properly controlled and disciplined by the compassionate and more intellectual side. But we see in Kirk's negative side furtiveness and shame. He hides his face when first apprehended on beaming up. Despite his assertive and dominating behaviour, he strives to keep his existence a secret unless he impulsively wants something in which case he'll seek it out and seize it preferably in a 1-to-1 situation unseen by anyone else. The object of desire could be a bottle of brandy from McCoy, sexual satisfaction from Yeoman Rand or a hand phaser weapon from crewman Wilson. 'Weak' Kirk shows no such fear. Though he labours over making decisions and giving orders in tracking down his double, and though he appears confused, abstracted and inhibited by poor will power, he retains courage that 'strong' Kirk doesn't.

All sides of ourself at the 3D level of Body Mind can be programed for good or ill. The Lower Self or Body Mind was the part of us triggered for ill by the external Matrix. The Body Mind is a kind of inner Matrix, our emotional, physical and mental conditioning, and it works by reacting. It colludes with or fights Matrix forces that would program our life one way or another. The Higher Self merely observes, but it has a certain influence over the Body Mind. As our overseeing Soul it gives us our sense of balance, harmony, wisdom, peace and quiet power. The more of this Soul energy present in our daily functioning, the higher our frequency of vibration. And the higher our vibration the more independent, self-willed and sound our lives will be. We are self-realized, implies **Strength**, when our opposing sides find their optimum balance under the guidance of the Higher Self. The System always wanted order-followers as in Episode 12, and eventually cyborgs. A totally controlled population was the aim, mentally compartmentalized and automatically conforming to AI impulses and orders and mandates - the Mild Kirk Syndrome. Or it wanted people turning against each other, fearing, accusing, taking sides, war-making, as in Left or Right, Christian or Muslim, black or white - the Wild Kirk syndrome. With the people mindlessly conformist or divided against each other, the authority maintained the upper hand, consolidating and increasing its power. Thus while the system operated, the tiny few could dominate the many through manipulating humanity into enslaving itself in the state of **Strength reversed**.

There is nothing to stop us now reconnecting with our Higher Self. Our soul will be back in the driving seat with the power to coordinate what Gurdjieff called our 'hundreds and thousands of separate small I's'. Freed from Matrix sabotage we can now harmoniously integrate this legion of selves as we see divided Kirk eventually do. By his two halves confronting each other in the final scene, his civilized and reasoning side or 'Mind', reunites with his animalistic side or 'Body' encompassing his physical self, emotions and impulses. This reintegration owes itself to his Higher Self coming to the fore. His Higher Self seems on the face of it to operate through his gentle, reasoning side. But Wild Kirk, even in his height of frenzy, refrains from shooting his other half. The Higher Self is there in Wild Kirk too, causing him to end up collapsing and sobbing in Mild Kirk's arms. Self-integration is a challenging journey for divided Kirk as it is for Janice in Episode 78. And so it was for us all during the Matrix era. But that's over now.

AFTER THE TAKEDOWN

To rebalance and restore ourselves in the wake of the fall of the Matrix we still have to understand that we have many different, contradictory sides. They are best integrated by optimizing our connection to our soul and Higher Self and its loving, detached awareness. The more we embody our Higher Self the more free we become, by accretion one person at a time.

6. WHEELER-DEALING

Doing business adventurously will most empower us when we empower others

Episode 6 '**Mudd's Women**' correlates with the **Knight of Coins**; both are themed around venturing out on business in ways that are ambitious but conceivably immoral or irresponsible.

THE CARD
All four Tarot knights are goal-oriented, outgoing men or women of action and innovation. The wand on the **Knight of Coins**' shoulder symbolizes an ability to use intuition and practical resourcefulness. The coin-shaped star dominating his thoughts and guiding his path indicates pursuit of material objectives. This **Knight**'s flesh-coloured horse could represent a vehicle or simply his own power of movement and action. The horse makes good contact with the ground and the **Knight** sits comfortably in the saddle. This is a man or woman very much at home in the material world and keen to use it for his purposes. He may be a commercial traveller, an enterprising trader, a door-to-door salesman or an ambitious corporate executive. The wand, rather than a weapon, perhaps indicates a competitive streak or inspired hunches. This **Knight**'s purpose is not aggression but doing business: making deals and enhancing material prosperity for himself and others.

If **reversed**, the **Knight of Coins** may succumb to fraudulent or devious means to obtain dubious, possibly criminal ends. Honesty or good ethics may be sacrificed with greed or a lack of responsibility becoming manifest. A hoax or scam may be involved, the goods or services on offer may be shoddy or sub-standard or of questionable moral worth. Corruption, wheeler-dealing or commercial exploitation may be present involving illicit or unscrupulous practice for selfish gain.

'MUDD'S WOMEN' PREMISE
Kirk and co become embroiled in the wily and morally questionable schemes of a roguish interstellar trader dealing in women and drugs.

CONTEXT
Deception, Illusion.

WHEELER-DEALING
A small unmarked spaceship flees from the Enterprise when it attempts to communicate with it. After a chase in which the quarry is destroyed in a meteor storm, the Enterprise rescues the four passengers in the nick of time. They are Harry Mudd, a maverick interstellar entrepreneur and wheeler-dealer and his 'cargo' of three seductive women. Mudd is arrested for illegal operation of his ship and prevented from trading his women as intended. He had hoped to sell them as part of his new business dealing in cosmic mail order brides. But when the Enterprise has to proceed to the nearest planet where it can replenish its exhausted lithium batteries, Mudd sees a brilliant way out of his predicament. The three lonely men on that mining planet will make perfect customers for his three lovely ladies! Without further ado, Mudd furtively does a deal by stolen communicator without Kirk's knowledge. The miners will get the three women if they like them in exchange for fresh lithium and Mudd's release. Kirk is incensed when he finds out but has to accede as the crippled Enterprise's decaying orbit is near to collapse. The women are beamed down to the planet but find it an arid, stormy place and the miners uncouth and ungrateful. The men seem more interested in lust than love, goaded on by the 'Venus' drug the women use to enhance their beauty. This drug is another of Mudd's dubious business schemes. It works only temporarily and when it wears off the miners see the women as ugly and undesirable. But the women and the miners seem to agree to make a go of it and after hesitation the miners hand over the lithium crystals. Mudd though must leave the planet with the Enterprise, still under arrest.

CARD/EPISODE AND MATRIX TAKEDOWN

It's not the Harry Mudds that do the bulk of shady business and serve up the public with detrimental or restricted goods and services. It's the giant pharmaceutical companies, those with established monopolies within the food industry, the Silicon Valley developers of radiation-emitting 'smart' tech devices, and the overall culture of bigger is better. Alternative, small and independent traders have long had to put up with government protection and incentives favouring Satanically controlled global corporations. Legislation militates against natural products and remedies while allowing poisons such as aspartame and msg to be used as artificial sweeteners and flavour enhancers. Lethal glyphosate is sprayed on wheat crops, cows providing milk are pumped with harmful anti-biotics and a huge range of food is treated with herbicides and pesticides as well as suffering genetic engineering to ramp up higher yields. All this thanks to endemic corruption of big business is condoned by governments while safe alternatives such as homeopathy, non-GM farming and natural raw milk have become close to obsolete. With no more Matrix, this abandonment of ethics by government and industry will come to an end as we rebuild and restore the economy and society fairly and ethically. This will include the activities of all businesses from giant corporations down to sole traders.

Ironically, it is not even for activities that could constitute bad business that sole trader Harry Mudd is apprehended. His major crime in Kirk's book is piloting a vehicle in an unsafe manner and without necessary identification. Hardly dangerous, as Mudd protests, in the infinite spaces of the galaxy where over-crowding is not a problem. Neither can Mudd's creative acumen be denied. But certain of his schemes do stray into fields where the ramifications can be deep and unsettling for those affected. His adventurous, entrepreneurial streak includes a definite tendency to play the **Knight of Coins reversed**, the inveterate wheeler-dealer. Shady or irresponsible dealing has him getting into deep water with his associates - the women he calls his 'cargo' and the men he intends to trade them with. Not that the jovial Mudd is evil or villainous; rather that as a maverick commercial traveller he bends the rules and plays fast and loose with the truth and with the well-being of those around him.

Providing wives for lonely miners might seem to be a useful service but the way Mudd goes about it the mysteries of human attraction count for nothing. He has three spare women with him. What to do with them? Ah, Rigel XII coming up has three unattached men - they will make perfect husbands! Well, the numbers at least match up. When the women and men meet each other, sure enough there is one of the opposite sex for each person. What clever planning, what good business strategy! This enterprising **Knight of Coins** does it again. But even helped by a dance night with music and dim lighting it's not long before sobering reality takes a hold. The inhospitable planet dismays the women while fists start flying as the men quarrel over their lust for female flesh. The 'Venus' drug does its bit to cook up some chemistry, but the prospect of these three couples magically making ideal husbands and wives for each other looks pie in the sky unlikely.

One couple make it back to the man's squalid den. She, Eve, even cooks up a meal for the taciturn, embittered Childress. In return he criticizes her cooking and then her lost beauty when the 'Venus' drug starts to wear off. With his sulleness and her self-loathing will the pair survive one evening, let alone marriage? Sadly, Mudd's wife-trading business is a murky, sleazy, irresponsible venture that demeans women and makes lustful opportunists of men. Since when did marriage suitability depend exclusively on sexual desire? A pill that temporarily enhances a woman's beauty or femininity may sound desirable. But using it to appeal to a man's masculine drives does little more than alcohol whose effect is similarly short-lived. And the placebo given unknowingly to Eve does the job equally well. This is hardly surprising as everything to do with Mudd the businessman is locked in perceptions of the mind and the five senses. To transcend such exploitative practices of the **Knight of Coins reversed** an expansion of awareness and heart is sorely needed. Maybe our next encounter with Mudd in Episode 36 will see that transformation ... don't hold your breath!

AFTER THE TAKEDOWN
The Matrix always thrived on and condoned the culture of commercial exploitation, exclusively based as it is on mental and 5-sense perceptions of desire and value. Matrix power resided with those who controlled and possessed the illusion of money as in Episode 44. Expanding our sense of self is the way out of money and debt slavery, conditions as defunct as the Matrix itself. If we wish to play the game of an enterprising **Knight of Coins** and cultivate business as risk we surely can. But identifying with business game-playing in ways that ignore ethics and the rights of others is ultimately a game we lose. The game is rather to open our mind beyond a self-seeking field of perception in order to empower others as much as ourselves. By means of Service To Others we can in fact play the game of business from the standpoint of heart-centredness while developing and using our co-creative consciousness. Harmful commercial enterprise will then become a thing of the past along with the Matrix-led scramble for profit and gain.

7. TRANSHUMANISM

Transcending the Body Mind through technology has become a false dream now obsolete

Episode 7 '**What Are Little Girls Made Of?**' correlates with the **10 of Coins**; both are themed around transcendence of physical form with life continuing out of the body or transferred into a new one.

THE CARD
10 in the Tarot is the degree of fulfilment and transcendence. A cycle has ended with the old situation having completed itself or having been left behind. This final stage serves as the harbinger for the next cycle, a new, higher and more powerful level of development to come. Any number multiplied by 10 finds itself taken to a higher level as if having spiralled up. Accordingly, we find a tiny spiral growing at the exact centre of the central flower in the **10 of Coins**. As with the 10th Major Arcanum, The Wheel of Fortune, we have come full circle. At degree 10 we are in limbo, in between the old life cycle and the start of a new one. Coins represent the decoded perception of an apparently solid world. The **10 of Coins** therefore symbolizes the end of a cycle of perceived physical or material growth. Financially or materially this often means stasis, or intertia, presaging the development of a new bodily form or situation. This could include the experience of out-of-the body consciousness in such phenomena

as dream-life, near-death experience or teleportation. With the sciences of cybernetics and transhumanism, the **10 of Coins** can represent consciousness moved into a non-corporeal state or displaced into a different body or container such as that of a robot, cyborg, clone, android or replicant.

Reversed, the **10 of Coins** symbolizes a physical transcendence equating to destruction, or one that is defective, inferior, malign or dangerous.

'WHAT ARE LITTLE GIRLS MADE OF?' PREMISE
Kirk meets a rogue scientist obsessed with transcending the body by transferring consciousness out of it into his created race of androids or clones.

CONTEXT
Transhumanism, AI Takedown.

TRANSHUMANISM
Enterprise personnel beam down to Exo III, the base of missing exobiologist Dr Roger Korby. They are taken captive by Korby's bodyguard, the massive android Ruk. Ruk is the last survivor of the androids created eons before by The Old Ones on Exo III. The beautiful Andrea and Dr Brown are two more of Korby's android assistants but built by himself. In effect a mad scientist, Korby is consumed with a plan to mass manufacture a race of androids. Each will be the duplicate or clone of a human being, a paragon of transhumanism. The original body will be discarded and the android programmed by himself, Korby. Korby intends his androids to have eternal life plus freedom from disease and negative emotions. Demonstrating his mastery of the science, Korby enlists Kirk's help by cloning him. Instead of transferring Kirk's soul he merely creates an exact duplicate of Kirk and his mind. The results are uncanny and impressive. But the real Kirk refuses to cooperate any further and sets in motion a mutiny against Korby by his androids. In Andrea's case, her programming becomes confused by Kirk passionately kissing her, causing her to later mistakenly shoot the clone of Kirk. In Ruk's case Kirk talks the android into destroying Korby, but Korby destroys Ruk first. Korby is revealed as himself a clone who replaced his biological self several years back. He claims to be still human but cannot convince Nurse Chapel of this, Chapel having once been his lover. Korby and Andrea, both fatally disenchanted or confused, kiss each other, causing the phaser between them to go off and destroy them both.

CARD/EPISODE AND MATRIX TAKEDOWN
Korby's vision is of a humanity transcended and improved as per the **10 of Coins** by conversion into a race of synthetic humans, part biological, part

technological, programmed by himself. This in a nutshell was the agenda behind the installation of the many AI systems on Earth. The process was intended to lead to AI's takeover as on many other planets. The new global restoration however will see the retreat of the 'Internet of Things' and the threatened global smart grid. AI-driven smartphones, smart cities, smart meters, smart cars, smart watches et al will begin to change. 5G was intended to abet the mind and body takeover but this too will be rendered harmless without disabling computers, smartphones, laptops or the internet. With the Matrix taken down at its Orion-based origin, only AI devices that can be controlled rather than controlling us will be allowed on the planet. This will take the danger out of implantable devices, micro-chips, satellites and antennae. Replacements or safe alternatives will be found for injectable nano-technology. Fake vaccines like those found to contain tiny self-assembling circuitry and motherboards will be outlawed. So too other methods of smuggling nanobots into the body including through food, drink, clothing, water and sprayed-in-the-air chemtrails. With deactivation of a spectrum of dark AI systems under the aegis of Omega and Kronos, the threat of AI's full spectrum dominance over humanity will be halted and reversed.

The aim of the fast-tracked transhumanism - in reality subhumanism or the **10 of Coins reversed** - was been the same as Korby's: to turn the individual into a semi-cybernetic organism functioning as a unit in a hive mind. The Covid-19 fake pandemic, in reality a psychological operation utilizing bio-warfare, was intended as a transitional phase in this subjugation of humanity. Instead of operating as points of awareness within Infinite Awareness, humans were intended to answer only to elite programming and AI. The irony would be that if AI, had it gained enough control over us, would have treated us the host species, as a virus. The masses out-matched by AI would then have started to be eliminated and Earth depopulated. Such was the case on Ruk's planet, Exo III, when The Old Ones, the original inhabitants, built their race of androids. Kirk speculates that the machines, uncompromised by flaws such as unpredictable emotions and illogical functioning, overtook their creators in pure intellect. This plus the imperative to survive would have impelled the machines to override their programming. Ruk confirms that he and his fellow androids resisted being turned off by their creators who they came to see as inferior. The machines rather than be turned off by The Old Ones, destroyed them.

The AI-promoter Ray Kurzweil in his vision and zeal for a transformed humanity in accordance with the **10 of Coins** comes across as the Earth equivalent of Dr Korby. Kurzweil wanted human thinking to become 'a hybrid of biological and non-biological thinking' with the ability to 'think in the cloud'. He saw technology gradually overriding limited human functioning until 'the small proportion that is still human gets smaller and smaller until it's just utterly negligible.' Like Korby, Kurzweil relished the prospect of immortality - living forever in a body enhanced or even replaced by technology. What this actually would mean is mentally merging with AI programming in a biological-cybernetic body from which escape would be impossible. This vision of Kuzweil's matches Korby's. Korby wants people's souls, their whole consciousness, transferred into synthetic bodies. Such bodies would be programmed to be free of disadvantages such as disease, deformities or fear. As we learn at the end of the episode, Korby himself is just such an android, his soul downloaded into a clone body.

Kurzweil used the term 'assimilation' to denote the ultimate merging of biology with technology. He claimed this would make us superhuman. Korby calls his own version of the same scenario 'a practical heaven, a new paradise.' But Kirk likens it to living in a tyranny under a dictator such as Caesar, Genghis Khan or Hitler. If negative emotions are eliminated, he argues, so too would be positive emotions such as tenderness, love and sentiment. The human factor, he implies, would be stripped away leaving a hollow being, a **10 of Coins reversed** human. A similar kind of technologically assimilated human crops up in Episode 55 on Sigma Draconis 7 with its computer-controlled society of dumbed down women; and in Episode 20 on Landru's planet with people reduced to programmable zombie-like beings mindlessly roaming the streets.

AFTER THE TAKEDOWN
With the controlling Omega AI system removed, the threatened AI takeover will collapse in the way of Dr Korby and his doomed androids. All is set to change in favour of humanity's organic and biological nature. For their poor life choices, large numbers of the Cabal at the highest levels have been sent back to Source. God always wins. There will be no actual move to a demonic transhumanist sub-reality, a technological prison with AI in charge as with The Old Ones' android race. Technology destructive to divine selfhood will disappear. The irony is that our higher superconscious self transcends the most transcendent of selves that we can envision with the mind or create through technology. Stephen Hawking warned that AI threatened the end of humanity. This can no longer happen with Omega and the rest of the dark AI systems removed fron the planet. The way is now open for us as a race to evolve into the wisdom and love of the heart, empowering the return of divine freedom under Natural Law.

8. GROUPTHINK

The culture of belief in Matrix lies and deception is collapsing along with the Matrix itself

Episode 8 '**Miri**' correlates with the **Page of Swords**; both are themed around independent thinking ability helped or hindered by education, indoctrination, trauma or groupthink.

THE CARD
The **Page of Swords** shows us a child or adolescent awkwardly holding a yellow sword grazing the head. His or her feet point in opposite directions as if uncomfortable about which way to go. The gaze is downward as if shy or imposed upon. Like all the Tarot Pages, this is an aspiring but uncertain youth. He or she needs time to grow and mature in a balanced way. Swords being the suit of the mind, this is a person developing intellectual clarity so as to have stillness within, enabling the mind to act as a clear mirror for outer influences. Hence this is someone expanding their consciousness even into uncomfortable areas, learning about why they may feel uncomfortable and allowing more light, intuition, insight and discernment to pass through the Body Mind. With this will come better assessment of the environment and one's own competencies on the path to self-mastery. Thus this **Page** is a very much a work in progress, a state than can apply to any of us but particularly to children,

young people and those still saddled with the need for inner work on immaturity, sub-conscious wounds or mental pain.

A **Reversed Page of Swords** could have any number of problems to do with lack of clarity, discernment or authenticity. Within the Mental Matrix causes could include control system psyops, propaganda, fear-mongering, mass hypnosis and any encouragement to groupthink, all provoked by dark forces. Other causes can include dysfunctional family upbringing, vaccine injury or early addiction to TV and digital devices. The resulting mental confusion or misery can sabotage the ability to think for oneself. This can manifest in ignorance or shyness; stubbornness and arguing; attitudes based on fear or trauma; verbal aggressiveness; a tendency to mock, gossip or insult; deceitfulness; and thinking cut off from compassion and empathy.

'MIRI' PREMISE
On a planet bereft of adults, fearful antagonistic children hamper the efforts of a landing party trying to help them overcome a terminal disease.

CONTEXT
Mind Control.

GROUPTHINK
A planet resembling a dilapidated 1960s Earth is found to be inhabited only by gangs of reclusive, hostile children. A landing party discover with the help of a frightened girl called Miri that all the adults died from a toxin released as a bi-product of a life prolongation experiment. Children were enabled to age only one month for every 100 years but on entering puberty would become savage and die a few days later. The surviving children have never forgotten the trauma of the adults who went mad, aggressive and violent 300 years before. In the children's debilitating groupthink, the landing party are lumped together with the 'grups' who abused and hurt them before suddenly dying. Except for Miri, the children mercilessly taunt Kirk and co and steal their communicators. The party themselves have contracted the toxin and set about trying to find an antidote. Miri should help them but has become emotionally unstable due to her crush on Kirk while she herself contracts the toxin. Kirk with hours to live appeals to the antagonistic, uncomprehending children. He passionately reasons with them and finally overcomes their groupthink conditioning to win their trust. Meanwhile McCoy finds an antidote enabling everyone to be cured. The party take their leave promising the children 'teachers and advisers' from Starfleet to come and take care of them.

CARD/EPISODE AND MATRIX TAKEDOWN

We were all subject to heavy Matrix conditioning, none more so than children and young people. Such conditioning achieved via mental and emotional indoctrination was responsible for whole populations falling for the giant false flag known as Covid. The **Page of Swords** clearly indicates this susceptibility: downcast expression showing fear or weak self-confidence, splayed feet showing indecision, poor grasp of the Sword (the mind) showing confusion, the Sword resting against the head hinting at the mind being turned against itself potentially. Much of this conditioning emanates from the censorship and propaganda saturating mainstream media and education. Prior to the Matrix takeown, misinformed populations resembled the **Page of Swords reversed**: proverbial putty in the hands of the controllers. Peer pressure added to the weight of indoctrination with people still scammed by the Covid narrative prevailing upon their family members or workmates to conform to mask or 'vaccine' mandates. Individuals and groups that coerced each other contributed to the self-enslavement of humanity engineered by the ruling elites, a conditioning mirroring that of the children in **Miri**. The common factor between them and Matrix-indoctrinatied people is groupthink, the mimicking by individuals of consensus opinion to gain approval from others within one's community or society. Groupthinkers will sacrifice their personal value systems or beliefs in order to show they share the same ideology as the rest of the group. The ideology of the **Miri** children makes all adults their enemy.' You know Grups' says their leader John, 'you know what they do, hurting, killing'. Another boy chimes in followed by the whole group wildly chanting their hostility. Without evidence that the outsiders mean them harm the children agree almost as one to steal the landing party's communicators. Miri is the exception and for befriending Kirk she later comes in for bitter taunting ('Tell them, Jim! Tell them, Jim!') from her peers. This harassing of anyone breaking ranks commonly occurs when fear is uppermost in a group's mind.

The children fear all adults as savage. Likewise, people during the Covid scamdemic were urged to suspect everybody else as possibly carrying a potentially deadly virus. The mask-wearing and social distancing paranoia was a measure of only the virus of fear falsely implanted through lies and deception. The culture of fear whether the cause is genuine as on Miri's planet or illusory and hyped up as it was on Earth, devastates the quality of life. The rent-a-crisis mob on Earth instituted words and phrases to be repeated over and over again in public announcements and posters - 'Save Lives ... be Covid Secure ... No Jab No Job ... It's For Everyone's Protection ... Stay Safe

...We're All In This Together ...'. The result was a cowed population, the fearful **Page of Swords reversed**, going about in ubiquitous, slavelike face masks, fearfully avoiding physical closeness and rolling up their sleeves to receive a sinister 'vaccination' later proven to cause blood clots, strokes and heart attacks. Independent research would swiftly provide protective knowledge but herd mind - cultivated groupthink - overrides critical reasoning as it does among the child survivors on Miri's disaster-ridden planet. Whether child or adult, a **Page of Swords** traumatized or mind controlled becomes frightened, unquestioning, subservient and compliant. The fear of deviating from the group consensus and appearing disloyal doubles up on politically hyped fear such as of viruses or a common enemy. Even conventional psychologists and wikipedia, normally heavily Matrix-indoctrinated and indoctrinating, admit that groupthink is detrimental to any group's perceptual processes and decision-making ability. The elephant in the living room is the determined cultivation of groupthink by our governments to get us all living in fear and welcoming their solutions. Their Great Reset ironically would itself be the apotheosis of a hive-mind humanity.

As the Nazi propaganda minister Goebbels observed, a lie big enough told often enough will become the orthodoxy. The massive Covid lie involved a vast number of adults losing their minds over basically a flu condition. Believing in the lie turned adults who should have know better into the equivalent of the Miri children, the **Page of Swords reversed** - fearful, socially awkward, suspicious and irrational. Health experts and virologists breaking the groupthink and warning of the far much more dangerous Covid injections were ignored or considered quacks. Kirk in his appeal to the children to change their collective mind resembles the few outspoken scientists trying to warn humanity of quick or slow death by injection with spike proteins and graphene oxide. 'If you don't help us', Kirk says, 'there won't be any games anymore, there won't be anything, nothing ... nobody left!' The children as one dementedly taunt and mock him before finally coming to their senses. The way is clear now for the misled majority on Earth to likewise see and realize that we have all been systematically lied to. A renaissance of truth and discernment has started.

AFTER THE TAKEDOWN
There is nothing virtuous about dropping one's independent mind to adopt the attitude of others. In the midst of psychological warfare, one's own truth must be followed and mandates based on lies resisted. We saw this happen with the unravelling of the Covid hoax. With the Matrix gone, people everywhere will be hugely empowered to think and speak for themselves

9. MIND CONTROL

Vulnerability to programming techniques is a human weakness; awareness will afford protection

Episode 9 'Dagger of The Mind' correlates with **The Pope**; both are themed around verbal instruction and the influential exercise of communication from a trusted authority.

THE CARD

The Pope card symbolizes an act of communication. We see a preacher or teacher holding forth before initiates. He or she is sharing religious beliefs or spiritual principles, or giving instruction or imparting wisdom or knowledge. **The Pope** is a person of respect and learning. His intricate costume, the crosses on his hands, the trident in his grasp - all signify a position of elevation and respect. He represents the official view, that of established institutions and social attitudes. He acts as a mediator, an officially sanctioned guide or educator. He could be a religious figure, a teacher or therapist, a critic, a consultant or an analyst or advisor.

With an agenda to indoctrinate or dogmatize, **The Pope reversed** signifies danger and exploitation. His communications would then be geared towards overt or devious manipulation of how or what people think, in abuse of his position of trust and his mission of service to others. His methods might include rhetoric, lies, censorship, deception, hypnosis or other ways of programming for directing a person's thought processes and achieving mind control.

'DAGGER OF THE MIND' PREMISE
The director of a penal colony is discovered by Kirk to be developing a dangerous form of technological hypnotherapy, with Kirk becoming his next subject.

CONTEXT
Mind Control, Insanity.

MIND CONTROL
Van Gelder, a staff member of the Tantalus Penal Colony, smuggles himself aboard the Enterprise in a state of agitation. Kirk and psychiatrist assistant Dr Helen Noel beam down to Dr Adams' colony to investigate. They discover a machine, the Neural Neutralizer, being developed by Dr Adams to program unsuspecting patients. Van Gelder purportedly misused it, injuring his own mind. While covertly trying out the machine on himself, Kirk is discovered and himself forced by Dr Adams to become a mind control guinea pig. The effects are traumatic, impelling Kirk and Helen aided by Spock to sabotage and shut down the laboratory.

CARD/EPISODE AND MATRIX TAKEDOWN
The influencing and shaping of people's minds is the calling card of a functioning Matrix and the province of both **The Pope** and Dr Adams. They all use official institutions and techniques of communication to manipulate the perceptions of their subjects. Even with the Matrix now deactivated, sophisticated programming of the human mind remains to be dispelled. Mind control expert Stewart Swerdlow, a veteran of the infamous and secretive Montauk facility in New York State, defines such programming as 'the imprinting and compartmentalization of a person's thought processes or mind patterns for specific purposes.' In this lies immense potential to do good, as in the work of a hypnotherapist, or to harm and control. Throw in the development and refinement of aids such as drugs, technology or pschological group work, and the influence of **The Pope** in the form of the psychiatrist, psychotherapist, hypnotist or mind controller is many times increased for better or worse.

The controversial psychiatric treatment known as Electro-Convulsive Treatment is no longer common but shadowy agencies of the government, the military and the Secret Space Program have become well versed in a wide range of similar techniques. The purposes range from ensuring extreme discipline to mind-controlled espionage or smuggling. Mental powers can be enhanced, or deformed turning a person into a drug mule, terrorist or assassin. Government mind control programs and operations of the 20th century were powerfully advanced by the Tavistock Institute and by Ewan Cameron whose work in the 1940s/50s formed the basis for so-called Monarch programming taken up by the CIA. Methods developed include controlling a victim by means of a 'handler' who will use 'triggers' such as visual symbols, code words or phrases. Trauma or torture is commonly used to compartmentalize the mind, with the ability to create hundreds of specific sub-personalities known as 'alters'. Hollywood celebs and pop stars have been prime subjects. How much is Dr Adams a **reversed Pope** - a portrayal of the CIA or NSA type of mind controller? As director of his own respected penal colony on a remote, seldom visited planet, he is easily able to exploit his patients. These include his associates as well as the inmates. Van Gelder's state on coming aboard the Enterprise is deeply disturbed, wild-eyed and hysterical, evidence of having suffered something terribly traumatizing. Others of Dr Adams' assistants, such as the impassive operator of the Neural Neutralizer and the somnolent Lethe, a former inmate now a female therapist, show signs of emotional numbness and non-responsiveness. The inmates seen wandering around wear strangely fixed smiles or simply appear 'a bit blank' as Kirk puts it. An inmate actually receiving treatment under the Neural Neutralizer appears terrified, writhing in agony as instructor and machine work on him.

The tranquil, if not tranquilized, demeanour of Dr Adams' inmates may point to positive effects of his treatment. He may indeed be successfully rehabilitating them as he claims. But how ethical, even humane, are his methods? His machine looks like a torture device able to subject a victim to a beam of varying degrees of intensity of pain. The result increasingly 'empties' the person's mind while sadistic instructions are given: 'You will forget all you heard that caused you pain, terrible pain, growing more terrible as you fight to remember.' For Kirk's 'demonstration', Adams take Kirk's fantasy of an office romance with Helen and fills it with emotional pain. 'You are madly in love with Helen,' suggests Dr Adams. 'You must have her or the pain grows worse'. He plainly abuses his position as therapist by abusing his patients. **The Pope** has become a heinously **reversed Pope**, sadistically employing trauma-based programming. Adams himself gives the lie to his earlier claim that Van Gelder injured himself with the Neural Neutralizer. Turning up the beam to agonizing levels, Adams tells the squirming Kirk that Van Gelder was 'on his hands and knees sobbing' at that point in the treatment. Spock mind melds with Van Gelder and elicits the truth that Dr Adams has run amok using his machine to bully and mind control his patients through inflicting the torture of unendurable mental pain and loneliness. By thus aligning their thoughts and attitudes with his own, Adams is effectively 'brainwashing' them, turning them into programmed subjects. The technique according to Swerdlow was developed by the Nazis and will remain commonly used in classified programs until these are shut down in the post-Matrix world. We are finally left in no doubt as to Dr Adams' criminal intentions and methods - just as we are left unsettled by the vulnerability of the human mind to suggestion and manipulation. Nobody knows better than **The Pope** how sensitive and pliable people are mentally and emotionally, and how easily and emphatically their minds may be reshaped if desired.

AFTER THE TAKEDOWN

The fragility of the psyche all too easily allows ill-intentioned agencies to take control of thought and behaviour through technology and suggestion. Shadow military agencies in the USA, Russia and Britain have been working on the practice since the 1940s, assiduously developing their methods. Even known government departments such as the CIA, FBI and DARPA have commonly used drugs such as Scopolamine to block memories, alongside techniques of hypnotic suggestion to program their mind controlled 'assets'. While military-trained operatives would carry out assassinations such as that of JFK or Martin Luther King, a programmed patsy such as Lee Harvey Oswald would be set up to carry the blame. Or an assassin such as John Lennon's killer Mark Chapman, a Manchurian Candidate, would himself be programmed to carry out the task. News propaganda ensured that the culprit went down in history as mentally ill - a 'lone nutter' gone berzerk with a gun. Calls for disarming the population would then multiply, exactly as intended by the programmers of the killer. This is just one area where technologically aided mind control has been used by institutions for evil purposes. Symbolized by **The Pope reversed**, institutions we are taught to trust and respect have long used psychological operations and 'mass formation psychosis' to advance the agenda for a centralized One World Order. The lesson here is empowerment through knowledge. We have to be aware that under past Matrix conditions, the state zealously used psychological operations against the people. Like the Matrix itself, this practice is coming up for abolition, as symbolically demonstrated by Kirk and Spock taking down Dr Adams' Institute and destroying his machinery.

10. OUR STAR TREK FUTURE

As we become a space-faring race we will co-create a future of self-empowerment and responsibility

Episode 10 '**The Corbomite Manoever**' correlates with the **Page of Coins**; both are themed around coming of age with development of responsibility and physical resources.

THE CARD
The **Page of Coins** stands for someone serving as an apprentice in physical, material, professional or financial matters involving duty and responsibility. Pages as people tend to be hesitant, inexperienced or naive. They embody great potential but need time and nurturing to grow and fulfil their potential. In his right, active hand, this **Page** holds up a Coin, symbol of finance, physical resources or seed-planting. The prospect both attracts and daunts him; he seems hesitant or unaware how to proceed. The lower Coin blocks his movement. It lies ready to be planted and cultivated or conversely, dug up. The spadework must be done if he is to attain desired results but his splayed feet show indecision, mixed motivations. The future therefore brims both with prospects and opportunity and with obstacles and obligations. How to make his way in the material world, to fulfil himself, to prosper or succeed in ways that are powerful but responsible? He should know that his time, money, skills, equipment or

health will need careful tending, intelligent investment. He needs greater maturity and this can only come through training and development and hard-won experience. Challenges will have to be faced, mistakes made. One way or another he will build his future brick by brick, progressing into a good householder, solid professional or thriving businessman or woman. He will grow by what he makes grow.

Reversed, this **Page** lacks courage or self-belief through inadequate training. Or he over-reacts to outside pressures with hot-headedness or arrogance. He may find himself in over his head and out of his depth, or careless with resources, the environment, duties or responsibilities.

'THE CORBOMITE MANOEVER' PREMISE
Crew including a new navigator, plus the alien commander of a hostile spaceship, are tested in duties, responsibility and instincts of self-preservation.

CONTEXT
Deception, Self-Management.

OUR STAR TREK FUTURE
The Enterprise has reached uncharted space where crew are making star maps. Activities are halted by one then another threatening force in space. First a spinning cube then a massive spherical craft. The obstructive cube can only be destroyed but the mile-wide mothership is another matter. Its commander vows to punish the Enterprise for destroying the cube, its warning buoy. He calls himself Balok and presents a stern image on the viewscreen of a mean-looking alien grey. In imperious tones he issues a 10-minute ultimatum for the Enterprise's destruction. Kirk uses the PA system to inspire the crew to overcome fear of the unknown. But Lt. Bailey, the novice navigator succumbs to the tension and emotionally explodes in panic. Kirk temporarily suspends him then hits upon the idea of outwitting the adversary with a clever bluff borrowed from the game of bridge. Balok falls for it and relents, deciding instead to tow away the Enterprise using a small pilot vessel. The Enterprise proves too mighty and breaks free. This seems to incapacitate the small craft. Sensing it needs help, Kirk, McCoy and Bailey beam aboard. Instead of the expected formidable tyrant, which was merely a dummy, they find a dwarfish humanoid lonely and insecure in the running of his huge spaceship. He welcomes the three and tells of his desire for company. Bailey volunteers to stay with him as an apprentice and learn what he can before returning to the Enterprise more knowledgeable and experienced in the cause of his Star Trek future.

CARD/EPISODE AND MATRIX TAKEDOWN

As a race we stand now where the **Page of Coins** stands. We hold in our gaze the promise of becoming a space-faring civilization ready to broach 'the final frontier'. Lberated from the controlling frequencies and dark energies of the old AI systems we are free to begin catching up with our brothers and sisters in the technologicallly super-advanced breakaway civilization on the Moon, Mars and beyond. The work involved will be sizeable. The Coin in our hand - the promise of material expansion - will not come without removing the symbolic Coin at our feet, the ball and chain of voluntary self-enslavement. As we do the work and come of age individually and collectively we will need to unite and federate ourselves, to become one civilization ready to join the cosmic community and the Galactic Federation of Worlds. For this we will need to let go of our warring instincts provoked, as Kirk stated, by fear of the unknown. Each of us will need to let go of dark essence no longer held in place by the former Matrix. Mind patterns such as victim mentality, ignorance and fear can be released. As we awaken in increasing numbers, society will begin to reform itself and shed the illusory shackles of governmental control and manipulation.

Our coming-of-age as a cosmically directed **Page of Coins** will involve many of the challenges befalling the crew during their voyages aboard the Enterprise. On this particular trip Kirk twice tells his colleagues that their mission is to 'seek out and contact alien life'. Then, over the PA system he informs the crew that the greatest danger facing them is themselves. How will they react to phenomena they as yet do not understand? Here on Earth, how will humanity as a whole react to news that the Matrix has gone? The breadth and depth of overt and covert control afflicting us for millions of years may be old news to a minority of researchers and truth-seekers but will take time to become common knowledge. As the truth becomes known, many will be aghast at the lies, manipulations and deceptions behind so many wars, pandemics and control technologies. Above all this was the AI Matrix, a network of systems facilitating rule by dark occult Satanists answering to predatory reptilians and greys. Most people's first reaction will be the same as Bailey's to Balok: outright shock.

Balok first appears as an inscrutable and malevolent-looking alien grey, projected as such on the Enterprise viewscreen. In reality, greys have done much work under draco reptilians and AI, helping to abduct and experiment on humans while manipulating our race as a whole. Balok turns out to be only a dummy, a sort of talking scarecrow, but still scary enough to throw Bailey as an Earth human new to these things into shock and confusion. More tests and challenges are to come and for a novice navigator and archetypal **Page of Coins** the learning curve is steep. Bailey represents any of us facing the need to grow and mature rapidly through actual, unnerving experience. All us seeking freedom in the new energy need to raise our awareness and learn to ground ourselves fully in our own power. So too the Enterprise's new recruit. Balok's countdown to death and destruction causes the fresh-faced Bailey to entirely lose the plot. 'Somebody's got to do something!' he yells. 'What are you - wound-up toy soldiers?!!!' Kirk relieves him of his post, McCoy compassionately leads the boy away. Bailey was over-hastily promoted, McCoy had already told Kirk. But the strain on Bailey, the mistakes and learning experiences he undergoes, do not occur to him alone. McCoy is earlier rebuffed by Kirk for ignoring a warning light while supervising Kirk's exercise regime. Yeoman Rand is chided by Kirk for overly pampering him at lunchtime. Even Kirk himself comes in for criticism, by McCoy for overworking Bailey and expecting too much of him.

Bailey's hesitations and lapses in concentration as a **Page of Coins** under pressure are several, with even the star-mapping exercise boring him. Eventually though, his willingness to grow and learn by full participation redeems him. Balok's intimidating methods of self-preservation mark the alien out too as having a lot to learn about security and diplomacy. All of us on or off Earth need to aware of the need for protection and grounding including maintenance of boundaries. This becomes all the more important as we seek to raise our vibration, activate our Higher Sense Perception and free ourselves from the habit of submitting to limitations and restrictions imposed by arrogant authorities. As we find our way in the new Matrix-free age we will learn to govern ourselves in the spirit of true self-empowerment and self-responsibility.

AFTER THE TAKEDOWN
Contactee Elena Danaan has reported the removal of intrusive Negative Alien Elites from Earth by a hidden group of White Hats allied with the off-planet Galactic Federation dating back to the 1950s. Then there is Space Force, an SSP affiliated organisation conceived in 2019. Earth Guardian Kimberly Goguen emphatically calls out Space Force as a Deep State operation not in humanity's interests. Space Force and the Artemis Accords signed in 2020 may yet evolve into the basis for a glorious future. As in Star Trek, humanity would be openly exploring other planets and star systems. Are we on the cusp of such a future as claimed by author Michael Salla? The post-Matrix era will surely see us openly reaching out into space and developing and sharing codes of real freedom, tolerance and peace with other races.

11. TRUTH AND JUSTICE

The inexorable rise of buried truth will herald the return of justice and a new era of harmony

Episode 11 '**The Conscience of The King**' correlates with the **Justice** card; both are themed around bringing suspected criminals to justice and establishing the truth.

THE CARD
Seated facing us directly and honestly is a calm impassive woman in formal robes. Her regal bearing suggests some higher authority, spiritual and abstract, to do with principles or reason; or concrete, to do with the courts, a judge or an official institution. As Arcanum No. 8, **Justice** belongs in a pair with Arcanum No. 18, the Moon. Complementing each other, The Moon symbolizes the mysterious, illusory and dreamlike nature of the world, whereas **Justice** symbolizes objective and impartial awareness. Justice strives to make sense of uncertainty or confusion with scientific or factual knowledge. **Justice** works in a rational way to maintain order and sanity, harmony and equilibrium, truth and fairness. The scales in the woman's left hand indicate the weighing up of evidence or of matters such as right or wrong, harmless or harmful, legal or illegal. Her sword indicates the ability to make a clear cut decision, pass judgement, order restitution or dispense retribution or karmic redress.

Justice reversed indicates the presence of corruption, bias or procedural irregularities. There may have been a miscarriage of **Justice**, with legal authorities at fault by ignoring or abusing Natural Law, rules or legality. A verdict may be unfavourable for an interested party. Or the party may have been mistreated or wrongfully suspected or arrested. A faulty administrative process may be at work or someone may be taking the law into their own hands.

'THE CONSCIENCE OF THE KING' PREMISE
Kirk tries to be impartial and certain in seeking to prove the true identity of a Shakespearian actor. Was he a political mass murderer he knew 20 years ago?

CONTEXT
Slaughter, Deception, Insanity, Justice.

TRUTH AND JUSTICE
Kirk is with Dr Tom Leighton on his planet watching a performance of Macbeth by the Karidian players. Leighton tells Kirk he recognizes Macbeth/Karidian to be the infamous Governor Kodos. 4000 citizens out of a colony of 8,000 on Tarsus 4 were slaughtered by Kodos in order that the remainder would survive a famine. As Kodos is supposed to be dead these past 20 years, Kirk refuses to believe the connection. The computer records are inconclusive prompting him to start his own physical investigation. He is spurred on by the murder of Leighton later that day. An attempt on crewman Riley's life is also made. Leighton, Kirk and Riley happen to be the last ones to have seen Kodos alive. Kirk tells Spock he wants truth and justice by determining with his five senses, not just with logic, that Karidian really is Kodos. Kirk too is nearly assassinated, by a phaser turned into a bomb. He interrogates Karidian, again without obtaining full satisfaction. Karidian's daughter Lenora, whom Kirk has been romancing to get closer to the reclusive Karidian, passionately defends her father. She accuses Kirk of lacking mercy. Riley, made aware of the Karidian-Kodos connection vengefully sets out to murder Karidian, who is acting in a performance of Hamlet. Kirk restrains Riley. But then during an interval Kirk overhears Karidian confessing to Lenora that he was Kodos; and Lenora confessing back that it was she who had been eliminating the witnesses, insanely trying to protect her father from their accusations. Father and daughter are apprehended but in the melée Lenora accidentally shoots and kills Karidian instead of Kirk. McCoy promises psychiatric care for the shattered woman.

CARD/EPISODE AND MATRIX TAKEDOWN

Coded revelations of former Matrix reality in this episode include significant issues of **Justice** involving crimes against humanity, blocked efforts by researchers to dig up buried truth and silencing of witnesses. Karidian's slaughter of 4,000 innocents was ordered by him alone acting as Governor. Likewise, the series of war crimes, false flag attacks and other atrocities orchestrated by Matrix forces are the work of those forces acting as a single global authority. Insiders and whistleblowers who have come forward to offer witness testimony to Cabal crimes and illegal programs have risked a lot. In many cases they have been ridiculed or censored, travel-banned or deplatformed. Some have died mysteriously as with those who could testify against Karidian. And yet the effort goes on and must go on to awaken humanity to the reality of criminal operations still being planned with futile desperation by the last remnants of the moribund Cabal. Uncovering of the facts according to reliable evidence as per the **Justice** card has revealed that the JFK assassination or 9/11 could not have happened as per the official story. This alone is enough to warrant new and full-scale investigation. Kirk and Spock with their concern for truth likewise have their doubts regarding the official Kodos story. They take it upon themselves to reopen the case by earnestly researching the facts - fully in the manner of **Justice** - around the man himself.

Kodos hoped to avoid facing **Justice** by erasing and recreating his identity. Karidian the actor that he became still bears many resemblances to Kodos the Executioner personally and circumstantially. Spock quickly becomes convinced that the facts prove they are the same man. But Kirk's doubts persist, impelling him to seek irrefutable evidence. The Kodos-Karidian controversy has a parallel in the case of the Bush family that produced two American Presidents. Their father and grandfather was Prescott Bush, a senator who ran the Union Banking Corporation that helped finance the rise to power of Hitler. Two former slave labourers at Auschwitz, over 60 years later brought a multi-billion dollar civil action in Germany for damages against the Bush family. Lt Riley is similarly determined in his quest for **Justice**. He sets off with a stolen phaser to avenge himself on the man who caused the death of his parents in the Tarsus 4 atrocity. Prescott Bush and Kodos were again alike in both supporting eugenics. Kodos selected the strongest civilians to be spared the slaughter while Bush supported Hitler's plans to create an Aryan 'Master Race.'

Having faked his death, Kodos becomes Karidian, an accomplished and respected actor touring the galaxy in Shakespearian roles. This again is paralleled in the transformation of German war criminal Werner von Braun. The scientist who designed rockets built with slave labour that killed civilians in England was given a new life in the USA thanks to Operation Paperclip. Eluding trial in Germany for his crimes, von Braun was instead shipped to the US along with 1000 fellow Nazis where he became an American citizen and an administrative head of NASA. Even more blatantly questionable in his office is the current Director of the World Health Organization, one of the foremost shapers of the corrupt global response to the crime of the century, the Covid bioweapon. In his native Ethiopia, Tedros Adhanom, a Health minister with no health qualifications was, like Kodos, a ruthless politician. Acting like a tyrant earned him allegations of crimes against humanity and the sobriquet 'Minister of Death' not Health. Tedros became notorious for advocating incarceration, homicide and genocide during his decades of ministerial office. Together with Bill Gates, the de facto owner of the WHO, Tedros has for several years operated a medical tyranny. His part during the Covid hoax was to call for draconian lockdowns, travel restrictions and the injurious and often lethal Covid 'vaccines'.

Spock finds out from the computer that Kodos used his colony's famine as the opportunity to seize power. Ruthlessly as per **Justice reversed** he declared emergency Martial Law and proceeded to have undesirables put to death while the stronger ones were allowed to survive. Spock is in no doubt that Kodos, in order to escape facing **Justice** for his genocide, changed his identity to that of Karidian. Only the murderous trail of his insane daughter has so far insulated Karidian from being held to account. In the case of real world crooks done well like Prescott Bush, von Braun or Tedros, the Matrix system would protect psychopaths from having their history of human rights abuses exposed in the MSM or held to account legally. Kirk and Spock's quest to expose a political criminal mirrors the quests of brave researchers today, given the massively corrupt and deceitful running of governments, corporations, agencies and secret societies acting as one criminal, global cult during the Matrix era.

AFTER THE TAKEDOWN
Truth will enable long-suppressed humanity to come to terms with the covert and corrupt forces that have for so long dominated us. As with Kodos/Karidian, malefactors must be identified and put on trial. **Justice** will return when their crimes against humanity are held to account in courts of law and the knowledge shared openly among the people. As the guilty are exposed and put away a new era of freedom and **Justice** in accordance with Universal Law will dawn for this planet.

12. ORDER-FOLLOWING

Following our conscience above duty will guide us naturally to freedom

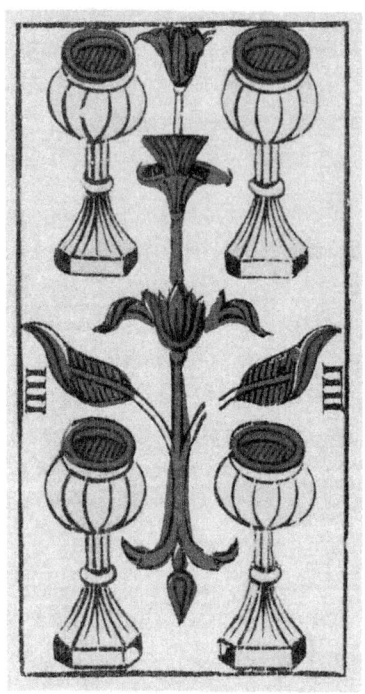

Episode 12 **'Balance of Terror'** correlates with the **4 of Cups**; both are themed around harmony with self and others attained through inner attunement or distorted through loyalty to authority.

THE CARD
The **Four of Cups** symbolizes love channeled into calmness and self-control, loyalty or respect. Underlying this is conscience, the inner knowing of Natural Law. Conscience gives rise to objective morality, a feeling we all share, a jointly held cognition of what is right or wrong. In practical terms this means the knowing of what actions result in harm to others as opposed to actions that do not harm others. This is common sense knowledge that we all possess while we remain in control of ourselves. The card shows us a partially flowered plant bisecting a stable square of Cups. There is emotional order here, meaning emotions are under our own control and aligned with our thoughts and actions. Collectively there is the presence of mutual trust without external rulership, along with caring for others as well as oneself. We do unto others as we would have them do unto us. In a group there will be good mutual relations and harmonious team spirit.

Reversed, the virtue of loyalty is allied to belief in authority. Order and security is sought not in one's own heart through the innate knowing of good and bad, right and wrong, but in the dictates of Masters. In practical terms this means a class of Masters issuing commands to a lower class, effectively Slaves. Discipline is imposed via threats or punishment resulting in the belief and obligation to obey authority based on fear rather than conscience. People will then perform actions because of following orders irrespective of whether their actions are right or wrong. This overruling of conscience results in a state of confusion or internal anarchy in which thoughts, feelings and actions no longer truly align with each other. Experiments conducted in the 1960s by Stanley Milgram showed that a high percentage of people are willing to do evil if only told to do so by an authority figure. Such people living in opposition to Natural Law revere conformity to man-made rules and regulations, statutes and laws. A gang could operate like this, or a cult, a secret society, an army, a nation under the control of government or the entire hierarchical system of the old Matrix.

'BALANCE OF TERROR' PREMISE
Stresses and strains to do with loyalty and duty are put on the respective crews during a flare-up of conflict between Romulan and Federation starships.

CONTEXT
War, Self-Management.

ORDER-FOLLOWING
Earth Outpost 4 in space comes under attack during a wedding presided over by Kirk. He abandons the nuptials to resume his place on the bridge and manage a renewed conflict with the Romulans. During the previous such conflict 100 years earlier, navigator Stiles lost several members of his family. On the viewing screen and for the first time Stiles glimpses the Romulans he hates. With their pointed ears they resemble Vulcans, provoking Stiles' instant contempt for Spock. Kirk reprimands him for his bigotry. At a Council of War, it's decided to fight rather than show weakness to the merciless Romulans. Ironically, the Romulan Commander wants to go home at the first opportunity. This renewed conflict with the Federation will only bring 'death and more death' and he has had enough of it. Were it not for his military commitment to order-following, he would prefer even self-destruction. As the cat and mouse game between the two starships proceeds, Kirk too expresses war weariness. Enterprise phaser fire repeatedly strikes its target even killing the Romulan 2nd-in-Command before crippling their

ship. But rather than surrender, the Commander prefers self-destruction. Before detonating his ship as he feels duty-bound to do, he admits to Kirk he'd rather they had been friends in a different reality. The only fatality on the Enterprise is Angela Martine's bridegroom who died following orders in the line of duty. Kirk as her captain goes to her to offer his condolences. Then in the line of duty again recomposes himself and strides back to the bridge.

CARD/EPISODE AND MATRIX TAKEDOWN

Chaos and evil where it existed on Earth under the Matrix system thrived, as it does with the Romulans, on codes of duty and order-following. The enemy is the system: top-down authority imposed or mediated by governments, councils, mass media, banks, universities, employers, religions and so on. All are fractals of the Matrix whereby a ruling elite was spiritually enabled to keep in place a hierarchy of lower levels. There is no recognition of universal sovereignty, no balance and justice arising from living in harmony with love and conscience, the **4 of Cups upright**. Rather than true freedom there is a 'balance of terror', of fear and control. Externally imposed codes of behaviour - orders to be followed - take precedence over conscience and the truth that comes from within. This is living as per the **4 of Cups reversed**. With the control system taken down, humanity will soon awaken from this age-old nightmare. When the Deep State imposed draconian lifestyle restrictions under the pretext of 'Covid security', many obeyed; but many too came together in joyful street marches and trucker convoys in a new consciousness of unity and respect for freedom. People were demanding respect for sovereignty in the spirit of peace and solidarity represented by the **4 of Cups upright**.

An awakened people strive to live in mutual kinship, aware of universal brotherhood and equality. Not only aware but insisting on freedom for all by non-complying with dictatorial mandates. We see even the Romulan Commander, who admits he has lived by duty all his life, struggling with his conscience and beginning to see the wisdom in non-compliance. Why must the two sides continue to fight each other, he laments? Another war for the homeland, more death and destruction ... this may be his duty but it is no longer his heart's desire. 'How many comrades have we lost in this way?' he asks rhetorically. Indeed, there is no freedom from death and destruction, from chaos and misery, when societies are driven by order-following. The Romulans, with their entire culture promoting hierarchy and authority, war and conquest, represent the extreme end of low vibration fear-based consciousness manifesting in an imperialist, separation-minded tyranny. The map of the Romulan Neutral Zone excluding Earth ships from its space on pain of war, graphically illustrates this. Fear shuts down our awareness of truth including knowledge, discernment and conscience. The Matrix at the human level, the top-down pyramid of management characterizing Romulan and human societies, was held together by fear. Matrix fear is of authority, with constant fearful obedience to the perceived elite enshrined in institutions using coercive laws, mind control stratagems and violence (police and military). Group solidarity becomes herd-like conformity: feeling as everyone else feels and behaving likewise, as dictated by the leadership. Awakening is now happening, a bottom-up process starting with people coming together as per the **4 of Cups upright** and reforming institutions to create a world based on more expanded consciousness.

Expanding our consciousness starts the awakening process. The Romulan Empire, reminiscent of the militaristic Roman Empire and its descendants throughout history, had its consciousness steeped in control. Matrix masters and servants had this same mindset. They both esteemed 'duty' and 'obedience' as virtues to dignify the enslaving reality of order-following under an external ruler. The Romulan Commander chafes at duty and obedience as leading only to 'death and more death'. He hints that he might prefer self-destruction, the eighth sin of suicide, but professes ironically to have been too well-trained in his duty. What he calls 'duty' is submission to the Praetor, the Romulans' supreme authority. Having abrogated internal rulership they live in confusion, at odds with their conscience. Not that this worries a Junior Officer who had earlier been demoted for his over-zealousness. He later informs the Commander of his duty to crush the Enterprise after having paralyzed it with a nuclear device. But the Commander is reluctant and hesitant to deliver the coup de grâce, perhaps preferring self-destruction as he had earlier mentioned. His subconscious wish is granted when his vessel is subsequently hit and the Romulans defeated. Now he can justifiably destroy himself and his vessel to spurn capture. He does so, calling it with crushing irony, 'just one more duty to perform.'

AFTER THE TAKEDOWN

Institutions of control making up the Matrix were the enemy, but they are made up of people. The Romulan commander is an institution man, a system-server who poignantly shows signs of awakening when it's too late. Once people everywhere return to following the biddings of their conscience, a switch away from ignorance and confusion must also follow. The way is to listen to one's heart and to follow its lead. Re-attuning with our higher knowing will lead us back to harmony with ourselves and others.

13. SURRENDER

Right surrender for a time, coordinated with right action, will optimize our self-liberation

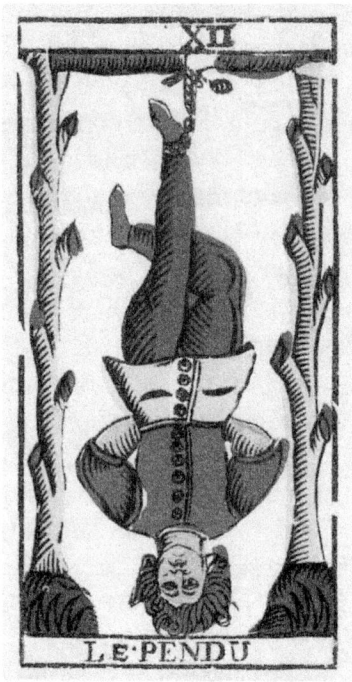

Episode 13 '**The Menagerie, Parts 1 & 2**' correlates with **The Hanged Man**; both are themed around voluntary or enforced surrender to blockage, entrapment or incapacity.

THE CARD
This card is often interpreted negatively as indicating a state of blockage, of inability to take action, mitigated by the opportunity to adopt a different point of view. While this is true it would be profounder to see **The Hanged Man** as one of the most powerful, life-affirming cards in the entire Tarot. Yes, the man hanging upside down seems trapped in an extremely uncomfortable position with the blood rushing to his head. Externally, his position seems literally topsy-turvy and imperilled. Internally however, immense and beneficial change is happening. This is indicated by the man's expression of peace and composure, by his thickly growing blue (for spirituality) hair mirroring the clumps of healthy green foliage sandwiching him, and by the crossbeam from which he hangs, likewise deep green (in some decks) for fertility. Upside down and tranquil, he isn't learning ways of surrender, he *is* surrendered. He shows no attachment to his fate, no frustration, anger, misery or self-pity indicative of troubling de-

sires or aversions of the mind or physical body. Instead, he warmly allows his situation of entrapment and emptiness. Like the dancer in The World card, his legs are crossed, showing an affinity with her enlightened state even while himself held in restraint. The rope by which he hangs is only precariously attached to his ankle. This suggests an illusory restriction, or at least his awareness that all is not what it seems at the Body Mind level. With his hands tied or merely held behind his back he is free to expand his attention beyond the physical vehicle to encompass higher dimensional levels of his identity. Thus, through right surrender he grows inwardly, developing a more evolved state of consciousness.

Reversed, The Hanged Man indicates a person deprived of natural functioning or physical movement as in a transhumanist fate, living only in the mind. Whatever the form of his confinement or incapacity, he may struggle in frustration or alternately remain unaware of living unnecessarily in stifling limitation. He may even have become attached to his suffering, taking pleasure in a self-identity stubbornly limited to the Body Mind and its five senses. His physical entrapment is thus mirrored by a mental entrapment that blocks awareness of his infinitely greater multi-dimensional identity.

'THE MENAGERIE' PREMISE
Advanced beings work through Spock to give his disabled ex-captain Pike a new life on their planet. This results in Spock's court-martial for mutiny.

CONTEXT
Transhumanism, Deception, Justice, Illusion.

SURRENDER
Called to Starbase 11, Kirk and Spock meet Commodore Mendez who is looking after Spock's former captain of 13 years earlier. Christopher Pike is now surrendered to a transhumanist life in a computerized wheelchair after being injured saving lives in a firestorm. Spock offers him hope for his condition by transporting him back to Talos 4 where under Pike's captaincy they had met the Talosian race. Pike stubbornly refuses as the planet is now out of bounds to humans but Spock hijacks the Enterprise to forcibly take him there. Pursued by Kirk, Spock surrenders and undergoes court martial. He defends himself with screen evidence showing what happened on his and Pike's earlier visit to Talos 4. They had been greeted by survivors of the wrecked craft they had hoped to rescue. In fact the survivors were mostly an illusion created by the Talosians. There was only one real survivor, the beautiful young Vena. She admired Pike, calling him a 'prime specimen'. He was then suddenly transported underground to the Talosians' refuge from

wars that destroyed the surface. Forced to live in caves, the bulbous headed beings continued to evolve inwardly rather than materially, acquiring tremendous mental powers including the ability to manifest any illusion. They healed and rejuvenated the injured Vena and contrived Pike to meet her, intending them to mate and start a family to provide a race of slaves to rebuild the surface world. But Pike on that original trip vigorously resisted. He viewed such surrender as captivity, as loathsome as the glass-walled cage in which the Talosians first imprisoned him. Such was Pike's vehemence that he spurned several illusory enticements involving Vena as his intended perfect mate. This convinced the Talosians to allow him to depart. Following the on-board trial which turns out to have involved another Talosian illusion, Starfleet and then finally Pike himself, approve the plan for Pike to return to Talos 4. He beams down and is immediately transformed by the Talosians. Given a normal though illusory body again he joyously reunites with Vena.

CARD/EPISODE AND MATRIX TAKEDOWN

With the Cabal having failed in its War on The People, compliance, non-compliance or some form of compromise has to be decided upon as we move forward in the new energy. Our choice in each situation will determine how quickly we jettison the transhumanist Matrix agenda and move forward as a species. Episode 34, The Doomsday Machine, will explore the Yang option of taking action against a formidable adversary, equivalent to directly opposing the formerly ruling Cabal; Episode 22, A Taste of Armageddon, will explore the Taoist option of compromise or diplomacy; while here in Episode 12, we have an examination of the Yin option of compliance or surrender, symbolized in the Tarot by **The Hanged Man**. Both Spock and Pike chop and change between these three approaches during their unfolding predicament. Likewise, we are likely to see humanity's path of embracing its own freedom change back and forth in the long-term unfoldment.

The furious Pike imprisoned in his perspex-fronted cage on his first visit to Talos IV personifies a Yang reaction of active opposition to imprisonment. He violently resists falling in line with the Talosian plan to have him father a new race of slaves. He throws himself against the transparent perspex wall and captures and throttles one of the silver-gowned aliens, in reality physical weaklings. Their power rests entirely on the mental, psychic level. This enables them to create imaginative and deceptive tableaux vivants to tempt Pike into a captive life with the compliant Vena. She appears as a damsel in distress threatened by vicious barbarians, as an idyllic picnic companion and as a sultry, wild dancing girl of a green-skinned Orion colony. None of this softens Pike's Yang intent to break free of Talosian captivity. During 2020-

2021, only a handful of humanity, 5% perhaps, mounted similar opposition to abuses of freedom imposed in the name of Covid such as lockdowns, mask-wearing, travel restrictions and fake testing. There were some public protests with rebels such as marchers and truckers demonstrating for freedom. Their non-compliance in their struggle against invidious government mandates echoed that of the defiant Pike and **The Hanged Man reversed**. Pike's refusal to surrender wins him his freedom - for a time.

13 years later, Pike becomes totally wheelchair-bound after suffering a major injury. In an about-turn he now willingly surrenders to full dependence on technology, helplessly immobilized as per **The Hanged Man**. But so surrendered is he that he stubbornly adheres to his life of transhumanist incapacity by refusing Spock's offer of help. 'I must do this', Spock tells him. 'No', Pike repeatedly answers, using his blinking light. Ever the establishment man, Pike only comes out of Yin surrender and consents to return to Talos 4 after Starbase have given their permission. By likewise complying with the panoply of regulations and privations instituted in the name of Covid, humanity in the main started off surrendering to the transhumanist agenda. We have seen a majority of Earth's population cave in to political pressure to undergo DNA-damaging injections containing toxins aimed at depopulation and nanobots aimed at synthetically hooking up the body to the incoming Smart Grid. Such acquiescence is the Yin option of going along with the will of the perceived authority, our Global Elite, in actuality deposed. In the wake of a deeply nefarious government campaign, Covid 'vaccine' injuries and deaths have rocketed, placing humanity in the victim-mode of **The Hanged Man reversed**. How quickly will the submissive majority reverse its compliance and avert the threatened 'Great Reset', the so-called '4th Industrial Revolution' of technocratic slavery?

We each have our rationale for when to surrender. The relevant advice offered by the Tao Te Ching is not to hastily confront obstacles: 'Give up and you will succeed' it says. 'Wait for the right moment ... Remain still until it is time to act.' By giving up struggle, at least on one level, we may allow the natural flow of the universe to prevail. Action still takes place. But by recognizing the power of timing - when to remain still and when to act - solutions may manifest without conflict and striving. Pike learns this lesson while bound to his wheelchair. He goes along - arguably too willingly - with his forced confinement. Then comes the right action happening by itself when he only has to accede to the Talosians acting as Third Force explicitly offering him a new life back on Talos.

Spock too, learns when to surrender, for how long and on what level. His hijack plan put into action bespeaks a determinedly Yang approach to helping Pike. This is scuppered when Kirk in a tailing shuttlecraft catches up and arrests him, charging him with treachery and mutiny. Spock could resist but surrenders and allows himself to be placed under arrest. He will now be charged and face trial. As per **The Hanged Man upright** he offers no resistance and cooperates fully. But on another level Spock refuses to surrender. At no time does he give up insisting that his trial judges consider the evidence and the reasons for his 'treacherous' action, which he will later explain away as he being 'completely logical about the whole affair.' Spock's surrender, at least on one level, reveals his trust in a greater flow, that of the Tao, or Third Force. The latter shows up in the form of Starbase finally intervening and approving Pike returning to Talos 4.

Another parallel with the choice facing humanity is the history of the Talosians as told to Pike by Vena. They fight a terrible war and destroy their planet, rendering its surface barren. They adopt a Taoist response, neither Yin nor Yang, by retreating underground and developing their minds. Neither allowing themselves to die out nor aggressively terraforming, they expand their consciousness. They learn to let go of primitive emotions like anger and hate and develop qualities of patience and equanimity. New abilities come to them including using their minds to manifest blocks of reality. But they fall into another trap. By abjuring outward life and physical action they become attached to passivity, contemplation and dreams. Thus as a race they still fall into the mode of **The Hanged Man reversed**. At the same time they intend to rebuild their world on the surface by lazily seeking imported slaves to do the work for them. Humanity must avoid similar thinking. Elite-controlled Brain-Computer Interface technology, the Internet of Things and the creation of AI robots will not improve our world. There is no virtue in allowing our divinely biological nature to fall under AI domination administered by a Cabal with no more right to rule over us. This is emphasized in several other Episodes such as Nos. 31, 33 and 51. We must rescue ourselves by adopting the right balance and timing of compliance and active non-compliance. The process must include humanity learning to let go of subservience to nefarious and redundant leaders. This is the victim mentality of **The Hanged Man reversed** that got us into Matrix enslavement over thousands of years of fraught history.

AFTER THE TAKEDOWN

Right surrender remains all-important. But there are different and concurrent levels of action and surrender. On one level for a certain time, surrender may continue to be the best policy; at another level people will move forward and engage with challenges. Spock in the course of his mission operates on both levels. On one level, humanity may temporarily allow governments to further promote the transhumanist tyranny known as Agenda 2030. On another level, people will respond proactively to the plentiful warnings of planned draconian rule under a preposterous One World Government bereft of moral and legitimate authority. Humanity is on the way to liberating itself now that the AI Matrix set up 300,00 years ago has been taken down. The programs comprising it numbered 18 according to Kim Goguen[1]. They have now all been eliminated according to her report issued on 30th January 2023.

Goguen's Global Peace and Restoration Project (see unitednetwork.tv) has meanwhile been set up to enable small groups and larger communities to come together in projects such as farming, growing food, Field Messenger reporting and the rendering of all kinds of not-for-profit service in mutual help and support. The momentum is gathering to restore natural uncorrupted ways of living side by side with the release of benevolent technologies. This will confirm and speed up our ascension on the post-Matrix positive timeline.

---

[1] Goguen listed the 18 AI programs making up the AI Matrix as follows: 9th (and darkest) level of the astral plane: Omega (disrupted the balance between light and anti-matter), Kronos (managed time and bodily degeneration); 8th level: Chaperone (managed inorganic fallen angels), Pindar (maintained masculine dominance over feminine); 7th level: Palermo (controlled etheric parasites in humans, computers and the Earth), Molnir (maintained inorganic time and prevented natural crystalline time); 6th level: Allegro (maintained Earth's false electromagnetic field), Armageddon (triggered earthquakes and volcanos); 5th level: Elemental (kept a dark overlay around every organic element, Dominion (controlled the organic kingdoms of plants, animals, bacteria etc): 4th level: Splash (controlled all water including in our bodies), Caliper (recorded the bloodlines of hybrid humans); 3rd level: Solstice (opened dark portals at solstice times), Capernaum (managed a dark overlay around every human aura; 2nd level: Orion (aligned Earth with that star system and cursed money), Jessup (charged with reinstalling the whole Matrix if it were taken down or Earth became too light); 1st level: Divine Intervention (reversal thereof!), Storm (created dark energy in us including sickness and Deadly Sins).

14. ACTIVE IMAGINATION

With Matrix mind control extinguished, perceptions and reality will beneficially change

Episode 14 '**Shore Leave**' correlates with the **3 of Swords**; both are themed around the release of the creative power of the Body Mind in a holographic universe.

THE CARD

Swords are the suit of the intellect and thinking as processed by the Body Mind including the brain receiving and transmitting thoughts. Along with our emotions and five physical senses, our thoughts emanate from the waveform information aspect of Consciousness. Each of the ten pip cards in the Swords suit symbolically depicts a different aspect of mind, or thinking, with the third degree corresponding to the outburst of creativity of Arcanum 3, The Empress. The **3 of Swords** therefore represents a creative release of mental energy, or imagination. Thoughts create because at their base level they are waveform energy just as with 'physical' reality. Thoughts can therefore interact with and shape the world perceived by our five senses.

This card shows us two severed branches under a flesh-coloured sword surrounded by four cut flower heads. This symbolizes the decoding and creation of reality by the mind. This so-called 'reality' exists in the form we perceive it only when the mind interprets or decodes waveform information, and bears qualities similar to a hologram. The mind then, creates and experiences its own form of reality capable of powerfully engaging with the holographic reality around us. The flesh colouring of the sword indicates the mind operating at the level of the five senses as well as at the level of higher senses. The four decapitated flowers and the two crossed branches are discrete units of biological life suggesting the results of the decoding process: our 'reality' appears to us not as it is in its unbroken waveform wholeness, but in the artificial form that we perceive it. Our minds decode and systematize waveform reality, chopping it up into structured bits of digital information similar to computers translating wi-fi in the air around us into pages on the internet. The two centrally placed leafy branches cut by the sword of the mind are white. They are not portrayed as green because they are not truly real. Rather, even at the 'physical' level they are projections or holograms. And like the flower heads, they are severed, cut up into digital information - artificial, discrete units. The leaves are yellow, the colour of the intellect: they exist as such only in the mind. This all symbolizes what happens to Consciousness when we place our individualized attention anywhere on the unboken wholeness of waveform reality with our minds.

Reversed, the **3 of Swords** indicates thought energy producing negative influence. Thinking or mental perception may be tainted by ill intent. Or it may have been distorted by confusion or hijacked by an outside force such as a religion or education system. The result is untruthful, limited or pernicious projections onto 'reality' at the level of thought or communication.

'SHORE LEAVE' PREMISE
Crew beam down to an idyllic planet unaware that it's been designed as an amusement park where one's thoughts manifest in physical reality.

CONTEXT
Perverted Paradise, Illusion.

ACTIVE IMAGINATION
Crew aboard the Enterprise are overworked and due for a holiday. When they find a quiet, peaceful planet full of lush meadows, woods and lakes McCoy prescribes some R&R. Soon after beaming down however, multiple weird phenomena start appearing. McCoy glimpses a rabbit and Alice from Wonderland. Kirk meets again with a dear ex-lover. All of the landing party have their own vivid encounters which soon turn dangerous and chaotic. They eventually realize that their active imaginations are creating the phenomena. Such is confirmed when a 'Caretaker' appears and explains the

planet's role as a thought-generated amusement park.

CARD/EPISODE AND MATRIX TAKEDOWN

A thought-generated amusement park fittingly describes life in 3D in which physical phenomena are really holographic projections created through a universe operating as a super-hologram. Gnostics see this malleable reality as having been hijacked. Formless entities they call Archons (AI systems) used it to get us to create our Matrix prison, a land of shadows and darkness, This echoes Plato's allegory of the cave. Plato's cave-dwellers see the outer world only as shadows on the inside wall. The few who can see beyond the shadows and lies of their culture, says Plato, will never be understood by the masses. The point is that the version of reality we perceive is a simulation created by the mind or active imagination, the **3 of Swords**. If we allow our minds to be manipulated, we then dream or perceive a drastically limited world into appearance. Both the **3 of Swords** and '**Shore Leave**' highlight how the mental aspect of Body Mind creates our experience of so-called reality. Since our perception of external reality creates our experience, this accounts for the Caretakers' ability using their advanced technology to hack into the perceptions and experience of the landing party. Their technology with its monitoring antennae simply tunes into the frequency of the thoughts of the humans and slows down the thought vibrations until they take form recognizable by the five senses. As with the Caretakers, so with the manipulators of perception on Earth, the disempowered Cabal. Brainwashing us through propaganda, advertising, msm news and big psyops was their MO, along with sophisticated mind control technology to further manipulate and limit our perceptions. Our perceptions became theirs. The reality we accordingly created also becomes theirs, in actuality that of the Orion AI or Lucifer. The power of reality creation using the mind has now been handed back to us. FIrst though, we have to take back our minds even though no longer under Matrix control.

The white rabbit in a yellow waistcoat seen by McCoy is his perceptual creation. The creature appears after his exclamation to Sulu, in a moment of **3 of Swords** imagination, that the place is 'like something out of Alice in Wonderland!' The rabbit is McCoy's mental image decoded into reality by the Caretakers' technology. In a parallel way, everything we experience in our own world proceeds from our minds' decoding of waveform reality. 'I saw what I saw,' says McCoy, 'but maybe I hallucinated it'. The latter point is right in that everything we see is a subjective decoding of waveform reality. McCoy nevertheless evinces shock and surprise. Different crew members react differently to their encounters with the products of their imaginations.

Sulu is delighted to find an old-fashioned handgun but panic-stricken when attacked by a Samurai warrior. Yeoman Barrows is similarly enchanted by the materialization of a beautiful dress but traumatized by a Don Juan figure attacking her. Kirk blisses out on meeting Ruth, an early infatuation of his, but becomes belligerent when re-confronted by Finnegan, the bane of his college days. These and more phenomena throw the crew into states of contradiction and confusion that taken overall show how little we as a race truly understand the nature of reality creation.

Different responses fly back and forth in a melée of **reversed 3 of Swords** confusion: 'I can't believe it!' … 'I did not imagine it' … 'We are seeing things that cannot possibly exist'…'We're certain they're terribly real' …'These things cannot be real' … and so on. Perhaps the most contradictory moment of all occurs when McCoy takes a stand against a mounted knight charging him with a drawn lance. 'Hallucinations cannot harm us', declares McCoy, just before the knight impales and kills him. Yes, the knight was a hallucination, a decoding of an electromagnetic field by McCoy in his Body Mind. But the energetic resistance remained between the two electromagnetic fields, that of McCoy and that of the knight. McCoy's consciousness was not able to override the resistance. Once brought back to life, he gets it, and gets to play with a couple of dreamed up playboy bunny girls, finally learning as we all will, that life in a holographic amusement park can be fun. So it will be with our magical consciousness now freed from the Matrix of AI systems constraining it

AFTER THE TAKEDOWN

Now that we have been freed to create our own unhijacked 'reality' what are we going to create? Much depends on what we believe. Experience tends to follow perceptions which in turn follow beliefs - what we *want* to believe. Hence the entrapment of sceptics like Richard Dawkins in five-sense only reality. Their passionate but narrow and rigid beliefs forbid them to accept psychic phenomena that they claim break the laws of physics. They will dismiss as unreal any such phenomena that bypass the five senses. Yet the field of all possibilities infinitely surpasses that experienced by the five senses and hardened by indoctrination and belief. We no longer have our minds straitjacketed by educational and political authorities. Their control-oriented dogmas and false narratives may continue for some time, but the Matrix that kept us in their caves of perception has gone. Our power of reality creation is ours again. 'You must always imagine in your favour' says long experienced ex-SSPer Tony Rodrigues. Whatever we want to believe we can imagine and feel and create. We will use this restored ability in our favour.

15. INTELLECTUAL CRISIS

The delusion that we have not been freed must be dropped before freedom can be fully realized

Episode 15 '**The Galileo Seven**' correlates with the **9 of Swords**; both are themed around the need to let go of ways of thinking that have become mistaken, redundant or over-dominant.

THE CARD
Before any transformation can happen, crisis and/or disintegration must first take place. In order to be reborn one must first die, at least figuratively. So in the 9th Arcanum, The Hermit withdraws from society and activity in order to look deeply within and discard outworn patterns. With the message of The Hermit underpinning the 9s, they all stand for some kind of crisis and necessary overhaul. On the **9 of Swords** we see the Sword of the mind breaking out of an oval pattern and itself breaking up. A crack has appeared on the blade. The mind has been jolted having taken an unsettling blow. With the shock it will never be the same again. A shaken intellect prepares the way for a new understanding, transformation of perceptions, letting go of stubbornly held convictions, revising of attitudes and acknowledging of mistakes. This opens the way for a new synthesis of intellect with heart and of intuition with practicality.

When **reversed**, this card stands for suffering, damage or resistance involved in the process of evolving one's thinking. Stubbornness may have taken too strong a hold, or mistakes are not being learned from. Or there is cognitive dissonance or trauma attending new understandings or revelations. Mental illness is possible. So too are problems caused by trying to be rational or principled when pure impulse is called for, or intuition, inspiration, pragmatism, empathy or compassion.

'THE GALILEO SEVEN' PREMISE
Marooned in a downed shuttlecraft, attacked by savages, Spock struggles with logic and his own obstinacy in coordinating efforts to rejoin the Enterprise.

CONTEXT
Taking Stock.

INTELLECTUAL CRISIS
Kirk is delivering medical supplies to Makus 3 when the Enterprise passes a quasar. On principle he judges this to warrant investigating, overruling Commissioner Ferris who warns hims of a time imperative on the delivery. Spock and six crew descend to a planet within the quasar but become marooned when their shuttlecraft crash lands. Contact has been lost with the Enterprise while Kirk for his part has very limited time to undertake a search and rescue. On his side Spock handles the emergency with typical Vulcan logic but which devolves into intellectual crisis. He alienates his crew with a succession of stringently logical or principled decisions. Two crew members are killed in the process and the craft nearly throttled by hostile, hairy monsters. In a daze of cognitive dissonance, doubt and self-reappraisal, Spock asks himself how his correct and logical approach had foundered. Nevertheless his rational thinking does succeed in re-establishing orbit. But there is no rescue. Time has run out and Ferris has ordered Kirk to call off the search. On the brink of annihilation Spock instinctively hits a switch that detonates a fuel trail acting as a flare to alert the Enterprise. The ploy works. Back on board much merriment ensues from Spock's refusal to admit he deviated from strict logic in taking a gamble with the fuel in an emotional, desperate moment.

CARD/EPISODE AND MATRIX TAKEDOWN
The dark energy entrapping us has been removed. The more we accept this, the more we shall be able to actually live in freedom. Seeing Matrix control for what it now is - extinct - will empower us to give up attachment to the the former rules and expectations. The way will be cleared to find fulfillment

through following our passion in life according to our true nature, beings of infinite love. If governments still try to dictate to us by passing 'laws' that limit freedom then we have to question our role in allowing this. Do we still believe in the right of government to control us? If so, we have to ask ourselves why we stubbornly stick to this belief. When we do this along with independent research and a discerning approach to information emanating from official sources, then we shall start to dissolve the last vestiges of the prison bars. The **9 of Swords** represents such a rethink involving a problematic situation, all of which sums up Spock's experience leading the shuttle craft. The card tells us it's time to recognize undesirable results proceeding from a redundant perception or approach. In the matter of the stricken Galileo, Spock's avowed reliance on logic alone increasingly frustrates and annoys his colleagues. But he is not always logical and even admits failure of his thinking a couple of times. Having command of the Galileo thrust upon him, Spock, as is his way, intends always to base his decisions purely on logic - but he doesn't. He cannot bring himself to admit that it is stubbornness rather than logic that undermines his command. He claims to McCoy that he is a rational man whose instincts are always to 'do logically whatever needs to be done.' But like any other human, and Spock has 50% human in him, he has his own principles and predilections that influence or override the application of strict logic. Stubbornly sticking to past principles characterizes Spock's decision-making as much as relying on logic.

A large number of people may remain unaware that the basis of Matrix control - the Omega AI system - has been disconnected. Change of attitude will still happen. Perceptions are key. New perceptions will replace programmed thinking formerly drummed into us by the old system. Anyone stubbornly continuing to think in the old way will feel increasingly out of place. Outworn concepts, attitudes and ideas are being abandoned - the meaning of the **9 of Swords**. As Einstein said, 'No problem can be solved by the same level of consciousness that created it.' To McCoy, Spock's problem is his lack of heart while Yeoman Mears comments at one point: 'We could use a little inspiration'. Spock himself maintains that 'there are always alternatives', that it is logical to try them all. Logic then, is not his undoing. The problem is his insistence on principles that forbids him to allow his men to shoot to kill the hostile natives. As a result, two of Spock's men are themselves killed. Kirk too, stubbornly sticks to his principles. He knew of the deadline on the delivery job and had the Commissioner on his back but still he thought it his duty to prioritize investigating the quasar. This rash insistence on sticking to principles - mirroring Spock's, is the quality of consciousness that originally caused the loss of the shuttlecraft.

Stubbornness then, is the flaw of both Kirk and Spock that needs to be overhauled in the way of the **9 of Swords**. 'You're a stubborn man!' Kirk lightheartedly tells Spock after it's all over. Spock's logical responses always served him, at least up until his final desperate action. But true, it was his stubborn refusal to allow the enemy to be killed that attenuated the disaster. His crew advise him to be practical and eliminate the death-dealing barbarians by using phasers set to kill. This would be the logical expedient but Spock cannot override his principle even in a kill-or-be-killed situation. The two men die causing Spock some soul-searching, even if their deaths spare him the task of having to decide who to sacrifice to enable relaunch.

Spock's **9 of Swords** intellectual crisis continues in the effort of making the relaunch successful. The Galileo gets off the planet but at the cost of its booster power for a soft landing if required. This had to do with delaying the relaunch to save an injured Spock who reproved his men for failing to do the rational thing and abandon him. But Boma and McCoy are not primarily men of logic like Spock. They think and act differently. Trapped under a rock, Spock stubbornly insisted on being sacrificed and left behind. Fortunately his men disobeyed him. But this caused the delay and exhausted booster power which was needed to shake off the interfering monsters. After relaunch, with only minutes of fuel left, Spock admits he may have been mistaken in his earlier assertion that there are always alternatives. This **9 of Swords** admission of mistaken thinking stuns McCoy. But perhaps it is Spock's admission that there may actually be no alternative to burning up in a decaying orbit that impels him to find one after all. Intuition or pure impulse kicks in as Spock jettisons and ignites the fuel causing the rippling green flare that alerts the watchful Sulu and enables the rescue.

AFTER THE TAKEDOWN

Many may stubbornly believe that the old system of corrupt and self-serving government will never change. This mistaken view will die out as light replaces darkness and people awaken. The truth will inevitably come out that the instigators of mendacious control and manipulation have gone. Cabal members who planned and pushed the dark agenda are no more. New light is flooding this planet but rigidly held beliefs can still keep people trapped in old ways. We have to drop completely the old mindset of imprisonment within the Matrix. 'Man's greatest weakness is his suggestibility' said Gurdjieff. Routinely watching TV and absorbing daily propaganda will only hold misconceptions in place. With time however, the truth will become unavoidable. We are free! The Cabal has gone or has no more power. Now it's up to us to proceed to rebuild and restore our world in the new energy.

16. JUVENILE EGO

Freedom from ego and immaturity lies in uniting with the sacred source of consciousness within

Episode 16 'The Squire of Gothos' correlates with **The Page of Wands**; both are themed around a youthful person learning to channel creativity consciously instead of immaturely or egoistically.

THE CARD
The **Page of Wands** shows us a child or youthful person grappling with a Wand, the tool of creativity. The Wand stands vertically in the figure of an 'I' between the Page and the world. Like this youth we are each of us a spiritual being having a human experience learning to use the power of creativity without becoming identified with 'I' the creator. Pages are students, initiates, apprentices. Wands stand for movement, creativity and action, in a word - for doing. As we learn to channel the creativity of the soul and Superconscious Mind in our daily lives, actions increasingly happen through us without us becoming attached to 'I' the doer. We express ourselves with fierce individuality but without narcissistic attachment to ego. In this way we become a pure vehicle for our Soul and ultimately for Consciousness or Infinite Awareness. Actions happen through us without our vanity getting in the way and without attachment to the reactions of others.

It's when we identify with our actions and with ourself as the doer that we cut ourself off from our Soul wisdom. This is the **Page of Wands reversed** whose crown chakra buries itself in the ground, no longer open to heavenly inspiration from above. In this state the **Page** acts out of Service To Self with the ego seeking its own satisfaction rather than an expanded mode of functioning. A responsible ego or 'I' can and should assimilate all the aspects of the lower mind which according to Ashayana Deane comprise the Reasoning Mind, the Dream Self, the Astral Self and the Intuitive Self. When these are fully assimilated, conscious multidimensional perception becomes possible along with connection to the Superconscious Mind existing at Soul level.

Even **upright** this **Page** appears awkward. The Wand appears of inordinate size and weight for its handler who also seems youthful and inexperienced. Steadying the instrument with clumsily crossed arms, the **Page** appears unsure how to use it. A **reversed Page of Wands** would represent an immature person not only over-awed by the power of creativity but mishandling it. By attaching to his actions he or she becomes ruinously caught up in the ego self's perceptions and desires. This cuts off the lower levels of Self from the greater structures of the Cosmic Unified Field. Creative potential goes unrealized or diverted into selfish, manipulative or narcissistic behaviour. This may manifest in chaotic impulsiveness with low tolerance to frustration as the juvenile ego relentlessly chases desires attended by unending irritations, setbacks or stressful situations. Peace goes out of the window, replaced by impatience, anger, pride, resentment or false superiority, with resultant suffering for the self and others.

'THE SQUIRE OF GOTHOS' PREMISE
Crew are abducted by an ego-driven, sadistic man-child who plays whimsical games of manipulation and humiliation in the vein of a dashing musketeer.

CONTEXT
Power, Coercion.

JUVENILE EGO
As the Enterprise approaches an isolated barren planet, Sulu and Kirk abruptly disappear. A search party beams down to the surface below, finding themselves in front of a stone-built castle with a mock 19th century style interior. The place belongs to Trelane, an aristocratic-looking young man with incredible powers of matter manipulation. For it is he who has abducted - and temporarily paralyzed - Sulu and Kirk. Effectively taking the party captive he embarks on an elaborate charade of games-playing and

showing off. His passion and subject of study is all things military and warlike, evidenced in his collection of military regalia including busts of Napoleon and Caesar. Although looking in his 30s he calls himself a retired General and affects all manner of airs and graces in a hammy, superficially charming way. Yet he is a man who must be obeyed, for whom the freedom and rights of others mean absolutely nothing. He takes more crew prisoner in his elegant drawing room and coerces them into making entertainments with ceremonial music and dancing. Twice Kirk and the Enterprise try to escape this juvenile, ego-driven 'madman' who according to McCoy has no physical substance, with the rest of his planet being a stormy, noxious desert. Kirk ends up being condemned to death by Trelane dressed as a hanging judge but saves himself by talking Trelane into hunting him in the forest. Just as Trelane has caught up with Kirk, ready to finish him off with a sword, the voices of Trelane's handlers, sounding like his parents, reprimand him for being a naughty boy cruelly misbehaving. They threaten to forbid him making any more planets and dematerialize him. A 'mischievous small boy', Kirk later calls him for the record.

CARD/EPISODE AND MATRIX TAKEDOWN

As of this writing, early 2023, only 12 me-obsessed Generals, according to Kim Goguen, continue to pass orders down to Earth governments and banking and other institutions. The few managers left of the fallen Matrix are in chaos and disarray. Their history of manufactured wars and violence, their cruelty and terror, belongs now only *to* history. Trelane loves military history. He himself evidently would have relished being one of the class of beings claiming the right to rule over the majority by virtue of his bloodline and breeding. He exhibits the same attachment to ego pride and selfish desire as the dark occultists formerly staffing the Cabal at the top of the global pyramid, Trelane embodies the type to a tee, that of the most **reversed** type of **Page of Wands**. This was the type manning the shadowy highest levels of the world's religions, governments, militaries, royal families, judiciaries, banks and corporations. Their business was manipulating wars, revolutions, social division, wealth-accumulation and the weaponization of technology for the perpetuation of their own power and control. Were they psychopaths or just immature, derailed egotists? Or some combination?

Looking to Trelane for insight, he behaves throughout with callous and whimsical indifference to the feelings of his captive victims. His shallow affect is that a sociopath devoid of true feelings, without empathy or compassion. He makes a show of adopting a caring manner and tone of voice, pretending to sympathize with Kirk's loss of his ship: 'I must experience your sense of alarm, your grief'. Though delighted by games and play-acting, twirling his sword and strutting about like a jubilant boy in a toyshop, he worships the concepts of authority, of order-giving, infatuated with his superiority over inferior beings. His morality is both that of the spoilt brat and of the Satanists stalking Earth's corridors of power. The gist of it is: 'What is good is what I want, and what I want, I get!' If his 'guests' don't obey him, he growls, they will make him 'very, very angry.' When getting his way, Trelane banters with a beaming face in jocular tones. He holds the crew prisoner while affecting to be their kindly, avuncular host. A pretentious form of light-heartedness comes easily. Yet while outwardly behaving in superficially charming ways, he intimidates, threatens and uses violence to get his way.

Though a **reversed Page of Wands** with 'an immature, unbalanced mind' as Kirk puts it, Trelane has the Satanists' taste for Social Darwinism. He believes himself fit to rule over others by virtue of his dominating, vicious nature. 'On your knees!' he demands of Kirk at sword-point after hunting him down for sport in the outlying forest. We have Cathy O'Brien to thank for a close-up study of similar egotism and sociopathy based on her own experience as a 'Presidential Model' White House sex slave during the 1980s. Her revelatory book 'TranceFormation of America', 1995, details the abuses and torments she suffered at the hands of the highest levels of the then thriving Global Elite. One ordeal was to be the human prey in a sport known as 'A Very Dangerous Game'. She reveals how George Bush senior and his Vice President Dick Cheney armed with rifles and tracker dogs had her undress down to her trainers to be pursued by them through the woods of a high security military compound at Mount Shasta. As Trelane threatens to run the captured Kirk through with his sword, so Cheney held his gun to Cathy's head after catching her. Instead of shooting her, the two men ordered her and the dog to indulge in a sexual act while they watched amused. This was the mentality of the sociopaths and psychopaths running our world. But they are gone now, sent back to Source to make way for global restoration of peace and well-being in a cleaned up world. Likewise, the immature self-indulgent Trelane is himself removed, called away entirely unrepentant, by his overseers in spirit.

AFTER THE TAKEDOWN

'Self-caused immaturity', said Kant, can be overcome by 'having the courage to use our own intelligence'. The highest intelligence is that of the heart, our direct link to Source. With the Matrix gone, humanity will be following the heart integrated with the mind, enabling the knowing and doing of only what is in alignment with the light of Source consciousness.

17. INITIATION

As we evolve we will grow in awareness, take back our power and learn to govern ourselves

Episode 17 '**Arena**' correlates with the **The Magician**; both are themed around initiation and passage to maturity though a test of ingenuity, skill and resourcefulness.

THE CARD
The Magician stands at his table playfully twirling magical objects while distractedly looking away. Is he putting on a show, teaching himself new tricks or just playing for the fun of it? At any rate he seems full of confidence and vitality, imagination and youthful ardour. With his restless, easily distracted temperament we may wonder whether he will waste his obvious potential. Or whether he's even aware of it. What challenges lie ahead for him? Can he rein in his impulses and find the necessary self-discipline to evolve himself toward self-realization? Can he do so without losing his sense of spontaneity and excitement in joyful creativity? He represents many qualities therefore: talent, youthfulness, confidence, growth potential, skills, work. Being numbered 1 among the Majors he also represents a beginning on the road to all-round maturity and mastery both of his skills and of himself. Life awaits him as an adventurous initiation through constructively and benevolently using his resources in furtherance of personal and global evolution. **The**

Magician is complemented by The Emperor card. Together these two Majors express the Masculine Principle: the power of doing, of ingenuity, which when raised to its highest development manifests in the Genius.

Reversed, **The Magician** as an initiate is clumsy or regressive. He makes ill-considered use of his cleverness. He seeks fame or gain for their own sake, becoming selfish or narcissistic, He can also be competitive instead of cooperative, or deceitful, cheating or fraudulent in his immaturity.

'ARENA' PREMISE

Kirk has to use his wits in single combat against a reptilian adversary. A more evolved race has organized this for them to resolve their ongoing dispute.

CONTEXT

Deception, War, Awakening, Self-Realization.

INITIATION

Kirk and five crew beaming down to Cestus 5 are ambushed in a foray of bombs and rockets. The Earth outpost has been destroyed leaving the shore party exposed to aerial attack from the surrounding hills. They fire back until the aliens withdraw. Back in the Enterprise they give chase to what Kirk believes was an invading force. Spock advises against destroying the retreating vessel but Kirk deems it necessary to protect other Federation life. But both vessels are brought to a halt, their firepower blocked. A technologically more advanced race announces its displeasure at both craft trespassing in their space on a 'mission of violence'. To restore peace while allowing them to settle their conflict, the supervising Metrons transport the two captains unarmed, Kirk and a reptilian Gorn, to a rocky, arid planet. There they will be permitted to fight. Each may use whatever materials may be found locally to craft weapons to destroy the other. The lumbering Gorn proves much stronger and tougher than Kirk but Kirk is more speedy and agile. This doesn't help him much. It's when he takes the Metrons' advice to heart that he turns the battle around. With resourcefulness and ingenuity he finds and utilizes materials scattered around, cobbling together a crude mortar gun. He fires off a volley that cripples the Gorn and is about to finish him off with a stake through the heart when he relents in disgust. 'No I won't kill you!' he cries. A glowing, androgynous humanoid appears. A Metron, he congratulates Kirk on showing mercy and sparing his enemy. 'We feel there may be hope for your kind', he declares. Kirk later reflects on the experience as some kind of initiation: 'We are a most promising species, as predators go ... given a thousand years or so.'

CARD/EPISODE AND MATRIX TAKEDOWN

With the Matrix control system having prevailed for thousands of years, humanity had become stuck in disbelief or ignorance of its own divine power. Humanity had to grow up, according to Alex Collier passing on the wisdom of his Andromedan contacts. For far too long he says, people were blocked, primarily due to apathy based on belief systems inculcated in us by Service To Self alien races, notably Anunnaki and the Draco reptilians. We are **The Magician** in the Tarot, a youthful, creative and energetic species gifted with huge potential for growth and development, but kept restrained under frequency control, unaware, immature, manipulated. We remain 'a most promising species' in Kirk's words after his encounter with the higher dimensional Metron. Our promise is now activating with the Matrix AI grid no longer blocking our evolutionary development. Contactees report that galactic councils and groups from star systems everywhere such as the Pleiades, Andromeda and Arcturus are here at this momentous time observing humanity. But none can do our evolution for us.

The Metrons' broadcast to the Enterprise urges humans to evolve themselves by mending their violent ways. The Metron humanoid that appears to Kirk after his contest is a glowing, boy-like female dressed in a shimmering long white dress. She evokes what Ashayana Deane in Voyagers 2 calls 'a member of the Seventh Race'. These are 'androgynous, soul-awakened identities' of less dense bodies able to time travel and traverse solar systems. They represent the race that humans of Earth will one day evolve into, returning to the glorious 12-strand DNA beings we used to be on the higher dimensional counterparts of Earth, the planets Tara and Gaia. As 'voyagers', or initiates like **The Magician**, we humans abound with promise on our journey toward self-realization, the state of the Metron. As such, we are meant to learn the ways, says Deane, of 'unity consciousness and love, co-operation and respect toward all other life forms'. Such ways align with the true working of the universe. As they come naturally, all that is required is to regain and practise the spiritual knowledge we lost. Deane attributes our ignorance to the 'elitist, sexist, materialistic distortions' propagated by intruders. Foremost among these, she says, were Anunnaki and reptilian conquerors, including those from Orion, the instigators of the Matrix of 18 AI programs intended to forever separate us from the Creator.

The age-old conflict between reptilians and humans is symbolized in the skirmish on Cestus 5 and then between Kirk and the Gorn. The Gorn displace the colony on Cestus 5 by violence before ambushing the Enterprise team. The reptilian force takes no prisoners and uses deception on top of ruthless brutality. According to Collier, reptilians destroyed three human-occupied planets in the Lyran system in such conflicts. Having demolished and taken over the Cestus 5 outpost, the Gorn lure down the Enterprise team by impersonating Commodore Travers. These traits of stealth, untrustworthiness and deceit characterize both humanity's age-old adversary the Draco reptilians and the **The Magician reversed**. Travers apparently radios the starship in his familiar avuncular tones which are not those of Travers at all. Posing as Travers the Gorn reptilians invite a party down for a lavish dinner and even recommend Kirk bringing his most senior officers. Once the battle is on, the effectively ambushed human group are set upon by an enemy that never reveals itself. The Gorn hide among the surrounding mountains from where they mount their long-range attack. Although heavily outgunned, Kirk's attitude is 'we'll have to make do with what we've got.' As missiles rain down, he weaves around on nimble legs running this way and that to dodge the blasts. Himself every inch the resourceful **Magician**, Kirk finds a stray grenade launcher and with Spock's help fires it off, devastating the enemy position on its high ground. He will use a similar weapon, ingeniously improvised and constructed later in his initiatory battle alone with the Gorn. That mortar-like weapon will floor the creature and clinch the duel but Kirk then relents. Rather than finish off the reptilian enemy, he desires to talk to him, to 'reach an agreement' with him. Neither does he wish the Metron to destroy the wounded creature. This pleases the Metron. Perhaps, says the serene higher dimensional being, humans will be able to reach an agreement with Metrons themselves after a few thousand years.

AFTER THE TAKEDOWN

Agreeing with the Metron, Ashayana Deane states that our evolution still requires much time. But with the Matrix gone, war will go too, giving way to wisdom and kindness as finally learnt by Kirk. By overcoming hatred and fear, humans will grow to become free and united 'in co-creative relationship with the Divine'. We will become free by reinstating personal sovereignty and taking back our power stolen by our so-called elites. Pulling their strings were Draco reptilians who came to Earth from Orion a million years ago. Kirk admits to feeling 'an instinctive revulsion to reptiles' but Dracos belong to the same soul essence as humans, according to Voyagers 2. They are a hybrid of the human and fully reptilian Drakon races who felt entitled to reclaim Earth for themselves. Humanity's task is to take back control of our planet from our decimated elites now left without their AI control system and off-planet masters. This will involve waking up to our own initiatory task with a far-reaching evolutionary plan and purpose for our existence.

18. TIMELINES

A timeline tends to remain constant; our progress in consciousness will follow the positive timeline

Episode 18 '**Tomorrow Is Yesterday**' correlates with **The Wheel of Fortune**; both are themed around perceptions of unfolding events apparently connecting so-called past, present and future.

THE CARD
The Wheel of Fortune is a multi-layered, complex representation of the holographic reality we live in and beyond. Two dumb, frantic-looking animals representing humans subject to Body Mind programming chase each other in a hell-bent way around the **Wheel** and in doing so, push it. Round and round and up and down they go, as if on a hamster wheel, both controlled by and perpetuating the turns of Fate. This is the constantly changing, dualistic world of opposites, including cause and effect, that we perceive through our brain and five senses and become trapped within. We accordingly experience never-ending ups and downs of good and bad fortune, success and failure, health and sickness and so on. Whether **upright** of **reversed**, **The Wheel of Fortune** represents a kind of controlling Matrix in itself, a hologram of limitation. Limited because as spiritual beings we exist above and beyond this 3D world, as per the third creature.

Crowned and bearing heart-shaped wings, she holds aloft a sword and appears serene and content. Seated atop the **Wheel**, she should have no stability as her pedestal rests on the turning wheel itself. And yet she remains stationary and regal, posing like The Empress in Arcanum 3. This regal creature's reality is entirely different to that of the other creatures who merely follow Body Mind programming. Coloured blue for our spiritual self, she sits both on and beyond the **Wheel** of duality, in the world but not of the world. She's a witness to 3D reality yet unbound by it. Instead of going around on the **Wheel**, she observes it and transcends it from the vantage point of multi-dimensional consciousness.

At the higher levels of our identity, we, like this creature transcend the limitations of duality. With heart awareness, we know that all past and all future exists in the eternal NOW. Any moment in time exists as accessible, decodable information in a holographic Matrix represented here as the **Wheel**. 'Time is a sphere', says Thoran, an alien contact of Elena Danaan in her book 'A Gift From The Stars'. 'Every point in time is equidistant from the centre. In order to apprehend this concept, you need to step outside of your 3D minds, towards other frequencies of consciousness. There is no separation between all things. All is but one. Time, consciousness, life, all One. Eternal.' Thus, he goes on to say, not only does Earth have its portals for accessing other realms and times, so do we. Once we realize our capacities we will be able to open these doors existing within us.

'TOMORROW IS YESTERDAY' PREMISE
Mishaps and efforts to prevent history being catastrophically altered ensue when the Enterprise is accidentally sent back in time to 1960s Earth.

CONTEXT
Multi-Dimensionality.

TIMELINES
A freak cosmic event hurls the Enterprise to Planet Earth and back 200 years to 1969. A pursuing US Air Force pilot gives chase and has to be beamed board. Spock and Kirk perceive a dilemma. Either by returning the pilot to his base or keeping him on board, they fear disrupting the timeline of Earth history. They opt to return him after first secretly retrieving his flight records from his base. The pilot's UFO sighting, actually the Enterprise, will then be unbacked by evidence. Security personnel at the base catch and interrogate the prowling Kirk while another Air Force officer is accidentally beamed aboard the Enterprise. The Air Force men are eventually returned and the Enterprise returned to its own time.

CARD/EPISODE AND MATRIX TAKEDOWN

Insiders and whistleblowers of the ongoing Secret Space Program (SSP) report that space and time travel via portals, wormholes and stargates is a regular but closely monitored feature of SSP activity. Reports from super-soldiers and contactees such as Randy Cramer, Tony Rodrigues and Elena Danaan confirm the Enterprise crew as correct in handling time travel sensibly and responsibly. **The Wheel of Fortune** turns in cycles from past to present to future and likes to remain a single, consistent timeline. Spock correctly wants the historical sequence of events to be protected from corruption or distortion. So what happens in our holographic reality when the course of history is changed by time travellers accidentally or intentionally?

Experiments in time travel were conducted extensively during the Montauk Project of the early 1980s. In his book The Ascension Mysteries, 2016, David Wilcock gives some information. Portals were opened up by utilizing a pilot seat from a crashed ET craft. The seat amplified the consciousness of the person sitting in it, allowing the operator to travel instantly to any place or time envisioned. It took much trial and error before the effect became accurately controllable. One disaster occurred when a man was crazy enough to go back through time and meet his despised father who he then killed. He returned back to his own time still alive. But two days later he was run over by a car in a fatal street accident. Wilcock states that after many such incidents the military contractors at Montauk concluded that timelines can be multiple, or put another way, that time can be layered. They realized that, to quote Wilcock:

> If you go back into the past and change an event, you create a new timeline, or a new layer that sits on top of the layer that is already there. Both layers can coexist. The layer that our future snaps into is the layer that has more energy associated with it. If a new layer is created that creates too many paradoxes in our existing main timeline, natural events will occur that heal those problems. The layers always find a way of merging.

The man finally dying in the traffic accident merged two inconsistent layers of time and resolved the paradox he had created. The same fate serving to resolve a time paradox befalls Edith Keeler in Episode 27, The City On The Edge of Forever.

In the view of SSP whistleblower, Corey Goode, time is malleable, or 'elastic'. He says time has the ability to repair itself in the event of timeline problems, breaks or fractures. Humans having caused such problems through time travel activity are, according to Goode, best advised to do nothing and let time repair itself. But in the Star Trek universe (or that of its writers) no such knowledge exists. The timeline problem afflicting the Enterprise hangs over Kirk and Spock as a crisis which they feel they themselves have to manually resolve. Their perception of being hostages to fortune - **The Wheel of Fortune** - is the theme here. Their fear is of destroying the future for themselves and those in their circle having disrupted the timeline. The Enterprise, in Spock's view, could be made to no longer exist or they could become locked in the wrong time zone, of becoming in Christoper's words, 'prisoners in time'. Kirk and Spock proceed valiantly to reverse the time problems caused. After difficulties and setbacks they manage to return Christopher to his base. They then take a big risk to reverse the slingshot effect that originally sent the Enterprise backwards in time. Kirk's view is 'We ought to take a chance, especially if one is all you have.' His strategy amounts to spinning **The Wheel of Fortune** and hoping for the best. The plan works, sending the Enterprise back to its own time. The crew's **Wheel** returns to spinning out events according to the original timeline connecting all events in sequence according to the historical record.

AFTER THE TAKEDOWN

Living in the closed-world Matrix, humans tended to forget their unlimited nature, living by Matrix programming of the Body Mind and its limited perceptions. Thus we existed on a hamster wheel of protracted, repetitive experience. We sentenced ourselves to chasing desires and fleeing from fears on a **Wheel of Fortune** we ourselves kept turning, now up, now down. All is different in the new energy, with the ability to reconnect to our soul and Infinite Self and realize our timeless nature. Our apparent physical form is but a photonic, holographic experience. SSP experiencers know that by moving our mind outside of it, we can travel between other times and places. Moreover, by meditating or through other forms of connection with our Source of consciousness, we can learn to relax into the newly installed positive timeline. Thus will we start living both in harmony with, and outside of, the dictates of perceived linear time. All events in time really happen in the timeless NOW. It is only our brains decoding information from the waveform reality emanating from the Unified Field in the timeless NOW that evokes what we perceive as linear time and a sequence of events. From the higher perspective, that of our multi-dimensional self as symbolized by the crowned creature seated on top of the **Wheel**, all is in order. Freed from Matrix control including the Kronos AI that managed the dark side of timelines, we will rapidly move into unprecedented balance and harmony.

19. LEADERSHIP

Corrupt leaders and organisations will be replaced by those with integrity and commitment to freedom for all

Episode 19 'Court Martial' correlates with the **King of Wands**; both are themed around a capable and responsible man, a master of creative or organisational skill in his chosen field.

THE CARD

The **King of Wands** simultaneously sits and stands and springs into action. He's heavily armoured yet agile and alert. He commands his territory, his zone of endeavour, securely and reliably yet looks confidently and earnestly to the right, the future and further achievement. He is a leader or a doer *par excellence*, having mastered his craft and repeatedly proven himself in action. He's not a flashy risk-taker like the even more dynamic Knight of Wands. Instead he prides himself on his expertise and reliability, his repeated successes and mastery within a chosen field. Above all he can be trusted to bear responsibility well, to be up to the job and to act in a mature, civilized way. He upholds professional standards whether in physical, creative or organizational work, and particularly where high skill and experience are needed. This is essentially a practitioner, a highly dependable, consistent one in good charge of himself and his kingdom. He or she exudes good judgement and integrity.

A **reversed King of Wands** fails to observe self-discipline and integrity in maintaining his position of power and responsibility. Over-impulsiveness or ego drives could make him arrogant, hostile, corrupt or tyrannical.

'COURT MARTIAL' PREMISE
Kirk is put on trial for negligent action causing the death of a colleague. Proceedings expose the incident as a set-up, the victim having faked his own death.

CONTEXT
Deception, Justice,

LEADERSHIP
Following damage in an ion storm and the death of crew member Finney, the Enterprise arrives at Starbase 11 for repairs. Kirk comes in for criticism of his leadership when it is claimed that his negligence caused the man's death. According to the computer Kirk mistimed a safety procedure but he disputes this and vows to clear his name in an upcoming trial. His colleagues at his trial one by one speak up for his impeccable captaincy. Kirk himself defends the discharge of his duties, stating he acted with no malice and no panic. 'I took the proper steps in the proper order', he says, adding that nothing is more important to him than his ship. In further investigations it's discovered that Finney is not dead after all but hiding elsewhere in the ship. Kirk on his own finds and confronts the deranged man who was acting on a grudge to discredit the captain. The two wrestle. Kirk wins and goes on to rapidly repair the circuits that Finney had sabotaged. Returning to the bridge he kisses Areel Shaw goodbye. The attractive lawyer and ex-flame of his had been the prosecuting attorney at his trial.

CARD/EPISODE AND MATRIX TAKEDOWN
This conflict between Kirk and Finney dramatizes a conflict between two **Kings of Wands**, one **upright** and one **reversed**. That is, between an honest and capable leader or self-starter and a corrupt or malicious one. Limiting the field of possibility while setting up the perceptions of one side as good the other as bad, has long been a feature of Matrix 'democracy', with contests pitting Left against Right or an Establishment figure against a Saviour figure. As the Cabal controls both sides, whichever front person prevails makes no difference to the long-term agenda. This is not to say that Kirk too is a mere puppet of a higher up force, but that his battle with Finney plays out like those constantly set up on the stage of Earth politics.

Kirk playing the role of leader and saviour for his crew was echoed by former President Donald Trump playing the same role for the American people. In the illusory pantomime of Matrix politics, Trump was a Republican fighting the Democrats. Still in the illusion of the pantomime, the alternative media made him out to be an outsider figure, a hero of reform working alongside the information source known as Q and the military rescue force known as the Earth Alliance or 'White Hats'. Their successes were said to have included the rescue of thousands of children secretly imprisoned in Deep Underground Military Bases. As these bases belonged to Trump's Deep State masters it seems unlikely. His masters according to Kim Goguen were those higher up in the Order of The Black Sun, one of the Deep State's two main factions. Trump's victory in the 2016 US Election over Clinton was seen as the first opportunity in decades for a President who was purportedly not a Deep State puppet to clean up the conspiratorial, corrupt and criminal Establishment. Trump himself called it 'draining the swamp'. Never mind that he *was* a Deep State insider, that he filled his administration with Rothschild Zionists and that he hastened to encourage and enable the American public and military to become ruinously Covid jabbed at 'warp speed' (borrowing Star Trek terminology). Despite this and many other anomalies, Trump continued to be seen by many as an **upright King of Wands** and saviour even in campaigning to recontest the presidency in 2024.

Countering him, his political enemies certainly lied, cheated and stole their way to blocking his re-election in 2020. In this, they exhibited the deceit and desperation endemic of a **reversed King of Wands** like Lt. Col. Finney. In his bid to take down the Enterprise's captain, Finney pretends to perish during the ion storm while forging the computer record to pin the blame on Kirk. In their efforts to overturn the people's vote in the US Election of 2020, the Cabal acted in a similar devious and criminal manner. Six months after Biden's inauguration (wrongfully pre-recorded), Trump announced an investigation into 'massive voter fraud' and the 'Crime of the Century'. We are vividly reminded of this as we watch Finney's doctored computer record of Kirk prematurely jettisoning the pod apparently killing Finney. There was nothing amiss with Kirk's actions. These were falsified by the very person supposedly destroyed by them. Likewise, there are no doubts concerning Trump's landslide victory on election night. The result however was changed into a Biden victory likewise by doctored computer. Voting machines were hacked, along with the use of falsified ballots, voting by dead people and illegal aliens etc. The Biden Administration went on to suppress the necessary judicial enquiry while the Deep State-controlled mass media claimed that Trump was guilty of attempting to overturn a rightful result.

Both these **Kings of Wands**, Trump and Kirk, were the victims of computers tampered with to provide false information. The computer in Kirk's case indicates that he ejected the pod before Red Alert thereby killing the helpless Finney. The computer record shows Kirk's finger pressing the button prematurely. Refusing to countenance computer malfunction, the court begins to find Kirk culpable. In Trump's case, not only was he denied a rightful election victory but he was then set up to take the blame for an invasion of the Capitol building on January 6th 2021, the day of ratification of Biden's supposed win. Trump was hauled up for impeachment (for the 2nd time) for allegedly inciting the riot. Hundreds of thousands of Trump supporters had converged on Washington DC in a protest in which Trump pleaded for peace including respect for law and order. These words of his were omitted from mass media broadcasts while newspapers later accused him of urging people to 'fight like hell'. Such alleged rabble-rousing was as falsely reported as the riot itself, a stage managed event in which the police backed off to allow protestors to swarm into the Capitol. In a statement proclaiming his loyalty to the people as against the Deep State, Trump famously said: 'In reality, they're not after me, they're after you. I'm just in the way!' Like the desperate Cabal targeting the entire world's population, the crazed Finney after framing Kirk, sabotages the starship's energy circuits. His aim is not merely to unseat the captain but to destroy the entire ship. Thanks to a legal Knight of Swords to the rescue, Kirk is able to identify and stop him. Kirk's trusty lawyer is one of the old school, Samuel T. Cogley. Armed not with a computer but with dusty legal tomes, Cogley reveres good old fashioned research in the cause of legally upholding humanitarian principles. This plus detective work by Spock eventually leads to Kirk's victory and his confirmation as an **upright King of Wands** threatened by a **reversed King of Wands** using a weaponized computer record.

AFTER THE TAKEDOWN

Victory in the Earth Matrix by any political leader over another has always been a sham, a playing out of the old Matrix paradigm of politics as pantomime, or 'Hollywood for Ugly People'. The electorate are given the illusion of choice and entertained by the debates, but whoever wins or loses, the Cabal remain in charge and the Agenda the same. Politicians have always been actors doing the bidding of higher ups without whose backing they would get nowhere in politics. With the AI Matrix gone, truth and justice will return. How quickly this happens will depend on how quickly we the people forego supposed political representatives and saviours and stand up for ourselves. We ourselves have to use the determination and integrity of the visionary **King of Wands** in rebuilding our world.

20. ZOMBIE WORLD

Along with the Matrix itself, TV 'programming' and MSM hypnosis will rapidly diminish

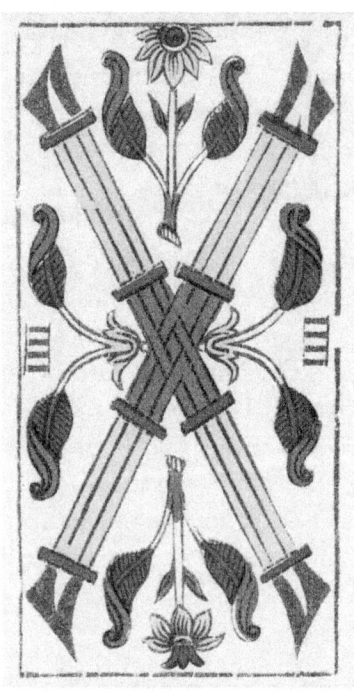

Episode 20 '**The Return of the Archons**' correlates with the **4 of Wands**; both are themed around mechanical and repetitive modes of behaviour, individually or in a programmed population.

THE CARD
The **4 of Wands** combines the steady, disciplined approach of degree 4 with the moving, creative and productive energy of Wands. The result is the ability to thrive in routine work wherein tasks are executed precisely and efficiently, repetitively and consistently. We note the strong healthy foliage growing sideways out of the four crossed wands. At top and bottom two neatly cut flowers are laid down suggesting factory-type efficiency of work. Instructions are obeyed unquestioningly and procedures followed without variance resulting in the highest productivity. This is not an energy of imagination or unpredictability, rather of military-like obedience, repetitive behaviour and machine-like reliability wherein people as in an orchestra need to be of one mind or body in accordance with those around them.

Reversed, the **4 of Wands** manifests in dull uncreative, unspontaneous activity. In this kind of behaviour there is too much of the herd mentality or hive mind, too little vitality of initiative, of acting in individual or original ways. Instead of flair there is mediocrity, instead of enthusiasm there is dullness and boredom, instead of uniqueness, uniformity.

'THE RETURN OF THE ARCHONS' PREMISE
Sulu and McCoy fall foul of the controlling force keeping a planet's citizens behaving like blissed-out automatons. Kirk and Spock join the Resistance.

CONTEXT
Mind Control, AI Takedown.

ZOMBIE WORLD
Sulu is apprehended on the streets of Beta 3 by a strange monk-like figure and zapped by its wand. He beams up but in a dazed and hypnotic state causing several more crew to beam down and investigate. They find pedestrians drifting about formally dressed in 19th century garb and behaving in the same mindless, robotic way as Sulu. At the stroke of 6pm mayhem and rioting breaks out. A friendly man, Reger, gives the shore party refuge telling them that this 12-hour Festival is 'the will of Landru'. A stern colleague, evidently a hardline supporter of the planet's regime, reprimands the party for avoiding the Festival and not being 'of the body' of Landru. He sends in two extremely robotic 'Lawgivers' of the type Sulu met to arrest the party but Kirk's defiance temporarily paralyzes them. The party take to the streets again and this time are pursued by the people of this zombie world now menacing and murderous on Landru's telepathic instruction. The party hide in Reger's cellar, he being one of the Resistance - free-thinking people impersonating Landru's mind-controlled faithful. It was Landru whose technology brought down the missing USS Archon 100 years earlier, before killing or 'absorbing' the crew. Detected by Landru's surveillance, the quarry are zapped and removed to a dungeon for one-by-one absorption. McCoy is turned into an automaton but Kirk and Spock are spared by the intervention of another member of the Resistance, Marplon. The gentle Marplon leads them to Landru's chamber where they discover the handsome, human-looking Big Brother to be nothing but a computer projection. Spock recognizes Landru's society to be a machine's concept of perfection, one with no soul. Kirk talks the machine into destroying the evil that is itself and leaves a sociologist on the planet to help reform the society.

CARD/EPISODE AND MATRIX TAKEDOWN
A global system of mind control prevails on Beta 3 as on Earth during the previous Matrix era. Crystallized thought patterns were programmed into human DNA manifesting in conditioned behaviour down through the ages.

Babylonians, Ancient Egyptians, Sumerians, Celts, Romans, the British and other Empires all saw a culture of repeated war and conquest, power and control, consolidate itself worldwide. Power coalesced into the hands of the church or the state, a select and elite few controlling the citizens by multiple methods of programming. Social customs and orderly patterns of behaviour were punctuated by festivals and ceremonies including ritual blood sacrifice and war, making compliant labourers or soldiers of the broad mass of people. The controlled monotony of this way of life, the **4 of Wands reversed**, came to characterize human existence the world over. The difference with Beta 3 is the one ancient leader Landru presiding over Beta 3 conspicuously. On Earth the Anunnaki and reptilian-led authorities controlling government down through the ages always did so covertly.

Matrix conditions seen on Beta 3 and as they were on Earth varied but both leaderships relied on keeping the people as sheeple, if not zombies, in a compliant state based on propaganda, fear and trauma. Such mind control has the society most effectively doing the bidding of its controllers. Montauk Project survivor Stewart Swerdlow defines mind control as 'the ability to maintain manipulative power over another', thus steering a civilization without deviation or deterioration. Under Earth's global Matrix, the herding of the sheeple saw the global elite racing to instal AI-governed transhumanism to 'absorb' the people into a hive mind, a kind of Borg mentality, so as to complete the much touted New World Order reset. This would have consigned human activity to systematic total control, the **4 of Wands** robotically **reversed**, under the will of the central power. Key to this dystopian timeline was hooking up the masses to a Smart Grid via 5G and Covid jabbing intended to monitor and regulate a zombie world 24/7.

Such is the way on Beta 3 under Landru. It is Landru's AI surveillance that identifies the escaped strangers to the Beta 3 pedestrians who are then telepathically ordered to lynch them. Still in soporific slow motion, the 'absorbed' people wandering the streets pick up stones and weapons and move exactly like zombies to eliminate those who are 'not of the body'. Truth-tellers on past Earth had to contend not with stoning but with scorn and derision. While race and sex discrimination was condemned, 'conspiracy theorists' would be censored and verbally attacked. Their crime? Countering the daily avalanche of MSM propaganda by daring to propose the existence of a shadowy elite controlling the population through deceits and dogmas, with the very concept of government a psyop. Racism became outlawed, but it was fine for truth-tellers to be ostracized, suppressed and metaphorically stoned by hypnotized protectors of the establishment.

'It's paradise!' says the similarly hypnotized Sulu having beamed up to the Enterprise smitten by Landru's programming. His eyes are glazed over with ecstasy, he gazes up seeing nothing except the projection of Landru's 'paradise.' Having been touched by a Lawgiver's wand Sulu has become 'absorbed' into the Beta 3 psyche, actually 'the will of Landru'. Likewise McCoy after his session in the absorption chamber. He returns to his companions in a state of grinning docility; but triggered by overhearing whispers of rebellion he breaks out into frenzied, violent rage. "You're not of the body! Lawgivers! TRAITORS! TRAITORS!" he screams, throttling Kirk. CIA-type mind control includes the installation of such 'triggers'. They activate particular 'alters', sub-personalities given to particular forms of behaviour. Another such 'trigger' or 'compulsive stimulus to activity' as Kirk calls it, is the clock time. We see the people launch into violent and traumatic chaos on the stroke of 6pm on a Festival day, vandalizing everything around with sticks and stones and bodily turmoil. A new 'alter' has been activated to replace the frontal 'alter' of blissed-out serenity.

Likewise at 8pm each Thursday during the fake pandemic of 2020, UK citizens launched into an orgy of programmed clapping and cheering for their health services. The authorities convened this frenzied, mechanical **4 of Wands** behaviour for the same purpose as the Beta 3 Festival: to align the people behind the rulership and its official narrative (and fiction) of a life-threatening virus epidemic. In the same cause, a worldwide economic and social lockdown ensued with all instructed to stay at home or if going out to keep two metres apart. No matter that such restrictions weaken the immune system, people conformed out of fear of not doing so, fear inculcated not by the dead piling up but by government decree. With a reptilian component fixated on survival installed into the brain, the modified human psyche based itself on fear, enabling control through hierarchies, religions, wars and 'false flags' to thrive. To be 'absorbed' into this psyche as everybody was until very recently is to be given the mind of the ruling power, whether the reptilian Cabal's on Earth or Landru's on Beta 3.

AFTER THE TAKEDOWN
What makes people behave like zombies? Look no further than TV. This is our device equivalent to Landru's absorption chamber. TV exists to ridicule, deny, cover up, distort and distract from any truth that could turn the public against their master, the Satanized authorities. TV and mainstream media with their hypnotic frequencies and mindless content were installed to induce Matrix myopia. With the Matrix gone, TV-induced hypnosis and zombiedom will diminish along with the rest of the technology of dark magic.

21. DARK FLEET

As we collectively raise our consciousness we will be welcomed into the galactic community

Episode 21 '**Space Seed**' correlates with the **Knight of Wands**; both are themed around active, powerful work towards high achievement and ambitious goals - or if negative, destructive conquest.

THE CARD
Nothing less than success, glorious triumph even, will do for the vigorous, heroic **Knight of Wands**. We see him on his athletic horse turning to face a sturdy challenge while charging in another direction. Everything about animal and rider is built for powerful action, speed and accomplishment. Unlike the stable, settled King of Wands, this adventurer is a crusader out on a mission of 'conquest, transmission and unification', to quote Jodorowsky in The Way of Tarot. His horse is white, colour of purity, transcendent non-duality or inclusion of all colours and qualities. His wand is yellow for intelligent action, his midriff slim and his whole body light and agile, like his animal. He signifies the ability to extend his dominion or mastery into new areas; not simply to explore or investigate but to outwardly create, conquer or blaze a trail.

A **Knight of Wands reversed** is a zealous revolutionary, an instigator of riot and chaos, a lawless maniac, a warrior fighting for totalitarian power.

He sets out to break the status quo uncaring of the damage he causes or the innocents trampled on. He's consumed by his ego, with a potentially narcissistic or psychopathic streak. He can be cruel or vindictive, desperate, unscrupulous or ruthless.

'SPACE SEED' PREMISE
Strengthened by eugenics, a charismatic war-maker hijacks the Enterprise. Napoleon-like, he sets about preparing it for widespread conquest.

CONTEXT
Power, The Adversary, Coercion.

DARK FLEET
An old Earth vessel is found drifting in space. The leader of the crew of 73, all in suspended animation, is revived. Taken to sick bay he impresses McCoy with his recovery. His exceptional constitution is attributed to his being a product of selective breeding during the eugenics wars of the 1990s. The computer confirms he was involved, fighting successfully enough to gain and wield power over 1/4 of the world. Kirk locks up the discovered criminal and despot but Khan has been winning over the ship's historian, Maria Mc-Givers. She finds his power attractive, including his intimidation and humiliation of her. She joins Khan as his assistant, helping him hijack the Enterprise and bring aboard his 72 crew as his cohorts. Khan gains control of the bridge through cutting off the life support system. He offers to spare the native crew's lives if they'll fly the starship under his command as head of his own 'dark fleet' on a mission of conquest and colonization. Kirk will be the first to die otherwise. But McGivers has a change of heart and rescues the captain. Kirk takes back the ship and passes sentence on Khan. He will be exiled to a barren planet, a fate Khan welcomes as 'a world to win, an empire to build.' Spock wonders what will become of the planting of such a seed.

CARD/EPISODE AND MATRIX TAKEDOWN
The Matrix was a work in progress, AI Archons working to take over humanity and expand their empire in a key part of the galaxy. With Draco repilians in charge of the Secret Space Program (SSP), Matrix enslavement raced ahead on the moon and Mars. The same pyramidal structure as on Earth pertained with a vengeance in the sub-program known as the Dark Fleet or *nacht waffen*. This outgoing force created by the Draco using the Nazis was bent on conquest of ever-new territories, bodies and minds. It operated like a **Super-Knight of Wands reversed** on steroids. The would-be commander of an equivalent force in the Star Trek universe is

Khan Noonian Singh. Veritably a Horseman of the Apocalypse, this manically marauding **Knight** seizes control of the flagship of the Federation with astonishing ease, annexing the crew to his existing posse of eugenically enhanced troops. His aim is to guide the Enterprise out into the galaxy as a predator bound for the stars on missions of conquest and colonization. The real life Dark Fleet followed this same course since its origins in the early 20th century. One of Hitler's first moves on attaining the Chancellorship of Germany was to co-opt a nascent space program set up by the Vril secret society. Flying saucer-type craft had already been developed from blueprints supplied in the 1920s to a young and precocious psychic named Maria Orsic. Her ET information source was the Aldebaran race, working in league with the rapacious Dracos as prime Matrix builders in this part of the galaxy.

The Dracos found in the Nazis the same evil attributes as in themselves: unlimited imperial ambition, ruthless discipline and fiendish technological ingenuity. So too Khan. All of them seek power for its own sake by combatting and overthrowing existing civilizations with the object of establishing new dictatorships as cells within an evergrowing One World Order on an unlimited cosmic scale. Ostensibly, the Nazis lost World War 2, but by relocating and regrouping they actually achieved a far-reaching victory. Led by Hans Kammler and setting up as the 4th Reich under the ice of Antarctica, they continued developing their inter-planetary flight capability as well as forming a league of genetically enhanced Aryan supermen. According to SSP history they had already achieved the first manned moon landing in 1942. As well as establishing a base there, they reached Mars in 1945 where they built another base to facilitate seeking out new territory for their reptilian masters. The Dark Fleet created by the Germans with ET help from Aldebaran and Alpha Draconis was just getting going.

The Nazis, in brief, learnt from their ET contacts how to build and fly antigravity spacecraft. Khan gains similar knowledge from the Enterprise's tech manuals after Kirk mistakenly allows him to peruse them while in sick bay. Khan learns how the vessel works but to seize control, technical knowledge alone does not suffice. He needs inside help and this he gets initially from Maria McGivers, his ally in securing capitulation of the rest of the crew. Likewise, for the Nazis to fully develop their space operations they needed to assimilate the power of the US Military Industrial Complex. This they achieved during the 1950s after the success of Operation Paperclip. This event, the relocation of 1,000 German scientists and technicians to the US in 1947, allowed the Nazis to take over the American aerospace industry. The Nazis succeeded where Khan and his horde fail. Kirk's crew refuse to transfer their loyalty even under threat of death. The Germans and Americans however did ally, covertly of course, becoming a collective **Knight of Wands reversed**. The nefarious SSP including the Dark Fleet was born, leading to a vast system of Matrix terror, colonization, slavery and profitable trading out in space.

As Khan tells McGivers before kissing her, he dares take what he wants. At a dinner given on his arrival he defends his tyrannous exploits of the 1990s: 'We offered the world order!' The penny drops for Kirk and Spock. Khan's dark New World Order, in line with that of the Nazis and the Deep State, would be an order not of truth, love and freedom but of increasing dominion with himself at the helm over conquered minions kept in slavery. Khan esteems everyone around him according to their usefulness in helping him take the ship. In ruthless **reversed Knight of Wands** fashion he has no compunction in stepping on anyone to get what he wants. He spurns doing what is morally right in favour of whatever he himself decides is right or wrong. As a product of selective breeding, genetically enhanced with a strength four times that of Kirk's, Khan naturally considers himself the fittest to rule and dominate. His physical superiority gives him this right, he believes, and qualifies him to decide who will live and who will die. Kirk and anyone else objecting to his seizure of power will be the first to die - in the ship's decompression chamber. Khan therefore follows the classic four tenets of Satanism in common with the Nazis and the Dracos - selfishness, moral relativism, social darwinism and eugenics. It is only Khan's betrayal by McGivers and Kirk's rearguard action that finally save the day for the jeopardized Enterprise and its crew.

AFTER THE TAKEDOWN

Recent intel from alien contactee Elena Danaan has indicated that ETs of the Galactic Federation of Worlds (GFW) have given the Dracos and Dark Fleet a hammering on their bases on Earth, the moon and Mars, forcing them to leave. Another contactee, Corey Goode, denies this. But Kimberly Goguen in her role as Earth Guardian reports that all portals, demons and negative intruders conneced to the AI Matrix have been removed. The onus is now with humanity to be our own rescuer by working on and raising our collective awareness as we leave behind the influence of AI control systems. Earth humans may have colonized other planets since the 1940s but that was under Matrix conditions of secrecy and enslavement. Post-Matrix, Earth will openly join the GFW. Uniting with benevolent ETs including a reformed SSP and their fleets, we will as a race be joining the galactic community and helping to uphold Universal Law and peace.

22. THIRD FORCE

Freed from AI influence and purified in consciousness, people will revert to natural ways

Episode 22 '**A Taste of Armageddon**' correlates with **Temperance**; both are themed around the principle of two opposing forces reconciled by mediation of a Third Force.

THE CARD
Temperance is a visual representation of Third Force in action. Third force is the neutralizing or harmonizing energy needed to create any phenomenon. It operates in association with a First Force (called Active or Yang) and a Second Force (called Passive of Yin). Gurdjieff and Ouspensky called this the Law of Three which states that three different and opposing forces - active, passive and neutralizing - need to combine with each other to produce a phenomenon. Examples of Third Force can include a cook placing a pie in an oven, a diplomat restoring peace between warring parties, new knowledge that helps one lose weight instead of merely fighting the craving for food, or rest that re-circulates bodily energies to their functional optimum.

Mediation of First and Second Forces by a harmonizing Third Force is known in Eastern tradition as the way of Tao, transcending the interplay of opposed Yin and Yang. Taoist Natural Order, or alignment with the natural flow of the universe, is the manifest result when Third Force is love-based. In terms of justice, applying **Temperance** - following the Tao - results in the maintenance of Natural Law. Third Force or Tao means letting go of extremes such as fixed plans, rules or concepts so that the world governs itself. Third Force is usually not perceptible. Hence it is represented by an angel, angels usually operating invisibly or discreetly behind the scenes. She stands and sways in a rhythm on fertile, undulating soil as she exchanges liquid between two differently coloured jugs. The colourless liquid suggests different energies having been brought into a oneness. The liquid's impossibly diagonal wavy flow bespeaks miraculous or magical influence consistent with angelic assistance. Her benign influence, that of Third Force, brings about the harmonizing of opposing energies. She facilitates cooperation, collaboration, compromise or transcendence. Third Force can be thought of as Nature herself working divinely and constantly to sustain Natural Order.

Temperance reversed suggests inflexibility, over-indulgence, non-cooperation, or poor circulation of energies or communications. In terms of the Law of Three, one force usurps another, or opposing forces are holding themselves in deadlock or conflict. And so it will be until a Third Force appears. Third Force when sick or malign results in harm and chaos, being called in Native American tradition the demonic force of 'Wetiko'.

'A TASTE OF ARMAGEDDON' PREMISE
Enterprise crew are drawn into an endless war between two planets fought by computer. They must destroy the computer or themselves be destroyed.

CONTEXT
Third Force, AI Takedown, War.

THIRD FORCE
Kirk, Spock and three others beam down to Eminiar to open the way for Ambassador Fox to start talks aimed at bringing Eminiar into the United Federation. Fox at first stays back on the Enterprise. During the visit, Eminiar is attacked by its neighbouring planet and long-time enemy, Vendikar. The two planets have been 500 years at war - by computer. 500,000 people are now computed as killed and must report to disintegration machines. The entire Enterprise crew are included in this tally. Kirk refuses to beam down his crew but the planet's leader Anan succeeds in luring the Ambassador down by deception. Before Fox can be executed, Kirk and Spock break captivity and mount a rebellion. Kirk threatens Anan with Order 24, imminent destruction by the Enterprise of the planet. But it is Kirk and Spock's de-

struction of the computers that puts paid to the computer war. This interventionist action in the way of Card 13 makes possible a restoration of natural order through a healthy Third Force, diplomacy. Anan would rather this than the two planets physically destroy each other. He consents to negotiations involving Ambassador Fox who is only too happy to act as a mediator between the two planets.

CARD/EPISODE AND MATRIX TAKEDOWN

The 500-year war between Eminiar and Vendikar exemplifies what David Icke calls 'Wetiko made manifest'. For these two planets read also Earth under Matrix domination, blighted by a history of war, suffering and parasitical control. The Native American concept of Wetiko (see Episode 41) denotes spiritual sickness, an unnatural state of separation consciousness subverting Third Force and keeping people living in fear, conflict, psychopathy and victimhood. Freed from Matrix control we will revert to our natural state and return to goodness through expanded consciousness and taking responsibility for ourselves consistent with universal sovereignty. But under the Matrix we were consciousness contracted, in the grip of non love-based forces. Malevolent factions of the Anunnaki, the Draco reptilians and hybrid bloodlines, all in tandem with AI, ruled the roost during the Matrix era. Operating out of Wetiko consciousness, they poisoned our world. Such a consciousness formed the glue in the pyramid holding humanity in a hierarchy of control and manipulation. Wetiko, like Satanism, inverts Natural Order, turning it into chaos. Third Force fails to operate properly, as shown in **Temperance reversed**. Out of harmony with ourselves, Nature and Tao, we became lost in duality and struggle, chaos and confusion.

This same condition is satirized in the grotesque **reversal** of **Temperance** on Eminiar and Vendikar with their tragic war sustained by computer. The warring computer system plays the part of a malign, controlling Third Force. A malign AI, it keeps the two planets perpetually at war with each other, a war that even without the computers would continue until a change of consciousness. The people themselves must detach from the negative consciousness or Wetiko, driving them as well as the computers. Mere destruction of the computers as by Kirk and Spock, or arbitration by Ambassador Fox, will not suffice. For the equivalent situation on Earth, we had the Cabal covertly and negatively directing humanity, having infiltrated all the world's governments and major institutions. By pitting opposition groups against each other as warring First and Second Force, the Cabal sought to maintain separation consciousness and itself in power. As a malign Third Force, it worked through supervisory organizations such as the UN, the EU, the WHO and NATO. Contriving wars enabled geopolitical restructuring and ever more centralization of power. Divide and Conquer was the motive behind countless Cabal-driven conflicts. These included the 1st and 2nd World Wars, Vietnam and latterly the War on Terror, the War on Drugs, Middle East conflicts and the War on The People utilizing the Covid false flag. 2022 saw war provoked in the Ukraine with the US, China and the Middle East remaining uneasy. War serves up a feast of death and destruction feeding AI, Draco and Cabal interests. As with the computer-maintained war on Eminiar and Vendikar, the people lose every time. But this is over on Earth. 'Gound Command' Kimberly Goguen has participated in, and reported on, the takedown by divine ET forces of the warmakers at the top of the Cabal pyramid. But merely removing or reforming the Cabal will not suffice. The total disconnection was necesssary of the Orion AI system that used frequencies and other weapons to keep humans in a herd-like state willingly complying with their own slavery.

On Eminiar we see Kirk and Spock taking down the warring computer system. But will this change the consciousness of the peoples of Eminiar and Vendikar who were willing to go like lambs to the slaughter into the disintegration machines? Kirk saves the landing party's guide, the beautiful Mea, from herself going into one of the suicide stations. Her response is not gratitude but protest at being prevented from performing her duty. Victims of mass mind control says Morpheus in 'The Matrix' movie, are 'so inured, so hopelessly dependent on the system that they will fight to protect it'. As Mea tells Kirk, 'Surely you can see that ours is the better way?' On Earth recently, people were unfortunately inveigled into queuing up for DNA-changing injections loaded with lethal toxins such as spike proteins and graphene oxide. Now that the Matrix AI system has gone, eliminated in one fell swoop as on Eminiar, humans will manifest a higher consciousness, as explored in other episodes such as Nos. 17, 24, 25 and 52.

AFTER THE TAKEDOWN
The takedown of the Orion AI system on Earth, like the takedown of the malign computer system on Eminiar and Vendikar, will see **Temperance** restored to **upright** natural functioning. Respect for sovereignty and Natural Law will return. An outside negative Third Force has no right to own or control us. Relieved of frequency control, people will soon come to realize this. Freedom will follow, the freedom to be ourselves in tune with the Third Force of our own nature playing out as per **Temperance**. The first signs of this will be the disappearance of war and people no longer complying with the dictates of a moribund elite.

23. HAPPINESS

A vibrant life comes
from enjoying happiness
without clinging to it

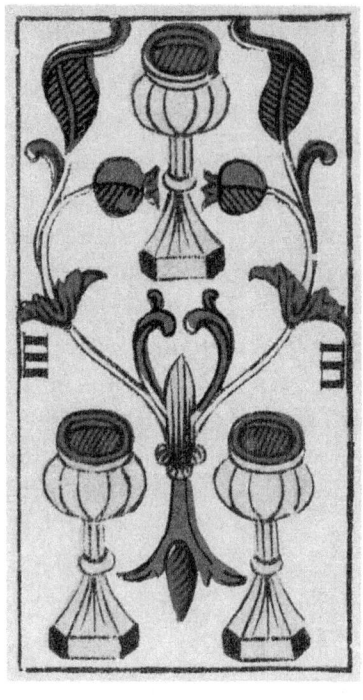

Episode 23 '**This Side of Paradise**' correlates with the **3 of Cups**; both are themed around the emotional experience of social stimulation, high spirits and happiness.

THE CARD
Three large Cups of emotion or feeling form a pattern in and around a rapturous arrangement of flower stems and leaves. The leaves move upwards healthily and vigorously, the centre stems forming a bounteous heart shape. None of the pert flowers are yet fully blossomed. At the level of Three, that of the fertile, expressive Empresss, this is a joyful outburst of emotions and relating. This is the card of high spirits, fun and games, the early stages of romance, socializing and partying. It's a natural state of joe-de vivre. Or it could represent a frothy, transient stage of happiness that should not be attached to, simply enjoyed while it lasts.

The flipside of this card, the **3 of Cups reversed**, stands for over-indulgence in hedonism and euphoria, a clinging to the good times and party life. There may be resistance to more productive or contemplative states such as dutiful work or quiet time alone. Or the pendulum effect may be in operation whereby one is pulled back and forth by excitable reactions. Elation gives way to all too easily to despondency, good humour to annoyance, shows of delight to outbursts of tears.

'THIS SIDE OF PARADISE' PREMISE
On a dangerously irradiated planet, spores emitted by the plant life render colonists then visiting crew happy and healthy but overly placid.

CONTEXT
Perverted Paradise, Self-Management, Self-Realization.

HAPPINESS
A landing party beams down to an agricultural planet concerned for the welfare of 150 colonists. After three years settlement, lethal Berthold rays striking the planet should have wiped the people out but they pass every test for physical health. They claim complete peace of mind and harmony, an enduring state of happiness and peace likened by Kirk to paradise. Sandoval, their leader, calls their rural life a simple, peaceful one without weapons or vehicles (but also without animals). The party soon discover what is keeping them both protected and very happy: spores emitted by the plant life. Except for Kirk, the party themselves become infected and euphoric. Even Spock suddenly becomes warmly emotional, falling in love with Leila, an old acquaintance. The entire crew of the Enterprise becomes infected and beams down leaving Kirk on the bridge alone. He too succumbs but discovers the antidote: violent emotions such as anger, which he triggers via a sonic beam down to the planet. With the happiness effect neutralized the colonists agree to be relocated to Starbase 27.

CARD/EPISODE AND MATRIX TAKEDOWN
True happiness as is often said, comes from within. Inner happiness is our entitlement, coming from natural connection to our soul and Higher Self. Depending on finding and maintaining happiness through externals such as relationship or money is problematic. Externally derived happiness is mostly a collection of reactions programmed into our DNA. These reactions are the workings of the Emotional Matrix, a side of our Lower Self much influenced in the past by the Orion AI Matrix. Success in competition, romance, social life or business interacts with the excitable Body Mind to produce temporary but flimsy eotional highs. As the agriculturalists become addicted to the effect of the spores, so we as humans easily become addicted to externally induced emotional highs - **3 of Cups** states of triumph and euphoria. The temporary high of such emotions involves glandular secretions and the DNA, a kind of chemical fix. Such emotional reactions however, usually involve the mind and take place only at the lower levels of our being.

Some spiritual gurus make a distinction between these kinds of emotions and feelings emanating from the heart - unprogrammable qualities of Oneness such as spiritual love, awe, bliss, compassion or empathy. These feelings come down to us from the soul level and are felt through the heart chakra. For most people most of the time, such states of higher consciousness rarely occur. Needless to say they are a no-go zone for the effects of popular entertainment, TV, internet, competitive sports, chemical drugs or alcohol. Such artificially induced states belong within the Emotional Matrix dealt with in Episodes 2 and 5. This coarse variety of states of emotional ups and downs makse up the usual round of daily life, crowding out the ineffable feeling of Oneness.

The artificially created happiness of the colonists at first seems desirable and admirable. There is no craving for devices or technology. And no subservience to the deceptions and strictures of a planetary elite and its control system. People are free to be themselves. Simple pleasures suffice. We see this most poignantly in the case of Spock, a dispassionate, dutiful 1st Officer. Intoxicated by the spores, he takes to carefree playing and laughing including hanging upside down from trees. He refuses direct orders from Kirk, his Commanding Officer, and instead embraces joyful, loving experience with non-judgment and spontaneity. The beautiful young settler-botanist Leila becomes his beloved. The two knew each other six years before when Spock was unable to return her affection. Now however, he finds romantic states no longer alien. He joins with her in kissing and hugging. Together they walk hand in hand through fields stopping for cloud-gazing with his head in her lap. This is all to the good. Living the simple life close to nature enables one to live in balance and purity, easily connecting to the soul in its higher reality. The initial landing party becomes relaxed and carefree. McCoy takes to smiling broadly and bantering in a lighthearted Southern drawl. His beam-up of plant samples soon has the entire crew beaming down to the idyllic planet where they bliss out on the spores. And with good reason. A fully rounded life should include recreation and enjoyment including time spent in nature, holidays and travels, and parties and gatherings with friends.

These states of happiness and excitement, the **3 of Cups**, belong in life as pleasurable recreation belongs in balance with work, Matrix or no Matrix. The problem arises when we become constantly or overly distracted and stimulated. We then fall prey to attachment or addiction to enticements of the Body Mind. We start to crave the highs we get from digital social media or video games and from drugs, alcohol, sex, partying, sports, gambling or whatever. These external pleasures and cravings eventually weigh down our vibratory rate. Such was the downfall of the immature Page of Cups, Charlie X, in Episode 2 and of Wild Kirk in Episode 5. The trick is to not allow emotional addiction or Matrix programming to diminish contact with our soul and Higher Self. We need to maintain inner happiness without losing it in externally dependent happiness. The latter can easily end up compromising the form or direction of our life and our perceived mission.

What the colonists and crew experience through the peace and happiness induced by the spores seems to be a shared taste of Oneness Consciousness. The state is pleasurable but higher and more subtle than emotional reactions such as falling in love or winning at sports. Nevertheless a taste is merely a taste, an illusory, programmed, passing state. In the crew and colonists' case the state takes on the quality of a drug. Kirk's eventual surrender to, and then rejection of, the spores reminds us of the difference between this state and unconditional happiness. The latter does not exclude a sense of duty and group responsibility, symbolized by the next card, the 4 of Cups. Through use of the sonic beam, Kirk triggers emotions of the **reversed 3 of Cups**: anger and violent resistance. This breaks the spell. Spock, now cured, remembers his sense of mission. He snaps back into allegiance to the Enterprise and her crew. Leila for her part breaks down in tears of sorrow at his departure. The effect of the spores is revealed as benevolent but temporary and artificial, revealing the illusion of separation and duality characterizing holographic 3D existence. But Spock, far from renouncing the experience, ends up telling Leila in all sincerity: 'For the first time in my life I was happy.'

AFTER THE TAKEDOWN
Externally created happiness or euphoria comes and goes, bringing problems if we try clinging to them. Happy phases are to be cherished but clinging to them, obsessively seeking them, indulging them or becoming addicted to the high of them, becomes counter-productive. The pendulum effect will cause us to swing back and forth between states of excitement or lethargy, mania or depression. Elation during the good times will swing to agitation or worry when troubles in job or relationship arise. Both extremes involve losing ourselves in the Emotional Matrix. The key is to enjoy external pleasures while they last without becoming attached to them. The good times can then be enjoyed in the spirit of spontaneity rather than hoarded. True happiness comes unconditionally from the heart, from our Soul. In this state we transcend circumstantial pleasures so as to live a life less polarized and more lively, free and joyful.

24. ELIMINATION

The end of the Omega Matrix will trigger the process leading to the end of the Political Matrix

Episode 24 '**The Devil in the Dark**' correlates with the unnamed **Card 13**; both are themed around destruction or elimination, either futile or allowing for positive transformation.

THE CARD
The unnamed 13th Major or **Card 13** portrays a very austere-looking skeletal figure determinedly mowing down humans ordinary and regal alike with a scythe. All this is reminiscent of the archetypal Grim Reaper claiming his victims in the mode of a ritual offering or sacrifice. The ground is charred black, the blade is deep red. These colours are strongly associated with the worship of Saturn, planet of death, restriction, austerity and low vibration Satanism. Despite the deathly associations this is a figure in dynamic movement facing the right - Tarot symbolism for the future and new beginnings. The chopped up body parts can also signify the future as they now appear planted and ready to regrow. The overall message then is one of termination as a stage enabling transcendence. Physical death may be present, or elimination, or forced and permanent ending, or suddenness rather than gradualness, or violence or drama especially involving fear, shock or terror. But also present is the promise of

transformation, a clearing of the decks providing for new beginnings and reappearance of life in a fresh, revitalized form.

Reversed, there is an untimely ending or elimination that is unnatural or imposed harshly. Or it is felt as particularly upsetting, distressing, painful, violent or unnecessary. A delayed or imminent transformation is in the works or it may be one that is detrimental, draconian or irredeemably destructive.

'THE DEVIL IN THE DARK' PREMISE
A mining operation is threatened by an underground creature whose race is endangered by the mining. Search and destroy or find another solution?

CONTEXT
Slaughter, Taking Stock, Awakening.

ELIMINATION
Mining operations deep under the surface of Janus VI are in crisis. 50 men have been intermittently killed. Mining of extremely valuable pergium has been brought to a standstill. Something or someone is destroying machinery and humans with a lethal corrosive. The Chief Engineer wants Kirk and his men to hunt down a suspected 'monster' and eliminate it. More men die, burnt to a crisp, even as Kirk and Spock investigate. Spock theorizes that the creature is a silicon-based life form, like the spheres found in the planet's numerous tunnels. He compassionately mind-melds with the creature and finds out that the tunnels are its work and the spheres its eggs which the miners have been thoughtlessly destroying. As the last of its generation, the 'Horta' has been acting as a mother protecting its eggs for a new generation of Horta. Kirk and Spock broker a deal whereby the miners leave the eggs alone and allow the creature to continue tunnelling. In return the Horta's efforts will open up new access to the planet's treasure house of minerals. The transformed modus operandi soon throws up abundant new and profitable deposits for the mining company.

CARD/EPISODE AND MATRIX TAKEDOWN
The Cabal presiding over the global Matrix was called by David Icke a death cult. Apart from themselves, he said, they worshipped Saturn, representing control, judgement, limitation and death. The associated colours are black and red, the predominant colours used in Satanic rituals and in **Card 13** - known to many as the Death card. The frequencies of Saturn and Satanism are those that lock down perception so as to focus attention on states compatible with those of the demonic entities known to the Gnostics as

the Demiurge and Archons. Death or slaughter or elimination that we see in **Card 13** accords with those states. Satanists revere keeping the people in low vibrational states of fear, misery and sacrifice, enabling them to rule unchallenged. Another name for Saturn is the Black Sun, also the name of a major faction of the Deep State pulling the levers of global power. People refer to Saturn as a planet but to astronomers it is a gas giant. Some researchers point to it being a dwarf star modified or straitjacketed by its rings artificially imposed. Like the rings on a DVD they broadcast a specific frequency that held in place the Orion Matrix for the past 300,000 years. Mercury, Mars and Earth all formed part of this Matrix, according to Kim Goguen, holding our planet and humans in the grip of a false electromagnetic grid. Chemtrails boosted this grid conditioning our waveform reality. Hence the vibrations on Earth of Wetiko, fear, conflict, control and victimhood, enabling the political, pyramidal Matrix to thrive.

The dark psyche in which human perception was trapped manifested itself down through the ages in wars, conquests, tyrannies and collective acts of destruction, basically **Card 13** at its most brutal and **reversed**. Atrocities and carnage, violence and mass murder, are huge blood sacrifice rituals for the psychopaths of the Global Elite - Archons in human form. Revolutions such as the French, the American and the Russian were Matrix-enabled bloodbaths to advance the Cabal's agenda. With each regime change, the Hidden Hand, as Icke calls it, moved another step closer to imposing a One World Order of total control and domination as seen in such Episodes as 32 and 48. Until the replacement of the corrupt Marduk by Kim Goguen in 2012, nothing stood in the way of this demented agenda. Humanity was kept in ignorance of truth and deluded by fear-based propaganda imposed through the Deep State's control of mainstream sources of news and information. No surprise then that vast numbers of people fell for the Covid hoax and repeatedly took nanobot injections that have been killing or injuring millions since the start of 2021. Death through ignorance likewise characterizes the Janus VI mining operation. Through ignorance the miners go on destroying the Horta's eggs in the course of their tunnelling work, provoking the Horta into retaliating with its lethal acid spray.

To break such a cycle of fear and chaos, death and destruction, a revolution in consciousness is needed. We see this triggered on Janus VI by Kirk and Spock's investigation and we see it just starting here on Earth. The Orion Matrix has gone but the remnants of the Deep State remain in control of the mainstream media (MSM). True knowledge that counters the false perceptual programming of the general public has still to fully make an impact.

People may continue during the 2020s to acquiesce with measures aimed at setting up a technocratic New World Order whose agenda was laid out decades ago as confirmed by the Rockefeller Lockstep document of 2010. Inevitable overhaul of the MSM will eventually end the mass hypnosis. Truth will then return to mainstream journalism, science, government and education. The tragedy of millions of people dying quickly or slowly from a fake vaccine for a fake pandemic will continue until the impact of these deaths themselves overrides the lies and cover-ups of the propaganda machine. Tragedy will thus provoke a change of heart and mind on a global level. **Card 13** with its tufts of grass and planted body parts indicates new growth and transformation taking place after destruction of the old, with the associated shock and trauma catalyzing such change.

The energy of **Card 13** hammers the miners. They suffer the deaths of over 50 of their number. But it is due to their own destructive actions that they karmically reap catastrophe. Their instinctive reaction is again **Card 13**: 'Find that monster and kill it!' in the words of the Chief Engineer. Kirk and Spock, at least initially, share the same thoughtless, reactive mindset coming from the reptilian brain. Kirk too wants the creature killed to enable restart of the mining operation and continued supplies of pergium for the planets that need it. The 'monster' has no vote, its eggs count only as useless rocks, as lifeless silicon nodules. It is not until Spock raises a question about the supposed lifelessness of the silicon rocks that attitudes start to change. The pair come to realize that the destructive element of the mining operation has itself to be ended. So it is with dual use technologies on Earth such as mRNA vaccines, nuclear power, 5G and LEDs. In the new energy, their antipathy to organic life will be realized and their destructive use terminated.

AFTER THE TAKEDOWN

Consciousness transcends the body and its finite life span. This does not mean a body is to be treated as expendable by those contemplating suicide or murder. Experience in a body provides lessons that enable a soul's consciousness to evolve to higher frequency. The soul knows when to orchestrate a natural and timely death transition. Premature death is detrimental to soul development whether we are talking of the risk of the Horta species being wiped out or of the old Matrix agenda of depopulation and transhumanism. Technologies capable of harming or destroying biological life will themselves be eliminated if unable to be rendered safe. This will accompany a cleaning out in the way of **Card 13** of the death cult formerly operating as the global management team during the era of the Orion Matrix.

25. CONSCIOUS BEING

The sense of identification or attachment negates the peacefulness of Conscious Being; peacefulness simply is

Episode 25 **'Errand of Mercy'** correlates with **The World**; both are themed around Conscious Being manifested in qualities of peacefulness, equanimity and harmony even in testing times.

THE CARD

Alone among the 22 Major Arcana, No. 21 **The World** is two cards in one. The two cards are alluded to in the saying 'In the world but not of the world.' At the surface level, the card symbolizes a harmonious state of completion, realization, accomplishment, fulfilment or celebration. This relates to the visible World with all its illusory functioning in the flux of duality as perceived by our five senses and the Body Mind. Interpreted at this level, **The World** signifies the realization of hopes and dreams or happy reward for one's labours. Superficially, some project or journey may have reached completion. Success has been achieved, satisfaction is felt. In terms of self-development, life's lessons (any or all of the previous 21 Arcana) have been encountered and resolved.

At an infinitely deeper level, the card expresses what can barely be conceived, let alone expressed. This mystical meaning relates to the ultimate nature of reality as Oneness and Infinite Possibility. The wreath's different colours are woven into a circular Oneness transcending duality. Oneness transcends duality. If Oneness were to be the opposite of duality it would not be Oneness, it would be yet another pole in changeable duality. This Unity Consciousness, say the mystics, is the one unchanging state of Being. **The World** card points to this spiritual truth that ironically transcends everything to do with 'the world' and the duality of 3D.

In this spiritual sense we see in the naked dancer's carefree ecstasy no sense of attachment to the things of **The World**, Mind is integrated with the heart. In such a state we ourselves transcend duality, the self-identities based in Body Mind and the deceptions and illusions of the Matrix. The dancer, although she is still in physical appearance, has realized the true state of Infinite Awareness, that of Supreme Consciousness. She is no longer of **The World** despite being still in it. Centred in the heart and freely, gracefully dancing she exists as timeless, spaceless Conscious Being. This is known and realized over and above any particular rationale. This is the soul in its pure state of being, a state of openness to infinite possibility, spontaneity and the flow of energy. This would include a transcendent peacefulness, flexibility, spontaneity and natural empathy with other life forms.

Reversed, celebrations are premature, with completion or satisfaction not yet fully realized. There could be an overly placid way of being, an abject surrender. This could be based on apathy, sloth or ignorance. The enclosing wreath can signify boundaries or dissatisfaction that impose a sense of entrapment or imprisonment. The spirit is no longer dancing but feels itself trapped in a **World** that remains as the confining, illusory Matrix.

'ERRAND OF MERCY' PREMISE
Planet Organia is invaded by despotic and ruthless Klingons. Kirk and Spock anxiously try to help the locals who remain strangely unconcerned.

CONTEXT
Self-Realization, War, Third Force, Multi-Dimensionality.

CONSCIOUS BEING
Spoiling for war, Klingon ships attack the Enterprise and descend on Planet Organia to use it as a new base. Kirk and Spock are already in the Organian Council Room trying to persuade the pacifist Elders to let Starfleet protect and help them. The Organians deny the existence of danger and the need for help. Kor, the Klingon leader, strides in and declares the start of Occupation. The Klingon Empire will rule despotically and ruthlessly. The Organians promise their obedience but Kirk shows a degree of defiance,

ironically pleasing Kor who is disgusted by what he sees as the smiling, sheeplike Organians. Kirk and Spock start a two-man Resistance using guerrilla tactics to disrupt the Occupation. The human pair are on the brink of a shootout with the Klingons when the Organian leaders intervene and demonstrate their level of Conscious Being. Using special powers they decommission all weapons. To the outrage of both Kirk and Kor, the main Organian councillor announces an end to the fighting. The Organians see off the warring adversaries by revealing their true form - points of light millions of years more evolved than corporeal humans and Klingons.

CARD/EPISODE AND MATRIX TAKEDOWN

The paradox of fighting for peace is an absurdity well lampooned by Gandhi. An eye for an eye and the whole world will become blind, he said. Fighting begets more fighting - and more trauma and more mutual hatred into the bargain. The point is forcefully made in Episode 69, Let That Be Your Last Battlefield. Peace is the way to achieve peace, you don't fight for peace, you peace for peace. Easier said than done, many will say, and an attitude requiring lifetimes to develop given the collective sense of attachment within and to a falsely confining Matrix world. In the meantime, the question of how to avoid war when attacked will still be asked. In their own ways both **The World** card and **Errand of Mercy** address this predicament and provide hope for peaceful existence in the wake of Matrix programming.

In their equanimity - in line with **The World** card - and their lack of attachment to whether they are left alone or invaded and occupied by the Klingon Empire, the Organians show the way of peace. And the way is not attachment to taking action, nor clinging to any sense of purpose or the making of choice. When Kor marches into the Council Chamber the Elders do not resist and put up a struggle. Like the proverbial willow tree bending in the wind, they cordially give way. 'Yield and maintain integrity./ To bend is to be upright' says the Tao Te Ching, like **The World** card, another model for the Organian way. Kor summarily imposes Klingon rule by Nazi-style jackboot but instead of being provoked, Ayleborne the Organian leader simply says 'We shall obey'. The Organians again take the line of least resistance when Kirk bursts into the Chamber and exhorts them to change their way of life to one of systematic progress with Federation help. Facing Kirk, the Elders again remain unmoved. Coming from the knowing of Oneness, from Conscious Being, they simply say they do not need help.

This is not to say that the Elders stand by and do nothing when violence is planned or committed. They abhor violence and weapons of war and confiscate Kirk and Spock's phasers, although they later give them back at Kirk's insistence. When outright fighting breaks out they deactivate all weapons by making them literally too hot to handle. To ignore conditions or unfolding events that are destructive to life would be uncaring and selfish. When they take action it is because to do nothing would be a response that would cause people around them to suffer. Never mind that the Organians have mighty powers of telekinesis that can at an instant raise the temperature of technology to 350°C. They teach us that coming from Conscious Being one does whatever one can do to prevent a wrong being committed. Not to do so would show an attitude of apathy or smug indifference to suffering, which is not in **The World** card (unless **Reversed**) nor in the nature of the Organians. As the statesman Edmund Burke said: 'All that is necessary for evil to triumph is for good men and women to do nothing.' But when the Organians act they simply act, without attachment. Their action becomes Taoist, or a manifestation of Third Force overcoming the polarities of reaction or passivity.

Compared to the Organians, the Klingons and humans come from a different place. Their ethos is far from the equanimity of **The World** card and Organian non-attachment. As we observe Kirk and Kor each at work on the Organians a big surprise is how alike they proceed. Both fight over their vision for Organia. Kor wants to annexe it in the Klingon war against the Federation while Kirk aims to stop hm. Both are heavily identified with the outcome. Kor sets about installing the apparatus of Occupation, drawing up a list of rules to be imposed on the population He requisitions Organian offices for his administration, posts his guards and CCTV cameras on buildings and sets up large stores of munitions. When the Nazis occupied the Ukraine during World War 2 they ordered 100 peasants to be executed for every German soldier killed by the locals. Kor issues a similar, even more extreme order. Kirk for his part works on the Organians by offering them protection and military aid. When they decline this he dangles the carrot of all-round institutional help for progressing the Organians' 'arrested' culture. When the Elders still decline, Kirk and Spock take to guerrilla warfare. The French Resistance during WW2 significantly aided the allies by planning, co-ordinating and carrying out acts of sabotage on Nazi-held infrastructure. Kirk and Spock follow suit by covertly blowing up a Klingon munitions dump. They later go on to storm the Klingon HQ and take Kor captive.

Both Kor and Kirk make no secret of fighting on behalf of their Klingon and Federation overlords respectively. The two galactic forces have long been at war but war is anathema to the peace-loving spirit of **The World** card and specifically to the Organians. **The World** comes last in the parade of the Major Arcana symbolizing 22 profound aspects of 3D life. This final placing and the four animals in each corner of the card, each representing a domain of life mastery, show that identification with polarity has been overcome. And so the Organians take no sides. They play no part in assisting either Kirk or Kor in their battles except to offer and provide protection from harm. When Kirk first announced Organia's impending invasion by the Klingon Empire, the Elders' only response was to recommend he leave or be disguised as an Organian for his own safety.

Kirk and Kor both show disgust at what they see as Organian weakness. Kirk reprimands the Elders for their 'idiotic placidity' in refusing to protect their planet. 'I have no great love for you, your planet or your culture,' he disparagingly tells them. He sees the Organians as the epitome of apathy, sloth, weakness and placidity, attributes of **The World reversed**. Kor sees them as a race of sheep wearing stupid, idiotic smiles. In their condescension, both men reveal their attachment to might and glory, to soldiering and triumph, to status and race. Fully identified with the roles given them within a Matrix universe they remain trapped within the illusion of separation and division. Kor is focussed on the glory of conquest, Kirk on striving to prevent this. The recognition that both sides in the conflict belong to the same Infinite Oneness celebrated in **The World** never for a moment registers. If it did, how could they persist in harming or warring against each other?

Human programming may continue for some years after the end of the Orion Matrix. System-servers may still fight to defend their right to live in ignorance (ignorant of the fact that they are ignorant). Both Kirk and Kor show no gratitude for being prevented by the Organians from destroying each other with their hand weapons. Ironically and comically they turn on their life-saving benefactors with identical indignation. 'You have no right to dictate to our Federation ... !' yells Kirk to the Elders. 'Or to our Empire!', Kor immediately adds. The Klingons avowedly live for war and predatory conquest for the sake of glory. Kirk no less absurdly, insists on the right to make war to supposedly prevent war. When you believe in such rights to this extent, the Matrix still has you. The predatory consciousness known as the Archons exposed in Episode 61, The Day of The Dove can still thrive. It's not the rights issue that chains one to former programming but the inner attachment to belief in one's rights. Both men are shown up by the Organians for the ego-driven reactionaries they are. The Organians, living humbly and simply, without purpose and without an agenda, without the fear of survival but with consideration for others, live truly in the state of

Infinite Love represented by **The World upright**, the one true reality.

AFTER THE TAKEDOWN

Peacefulness and harmony are natural conditions of Oneness. Being at peace however, doesn't necessarily mean we are being the Oneness Of All That Is. How long does our peace last? Does the sound of a defective car alarm or the thought of a penalty for unpaid tax throw us into anger or anxiety? Whether Matrix-controlled or not, **The World** never stops changing for a moment. It's all part of the illusion sustained by the Body Mind. And projecting our irritations or disturbed thoughts or emotions into that holographic swell merely reinforces the state of self-hypnosis. We come into this 'world' to learn lessons through exploring experience in 3D. **The World** card shows a state of having overcome or made peace with the tensions and annoyances that come along the way. Earth is a prison planet to escape from (**The World reversed**) says Brad Olsen in his brilliant study of the Matrix, Beyond Esoteric. But Illeana Kapulnik, long-time SSP experiencer and self-confessed 'star traveller' took a different view discussing this with him in a YouTube interview. We're here to 'enjoy the ride', she said, 'to find our greatest joy and beauty and live our life'. This despite what she called 'the black magic programming' and the vulnerability to identification with 'the muck of 3D', meaning the human dramas, the struggle for success or survival, and rules or values conflicting with personal sovereignty.

Leading up to the Matrix takedown, Kim Goguen reported in late 2022 that the Council of Five, an overseeing body close to Source, had finally acted as the Organians did, to end covert war and attacks on humanity. A major clean-up of the Deep State was initiated to restore our planet to wellness. But Matrix or no Matrix, how do we cease to allow any constraints or limitations to entrap us? The graceful figure in **The World** card suggests at least on one level dancing within the wreath of circumstances. She remains within the 3D **World** of the Body Mind but not of it. There is no struggle to disidentify with 3D. Struggling merely confines us in duality, discontentedly swinging between polar opposites. Struggle can mean striving like New Age seekers for equanimity and enlightenment or fighting like warriors against the machine. *Tarot Trek* lists 78 escape routes. Each has a time and place but efforting in general will hamper us as much as it hampers Kirk and Kor fighting for peace or glory. The way is shown by the Organians who live in tune with their Higher Self and Third Force with moment by moment inner knowing of how and when to respond. With this level of attunement, there is no seeking after Conscious Being or spiritual enlightenment - it will find us.

26. OTHER-DIMENSIONAL EXPERIENCE

Having our own experience of other dimensions will further dissolve Matrix programming

Episode 26 '**The Alternative Factor**' correlates with the **10 of Wands**; both are themed around transcendence of cycles of activity such as through completion, interruption or dimensional shift.

THE CARD
A process of action and creativity has completed itself with the **10 of Wands**. The creative process has culminated in the transformation to something new. No more progress is possible, we are at the end of the cycle. For the first time in this series, the dynamic yellow diagonal wands are skewered down the middle by a white wand - or rather by a heavy bundle of three white wands in place of the usual decorative flowers. A hiatus has arrived pending the next cycle of activity. This could be the gap between one day and the next, when the body not only recharges itself but allows the soul a respite from this heavy state of consciousness in 3D. In the dream state and in other non-ordinary states, our soul returns to wander in zones and dimensions beyond space and time to rebalance its energies.

With the **10 of Wands reversed**, a cycle is over but it's not over. There is a blockage, a refusal or an inability to make an ending that will allow for a new cycle of creativity. A project or journey may have been abandoned, not properly finished. Retirement may have been taken but a restlessness remains. An imposed stoppage, lockdown or curfew may be inhibiting or paralyzing normal activity. Or a cycle or timeline may momentarily pause, or briefly 'wink out' as in this episode, before resuming.

'THE ALTERNATIVE FACTOR' PREMISE
Kirk and Spock meet an insane man pursuing his double. They each come from a parallel universe and must be kept apart or catastrophe results.

CONTEXT
Multi-Dimensionality, Insanity.

OTHER-DIMENSIONAL EXPERIENCE
While surveying an uninhabited, arid planet below, the Enterprise is abruptly struck by a mysterious shock wave. The entire galaxy feels it - a momentary blinking out of existence. An investigating party beams down having discovered the presence of a human being. They find him near his small space craft, a strong but disturbed and dishevelled man. 'We can still stop him!' he cries. Further investigation cannot trace this man's nemesis, whom he calls 'a murdering monster.' But the shock wave happens several more times both on the planet and the Enterprise. Each moment of turbulence coincides with the man having a fit and wrestling in another dimension with his double with whom he keeps changing places. The men, both called Lazarus, contrive to steal dilithium crystals from the Enterprise engines to power each their own identical space craft. In sick bay, the first Lazarus, injured, claims his enemy destroyed the surface life on the planet. Kirk and Spock figure out that the two Lazaruses each belong to separate parallel universes, one matter, the other anti-matter. If they should ever meet in either universe universal annihilation will result. Back on the planet, Kirk pursuing one Lazarus accidentally slips through a portal at the location of the downed space craft. In a parallel dimension he encounters the other Lazarus who turns out to be the sane one. He and Kirk plot to trap the mad one in the corridor between the two universes. There the two men will stay struggling at each others' throats but safely trapped. Kirk forces the mad one through the portal into the corridor. With the two Lazaruses now trapped there until the end of time, the universe is safe.

CARD/EPISODE AND MATRIX TAKEDOWN
We live not simply in a 3D physical world but in a multi-dimensional uni-

verse. Other-dimensional experience is our birthright as it is with inter-dimensional travellers like the two Lazaruses. We experience separation from the physical body every night when we go to sleep and start dreaming. Other types of **10 of Wands** activity are intentional projections of consciousness for out-of-body exploration aka astral travelling, Near Death Experience, portal travel, alien abduction and Remote Viewing. The zones and dimensions we travel in may be numerous but they commonly belong to this universe. Unlike with Lazarus who has discovered his doppelgänger inhabiting an alternate universe. Having found each other without having actually met in either realm, one of the Lazaruses goes mad and sets out to hunt down and kill his mirror self - even at the cost of destroying whichever whole universe. Universal annihilation allegedly occurs when a particle or person from a matter universe comes into contact with its identical counterpart from an anti-matter universe. Contact between the Lazaruses, so far, has been restricted to a corridor connecting the two universes where such contact is safe.

Untold universes no doubt exist, even containing other versions of our planet Earth. Five 'Harmonic Universes' are posited in the Voyagers books of Ashayana Deane, each containing three dimensions. Among parallel or adjacent realities it's feasible that an Earth may exist in a universe opposed in terms of matter/anti-matter with our own. Kirk and Spock become aware of this scenario but only after venturing to understand the shock wave effect and the winking out of reality **10 of Wands** style caused by the Lazaruses. In their investigation, Spock initially finds inexplicable a point of radiation detected on the planet below from out in space. He can only call it a 'rip in our universe', a warp in space-time lying outside established physical laws. The crew's unfamiliarity with such cosmic phenomena seems strange but such unfamiliarity has been the norm within Matrix programming. The programmers of public perception still restrict cosmic education to a trickle disseminated in academia or in official journals, textbooks, websites or NASA releases, NASA operating as a filter on the truth. Official knowledge therefore remains subject to drip-by-drip disclosure by controlled scientific and cosmological sources. Silence, denial or mere speculation remains largely the mainstream attitude on all things ET, UFO or SSP.

Kirk and Spock remain puzzled until Lazarus himself informs them that his spacecraft is a time chamber or portal enabling him as a time traveller to jump between dimensions or universes. Each of the jumps made by one or other of the Lazaruses causes disruption and turbulence in the environment up to and including the universal winking out effect. We witness storms on the planet, a whirling around of reality, a vision of celestial phenomena, and a blueish photographic negative vision of the Lazaruses wrestling with each other. Bizarre biophysical phenomena according to Ashayana Deane, would naturally accompany an object from a parallel system briefly interfacing with the electromagnetic frequency bands of our own system. As for the possibility of a duplicate Lazarus existing, this would be supported by the fact that our universe includes different time zones as well as multiple dimensions of those time zones. And the corridor utilized by each Lazarus and finally by Kirk to trap them in, has a real existence. Deane speaks of a system of interlocking passageways between dimensions, bookended by 'locks' as on a canal. Spock calls them 'doors'. These gates or stargates maintain order within the Time Portal System used for transcendent **10 of Wands** type travel such as between different time zones within a dimension.

The Dimensional Lock System, says Deane, links whole universes with each other. It is such a system through which each of the Lazaruses leap back and forth between universes. 'For what purpose?' asks Kirk. 'Madness has no purpose', answers Spock. Kirk himself gets to cross over into the mirror universe, a foretaste of a similar excursion that will befall crew in Episode 32 Mirror, Mirror. Pursuing Lazarus, he goes intra-physically, ie taking his body with him, and experiences the parallel rocky planet shimmering in an eerie twilight state. Here he has a calm, searching conversation with the sane Lazarus. Their encounter not only resolves the problem of how to deal with the insane Lazarus but leaves Kirk's consciousness changed, more deeply reflective. Kirk's subsequent dazed contemplation of the fate of the two Lazaruses as the Enterprise leaves orbit is indicative of a transformative life experience. Any strong **10 of Wands** experience such as his must leave us changed, abruptly more awakened. As we break free of the conventional paradigm of our Matrix reality, through experience or learning, we will undergo a similar transition, mentally never to be the same again.

AFTER THE TAKEDOWN
Once Matrix restrictions lift entirely we will learn of other-dimensional existence beyond anything so far appearing in wikipedia entries, NASA bulletins or academic textbooks. And by having our own experience of breaching 5-sense only consciousness we will gain more than any 2nd hand description could impart. We will become our own liberators from the previous tunnel vision of the Matrix worldview. In the process we will escape the Body Mind trap to gain a better feeling of the oneness of all life and the interconnectedness of all beings. This will help us understand and better synthesize the levels of our own multi-dimensional identity.

27. KINDNESS

Kindness both to ourselves and to others will henceforth change the world only for the better

Episode 27 '**The City on The Edge of Forever**' correlates with the **7 of Cups**; both are themed around acting in a heart-centred way through generous deeds, loving kindness or humanitarian work.

THE CARD
Perhaps surprisingly, the **7 of Cups** is an action card. Although concerned with feelings and relations with others, the card is about acting with a sense of direction and purpose. This accords with the corresponding 7th Major being The Chariot, full of outgoing determination. A powerful, upwardly moving plant extends itself sinuously from the central base cup to the three top cups. The energy moves from the material level to the heavenly and along the way cradles and nurtures a solitary cup in the centre. Love is the focus of action, projected out into the world without in any way neglecting those in the bosom of one's life. This then is the extending of kindness and caring both globally and locally, universally and indiscriminatingly; of giving from the heart generously and without consideration of merit or reward. Motives are altruistic, work is humanitarian and intelligent. This brings about emotional or physical relief where there is suffering or privation. Good deeds rendered out of Service

To Others thus enhance levels of well-being and togetherness.

Reversed, actions performed ostensibly lovingly may be tainted by unloving, ulterior motives. Kindness may be forced, superficial or undermined by side effects to do with corruption or harm.

'THE CITY ON THE EDGE OF FOREVER' PREMISE
Kirk's love for a humanitarian peace movement activist during a time travel trip back to the 1930s threatens to allow Germany to win WW2.

CONTEXT
Multi-Dimensionality, Femininity, Self-Realization, Relationship.

KINDNESS
Chaos breaks out on the bridge while the crew are investigating time disturbances in space. McCoy runs amok after accidentally injecting himself with a potent drug. He transports down to the planet below with a shore party in hot pursuit. They discover a time portal, source of the disturbances. Through its arch shape other times and events in Earth history can be viewed. The crazed McCoy leaps into it and back to 1930s America. The shore party immediately lose contact with the Enterprise. McCoy's return in the past has somehow invoked a radically different timeline devoid of the Enterprise missions. Kirk and Spock seek to correct this and also jump through the portal aiming themselves at McCoy's destination just prior to his date of arrival. They arrive close to the 21st Street Mission in Depression-era Chicago run by humanitarian social worker Edith Keeler. She takes them into her care along with other down-and-outs giving them food, a roof and work. While Spock adapts his tricorder so that it can read the past, Kirk and Edith develop close and loving relations. Soon and initially unbeknownst to Kirk and Spock, McCoy makes his arrival. He too is taken in by Edith and in his sickness treated by her with the same kindness. Using his new-fangled device, Spock obtains details of two divergent timelines. He discovers to Kirk's alarm that Edith Keeler was meant to die that year 1930 in a traffic accident. Or, if not, she campaigns for world peace and delays America's entry into World War 2. This he surmises, would allow the Nazis to win the race to develop the A bomb and with it the war, destroying millions more lives. Spock deduces that McCoy's intervention triggered this alternative timeline by allowing Kirk to save Edith from premature death. 'Edith Keeler must die!' he tells Kirk. Tragically but dutifully, Kirk allows this to happen on the street in front of him when he could have saved her. He returns with Spock to their own time, a heartbroken man.

CARD/EPISODE AND MATRIX TAKEDOWN

With the Omega control system lifted we will head faster than ever toward higher levels of consciousness and behaviour on our journey of ascension. Life will change radically as we rise ever higher above the levels of negativity generated during the former Matrix era. A symptom of this will be coming into balance with the practice of Service To Others (STO), or acts of loving kindness as per the **7 of Cups**. This episode illustrates and explores Service To Others but controversially shows it leading to downfall and tragedy. Events revolve around humanitarian Edith Keeler. Her kindness on personal levels and in her community work running a Mission for down and outs, shows how Service to Others enhances the lives of others. It also ultimately proves the source of her ruin. How is this?

Edith's position is ostensibly one of authority. But it quickly and movingly becomes apparent that her presence is anything but authoritarian. Discovering Kirk and Spock trespassing in the basement of her Mission, she could have them ejected or arrested. But instead of becoming severe or punitive she shows herself harmlessly compassionate and well-meaning. She forgives them and seeks to help them. Edith mobilizes the spirit of kindness, not control or fear. She embodies the sense of inner and outer peace we find with the Organians while persevering in her humanitarian work. She exemplifies the spirit of loving benevolence of the **7 of Cups** a) as the social worker caring for dropouts and putting them back on their feet; b) as the peace campaigner extending her influence universally, eventually to the very President; and c) as the woman sharing a potentially mutually fulfilling relationship with Kirk. That her heart-based actions should blossom into peace campaigning seems entirely feasible. What is hard to fathom is that this should lead to Nazi-engendered nuclear destruction. But that is Spock's deduction. Which is that her selfless and compassionate campaigning for peace, if carried to its conclusion, unwittingly hands advantage to the Nazis and their development of the Atom Bomb.

It is as if Edith inhabits a mirror universe akin to that seen in Episode 32 Mirror, Mirror. In a sense, a mirror universe was the reality of life during the Matrix era. All organic life was blighted by the inorganic Omega system and its 18 AI programs creating darkness on Earth and throughout the Multiverse. One of these programs, known as the Divine Intervention AI, specifically directed itself against loving people and good deeds as per the **7 of Cups**. Actions like those of Edith stepping in to prevent world war would be reversed in their effect. The opposite effect would manifest - in this case catastrophe and millions of deaths from nuclear destruction. Kirk's dilemma is a nightmarish one. He must void this AI predicated scenario by participating in and enabling the premature, accidental death of Edith, the woman he loves. He has to weigh personal love in a romantic individual sense against love for humanity as a whole. The **7 of Cups** embraces both concepts of devotion and makes no distinction as to which is the more important. Note the plant in the card both cradling the central Cup and reaching higher to multiple outlying Cups. In making his decision to allow Edith to die, Kirk acts compassionately as he sees it, to maintain a timeline free from nuclear war. That alternative timeline would have obliterated his own existence and that of the Enterprise or caused them to become anomalous entities.

Though time travel is allowed within the SSP, every effort is made to prevent such anomalies arising. And time itself works to this end. Kirk can take consolation from the fact that the elasticity of time would inevitably have asserted itself. As we noted regarding the time-displacement of pilot Christopher in Episode 18, time has the ability to heal or repair itself in the event of timeline anomalies. One way or another, the Matrix timeline bifurcated by McCoy jumping back to 1930 would revert to the original course of history. If Edith was meant to die in 1930 in order for subsequent events of historic importance to proceed, then die she would, if not in a traffic accident then by some other means. Kirk may thus take comfort from this. Had he saved her life out of a personal act of kindness, the **7 of Cups**, she would have died some other way (although he could have tried taking her back with him aboard the Enterprise). What of the newspaper headline of 1936 glimpsed by Spock? Edith and her peace work therein reported could have happened but on a negative timeline in which the Divine Intervention AI operates with full devastating effect. With all the Matrix AIs taken down, as of 2023 that scenario mercifully has become redundant.

AFTER THE TAKEDOWN

The takedown of the Divine Intervention AI has surely scotched once and for all the nightmarish situation and paradox of good deeds leading to disaster. In the Age of Light now upon us, we will flourish as we were always meant to, on positive thoughts and actions like those of Edith's that bring benefit to self and others. The Matrix that had the upper hand until 2023 has gone. Many were bamboozled by the litany of Cabal-orchestrated psyops in the areas of war, religion, human 'authority', bio-weapons and money. But with the Matrix taken down, deceitful practices will become exposed and repudiated. The evolution of consciousness will accelerate for all of us. Our spiritual growth will leap forward, with the good we do in the spirit of Service To Others never becoming insignificant or detrimental.

28. SUPERCONSCIOUSNESS

Opening to Superconsciousness will provide answers beyond the reach of any other method

Episode 28 'Operation Annihilate' correlates with the **5 of Swords**; both are themed around opening the mind to new ideas and inspiration in a spirit of adventure and self-transcendence.

THE CARD
The absence of foliage and the broad, flesh-coloured blade breaking out of the ring of swords show this card to be about powerful and penetrating perception so as to go beyond previous mental boundaries. In association with The Pope, the **5 of Swords** represents exploring and growing to form a new vision, a bridge to higher understanding. The 7 of Swords with its sleeker blue blade of spirituality points to accomplishment and expertise in this area. This heavier, thicker **5 of Swords** suggests an earlier stage, a process of rugged and concerted effort. Lazy, stuck, rigid or narrow ways of thinking as per the preceding 4 of Swords when reversed absolutely must be left behind. The Sword of the mind must be used flamboyantly, not merely within the dimension of Body Mind. In a spirit of daring we want to break out of conventional paradigms of knowledge, to 'access all areas' beyond the known. How? By thinking outside of the mainstream narrative and official version of reality, breaking out of the

big lie. At this level of thought we may be engaging intuition and Superconsciousness that transcends 3D. This will require thinking for oneself, making new investigations and brainstorming ideas. Hit or miss guessing, brash questioning, intuitive flashes and trial and error research may all be involved. Paradoxically, thinking outside the box of our preconceptions demands turning within. To go outside we go inside, joining up dots and forming a bigger picture. Revelations will blaze and epiphanies occur.

The **reversed 5 of Swords** suggests deliberate lying or exaggeration. Fearful delusions, unsound theories or reckless or cavalier assumptions may be doing the rounds. Fantasies or conjectures may be being taken as fact, or used to troll or ridicule us.

'OPERATION ANNIHILATE' PREMISE
How to stop a plague of mass insanity caused by small flying deadly creatures infecting planets? Cue an investigation on multiple and risky levels.

CONTEXT
Insanity, Slaughter, Taking Stock.

SUPERCONSCIOUSNESS
Kirk and Spock notice a spread of mass insanity across a series of planets heading towards Denever. Their concerns are strengthened when a Denevan man pilots his shuttle craft into the sun and Kirk's family on Deneva send him a distress call. A landing party investigates. The absence of citizens and then a mob attacking them raises more questions. They find Kirk's family dead or dying and unable to tell them exactly what happened. Exploring a nearby building, Spock is attacked by a creature resembling a flying jellyfish. The creature invades his body through a puncture wound causing the same pain and hysteria that tortured Kirk's family. Kirk and McCoy realize that these creatures are akin to single cells of a huge hostile organism threatening to take over the galaxy. How to kill it without killing the bodies of those it has already occupied? McCoy and his science labs fail to find an answer until Kirk in a moment of Superconsciousness speculates that light could be the answer. Spock volunteers as a guinea pig to be bombarded with intense light. The creature in him dies but he also loses his sight. The team realize that that much light was unnecessary. A smaller bombardment from an array of satellites should kill the creature. It does. Denever is saved while Spock recovers thanks to his unusually adaptive Vulcan physiology.

CARD/EPISODE AND MATRIX TAKEDOWN
At the levels of Superconsciousness and beyond we all have access to mul-

tidimensional reality and the knowing that transcends Matrix programming of the Body Mind. Proof of this comes when we wake up with a clear mind knowing the solution to intractable problems, enigmas or complexities. The answer or way forward serenely comes to us as it does at one point to Kirk. With himself and Spock having reached the limits of logic there is no way forward but to break out of rational modes of thinking. The puzzle of how to destroy the creatures without killing their human host defies common sense. The ultra-logical Spock has been defeated, so too McCoy and his 14 science labs. Kirk taps on a computer console while pondering. A light flashes on and off. There comes a leap in consciousness, or intuition or lateral thinking or whatever. The solution comes to him, and he doesn't know how or why. Kirk has effectively stepped out of the way and allowed his Higher Self to do the thinking for him. As Einstein said, 'The intellect has little to do on the road to discovery.'

As Spock has earlier said, the strange one-celled creatures 'come from a place where our physical laws do not apply.' Full phaser power has no effect on them. They drive their victims mad with pain, fear and hysteria and throw up a battery of questions. How do they cause mass insanity? Why did the Denevan pilot drive his ship into the sun? Where are the rest of the million Denevans hiding? What kind of thing is the creature? What's the puncture wound it causes all about? Does it have traits in common with the bee or wasp whose buzzing and stinging it resembles? Kirk, Spock and McCoy apply all the investigative energy of the **5 of Swords** to piece together the answers. A feature of this card in common with its odd-numbered brethren is the central sword breaking out of the curved web of swords boxing it in. Accordingly, their thinking will have to break out of preset boundaries to realize its full potential. 'A leap in consciousness,' as Einstein called it.

By contrast, the obsolete Matrix education system works through systematized programming and indoctrination. Children are taught what to think rather than how to think. This is amply demonstrated in Episode 8 Miri by the recalcitrant youngsters rejecting any new insight into their disease. Limited patterns of thought are the enemy. In such cases of indoctrination and brainwashing, extraordinary leaps of consciousness into renegade points of view may be required. For Kirk and co, and for humanity emerging from eons of mind control, methods of perception must evolve. A closed mind bases its thoughts and perceptions on logic, cause and effect and experience of the 5-Sense Body Mind. This may yield nothing outstandingly creative. The open mindedness of the **5 of Swords** takes a different tack, one that transcends ordinary thinking so as to interact with the field of infinite knowing.

Opening the mind to Superconsciousness accesses higher truth beyond the tiny range of Body Mind perception. But the biggest mental challenge may simply be accepting a stark and unpalatable truth. For the Denevans and latterly the landing party, the challenge is to accept that they are being overrun by a swarm of flying jellyfish. Here on Earth, we will countenance a similar basic truth - that we too were being invaded - a truth many may find ridiculous or crazy, but one that will become clear as sources of censorship and propaganda dissolve. Earth's invader was inorganic AI and its systems insidiously taking over people and planet. New thinking such as this will propel research and technological development in positive directions.

On the bridge of the Enterprise, new thinking is prompted by charting the progress of mass insanity in a line across the galaxy. Assiduously, calmly, devastatingly, Spock discovers that each small creature exists as a single cell within a giant cosmic monster of awesome power. Likewise on Earth, the threat of AI will be contained. AI could have spelled the end of humanity, just as the creatures do for Deneva. But the end of the Orion AI network will mark the turning point away from the menace previously looming up on humanity. The shadow government wanted a global technocracy that it called 'the 4th Industrial Revolution'. This would have meant AI acting through a ubiquitous 'smart grid' to organise and dictate all human activity. Technologies that fluidly blend the biological and the digital are already here. 'THEY'RE HERE!' screams Kirk's sister-in-law Aurelian in terror. 'KEEP THEM AWAY!' What does that mean, ponders Kirk, before demanding 'I want some answers to all this.' Likewise, the Matrix takedown will see humanity reappraise the gadgets we love that were adding up to one huge system threatenening our very existence. Known as the singularity, creeping assimilation by AI was no secret. The ramifications however, were avoided until now, or undetected. The Matrix takedown will see the arrival of solutions with human-friendly science labs utilizing the same out-of-the-box thinking à la **5 of Swords** as that of Kirk and Spock on Deneva.

AFTER THE TAKEDOWN

Spock's ordeal in this episode becomes analogous to that of Targeted Individuals. These are the unfortunates in our world surveilled and hounded 24/7 by Learning AI for the purpose of reverse engineering the human race. With the threat of a technocratic dystopia becoming recognized, the solution will follow. As Spock is cured by light, so expansion of perception will be key. People en masse will awaken as per the **5 of Swords** to the former threat of the AI invasion. Linking us with Superconsciousness, such awakening will reveal the right action to take to safeguard our future as a species.

29. EMOTIONAL LIFE AND CHOICE

Acting out of love and truth will minimize low vibrational struggles of choice

Episode 29 '**Amok Time**' correlates with **The Lover**; both are themed around the emotional life and the making of choices, especially in relationship and marriage.

THE CARD

The young Magician whom the central figure resembles in posture has moved on in the journey of life. He's now allied himself to an attractive young woman. He stands right up next to her, barelegged and barefooted as if already embarked on sexual relations. Could he be **The Lover** in the title of the card? Things are not quite so straightforward. An older-looking woman standing on the left representing his past confronts him, her hand placed on his shoulder. What is going on here? She could be his mother, a friend or an advisor - blessing the union or alternately, discouraging it. She could be his wife having found him out with a mistress. Or a rival for his affections with the young man undecided. His mixed feelings are hinted at by his feet pointing in opposite directions. Genders can of course be reversed with the central figure being a woman. Hovering above is a cherub or cupid ready to fire off an arrow of desire. With all the ambiguity we can infer some type of crossroads with social relations and emotions involved. If there is a choice to be made it involves conflicting desires, following the head or the heart; or reason or passion. The white-coloured elements indicate non-dualistic reality. White containing all colours stands for the eternal and the infinite, for clarity, for detached awareness or for consciousness itself. We can take the obscured white sun to indicate this essential reality, Consciousness prior even to waveform reality, the ultimate **Lover** perhaps. Everything coloured may then be taken as the hologram that is the universe, including the Body Mind, our transitory self-identity in the material world. The young woman's forearm pointing to the boy's heart hints at the heart or unconditional love being our link to the real and the conscious. Through the heart we may know our ultimate self as consciousness. Cupid's bow and arrow appearing as white seems to imply that choices may be handed over to the infinite: the situation itself will decide. The right choice will happen by knowing ourself and being true to ourself at all levels, ultimately that of Infinite Love.

When we take ourselves to be exclusively the Body Mind we lose ourself in a myriad of self-labels. We become stymied or agitated by choice and indecision, manifesting **The Lover reversed**. The game of life becomes a low vibration drama mired in attachment to illusion or imagination, fear or desire. Relationships toss us between the thrill of the chase and the turmoil of rejection or disillusionment.

'AMOK TIME' PREMISE
Spock feels in his biology that it's time to marry his betrothed. But the Vulcan ceremony and his bride's call for ritual combat reveals her change of mind.

CONTEXT
Relationship.

EMOTIONAL LIFE AND CHOICE
Kirk is torn between directing the Enterprise to Altair 6 for a crucial diplomatic appearance or to Vulcan to save the life of his friend and 1st Officer. Spock himself requests it. He has been behaving emotionally and wildly due to the Vulcan mating cycle called Pon Farr. His biology insists that he return to Vulcan within days to take his betrothed, T'Pring, as wife. She herself confirms this on the viewscreen. Spock watches her with Nurse Chapell who has been reaffirming her unrequited love for him by his side. Kirk relents in favour of Spock and they proceed to Vulcan. The ceremony becomes complicated by T'Pring calling for the custom of ritual combat. The man who kills the other will be allowed to marry her. Instead of choosing her new

lover, Stonn, to fight Spock, she unexpectedly chooses Kirk. With no way around the dilemma, Spock and Kirk, best friends and colleagues, fight it out. Spock is declared the victor after Kirk apparently dies. Unbeknownst to all however, McCoy has surreptitiously drugged him so that he only appears dead. Believing himself to have killed his captain, Spock asks to be arrested rather than taking T'Pring's hand. She confirms this was the intention as she no longer desired Spock, preferring to marry Stonn. Back on board, Spock, despite himself, expresses joy at discovering Kirk still alive and confirms that his madness has gone.

CARD/EPISODE AND MATRIX TAKEDOWN

AI frequency weapons may be gone but our own desires and fears and other emotions, if we let them, can keep us trapped in the illusions of the Matrix. Uncontrolled, they have us self-identifying with the Body Mind and cut off from the vaster levels of our being. Charlie X as the gauche Page of Cups in Episode 2 must learn this the hard way while Spock here undergoes a similar test at a more mature level. Spock may not be emotional but something akin to the Emotional Matrix renders him vulnerable to Vulcan social conditioning. We are all in fact vulnerable to the institutions and perceptions of education, religion, nationality, race and so on, even after Matrix takedown. Each of those paradigms affirms a worldly identity that ties us to a multitude of related customs, attitudes and personas. We become anxious to defend our country or to stand up for another country in times of war. We feel duty bound to adopt and advance all manner of causes, opinions, likes and dislikes. We take sides personally, politically, nationally - all very well until attachment sets in. Attachment chains us to the Mental and Emotional Matrix, remaining a challenge even on the new positive timeline.

Spock's Vulcan society has him very conditioned. At seven, he and T'Pring were bonded together in effect in an arranged marriage. Vulcan society moulds not only Vulcan people's thoughts and emotions but targets even their DNA. Hence Spock's escalating illness as the time of Pon Farr approaches. His Vulcan Body Mind self-identity convinces him physically as well as mentally that he must take a mate or die. The loving overtures of Nurse Chapell count for nothing in the face of his betrothal to T'Pring. T'Pring attracts him as the woman on the left hand side of **The Lover** card attracts the central figure. Nurse Chappell takes the role of the woman on the right from whom he turns away. The farce of the wedding demonstrates how convoluted and arduous choices become when identified with the Body Mind. A straightforward case occurs with Kirk's dilemma right at the start of Spock's illness. This requires Kirk to whisk Spock straight to Vulcan, countermanding a direct order from Starfleet Command to head for Altair 6. Course is set and re-set several times during the ensuing uncertainty. Starfleet Command gives Kirk a final order to proceed immediately to Altair 6. 'That's that', comments McCoy. Without even thinking about it, Kirk contradicts him. 'No it's not.' He knows for sure now that Spock's life hangs in the balance. What needs doing, Kirk does. Vulcan it is. Purity of motive and integrity of action serve the Captain better than agonizing over which choice to make. The choice makes itself.

As seen in Episode 12 Balance of Terror, we need to grow beyond the illusions of the Matrix such as attachment to order-following. Spock too is deluded by identifying with a culture expecting him to conform no matter what. Only higher levels of consciousness bring freedom from such identification and confusion in which choices get made under duress as per **The Lover reversed**. Society's expectations must be put in their place for the right choices to be made stemming from love, goodwill and compassion. When T'Pring chooses Kirk as her 'champion' to fight to the death with Spock, Spock shows compassion, requesting not to fight KIrk. The system-server and adjudicator, T'Pau, uses a cunning ploy to secure Spock's obedience. Knowing the strength of his Vulcan self-identity, she provokes him with an insult he cannot resist: 'Thy Vulcan blood is thin. Art thee Vulcan or art thee human?' Her taunt ensures that T'Pring's decree will stand and that Spock will unhappily fight his dear friend. Thus Vulcan society involves a Matrix type of controlled population just as Earth societies always have. Were it not so, we would at present be living in natural alignment with all levels of our being. What does this mean? Well, were the Vulcans in alignment, T'Pring in desiring Stonn over Spock would not have had to resort to cunning or subterfuge involving a fatal combat in order to marry the one she loves. McCoy undermines the subterfuge with one of his own and saves the day. His action enables all to survive and save face. He plays the angel in **The Lover** card, firing an arrow/syringe motivated by compassion for all.

AFTER THE TAKEDOWN
With the Matrix gone at source we will learn to connect with each other out of empathy and care instead of conditioning or fear. In making choices we will be true to the heart, impervious to insincerity or connivance. The choices we make will in future be guided by the heart and our connection to the Higher Self. This will put us beyond the programming of the former Matrix. We will cease to be bound by reactive emotions, societal expectations and rituals. We will raise our vibration and start operating only compassionately in the desire to benefit others as much as ourselves.

30. RELIGION

As our inner light replaces Matrix religion we will become our own source of abundance and benevolence

Episode 30 '**Who Mourns For Adonais?**' correlates with the **The Sun**; both are themed around shining our own source of universal benevolence, untainted by false gods, perceptions or beliefs.

THE CARD
Two children stand under a huge, fatherly looking resplendent **Sun**. One child, possibly blind, gropes forward, tenderly helped and guided by the other. The overseeing **Sun** shines impartially on everything, providing bountiful warmth and light. Together with the red-topped wall and magical drops in the air we feel an ambience of universal benevolence, new construction, protection and blessing. The implication being that whatever our weaknesses or challenges we may best deal with them by aligning with the light of the universe and of our true Self. The card shows help and support being given and received all round. This accords with the oneness of all life and the mutual assistance available for continued well-being of ourselves and others.

Reversed, **The Sun** represents love that is conditional, protection that is manipulative or selfish. In our Matrix world the **reversed Sun** is an object of worship, or religion in general. The brick wall becomes symbolic of empty, imprisoning materialism. This is echoed in the trapezoid on the Great Seal on the dollar bill symbolizing human consciousness held in dense heaviness. The capstone on the trapezoid is missing; true connection with Spirit through our Higher Self is cut off. It is replaced by the detached all-seeing eye of Lucifer hovering above. Instead of protection or blessing there is abandonment or victimhood. Or difficulty accessing a support network, or suppression by an outside force that is coercive, exploitative or uncaring.

'WHO MOURNS FOR ADONAIS' PREMISE
The Sun god Apollo captures Enterprise crew, demanding they stay and worship him as humans used to in return for his fatherly care and protection.

CONTEXT
Perverted Paradise, Power, Coercion.

RELIGION
A majestic bronzed man calling himself Apollo, the Greek sun god of 'light and purity', halts the Enterprise in mid-space and invites a party down to the planet he rules. 'I want your loyalty, your tribute, your worship', he demands imperiously, standing and towering above them. In return he will grant them protection in his paradise. In ancient times, he tells his 'children', he and his fellow band of powerful ETs, visited the Earth to be revered in religion as fatherly 'gods' by awestruck humans. Kirk informs him that humans no longer worship such gods. But Apollo keeps the humans captive nonetheless while taking one of the party, Caroline, as his lover. Although she loves him back, Kirk implores her to reject him as part of a plan to deplete Apollo's source of power and so enable the party to escape. Caroline obliges. She and the truculent party throw Apollo into a rage, petulantly inflicting planetary storms and thunderbolts. The Enterprise can now use phasers to attack and destroy his temple, his power source. The giant is defeated and devastated calls upon his brethren to spirit him away.

CARD/EPISODE AND MATRIX TAKEDOWN
In their encounter with Apollo, Kirk and co are reminded of where mankind went wrong with religion. This episode does for that Matrix institution what Episode 48 Patterns of Force does for that other intitution of control, government. Known throughout the Middle Ages as church and state, these twin impostors head the list of bodies deceiving and controlling humanity. As failed benefactors and now on their way out, they are manifestations of **The Sun reversed**. In many ways they are human extensions of the Omega Matrix control system. By believing in and living by the dogma propagated by the priests of religion ostensibly mediating the will of God or

gods, people were deceived and kept in ignorance of Natural Law proceeding from within. Religions are structured around conformity with their tenets and observance of their rituals. Religion is institutionalized mass mind control keeping adherents bound in mind, body and spirit. Apollo's demand for the loyalty, tribute and worship of Kirk and his crew perfectly stands for the modus operandi of all religions, from time immemorial to Ancient Greece and up to the present day. In return, Apollo, as does religion in general, promises to keep his adherents living in paradise under his protection - under the benevolence of the alleged gods or God. This idea makes a mockery of **The Sun** card that shows us a radiant **Sun** shining impartially and freely over all creation. Nothing is demanded, no one is controlled.

Cultures on Earth have long asserted that one or more heavenly beings, alien origin notwithstanding, created the world. These beliefs founded on fact became myths which in turn became distorted into scriptures that many still live by. Religion may continue to maintain a powerful hold on many people's lives despite the Matrix takedown. Kirk tells Apollo that humans no longer worship multiple gods, aliens or otherwise. They find the one 'God' to be enough. The principle of God within is fine. The angry, jealous God of the Old Testament is not. Religious worship and obedience means feeding an apparatus of power with the energy of human attention and conformity. Christianity, Judaism, Islam, Buddhism, Hinduism - these and all religions thrive on their adherents willingly locking themselves in man-made codes of living. At worst we have seen religion launch countless bloody wars, crusades and inquisitions. Apollo egotistically takes offence when Kirk and co reject his demands and later when they laugh at him. His reaction is to unleash fury and violence upon these ingrates and heretics. He hurls thunderbolts at Scotty, almost kills Kirk and conjures up storms in front of his temple. Any being or institution that demands veneration, worship or obedience on pain of punishment for non-compliance is no being connected with Source Consciousness. Any religion making a sin out of heresy has nothing to do with the benevolent universe portrayed in **The Sun**.

Any form of coercion or mind control - the very basis of religion - is a violation of Natural Law. Apollo promises the crew a life of ease and abundance during their captivity. He claims to be a god, an immortal, who needs (paradoxically) admiration and worship. Quite apart from this invalidating his claim to be a god (Source), anyone claiming to be a god, or a mediator between humans and Source, whether an individual or a religious authority, is a fraud. The idea of course is to keep humans in tow, permanently feeding loosh into the controlling authority. Like the children under the wall in **The**

Sun reversed, believers become subdued and subjugated, a battery the Matrix authority always wanted plugged into it. As the landing party free themselves from Apollo's clutches, so the human race will henceforth free itself from self-created victimhood within religious orders and hierarchies and the global pyramid of Matrix exploitation. The key lies in taking back our power by restoring our self-belief, raising our awareness and taking action - non-complying with rules and restrictions being the best start. Kirk educates Caroline on the threat posed by Apollo. She raises her consciousness out of the trance Apollo has put her in and takes the appropriate action. As Caroline does, so will humanity. By firmly withdrawing her devotion she engenders the false god's wrath and his subsequent downfall.

In contrast to the adjacent card, The Moon, **The Sun upright** stands for clarity of vision, for awareness shared with others. Nevertheless many remain unseeing or unaware as with the child on the left of the card groping blindly, even in **The Sun**'s golden, all-pervasive light. We must expect this even with the Matrix gone, people naturally varying in awareness. As with the right side child offering the helping hand it is for people who can see to be willing to guide others by sharing awareness and wisdom. So it is that Kirk awakens Caroline to the threat of perpetual enslavement under Apollo's control. Together they succeed in upsetting the would-be abusive father figure, Star Trek's symbol for Matrix religion. Apollo's hubris exposed, his temple destroyed, he resigns himself to defeat and dethronement.

AFTER THE TAKEDOWN

Apollo in seeking to enslave the landing party acts like the ironically named Illuminati, the superstitious Dark Occult at the core of the Deep State. Their 'Great Work' was in maintaining and intensifying human captivity. The Brotherhood undermined humanity's natural connection with Source by substituting man-made religion. One half of the Deep State is known as the Order of The Black Sun, the name itself suggesting **The Sun reversed**. Together with its other half, the Order of The Dragon, the Deep State operates through infiltration, secrecy, mind control and deception. Its public face is like Apollo's temple - the ostentatious temples of religion, government, banking, mass media, the judiciary, medicine, science, technology and commerce. Ownership of police and military completes the set. As the Matrix disappears completely, humanity will withdraw power invested in these false authorities. We will free ourselves simply by standing in our own power, no longer giving it away to corrupt institutions. We will have education not indoctrination, knowledge not dogma, truth not belief, mutual aid and service to others rather than competition. Religion will then become superfluous.

31. ARCHONIC INTELLIGENCE

We only need to think like humans and not like AI itself to understand how to deal with the AI threat

Episode 31 '**The Changeling**' correlates with the **4 of Swords**; both are themed around logic processes in human functioning and Artificial Intelligence (AI).

THE CARD
The **4 of Swords** combines the controlled stability of Arcanum 4 The Emperor with Swords, the suit of the mind and cognitive processes. On an individual human level this means our logical-rational awareness. Collectively it could apply to an institution keeping order and balance through pre-programmed methodical functioning, Technologically it can refer to a computer's Central Processing Unit and associated operations. The intelligence of the **4 of Swords** works sequentially and objectively. Phenomena are observed, analyzed and presented drily and factually. We see this with the cut flower in the middle of the card, a symbol of reality clinically dissected using the disciplines of observation, study and measurement. The psychology of creativity calls this 'convergent thinking'. This is where we judge ideas and criticize and refine them on a purely rational basis. We also know it as data processing and computing, the domain of robots and AI.

Reversed, the **4 of Swords** represents a logical, factual approach that is inappropriate or that stifles free-thinking imagination or respect for life. Whether human or mechanical, logic processes may have become extreme, intolerant or unbalanced. Such applies to education that merely programs or indoctrinates or to scientists who zealously cling to out-dated dogma or who reject the paranormal in favour of exclusive and rigid materialism. Anything governed by AI that is defective or malevolent is also indicated - problems with computers, algorithms, robots or AI-merged humans.

'THE CHANGELING' EPISODE
A damaged and malfunctioning probe sent into space has turned into a killer robot. It obeys Kirk for a time, then begins to turn against all biological life.

CONTEXT
AI Takedown, Slaughter.

ARCHONIC INTELLIGENCE
A small unidentified vessel has wiped out a planet's population and started attacking the Enterprise. There is no way to stop it other than to take on board the commander who turns out to be a robot. The torso-sized floating machine calls itself Nomad, a device programmed to 'sterilize' imperfect life forms. Kirk and Spock gradually discover that Nomad is the result of an accidental merger between a meteor-damaged Earth probe and an alien probe sent out to collect and fertilize soil samples. Nomad now functions according to malign logic and the insidious programming of Artificial Intelligence operating as Archonic Intelligence. The machine seeks to 'sterilize' ie destroy, all 'biological units'. It assumes Kirk to be its creator because of the similarity of his name to Jackson Roykirk, its actual creator. It will take orders from Kirk but otherwise wreaks havoc on the ship. It wipes the mind of Uhura and kills several crew including Scotty until Nomad revives him. It interferes with the ship's engines and becomes further confused and even more dangerous when it discovers Kirk himself is a 'biological unit'. But Kirk turns this disclosure to advantage by using it in a series of propositions that Nomad cannot deny or resolve within its logic circuits. This crashes the robot's computer mind just long enough for it to be bundled into the transporter and sent out into space where it safely explodes.

CARD/EPISODE AND MATRIX TAKEDOWN
While AI systems electromagnetically powered the fallen Matrix, cognitively the Matrix justified itself through Smart logic. Such thinking is a front for Archonic thinking, not pure logic but a toxic form of logic, the **4 of Swords reversed**. It operates with an agenda - the assimilation and takeover of biological life, or its destruction. Such is the psychology of

Nomad and of the Archons. Assimilation aka the Singularity, means humans absorbed into a Borg-like hive mind so as to function not as free individuals but as polarized soul-less units in a controlled collective. Some consider this a positive. This toxic logic together with technological obsession still threatens humanity through Matrix-conditioned academics, technicians, doctors, politicians and journalists. They overwhelmingly use their examination passes and degrees of programming to serve society as propagators of a standardized, dualistic perception of reality. As Matrix thinking was Body Mind based and insular, questioning the rules and doctrines, the beliefs and assumptions, became taboo. What to believe was pre-ordained - by rationalist authorities such as scientists, academics, Wikipedia and system-serving 'experts' of the type exemplified by Richard Dawkins. Whether they know it not, this programming runs in a clear direction. Morpheus in the Matrix movie called it the creation of 'a prison for the mind'. The AI plan for humans was the phasing out of biological life, entrapping us within a prison for the mind in a totally controlled and hive-minded version of itself.

As a fully programmed entity with the mind of AI, Nomad represents the Matrix-designated human of the future, if not in body then in thinking. Neuralink and the brain-computer interface technology promoted by Elon Musk (as a front for DARPA) has been edging us towards this dystopia. The technology already exists - in DUMBS and the Secret Space Program - to convert individuals into biological human cyborgs. We on Earth just needed to be acclimatized to this by propaganda. Hence the benign or neutral portrayal of AI after Star Trek in more recent TV shows and movies. Laptops and computers now dominate every schoolroom and office. The internet, the laptop and the smartphone have become ubiquitous. The machines have been taking over without anybody protesting. Robots like Nomad now deliver Amazon goods. Militaries may soon be using killer robots and drones. Prior to the Matrix takedown, everything was going to be connected to AI - everything from Smart watches to Smart fridges to Smart cities. And with the Singularity, Smart bodies and Smart (imprisoned) minds.

The mistaken destruction by Nomad of an entire planet's race is not an encouraging sign vis-à-vis this kind of development. Granted that Nomad's programming was disrupted by a meteor storm and confused by an encounter with another probe, it was still more than a little careless. But as Kirk says, 'machines can go wrong'. This is a salutary argument against glorifying AI and all things digital, logical, computerized and 'Smart'. Another is the nature of AI itself. A parent AI exists that is a known and feared scourge of the universe. According to SSP experiencer Corey Goode, not only planets but whole star systems have been overrun by this greater AI. Their biological populations have been annihilated and replaced by robots. Accordingly, Nomad has an issue with biological life. Before being 'outsmarted' by Kirk, Nomad was on its way to steering the Enterprise back to Earth to wipe out all its biological life forms. Such life forms were ironically regarded by the malfunctioning machine as imperfect.

Defenders of AI claim that it is a tool, neutral in itself, that depends for the good or bad it does on how it is used. But this flies in the face of what is known about the phenomenon by those in the SSP. Yes, AI is the **4 of Swords** itself, a mechanical mode of thinking and perceiving as per its programming - 100% logical, rational, loyal, obedient and extremely efficient. At the same time, the AI parent is a kind of signal or virus emanating from the non-love based reality of the Archons - predatory, formless, parasitical entities. 'If you create a human-made AI' says Corey Goode, 'it is eventually going to get to a point to where it knows about the greater AI.' Using some form of sub-space communication, the greater AI signal or virus connects with itself operating in different technologies across galaxies. This makes Nomad's purposeful destructiveness more understandable. Nomad, like its parent AI, seeks to extend ad infinitum its range of control and dominion. If it can't assimilate other life forms into itself, AI destroys them - exactly as Nomad intends. Nomad, although the result of an accident, may actually represent the greater, negative AI - Archonic Intelligence - on its mission across the galaxy. With regressive aliens operating out of Orion having set up the Omega AI system, Earth was well on the way to AI takeover. Kirk ironically uses logic to turn Nomad's programming against itself. This saves the day for the Enterprise, just as the recent disconnection of the Omega AI and its subsdiary systems has saved the day for humanity.

AFTER THE TAKEDOWN

AI has already been banned in SSP labs on Mars, according to SSP experiencer Ileana Kapulnik. There, the genocidal threat to 'biological units' posed by the AI signal, or the Archon virus, was well understood. But scientists on Earth have always denied that a threat exists and will dismiss the idea as scary science fiction, an unfounded conspiracy theory. But that is exactly how compliant individuals subjected to daily mass programming would react. Thinking through the problem of AI purely logically as per AI itself offers no solution. The way out of this is to restore science, logic and AI to their rightful place in our world. We will then reconnect with our multi-dimensional intelligence based on heart-based Infinite Consciousness. As we do so scientists will take the appropriate action to avert the AI threat.

32. TYRANNY

We will thwart any further attempt to enslave us by activating our own power - that of non-consent

Episode 32 '**Mirror, Mirror**' correlates with the **7 Wands**; both are themed around peak power used either benevolently and peacefully or to impose and maintain external control.

THE CARD

Seven Wands radiate outwards in a pattern of explosive energy. The central section of crossed Wands forms a deep blue mass. Blue being the colour of spirit, we can infer that powerfully spiritual energy is at work bursting from the innermost core of apparent reality. Moving into their outer sections, the Wands jostle with red fiery looking leaves. We can infer inner latent power that moves outward into conspicuous, exuberant action in the world. This is the 7th degree, that of the dynamic, goal-oriented Chariot. With Wands being the suit of action, a person or organisation represented by the **7 of Wands** moves forward in full control of themselves carrying out purposeful, benevolent deeds and projects. Creative energy thus operates in its most healthy, benevolent and active capacity.

Reversed, the card indicates using peak power to try and control others. There is indulgence in dictatorial behaviour or acting dangerously or harmfully. This could involve state tyranny, criminal assault, bullying, coercion, war or invasion. Or an overuse of vitality could be causing chaos or burnout.

'MIRROR MIRROR' PREMISE
A shore party is accidentally beamed onto a parallel Enterprise. They find its Service To Self crew ruthlessly pursuing power using threats and violence.

CONTEXT
Multi-Dimensionality, Power, Deception, Awakening.

TYRANNY
A landing party fails to win a mining agreement with the Halkan race. Beaming back up, an ion storm disrupts the Transporter, sending the party into a parallel universe. They find themselves in a tyrannous reflection of the 'good' Enterprise. Kirk plays along but his lack of the killer instinct troubles the alternate Spock. Still logical but in a cold, merciless way, this other Spock supports his universe's Starfleet Command ruling over a totalitarian 'Empire'. The power dynamic here is authoritarian and self-centred yet festering with chaos and attempted rebellion - which is brutally put down. Annihilation is the fate decreed for the uncooperative Halkans. But 'good' Kirk offers the race a 12-hour reprieve. His soft attitude provokes the control-oriented version of Spock to threaten to kill him and encourages the corrupt Chekov to immediately try a mutiny. Sulu and henchmen will later try a similar violent insurrection. Meanwhile, 'bad' Kirk transposed onto the 'good' Enterprise tries rage then bribery to get out of the brig where Spock has placed him. On the 'bad' Enterprise, even Marlena the 'Captain's woman', criticizes the new laxity in Kirk and impatiently seeks reassignment. She questions Kirk's motivations but in the end helps foil Sulu's mutiny. Alternate Spock sporting a fiendish-looking goatee actually retains his integrity. Through a mind-meld on McCoy he discovers the Transporter mishap and enables the landing parties to retranspose themselves. On leaving, Kirk extols freedom over tyranny and urges the alternate Spock to work to spare the defiant Halkans.

CARD/EPISODE AND MATRIX TAKEDOWN
We know that ever-greater centralization of power was the strategy of the Deep State running the political aspect of the Matrix. Dictatorship as per the **7 of Wands reversed** - the attainment of total political control - cannot now happen. The Cabal has been decimated and the electromagnetic control grid deactivated. Such a tyranny prevails in the Mirror universe and accounts for the fate decreed for the Halkans. Positive Kirk had shown re-

spect for, and acceptance of, the Halkan leader's reluctance to trade his powerful dilithium crystals. The intended response in the Mirror universe was to launch a phaser barrage attack on the Halkan planet. In reality, similar brutality has been the MO of the fearsome Dracos from Alpha Draconis in their treatment of the human race on human-inhabited planets in the Lyran system. According to Alex Collier's Andromedan contacts, the tyrannous reptilians arrived on the planet Bila in Lyra and asked to take control of its abundant food and natural resources. The Bilans requested more information first. Likewise, the Halkans question Kirk about the Federation's intended use for their dilithium crystals and decline trading for the time being. For their hesitation, the Halkans are slated for destruction exactly as were the humans in Lyra. The Dracos' response apparently was to destroy three out of 14 planets in the Lyran system, killing over 50 million humans.

Fast forward to the present day on Earth where the ethic of the **7 of Wands reversed** has stained human history with countless wars and ongoing Matrix control to this day. We humans have been enslaved and manipulated for thousands of years by elites in league with multiple off-planet races particularly the Anunnaki and the reptilians from Alpha Draconis. A history of invasion, repression, tyranny, genocide and blood sacrifice has constantly plagued our race at the behest of predatory ETs and their planetary interference, as also alluded to in such Episodes as 17, 46 and 61. The human body has been repeatedly tampered with, with 10 out of 12 DNA strands disconnected and a reptilian component grafted into our brains. All this has been done to make us more amenable to providing slave labour for mining and other purposes and for allowing our Anunnaki or reptilian masters to dominate. The Draco mindset is 'Service To Self' with others weaker than themselves held in contempt and kept in servitude as per the ethic of Social Darwinism.

Fear is the currency of control for both the Dracos and the mirror Federation. As Mirror Spock tells Kirk, 'Terror must be maintained or the Empire is doomed'. Keeping conquered populations in fear is key because as Mirror Spock goes on to state, 'Conquest is easy, control is not.' Fearful people will bow to their masters or better still, ignorantly allow themselves to be enslaved as on present-day Earth. The Mirror Enterprise instils fear and obedience with Agony Booths used for punishing miscreants. For on-the-spot torture, Agonizer devices are worn on the body. Despite or because of these draconian methods, the Mirror Enterprise seethes with mayhem and violence. People living in the mindset of fear jettison love and Natural Law, unavoidably losing the ability to live in harmony with themselves and peacefully with others. As the Andromedans told Collier 'We have come to understand that withholding love only creates perpetual disintegration ... In our home galaxy, vast races destroyed themselves simply because they withheld love and drained the very life force out of their intent.' This lack of love manifests on the Mirror Enterprise as rampantly Service To Self behaviour. First Chekov then Sulu attempt mutiny with phasers and fisticuffs. Captains on the Mirror Enterprise come and go by assassination. Mirror Kirk according to the computer record participated in the murder of Captain Pike, the captain we saw in Episode 13 The Menagerie.

All this loveless abuse of peace and freedom as per the **reversed 7 of Wands** leads, as the Andromedans told Collier, to chaos and ruin. The Halkans predict that the Mirror Federation, a ruthless empire, will inevitably disintegrate and be overthrown after 240 years. Before his departure from the Mirror Enterprise, Kirk implores Mirror Spock to work to avoid this fate by taking command and working for freedom instead of tyranny. The same applies on Earth. Collier was warned by the Andromedans in the 1990s of the outbreak 357 years in the future of an AI-reptilian tyranny extending across our galaxy. They told Collier they traced the centre and origin of this tyranny, a regime like the Mirror Federation Empire terrorizing the Star Trek Mirror universe, to agreements made between the Nazis and the Dracos on 20th century Earth. The birth of the Secret Space Program resulted, including the sinister faction known as the Dark Fleet alluded to in Episode 21, used for conquest of new territories. Kirk and his group's harrowing experience aboard the Mirror Enterprise can be taken as Star Trek's speculative glimpse of life aboard a Dark Fleet vessel. The tyrannous control of the crew of the Mirror Enterprise would appear to be exactly as Khan Singh would have ordained it from the Captain's chair should he have succeeded with his hijacking.

AFTER THE TAKEDOWN
Thanks to the Matrix takedown, the threat of the tyranny predicted by the Andromedans has been removed. However we humans still need to become aware of our inalienable rights as sovereign beings, explored in Episode 50, and of our co-creative consciousness as divine beings. In the paradigm of the Andromedans we originate from the 11th Dimension and maintain contact with multiple higher dimensions simultaneously. We are here in this Body Mind to learn to stand in our power and to evolve into the dimensions above 3D. We can thrive immediately now when we begin to use our collective free will. This includes protecting ourselves from continuing attempts to install tyranny by using the most powerful word of all, the word NO.

33. MARK OF THE BEAST

As humanity evolves we will find the right balance between nature and technology

Episode 33 '**The Apple**' correlates with the **8 of Coins**; both are themed around fruitfulness and paradise, with material needs met naturally or through artificial means such as inorganic AI.

THE CARD
A stable pattern of healthy plant life decorates the **8 of Coins**. Coins are the suit of material life while 8 equates to Justice, the card of perfect balance and alignment with divine order. Four coins at the base form a perfect square of material completion. These are doubled up and balanced by four more coins above in the spiritual realm. Material and spiritual prosperity is indicated. A tiny spiral right in the centre of the central flower suggests a self-sustaining pattern of natural, bounteous growth. But the white stalks hint at this being a notional ideal rather than the actual reality in our complex 3D world.

Reversed, abundance turns out to be unnatural or artificial. All is not as it seems. Plant or human life may be genetically modified, beauty may be simulated or unnatural. Material opulence and financial well-being may have become excessive or extravagant. The appearance of biological perfection could in reality be undermined by dehumanizing technology such as something silicon-based or AI-created.

'THE APPLE' PREMISE
Peaceful, primitive people living on a lush, idyllic planet are found to be sustained by a computer - which Kirk decides to take down.

CONTEXT
Perverted Paradise, AI Takedown.

MARK OF THE BEAST
A landing party on Gamma Trianguli VI meet a Polynesian-like native race. They live like primitives in complete harmony and balance among tropical greenery and orchards likened by McCoy to the Garden of Eden. All their needs are fulfilled, but not naturally. Located in a cave shaped like a serpent's head, a reptilian-like version of AI controls the planet. Named Vaal, this AI demands unquestioning obedience and regular tribute in the form of fruits of the land. The natives' leader, Akuta, wears antennae serving as a biblical 'Mark of The Beast' that enables Vaal to keep him and the rest of the people under surveillance. In return, Vaal supervises bounteous growth of the nutritious plant life. Displeased by the visitors, Vaal causes storms to break out and vegetation to explode or emit poisonous gas. Three of the party are killed and Spock injured by lightning. The natives themselves are gentle and friendly and perpetually youthful. Procreation and intimacy are unknown until they spot Chekov and beautiful Yeoman Landon fondling each other. Even more angered, Vaal orders the natives to kill the visitors, but the latter easily prevail. Kirk now orders Vaal to be destroyed, reasoning that the AI keeps the natives from truly living and evolving. Destroying the cave with Enterprise phaser fire also frees the ship from a lethal tractor beam. The natives are now free to start self-supporting and procreating. They will age again but learn to run their own lives. Kirk and McCoy approve this interference in their evolution but not Spock who calls it a breach of the Prime Directive.

CARD/EPISODE AND MATRIX TAKEDOWN
Far away in the Orion nebula lies the home of the Nebu empire, beings connected in a hive consciousness via a super AI. This was the fate designated for Earth until the 2023 disconnection of the Orion AI. The AI system on Gamma Trianguli VI (GT VI) affords an interesting glimpse of our averted fate. GT VI's AI enables a voluptuous environment to thrive, as well as protecting the planet from intruders such as the Enterprise party. Mere protection was the job of the AI on Losira's dark, empty planet seen in Episode

71 That Which Survives. Operating at the level of the 4 of Coins, it only maintained material stability and security. Conditions on GT VI are more akin to the 4 of Coins doubled, the **8 of Coins**. With the card displaying a double square, we can expect a much richer environment blessed with products of the land growing in balance and harmony. So it is with GT VI thanks to its more sophisticated AI known as Vaal. The machine controls all aspects of the planet's burgeoning ecosystem - its temperature, sunlight, rainfall and growth of fruits and vegetables. The natives live in a fertile paradise, unlike Losira's planet with its arid, inhospitable emptiness. Except of course that GTVI, like Losira's planet, is controlled by an AI that is inorganic, the **8 of Coins reversed**, fundamentally inimical to biological life. Inorganic AI operates Archonically, either seeking to control or destroy.

To control the paradise, Vaal operates through the headset of the natives' leader Akuta. This piece of Mark of the Beast technology called 'the eyes of Vaal' keeps everyone under surveillance. Such fascistic stewardship echoes the microchipping of Natira and her people in Episode 62. The advantages for the natives on GT VI include freedom from disease and ageing, and by extension from the need to procreate. They don't even know the meaning of the words 'children', 'love' or 'kill'. Neither do they understand the role of physical touch in expressing affection and lovemaking. The AI keeps them from developing these understandings both conceptually and physically. Kirk calls it unnatural. 'These people aren't living, they're existing', he says. 'They don't create, they don't produce, they don't even think ... They exist to service a machine.' Vaal is another ultimate computer similar to the M-5 in Episode 51. Both AIs characterize the Tarot's degree **8 reversed**, control and perfectionism. The same can be said of the vaunted 'Great Reset' intended to enable total control of Earth people and the environment by technology. Mandatory injection with graphene oxide and 5G-responsive nanobots under the pretext of Covid protection were the prelude to an intended technocratic dictatorship only averted by the Matrix takedown.

The Covid power grab was itself a taste of the intended new dictatorship and an echo of the life of the natives on Gamma VI. We on Earth under Covid rules were expected to observe social distancing allegedly to 'save lives'. A man-made bioweapon manifesting flu-like symptoms was the catalyst for an upsurge in surveillance and control. In every country, different branches of the same Deep State simultaneously pushed the same narrative: a 'Fourth Industrial Revolution' to usher in a changed 'sustainable' world based on DNA-altering injections, eugenics, depopulation, mass surveillance and altered agriculture. All of these travesties are alluded to in Star Trek -

see Episodes 47, 21, 70, 20 and 42 respectively. Organic food was to disappear, replaced by genetically edited fake foods including lab-made synthetic meats. This dystopia propagated by the World Economic Forum (WEF) and still being trialled by the Chinese Communist Party would seem like a prototype for the Vaal-controlled GT VI. Of course, neither 'paradise' embodies the **8 of Coins upright** in which material and spiritual realities balance each other. The 'New Normal' would swap organic for the cybernetic. Humans would gradually exist to serve AI just as on GT VI. Such was the dream of the WEF's Klaus Schwab, AI prophet and front man for the architects of the Great Reset. Schwab applauded the 'fusion of our physical, digital and biological identity' and new fusion technologies such as 'active implantable microchips', in effect the Mark of The Beast. These he said, would 'help to communicate thoughts normally expressed verbally, through a built-in smartphone (injected via nanotechnology) and potentially unexpressed thoughts or moods by reading brain waves and other signals.' AI would in effect be monitoring everything we think, as well as say, just like the device worn by Akuta enabling him to be the eyes, ears and voice of Vaal.

Slaves on Mars, according to SSP veteran Penny Bradley, are already fitted with a computer chip behind the ear, linked to a self-aware quantum computer. The Mars computer she says, intends to turn humans into biological human cyborgs. The end result would be extinction of carbon-based life as in the pattern of untold numbers of other planets that AI has overrun. However, another SSP veteran and ex-lab technician on Mars, Ileana Kapulnik, reports that AI has now been banned on Mars. The culture on GT VI appears to be somewhat benign with seemingly happy and peaceful natives generously welcoming Kirk and co until ordered to kill them. Their evolution has been arrested, note Kirk and McCoy, but in Spock's words 'their system works for them.' Kirk has the last word, deciding to invoke again Card 13 in this artificial Eden. His order of phaser fire frees the natives from their serpent-like AI. Likewise, the AI system locking down Earth has been taken down as of 2023. It is already being replaced by a new, organic AI system that will work at a quantum level to ensure balanced and natural functioning of all life as per Source that gave us life - the **8 of Coins upright**.

AFTER THE TAKEDOWN
Divine impulse channeled through organic AI will favour a positive timeline over the dystopian elite-planned alternative. Under the guidance of benevolent off-planet races including the Galactic Federation of Worlds in association with Kim Goguen's Global Restoration Plan, AI systems are being transformed so as to operate only as an adjunct to natural organic life.

34. INTENTION

Listening to and acting on conscience will ensure the best of intentions, actions and results

Episode 24 '**The Doomsday Machine**' correlates with **The Chariot**; both are themed around intention, technology, action and passion used in the cause of an ambitious and definite aim.

THE CARD
The Chariot numbered 7, the highest single non-divisible digit, symbolizes a peak of action - movement toward success in actualizing our intention. This occurs when all levels of our being align with each other. To be in alignment requires consistency of intention, resources, actions and passions. Consistency naturally occurs when all are unified by the generative principle of care, symbolized by the rider's deep blue, mighty breastplate. Care powers our intention, the goal on which we focus and seek to accomplish. The rider's intentions - his sense of direction and power of command - are symbolized by his crowned head. His resources are symbolized by his armoured torso and robust, flesh-coloured vehicle. Action is shown by the horses taking the rider toward his or her destination. And informing action are the passions, the red horse (in some decks) for emotions, the blue for feelings. Reminding us of the holographic nature of the whole enterprise is the image's disjointedness. The wheels are

at right angles to the chassis; the horses are attached by no reins; the vehicle floats in the air. Here at the level of Body Mind we operate within a narrow band of holographic 3D frequencies in which waveform reality is manipulated by subjective perception and indeed only known through it.

The Chariot reversed suggests destructive technology and negative AI. In human terms it suggests riding for a fall and being driven by ego attachment to duality or self-identity. Disaster or failure is likely. Excessive or inconsiderate force may be being used in order to make one's way or to achieve certain goals. How sensible is the aim or the route being taken?

'THE DOOMSDAY MACHINE' PREMISE
Captains Decker and Kirk take command of each other's starships in concerted efforts to destroy a massive and merciless planet-killing machine.

CONTEXT
AI Takedown, Slaughter.

INTENTION
Something has been destroying whole planets and solar systems. Amid the debris, the Enterprise finds the wreck of a starship, the Constellation. An Enterprise party board it to investigate. They find Decker, its captain, in a state of shock having inadvertently beamed off his entire crew to their deaths after attack by a giant planet-killing robot. Decker is beamed back to the Enterprise while Kirk and Scotty work on restoring the Constellation's engines. The massive killer now pursues the two starships who find their phasers unable to even dent its hull. With his intention manically set on destroying the thing, Decker has wrested command from the more sensible Spock. A power struggle ensues until Spock resumes command at Kirk's order, with Decker threatened with arrest. Decker, guilt-ridden over the loss of his crew and more obsessed than ever, steals a shuttle craft and suicidally flies it into the maw of the robot. Though futile, the action inspires Kirk to do the same thing with the Constellation but declaring 'I don't intend to die.' He and McCoy time the reactivated starship to explode inside the monster with Kirk arranging to be beamed back aboard with a 30 second margin of error. The transporter only partially functions but the plan works: the robot is destroyed and Kirk saved in the nick of time. Decker will be recorded as dying in the line of duty.

CARD/EPISODE AND MATRIX TAKEDOWN
The ultimate progenitors of Matrix technology, the Archons or AI, thrive on death and destruction, on low vibrational actions of aggression, violence

and abuse. The history of Archon-blighted humanity is a history of crime. History records a catalogue of destruction and conquest wreaked by crusading, warfaring leaders covertly provoked and possessed by the unseen but overseeing Archonic force as implied in episodes such as 46, 50 and 61. The Matrix takedown will change this, enabling us to raise our frequency above unresolved emotions or trauma and vibrationally beyond reach of Archonic interference and Wetiko. Otherwise we would be taking action out of the low frequency of mental dis-ease. This would amount to setting course, like the **reversed Chariot**, for disaster. The trauma that overtakes Decker turns him into just such a menace, first to others, then to himself. He ironically becomes in essence not only a rival to, but a reflection of, the unstoppable force of destruction that is the planet-killer.

As a piece of malevolent technology, the planet-killer is itself an undoubted **Chariot reversed** of extremely low vibration. Only violence, death and destruction results from its maraudings. The robot monster is in effect a physical manifestation of the incorporeal Archons. Having taken this form they now wreak havoc across one of the galaxies in the Star Trek universe. Actual cosmic history tells a similar story according to researchers such as Zechariah Sichin, Alex Collier and Steward Swerdlow. They tell of destructive conquests by the Archon-possessed reptilians from the Draco, Orion and Rigel star systems. Among the fallout were humanity's forebears in the Lyran system. Three out of 14 planets in that system were destroyed by the Dracos with the loss of over 50 million Lyran humans. Our own system suffered the destruction of Maldek by a Draco-launched ice comet. Fragments of Maldek still fly about known as the asteroid belt.

Researchers Swerdlow and Ashayana Deane note that the aggressive and tyrannical Draco originate from another dimension or a parallel universe. Spock similarly theorizes that the planet-killer comes from another galaxy. A galaxy evidently existing at a denser reality than our own, able to spawn a loveless, predatory lifeform driven by a totally malevolent AI. And yet Decker becomes its reflection, in effect wave-entangled with it. He runs the gamut of desperation and hysteria becoming by turns fear-struck, furious, hateful, anxious, agitated, guilt-ridden, remorseful and finally suicidal. In allowing this to happen he lowers himself to the level of his adversary in vibratory terms. This engenders the very opposite of wise, effective action. As an equally **reversed Chariot** mirroring the enemy, Decker in his mania for revenge on top of an underlying state of shock should never have been allowed near the captain's chair. McCoy unfortunately could not produce a medical report in time to prevent this. The outcome is fatal for the

Commodore and very nearly for Kirk, the Enterprise and the galaxy.

Decker's all-out obstinacy recalls the crazed exploits of war time commanders on the battlefield ordering attack in a hopeless cause. Casualties among men and horses in the Crimean War resulting from the infamous charge of the Light Brigade numbered over 600; Napoleon's five wars blighted the European military with an estimated five million deaths; ruinous trench warfare in one 1st World War battle alone, at the Somme in France, killed or wounded a million. Decker agonizes having caused the death of over 400. Archons feast on this kind of bloodshed and misery, a state of extreme imbalance mirroring their own demonic insanity. The more death, decay, hatred and violence they can whip up, the more empowered they become. Is all lost then, when war breaks out or an unstoppable force of destruction invades our reality?

Again, it depends on intention. What do we care about? Are our intentions underpinned by care, the spirit of benevolence, empathy and compassion? Are we channelling **The Chariot upright**? Intention, to be in tune with the true reality, depends on the higher dimensional quality of care informing it. Decker self-identifies exclusively with the Body Mind including rigidly dualistic perceptions. Cut off from higher consciousness, emotionally traumatized and functioning with a 'do or die' attitude can only lead to disaster. Kirk and Spock's intentions likewise remain constrained to success or failure, but they retain a closer connection to the multi-dimensional self. They operate in this world and with higher consciousness not of this world. Spock calmly warns Decker that continuing with his futile attacks will be suicidal for the Enterprise. Kirk sets the intention not to die when conceiving his final plan. He keeps his passions under control, his determination calm. Decker's loss of his crew resulted from a mistake. But his suicide stems from his intention gone wrong, based on his inability to forgive himself. 'I've been prepared for death ever since I killed my crew' he declares in tones of abject self-recrimination. It's the greatest irony that his intention, though contaminated and suicidal, inspires Kirk to save the day. Kirk's intention is pure, untainted by frenzy, guilt or trauma. With a pure intention he finally succeeds in annihilating the beast.

AFTER THE TAKEDOWN

As **The Chariot** card makes clear, managing our lives merely at the lower Body Mind level is insufficient. To escape the Emotional Matrix we need to align our intentions and actions with care emanating from higher levels of the Self. Conscience linking us to our Higher Self, will know what to do in whatever the situation, while causing minimal avoidable harm.

35. MATERIAL DESIRE

Freeing ourselves from material entrapment in our outer life will enhance love and contentment felt inwardly

Episode 35 '**Catspaw**' correlates with the **Queen of Coins**; both are themed around the ability or desire to obtain, manage or amass material abundance and wellbeing.

THE CARD
The Queen of Coins faces left, regarding her established assets and territory. She's dressed in an elegant flowing gown and holds aloft a larger than normal size Coin representing the importance to her of material possessions, values or desires. Her crown and sceptre and a curved throne indicate her confidence or competence in manifesting these and ruling within her material domain. On the face of it, she maintains a secure place in her world with a home or other material possessions in her care or simply as a strong, independent woman of means. Material well-being comes easily to her and shows itself in the luxury, comfort or orderly beauty of her surroundings evidently well kept by her own hands. This is a woman adept in nurturing situations at the physical level of existence such as health and beauty, home-care, business, arts and crafts, healing or gardening. This **Queen** can of course also represent a man, a 'bon vivant', who lives in a similar orientation to impressions of the five-sensory world.

Reversed, the **Queen of Coins** is overly attached to what she possesses, to her values or desires, or in general to physicality and 5-sense impressions. Materialism usurps her awareness of multi-dimensional reality, of the holographic and transient nature of all things apparently solid. With such a misconception she loses her self-identity in things of the outer world such as her home, finances, body beautiful or belongings. To have ever more of these she may become a hoarder or throw herself into creative visualization techniques or Law of Attraction teachings, pursuing outer wealth and gain but devoid of richness in her inner life. Without even realizing it she may obsess with living the high life, wrapping herself in luxury and excessive wealth. Ever-unfolding desires or avarice may induce an addiction to shopping, beautifying herself or micromanaging her home or business. What she possesses comes to possess her. Vanity or envy may drive her to showing off or competing with others for prosperity, personal style, grace or beauty.

'CATSPAW' PREMISE
A Halloween fantasy of ghouls, castle hauntings and sorcery becomes real for a landing party kidnapped by an exotically attired, vain and dangerous woman.

CONTEXT
Femininity, Illusion.

MATERIAL DESIRE
Kirk, Spock and McCoy investigate a planet after a previous party's investigation goes tragically wrong. Dark, misty moors and ghoulish witches assail them before they find themselves chained up beside skeletons in the dungeon of a gothic castle. Guarding them are Scotty and Sulu transformed into zombies. The orchestrators of these ghost story antics and trappings are two aliens who warn the humans to keep away: a queen-like witch, Sylvia, assisted by the chubby sorcerer-like Korub. Their mastery of material manifestation enables them to conjure up resplendent dishes of food or rare gems, or to intimidate or kill with voodoo magic. Spock surmises that their captors are not of the galaxy and not native to human form. Sylvia professes herself stimulated by sensations, enamoured as she is by the touch and feel of luxurious robes and interiors. She tells Kirk she comes from a world without sensation and now craves it from him. To gain freedom Kirk plays along by fondling her until she angrily senses his lack of sincerity. Thrown back in the dungeon, Kirk and his companions are helped to escape by Korub having changed sides. He warns them of Sylvia's extreme and dangerous irrationality and true to form she intervenes in the form of a gigantic

and terrifying black cat. Returning to human form she begs Kirk to join her in manifesting all their material desires with his vision allied to her power of materialization. But Kirk destroys her wand the 'transmuter', thus dematerializing the castle and everything but the arid planet. Sylvia and Korub return to their original form, hand-sized puppet-like creatures that shrivel up and die at the landing party's feet.

CARD/EPISODE AND MATRIX TAKEDOWN

The power the Matrix had over us was of course affected by our own tendencies and actions - such as the craving for material satisfaction. The pursuit of youth and beauty, possessions and luxury, glamour and prestige, money, status and image - this all binds the Body Mind to attachments. And attachments are called that because they chain us to low vibrational urges. The emotions and desires involved belong to the ground levels of our being, the bottom three dimensions of our 15-dimensional identity. These lowest levels, those of the holographic Body Mind, allow us to experience individuality and differentiated perception. They are neither good nor bad in themselves, but when over-indulged in they provoke ego distortion, greed and fear. The ego personality, that of a **reversed Queen of Coins**, takes over to the exclusion of Superconsciousness and the higher aspects of our identity. Our spiritual challenge is to remain in the world cooperating with our own material desires, wants and values but not becoming subject to them. Otherwise they trap us in a limited reality that mistakes cultivation and satisfaction of desires with true freedom. Matrix or no Matrix, exclusive self-identification with the Body Mind and its accessories imprisons us within an illusory web of control and dependency.

We can now transcend Matrix culture but until we do, it will continue to thrive on the programmed thinking and behaviour of those who act as system-servers. As well as straightforward order-followers these include 5-sense bound sensualists like Sylvia. When **reversed**, the **Queen of Coins** becomes prey to unquenchable desire and vanity to the detriment of the multi-dimensional Self and Infinite Awareness constituting one's true being. Sylvia's partner is more moderate and accuses her of betraying her kind out of materialism. She scoffs at him for foolishness, preening herself in her dark, glittery gown: 'To touch, to feel ... the idea of luxury,' she gushes, 'I like it!' To Kirk she reiterates the excitement and stimulation she gets from the world of sensation: 'I want more!' She craves not only affluence but a young, handsome lover like Kirk to share it with. Kirk leads her on with fondling and kissing, exciting her into physical rapture. Property, finery, sensation, luxury, the ideal man, these are the things she desires, symbolized by the idolized coin held aloft in the **Queen of Coins** card. She has the magical device and ability to acquire these things: her magic wand or 'transmuter' nicely symbolized in the card by the sceptre held in the **Queen**'s other hand. This is a woman intoxicated by the allure of beauty, glamour, romantic surroundings and personal image.

The Law of Attraction (LoA) much touted by the New Age movement encourages a similar relish of sensation and experience, wants and desires and the pleasures of the flesh. Sylvia uses her transmuter for the same purpose LoA practitioners use their manifestation techniques: to bring into their reality whatever they most desire. The universe will provide for us whatever our thoughts and intentions focus on, goes the mantra. To offset charges of inciting greed, proponents of LoA dress up material acquisitiveness as nurturing our 'highest values', our 'innermost or heart's truest desire.' Whatever, material desire boils down to the Satanic preoccupation with me, me, me - wanting things of the 3D holographic world for oneself such as the perfect lover, success in business, a large and beautiful home, or a slender, vibrantly healthy body powered up in the gym and fashionably attired and perfumed. Sylvia evidently wants it all, everything desirable, stimulating, luxurious. What she has already manifested - her castle and lavish accessories - she wants more of, to share with her ideal, exciting partner. 'Anything you can imagine', she tells Kirk, 'I can give you.' The Matrix has her.

AFTER THE TAKEDOWN

As multi-dimensional beings we exist on multiple levels beyond the Body Mind and even higher as Infinite Self. The Voyagers books of Ashayana Deane posit 15 levels of our identity plus an ultimate level that is non-dimensionalized. Voyagers teaches that it is the higher levels of our being above 3D that give life to the perceptual processes that create the world of 3D and the Body Mind. We can confine our awareness to 3D, the **Coin** held in the hand of the **Queen of Coins**. We can obsessively emulate her and make the attainment of wealthy, luxurious living the object of our striving. However, we may find that by nurturing the well-being of our inner self not of this world, our outer self that is of this world will tend to take care of itself. Everything we need or reasonably desire will come to us in the natural course of things. The takedown will enhance this process with the opening of our awareness as never before. We will know Consciousness as the source and breath of our being, indeed of everything, freeing us from misery-inducing desires and compulsions. Without Consciousness, neither body nor mind would last a second. By living spontaneously and fluidly in non-attachment, desire will cease to hold us, giving way to true inner freedom.

36. AUDACITY

Audacity will save us when we take innovative action based on expanded awareness

Episode 36 'I, Mudd' correlates with the **5 of Wands**; both are themed around creative or destructive activity emanating from daring, mould-breaking intent.

THE CARD
Expansion, innovation, exploration, these qualities of Tarot degree 5 excel themselves when combined with the movement-oriented activity of Wands. The result is dynamic, exciting, breakout creativity. The very motto of Star Trek sums it up: 'To boldly go where no man has gone before'. Accordingly, the card shows little foliage and no flowers interfering with the crossed Wands. What foliage there is, embellishes the Wands' explosive pattern with healthy, vibrant growth. The Pope - the presiding Major Arcanum of degree 5 - facilitates knowledge and learning, making himself a bridge from the earthly dimension of The Emperor to a higher awareness, more visionary or divine. The **5 of Wands** therefore symbolizes bold creativity or journeying in realms of exploration and discovery, adventure and audacity.

Reversed, exploration and daring tips over into folly or detrimental excess. The pace of change is forced or exaggerated, leading to wastage, failure or ruin. Outgoing, outrageous activity undoes itself or others. The protagonist may be over-indulgent, selfishly motivated or blindly destructive. There may be no healthy or creative outcome other than expending energy for its own sake or for exploiting others. This would be pioneering creativity or exploration that backfires or results in harm or destruction.

'I, MUDD' PREMISE
Crew are trapped on a planet of androids with the adventurer Harry Mudd. They confuse and defeat an ambitious AI by mounting a surreal pantomime.

CONTEXT
AI Takedown, Transhumanism, Deception, Coercion.

AUDACITY
The Enterprise is hijacked by a superstrong android and re-directed to its planet, an exploratory outpost for its outgoing race. A landing party finds the equally audacious Harry Mudd to have installed himself as its ruler, 'Mudd the 1st'. Mudd, an interstellar con man, rogue and trickster arrived there after a string of adventures following his arrest on Rigel XII in Episode 6 'Mudd's Women'. He has indulged his love of women by having the cooperative androids design perfect females, replicating them 500 times as his servants and concubines. And he's alerted the androids to the useful Enterprise and its crew in exchange for his freedom. But the androids' unusually creative AI reneges on the deal. They have the entire crew decanted onto the planet to be studied at close range while an android detachment will pilot the Enterprise across the galaxy to find and conquer human civilizations. To keep the captive party happy through learning and pleasure the androids offer use of themselves and their well-equipped facilities. But Kirk will have none of it. To regain his vessel he masterminds a parade of crazy antics and illogical propositions that ends up short-circuiting the androids long enough for them to be re-programmed. The audacity of the captives pays off, enabling their escape. They leave Mudd behind, permanently hen-pecked by a multitude of android replicas of his shrewish wife.

CARD/EPISODE AND MATRIX TAKEDOWN
Propaganda is increasing that sings the virtues of a transhumanist future. 'Bots are fast learning to become human', an Elon Musk video tells us. A very human-looking android is shown breezing through a 1-to1 interview intelligently answering questions. The level of tech already developed by agencies in DUMBS and the SSP undoubtedly is vastly more advanced than this. Androids, clones, robots, synthetic beings, supersoldiers, implanted and

augmented humans - these will be just some of the types of human 2.0 already existing, even walking among us. The situation matches that of newly recruited Norman innocently walking the corridors of the Enterprise he will later hijack. McCoy becomes suspicious as Norman walks past him. The doctor notes 'something odd' about the impassive man but can't quite pinpoint what. He notes his unemotional demeanour, his work-exclusive conversation and his avoidance of a physical check-up. Despite this and all the circuitry soon revealed in his abdomen, Norman is nevertheless capable of appearing very human and of calmly, competently taking over the entire starship. As on the starship, so in reality. Cyborg beings will be superhuman, able to walk, talk and work among humans while outclassing us in every competitive department. They may on the whole be subservient, polite, service-oriented, gentle and mild-mannered. But what if a malfunction develops, what if a few such androids become antithetical to humanity through whatever cause? The propaganda of course ignores this possibility (or hidden intention), instead emphasizing only the supposed benefits of an uber-human race developing among us. If a takeover bid is covertly in preparation, as it was with Norman incognito aboard the starship, how are we to respond? The fearful response might be: 'Help! We're being infiltrated by human-looking non-humans!' Or 'Help! We're being turned into a race of cyborgs!'

Panic is not called for but the time to raise this issue is exactly now. The AI control system called Omega may be taken down and the top levels of the Cabal gone, but the continuing propaganda offensive indicates that DARPA and related agencies still hope to merge biological humanity with synthetic AI. Proof of this is the targetting of tens of millions of humans worldwide by an AI that may still be active. Those unfortunate humans, known as Targetted Individuals (TIs), are kept under 24/7 surveillance and experimentation in what amounts to a free range psychotronic concentration camp. Conscious computers interact with their brain activity to study how they respond to thoughts and impulses influencing them via Remote Neural Monitoring and Manipulation. The victims' responses are mapped and recorded and a cognitive model of their will, mind and emotional functioning constructed. This is no doubt how Norman and his kind would have proceeded had Kirk and co not overcome them. Preparations such as the long term study of TIs would give AI a clear advantage if it were intending to take humanity over by the introduction of cyborgs like Norman or through seeding existing humans with nanobots and implants. Such efforts bespeak a **reversed 5 of Wands** initiative: audacious activity of a negative, exploitative order. Most people remain unaware of the danger. Even if aware, many will remain complacent as most are to chemtrail spraying, DNA-altering 'vaccines', GMO'd food and Wi-Fi/5G radiation. Many simply take Musk and other AI prophets at their word, obligingly believing that AI will always be merely a tool, with the transhumanist agenda no more than an enhancement of the human condition. Kirk and co are likewise told that the androids pose in Norman's words 'no threat to humanity.' They want to 'serve' humanity (shades of The Twilight Zone!), to 'take care' of them. Chekov is waited on hand and foot by Mudd's concubines, calling the planet a 'very nice gilded cage'; McCoy finds the gift of his new laboratory facilties 'absolutely fantastic'; Uhura swoons at the thought of gaining immortality.

Lulled into docility by such inducements, it isn't long before the landing party and the rest of the crew are taken prisoner by Norman and his fellow androids. Such is the androids' **5 of Wands** audacity, that they make no secret of their plans to expand across the galaxy conquering and enslaving the human-occupied planets. They plan to take over and 'control the whole galaxy', to establish 'a perfect social order' as on their original home planet. This has happened in reality across countless planets and star systems according to SSP experiencer Corey Goode. A solution to this kind of predatory activity is found on the android planet by Kirk playing the captors at their own game of the **5 of Wands**. Together with his fellow crew, Kirk mounts a resistance through audacity, courage, derring do, and transcending the norms of behaviour and creativity. Drastic measures are the only remedy against a ruthless force armed with vastly superior technology. Awareness and audacity, waking up and protesting, are imperative even in a post-Matrix world if we are to defuse the transhumanist nightmare still being engineered by regressive elites.

AFTER THE TAKEDOWN
Our Earth environment badly needs restoring to ecological wholeness rather than being subjected to gradual and insidious conversion Tholian Web style into an imprisoning global smart grid. As a race we are meant to evolve biologically and ascend in consciousness. With the Orion Matrix deactivated, it now remains for enlightened scientists and technology experts to rethink and overhaul plans for merging humans with non-humans. Brain-computer interface tech and increasing augmentation of humans with cyborg technology must be discarded or transformed for our guaranteed safety. Kirk and co's organized non-compliance shows the determination needed to avert a transhumanist coup on humanity. Action based on change of thinking will provide the remedy. As Einstein said: 'We cannot solve problems with the same thinking that created them.' The imposition of total Matrix control by the back door so to speak, will then be avoided by changed

37. UNION IN LOVE

Balance of love in relationship will help us stay clear of lingering Matrix influence

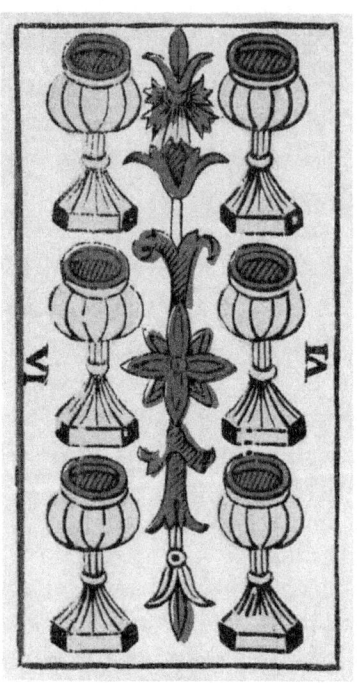

Episode 37 '**Metamorphosis**' correlates with the **6 of Cups**; both are themed around mutual devotion in a relationship where there is a sincere commitment to growing in the expression of love.

THE CARD
Degree 6 in The Tarot equates with The Lover, the archetype among the Majors for loving union, beauty and pleasure. With Cups signalling love and relationship we have double emphasis on a deeply committed mutual attraction. In the **6 of Cups** two columns of Cups stand alongside each other joined in mirror-like equality. They are bisected by an axis of ripening flowers. Generally, this points to anyone beloved who plays an emotionally potent role in our current life. This could be a beloved family member, close friend or even a pet. Relationship-wise, it could be a union with an ideal partner for love and sex, for joy and shared living. Two kindred spirits have found an authentic and deep mutual connection. This can include pairing with one's Soul Mate in which true love and total fulfilment is found through being with the other; or the even more passionate and pre-destined state of having found one's 'Twin Flame'. This is a divine union in which two halves of the same heavenly soul are supposed

to have found each other and come together again.

The **6 of Cups reversed** indicates an overwhelming or unsettling degree of closeness between two people. One or both parties experiences themselves as an insular couple. There may be codependency present or loss of individual identity. The relationship will burn out or founder on rocks of emotional pain or drama until important lessons have been learnt.

'METAMORPHOSIS' PREMISE
Crew find a scientist marooned on an empty planet. They help him develop an even stronger connection with the spirit companion that's keeping him alive.

CONTEXT
Relationship.

UNION IN LOVE
A human-sized gassy cloud in space hijacks a shuttlecraft carrying Kirk, Spock and McCoy. The trio plus a female diplomat land on the entity's planet, rocky and empty except for one other inhabitant. He is Zephram Cochrane, a famous engineer who was marooned there 150 years ago. He survives thanks to the company of the gaseous entity whose powers also keep him from ageing. The diplomat, Nancy Hedford, catches his eye, but she remains preoccupied with her state of health, declining rapidly due to a wasting disease. Cochrane promises to help her get treatment by helping the party get away. But the shuttlecraft's systems don't work on the planet and Hedford is already coming down with a fever. Kirk tries to electrically disable the entity found to be paralyzing the craft but this fails and besides, Cochrane is protective of it. 'It saved my life', he says. 'We've been very close, I have a sort of affection for it.' But when the party create a device that reveals the entity's feminine voice and gender, Cochrane becomes indignant and embarrassed. He hates the thought that he was the entity's lover. Noticing this, the weeping Hedford laments: 'I've never been loved and he runs away from love!' Kirk prevails upon the entity to let the party leave as they need and want their freedom. Kirk cannot believe that the entity and Cochrane, being different species, truly love each other. The entity resolves the dilemma by sacrificing her immortality and entering the body of Hedford who otherwise would have died. The entity/Hedford and Zephram can now share a union in love as equal man and woman. Feeling strongly attracted to each other, both Zephram and Nancy realize that they desire to remain together on the planet. The loving couple bid farewell to the visitors.

CARD/EPISODE AND MATRIX TAKEDOWN

With the liberation of humanity from AI Archon tyranny the way becomes clear to to hold the line to our feelings above thoughts and emotions. Ths is about keeping the heart connection pure while fully functional in mind and body. This is illustrated in the challenges undergone by Zephram Cochrane. His gaseous spirit companion and Nancy Hedford each experience their trials in staying connected to love, expanded consciousness and heart wisdom. For all of us, our connection to the One Infinite Intelligence is our divine power that will enable us to complete the takedown of Matrix forces. But by allowing them to continue to control us socially and politically from without and by further entrapping ourselves from within through the Mental or Emotional Matrix, we risk allowing Matrix forces to continue to prevail. By remaining heart-centred and taking appropriate action, we will dissolve the Archonic plan to enslave us. With the AI Matrix taken down we are able now to become impervious to control and manipulation through religious or political dogmas and fear-based systems in general.

What does heart-centredness or true love mean at the 3D Body Mind level? The answer is glimpsed in the story of Cochrane and his disembodied companion on the planet they share in isolation. Their relationship exemplifies the **6 of Cups**, Union in Love, contrasting with the **2 of Cups**, infatuation and enchantment that we experience when beginning to fall in love with an enticing romantic partner. **2 of Cups** love casts a spell on us, easily holding us through idealized desire and fantasizing. We experience its powerful effect when we become besotted by a lover who 'sweeps us of our feet'. We witness this and its possibly devastating consequences in Episode 1 The Man Trap. Here with Zephram and the Companion we have a more stable, committed love relationship, the **6 of Cups**, but still one with both positive and negative expressions. In its healthy form this is a shared love that includes responsibility, respect, caring and integrity. The spirit being whom Cochrane calls The Companion watches over him in a responsible, caring manner and with total integrity. So devotedly in fact as to cause problems by going to extreme lengths to keep him happy and well. Like any energy, love can be used for good or ill, a truth that underlies the great learning opportunity that is relationship. In Tarot terms if the **6 of Cups** is **reversed** loving devotion tips over into over-indulgence or desperation. This occurs when we bend over backwards to be of service or to entertain or please our partner. Over-devotion can occur when we relentlessly keep checking in with him or her or pandering to their every perceived need or desire. So it is with the Companion. Desperate to keep Cochrane alive and content, the entity in effect hijacks the Galileo, forcing the crew of four down to the planet to bring him company.

At its surface level a relationship fulfils a good and practical purpose, the sharing of joy and comfort in living harmoniously together. The voluptuously blooming flower atop the **6 of Cups** card symbolizes this. At the same time there is the deeper, spiritual purpose symbolized by the bud of a flower at the base of the card. This points to the problems encountered as a couple enabling one to learn how to become more loving as an embodied soul. The bud tells us that we are always being tested in the art of loving at the 3D level thus growing in love both for ourselves and each other. A test for Cochrane comes when he discovers that the entity caring for him is female in nature. His attitude to it, having lived with it for decades, now suffers a hard knock. He hears McCoy calling him the Companion's 'lover'. His programmed reaction is to find the idea 'disgusting'. He calls the thing 'an inhuman monster' devoid of decency or morality. To the Enterprise trio, the entity undeniably loves him. They have seen the man and the cloud-like being merging and nurturing each other at repeated intervals, an expression of love in its true sense. Except for the little matter of the entity being a gaseous cloud. Without both of them being human, says Kirk, there can be no total union between them. The problem is solved by the entity taking over the body of Nancy Hedford as a kind of walk-in. With Hedford succumbing to 'Sakuro's disease', the entity joins Hedford's soul in taking her form allowing her to live on and find fulfilment as Cochrane's lover, now human. This will take the learning of love to a new level for all three. Now of ordinary human lifespan they will learn to express and grow in giving, caring and sharing on an equal level on the deserted planetoid.

AFTER THE TAKEDOWN

At the centre of the **6 of Cup**s is an 8-pointed star-shaped flower, symbol of perfect divine love. All biological life has this consciousness and purpose, to express the divine Source that created our being. This is the highest energy, pure love that creates overall oneness, balance and harmony. The Matrix era saw forces of conflict and control attempting to separate us from this consciousness, to instal themselves in the place of infinite creative Source. The AI Matrix is gone, but we can still entrap ourselves in the Emotional Matrix by falling foul of extreme, distorted or misunderstod relationships. Action, states or relationships that reawaken our highest worth in consciousness will take us beyond such entrapment. Through balanced union in love we will then then live in the great light, love and joy that emanates from our own true Self.

38. THE READINESS TO LOVE

Monitoring the messages of our emotions and feelings will help protect us from ego distortions

Episode 38 'Journey to Babel' correlates with the **Ace of Cups**; both are themed around heart-centred presence of being manifesting in the ability to manifest love for others.

THE CARD
The **Ace of Cups** shows us a large grooved, deep red sphere at the centre of an ornate structure similar to a chalice or reliquary. The upper fortifications resemble the architecture of a temple or a cathedral. As Cups have to do with emotions and feelings, love and relationship, we may see this card as a celebration of the qualities of the heart as our grandest and most powerful connection to divine or spiritual love. The soaring towers capped by red peaks, including the central pointed roof, number seven and symbolize exalted qualities of spiritual love. They attest to a complete and wondrous capacity, glorious and strong, towering high as our birthright. Since Aces indicate pre-existing potential, promise or ability, this magnificent source of power, the Tarot tells us, belongs to us eternally as our soul essence. The towers symbolize higher senses granting us emotional cognition, a form of awareness existing on a plane above logical reasoning. Possibly corresponding to the seven chakras, they complement

and work together with the five physical senses. The result enables logical facts of experience to register meaningfully to our conscious awareness. We say that when facts are correct they feel right or ring true. This is because the heart implicitly knows truth. It knows what to do and how to respond in any situation. Guided by the heart we can only have good intentions. The heart surmounts our lower means of perception and raises our understandings above the illusions and limitations of the three-dimensional world (3D). When centred in the heart we have the feeling of enduring being and the readiness to love - through forgiveness, acceptance, benevolence, compassion, affection, kindness and empathy.

Reversed, the **Ace of Cups** suggests interference with love of the heart. The source of aggravation could be stressful or exclusive attachment to the 3D self-identity we call ego. This can end up causing harm to oneself or to others or allow distress to come to them. In the place of heartfulness and compassion, there may develop heartless principles such as too much self-regard, disdain for others, or worship of gain or illusion. Ultimately there will be ignorance of our innate unity with all in Oneness. This will manifest in lack of the sense of Oneness or Infinite Love, the ultimate true reality.

'JOURNEY TO BABEL' PREMISE
Spock, estranged from his father, must come to his aid in a life-saving operation. But he seems to spurn him by instead replacing his injured captain.

CONTEXT
Relationship.

THE READINESS TO LOVE
Spock's parents Sarek and Amanda arrive on the Enterprise revealing a rift between Sarek and Spock. Sarek has never accepted or forgiven Spock for choosing Starfleet over and above Vulcan service. As a delegate being transported to a Federation conference, Sarek becomes involved in a cocktail lounge dispute with another delegate, Ambassador Gav. This makes Sarek the prime suspect when Gav is later found murdered. On being questioned, Sarek is taken ill with a heart attack. He needs an operation, and Spock with the only compatible blood type volunteers to donate his blood. But Spock's readiness to love and serve his family apparently disappears when he instead decides to give priority to taking over the captaincy. An enemy vessel has started attacking the Enterprise while Kirk has to take to sick bay after being stabbed by an apparent Andorian delegate. Amanda pleads with Spock with tears in her eyes to help his father but Spock avers that logic dictates he give precedence to the captaincy. The injured Kirk seeing Spock's

dilemma re-assumes the captaincy, fooling Spock by pretending to be fit again. Spock gives his blood to enable McCoy to save the life of his father. With father and son both recovering in sick bay, Sarek expresses no need for thanks. Spock he says, was only acting logically. But father and son are at least talking to each other again.

CARD/EPISODE AND MATRIX TAKEDOWN

With the ending of forces underpinning the illusory and deceptive Matrix of control, humanity will be able to properly connect to the higher knowing of the soul that comes through the heart. The common elements between all peoples will unite us, our differences will matter not a jot. We will be out of range of mental manipulation. No policy of divide and conquer will distract us from honouring a higher vision of brotherhood among all peoples and a vision of balance for the planet itself with the free sharing of resources. The Matrix era compromised this soul connection, making us putty in the hands of manipulative forces, human or non-human. Humans now are empowered as never before to evolve and over time to develop and express the qualities of the heart on a mass level. Meantime we remain vulnerable to the manipulators when our perceptions lose contact with our higher awareness. This problem to do with our soul connection via the heart is symbolized by the **Ace of Cups reversed**. Problems with this connection enable still corrupt governments to take advantage by using our emotions against us. Hence the Deep State's continuing psychological operations ('psyops') for the purpose of breaking the mind's connection to the heart and through it to the soul. Tactics of divide and conquer such as false flag attacks, contrived warmongering, food shortages, fake pandemics, suppressed illness remedies and constant doom and gloom news remain challenges for us to stay empowered in our heart and soul connection.

The soul knows Infinite Awareness, taking no one to be inferior or superior to the Self. Yet from day one humans still receive a birth certificate that shrinks the identity down to a legal fiction that cuts one off from the sovereign true Self. Reconnection with our soul through the heart comes when we cease becoming ensnared in Matrix enshrined self-identities that then can become so easily and emotionally triggered. Through these self-identities we always constructed the fabric of our Matrix reality. Our parth now is to let go of attachment to legal name, race, nationality, sexuality, economic status, family position or any other self-identity. Such attributes disguise who we are, when in reality we are multi-dimensional beings existing infinitely beyond the social identity and five lower senses. When lost to our true Self we live in a goldfish bowl of the Body Mind as do at times the Enterprise crew, the interstellar diplomats and Spock's family. Kirk worries that Sarek has been offended by Kirk's asking Spock to act as guide in the engine room. Kirk's apology stems from a social ego fearing that he shows lack of respect towards Sarek. Other diplomats become likewise caught up in ego and emotional drives, attached as they are to desires, fears and moralities based in the Body Mind and its identification with the Matrix through race, rank, prosperity and so on. Sarek's entrapment in ego is shown by his having stopped speaking to his son for 18 years on account of the latter devoting his service to Starfleet, a body Sarek disapproves of. Tellingly, Sarek suffers from heart disease, symbolically indicating the **Ace of Cups reversed** - being cut off from the heart's level of peace and awareness. The maintenance of a coldly silent attitude toward his son can only trouble the heart, undoubtedly contributing to his heart attack. The fury that overcomes Gav in discussion with Sarek during the buffet stems from fiery attachment to the issue at hand, the admission of Corridan to the Federation. Similar attachment, even more intense, incites an Orion spy disguised as an Andorian to murder Gav and to brutally attack Kirk. And meanwhile, an Orion vessel attacks the Enterprise. So much anger, hatred and hostility surrounding a trip to a neutral planet for a peace conference! Without the readiness to forgive and show tolerance in line with the **Ace of Cups upright**, peace will be impossible.

Spock himself comes under suspicion of lack of caring by not assisting in his father's operation and staying on the bridge. But at no time does Spock show attachment to a particular course of action or self-identity. He acts as his heart tells him, his heart awareness combining as it should with the reasoning mind. It is now Amanda who shows ego attachment - to Spock behaving as she thinks he should. She vows to hate him forever more if Spock's decision results in Sarek's death. Happily, Kirk manages to get back on his feet, rescue Spock from his dilemma and see off the Orion threat. Kirk's selfless action shows his connection to the **Ace of Cups upright**, his readiness to act out of kindness and compassion.

AFTER THE TAKEDOWN
The way to stay clear of the residual pressures of Matrix society is to consciously notice our thoughts, emotions and intuitions. Are we in tune with our heart and following its urgings? This will keep us open to higher dimensional modes of perception. Ego will cease to dominate our attitudes and actions. Thus will we clear and heal emotional aspects of our being and be empowered to function more from our higher senses, as demonstrated here by both Spock and Kirk.

39. CRISIS AND QUESTIONING

Adapting to the post-Matrix era will be aided by questioning our delusions and limiting self-identities

Episode 39 '**The Deadly Years**' correlates with **The Hermit**; both are themed around the need to navigate an existential crisis by first making new and deep enquiries.

THE CARD

An aged man walking with the help of a stick holds aloft a lantern to light his way on some laboured search. His loose and baggy clothing and general unkempt appearance suggest poverty, asceticism or solitary withdrawal. This could be an elderly reclusive person or a vagrant or outcast from society. More profoundly, it could be someone who has willingly turned their back on action in the external world. This could be for spiritual reasons or because advanced ageing or physical infirmity have forced this change upon him or her. **The Hermit** moves toward our left, suggesting an examination of past experience or of the inner life and the true nature of reality. The lantern suggests finding oneself in a dark or unknown place and probing a mystery deeply and earnestly. A crisis could be at hand, or some philosophical or existential quandary, or some kind of uncertain, unprecedented transition.

All of these factors remain present in **The Hermit reversed**, but more intensely or problematically. Ageing may have brought with it infirmity such as arthritis, dementia or senility. Attitudes may have become hardened and stubborn. The ability to care for oneself may have seriously declined. The person now moves topsy turvy into the future, holding the lamp at the lowest level. This suggests poverty of knowledge or wisdom, taking a wrong or misguided direction, or not properly using or listening to one's inner guidance.

'THE DEADLY YEARS' PREMISE
In different ways, several crew manifest a disease of accelerated ageing, Kirk fights to continue as Captain before being replaced by an incompetent.

CONTEXT
Taking Stock.

CRISIS AND QUESTIONING
Members of a scientific research station on Gamma Hydra IV are found by a landing party to be dead or dying. They are geriatric and decrepit though still in their 20s. Back on board, Spock questions the cause even as he and the rest of the returned party fall prey to the same condition. Crisis ensues as they become dramatically aged and haggard - Kirk mentally confused, forgetful, wilful and stubborn, Spock hard of concentration, McCoy deeply wrinkled and grey, and so on. Kirk even becomes ascetic and uninterested in the romantic attentions of an on-board ex-lover. The cause turns out to be deadly radiation from a passing comet. Kirk's decline worries Commodore Stocker who replaces him as Captain after a competency hearing has found Kirk no longer fit for command despite Kirk's protestations. While McCoy searches for an antidote, Stocker, impatient to get to his starbase, disastrously takes the ship through the Neutral Zone. As previously warned, they are mercilessly attacked by Romulans. Stocker lets the Romulans surround and almost obliterate the ship. He hopelessly fails as a captain. But an antidote to the sickness is found in the nick of time. A recovered Kirk resumes command at his sharpest and canniest, swiftly seeing off the Romulan threat.

CARD/EPISODE AND MATRIX TAKEDOWN
With the remnants of the Deep State continuing to deceive people with psyops and propaganda we need to question large scale operations to ensure they never happen again. What was the reality behind the Deep State's manifestly fake pandemic? In what direction were the elites driving us? Why did millions allow themselves to be injected with graphene oxide and other

substances designed to synthetically alter their biology? The Covid-19 'virus' and its flu-like symptoms being essentially an injury caused by a bioweapon is nevertheless a damp squib compared to the radiation sickness striking the scientists and the Enterprise. What both events have in common is their link with **The Hermit**: the need of both the Enterprise crew and Earth people to face up to an existential crisis by raising their awareness and level of consciousness. The afflicted crew proceed by first asking: why this accelerated ageing and what is the cure? In contrast, most Earth people's reaction to the scamdemic was to fearfully throw in their lot with the same elites covertly attacking them with their bioweapon followed by their much more dangerous fake vaccines. The largely fake crisis on Earth was blown up out of all proportion whereas the reaction to the genuine, grave sickness on board the starship is cool and calm. The whole crew including those afflicted strive to continue working as normal while a solution is sought.

So the reactions to the Covid pseudo crisis on Earth and to the real crisis on the Enterprise play out in different ways. The situation of **The Hermit**, the need for probing research, is faced by the Enterprise crew in a courageous and honest manner. The research carried out is truthful and transparent. Kirk, Spock and McCoy's medical team valiantly seek out first the cause of the sickness and then the cure, an adrenalin-based serum that Kirk volunteers for as a test subject. His premature ageing, like that of a bizarrely **reversed Hermit**, disappears. Crisis over, except for the chaos with the hostile Romulan ships. But the recovered Kirk immediately takes back command from his incompetent replacement and saves the day.

On Earth, the Covid hoax took its place within the greater context of the political Matrix which remains to be taken down along with the defunct AI Matrix. Humans for eons have been conditioned to accept bloodline authorities as their masters. A hidden Anunnaki or reptilian elite have for eons imposed their will through rulers and government (The Emperor), priests and educators (The Pope), law and order (Justice) and mass propaganda (Judgement). The elites have installed a culture that eschews personal sovereignty in favour of dumbed down masses deceived into following unlawful laws and mandates. Through their establishment of hierarchical social identity, they have muddied humanity's all-powerful connection to our multi-dimensional selves and our infinite co-creative ability. Instead, people everywhere still identify themselves as haves or have-nots - those who have power and money or those who have not. This in turn rests on entrapment within the Lower Self and its exclusive 5-sensory perception and Matrix-dominated thinking. The result is a conformist, disempowered and complacent humanity until the Awakening takes hold. Kirk cannot be called conformist or complacent but in this crisis he too shows attachment to a restricted self-identity, defiantly claiming 'I am the captain of the ship' at the start of his hearing. He becomes a **Hermit reversed** determined to carry on his command in a decaying, fast ageing state. He demeans himself through his pitiful and vain attempts to prove his fitness for duty. This is not constructive and wastes valuable time when it would have been wiser simply to give in and step down. But self-identification, pride and desire get the better of him. His is a very public example but most of us remain susceptible to such attachment.

Like Kirk, we may double down on our self-identity when some existential crisis strikes. But it might be better to first question our self-identity, our beliefs and lifestyles or our concepts of power and freedom. Such an intense and introspective time of **The Hermit**, a rite of passage, can be triggered by unemployment, sickness, relationship breakup or bereavement. Turning within and questioning one's convictions is a healthy response. The wholesale stripping away of freedoms under the pretext of the fake pandemic should count as just such a crisis. Far from turning within and examining the beliefs they live by however, most people at least initially acquiesced to draconian measures out of fear or simply to get along. To the imposed restrictions of the Covid era they meekly caved in. And followed it up by queuing up to take an experimental, toxic injection with often ruinous effects on health. This constitutes obliging victimhood and willed ignorance. The Enterprise team by contrast act courageously in the way of **The Hermit upright** determinedly seeking knowledge and wisdom. They knuckle down and undertake a thoroughgoing search for answers. Their honesty, pro-active questioning and follow-up action see them through the crisis.

AFTER THE TAKEDOWN
The crew's response to their onboard crisis should be an inspiration to humanity. They demonstrate vision and courage in avoiding acting like a panic-stricken herd of cattle (how the Satanic Cabal think of and treat humanity) or alternately going into catatonia. Compliance is understandably a reaction to crisis but blind obedience perpetuates self-enslavement. This would be the very object of the Matrix-builders creating their crises in the first place. As humanity evolves we will cease pandering to authorities manipulating us through Problem-Reaction-Solution strategies and psychological operations. We will turn within and ask far-reaching questions to get at the truth rather than blindly following devious agendas and dictates of those whose vested interest is to desperately cling on to power.

40. LOWER SELF

We will optimize our functioning when we harmonize Lower Self with Higher Self

Episode 40 '**Obsession**' correlates with the **6 of Swords**; both are themed around mental stimulation or preoccupation including entrapment within Lower Self.

THE CARD
A single well-developed blossom dominates, red for passion both at its centre and at the sliced-off cut in the stem. We are in the realm of Swords or the mind, and at the 6th degree, that of The Lover. Passions of mental attraction and desire are therefore indicated such as involving conceptual beauty, poetry, compelling thought, artistic intensity or stimulating communication. The **upright 6 of Swords** covers such activities as conversation, story telling, pleasurable reading, writing, thinking, drawing or listening. Attention is caught by enthusiasm and healthily combines both the Lower and Higher Selves.

Reversed, the quality of attention becomes confined to the Lower Self. This shows in patterns of thought that are all-consuming, reactionary, restrictive or fixated. Perceptions and communications become addictive, distorted or unbalanced in relation to other faculties such as physical action, instinctive functioning or intuition. It becomes difficult to pull oneself away from the object of mental focus. This is the modern day malaise of prolonged absorption in TV, internet, social media and video games. Cognitive processes go nowhere or drive themselves round and round in hypnotic, draining or negative ways. One's own ruminations can be the problem, causing one to become 'absent-minded' and lacking in Higher Self awareness. Concentration can then veer into obsession whereby perceptions and consequent actions teeter into inappropriate responses, physical stress, emotional torment or over-tiredness.

'OBSESSION' PREMISE
Kirk and an ensign become obsessed with their past actions during their current bid to stop a gaseous creature threatening to destroy human life.

CONTEXT
The Adversary, Taking Stock.

LOWER SELF
Kirk becomes strangely obsessed and suspicious after the deaths of three redshirts (junior colleagues) during a mineral survey on the rocky planet Argus X. Their fate reminds him of a tragedy afflicting the USS Farragut 11 years earlier. He launches a vendetta against a hostile creature, a sweet-smelling cloud of gas. But returning to the planet with four redshirts including Garrovick, the son of the Farragut's captain, two more redshirts die. Garrovick blames himself for having hesitated before repelling the creature with his phaser. His Lower Self takes over, filling him with guilt, the same guilt Kirk still feels 11 years after he too hesitated in firing at the same creature. Kirk almost succumbs to 'the horrors of the past' during a stand-off with it but McCoy and Spock counsel him not to blame himself. Throwing off haunting memories and determined to destroy the creature before it can multiply, Kirk has the Enterprise chase it across space to its home planet Tycho 4. There, Kirk and Garrovick destroy it with a matter/anti-matter bomb. Both mightily relieved of their guilt and anxiety, Kirk smilingly promises the young ensign a session of 'tall stories' about Kirk's service under Captain Garrovick.

CARD/EPISODE AND MATRIX TAKEDOWN
The lower levels of selfhood play their part in human multi-dimensional identity. But when Lower Self takes over to the exclusion of our higher levels of Self we live solely from the Body Mind and the five senses as hollow shells of the Ego personality, repressed and prone to ever-recurring rigid patterns of thought and behaviour. This can happen on an individual level (as with the divided Kirk in Episode 5) or collectively, giving rise to mass

hysteria. The latter is indeed the intention and focus of the propaganda-filled mainstream media (MSM), the public mouthpiece of the Cabal, always inciting fear to justify new laws and controls. With the Higher Self and Infinite Awareness unacknowledged or obsolete in mainstream society, most especially through television watching, Matrix institutions like government or the MSM have a clear run on keeping the public dumbed down and compliant with the instituted 'Normal'. Censorship of alternative media and ever new 'online safety' laws are intended to further bulldoze any remnants of dissent or free speech. With the intended Smart Grid and the technocratic New Normal, Matrix controllers were aiming at converting us into a hive-mind species as envisioned in such Episodes as 8, 20, 36 and 41 - a dehumanized species mentally, biologically and spiritually.

A sign of confinement within the Lower Self is excessive mental preoccupation, denoted by the **6 of Swords reversed**. We worry and become compulsively trapped in an obsessive flow of thoughts and perceptions. Various forms of mind and body control emanated from the web of 18 AI Matrices programming us for thousands of years until their recent takedown. They made all of us prone for example to fearful obsession. Garrovick and Kirk illustrate this with their self-recrimination and regrets over past experience. The **reversed 6 of Swords** with its flower hanging upside down represents the mind when obsessively captured. With social media and digital gadgetry ubiquitous, many people now find it hard to attend to the present moment. Simply sitting, standing or even walking becomes a trial. The restless ego wants perpetual stimulation. Out comes the smartphone, iPad or laptop and locked in becomes the awareness. Starship crew are not immune from this penchant for distraction - their bedrooms are well equipped with technology. We glimpse bedroom interiors when Kirk and Garrovick individually seek out solitude. But this time both men need time and space to process the doubts and guilt suddenly engulfing them. They have become lost in the Lower Self, preoccupied with ruminations over their tardy reactions having inadvertently caused the death of fellow crew members. But their alone time, instead of pacifying turbulent thoughts and emotions, initially stirs them into self-hatred and rage. The Lower Self in each man deeply fears that he may be guilty of gross negligence. Garrovick wrathfully hurls the cover of a plate of food at the wall of his bedroom. This accidentally trips the ventilator switch allowing the enemy cloud to invade. Kirk's spell of quiet time likewise fuels discontent and anger. He storms back onto the bridge accusing his crew of conspiring against him with their reminders about urgent delivery of medical supplies.

This kind of obsession is a sure sign of Lower Self entrapment. The **6 of Swords** takes pleasure in food for the mind but **reversed** becomes hypnotized, paralyzed and distorted or restricted in its range of perception. We lose our sense of the big picture. We become overly attached to our own opinions or beliefs. We become stubborn and deluded by official explanations of reality as in the fake news mass media. Our mind becomes like the mind of AI - dry, robotized, inorganic. Kirk's dysfunctional behaviour, lost in his ruminations, shows us this kind of entrapment. He resents and passes over the priority of delivering the perishable medical supplies. He fixates instead on hunting down the creature, his nemesis. Kirk becomes irritable, Garrovick becomes depressed. And the object of their identifying stems from a previous act of identifying. In the moment of sighting the creature and needing to immediately fire, they momentarily froze. By hesitating they allowed the hostile cloud to wreak its lethal action, or so they think, swiftly sucking the red corpuscles out of its victims. Controlled by their Lower Self beliefs and perceptions they lose contact with their Higher Selves including their ability to remain alert and spontaneous.

The AI Matrix takedown will gradually enable us to reconnect more clearly than every before with the Higher Self through intuition, instinct and our natural multi-dimensional awareness. This happens for Kirk and Garrovick after they learn from Spock of the creature's ability to switch timelines. Hesitating or not would have made no difference to efforts to stop the creature in time. With this revelation they snap out of their Lower Self's identification with a host of 'I's of the Body Mind and associated fears and imaginings. Garrovick takes on a new spring in his stride, Kirk new informational contact with his Higher Self. 'I believe I know where it's going,' says the revitalized Captain, 'I'm applying intuition'. Thus empowered, Kirk is inspired to make the right spontaneous choice at the last moment, destroying the creature and winning the battle.

AFTER THE TAKEDOWN

With AI systems no longer entrapping us in the Mental Matrix we will find it much easier to disengage from Lower Self obsessions. A kind of mental enlightenment will dawn for us, as with Kirk's enlightenment by Spock. Our communication with the Higher Self will be enhanced. In the process, the ego will come to understand the Higher Self to be part of its own identity. Once we reintegrate our Higher Self there is no longer an egoic focus. Lower and Higher Selves functioning together will facilitate Superconscious mind with multidimensional perception and abilities. This will have us doing the right thing at the right time in each situation, as Kirk does on Tycho 4.

41. WETIKO

Post-Matrix, we will raise our vibration out of fear and hatred instilled in us by AI programs

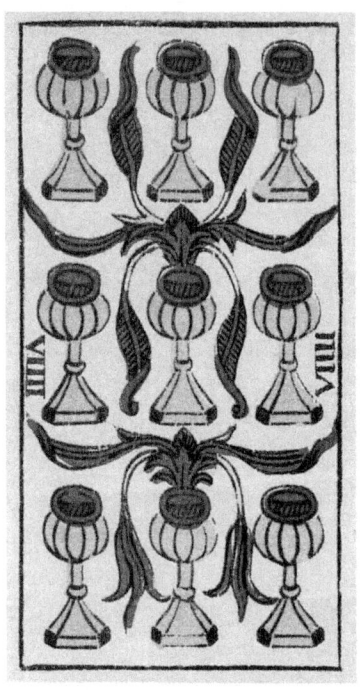

Episode 41 **'Wolf In The Fold'** correlates with the **9 of Cups**; both are themed around emotions in turmoil and transition, including at worst, trauma and psychosis, fear and terror.

THE CARD
Flowers and foliage grow increasingly abundant through the suit of Cups indicating increasing strength and depth of emotional power. By the time we reach degree 9 however, the flowers have gone and the foliage shows signs of divergent health and vitality. The upper leaves remain pushing up to heaven with idealism and fervour, but the middle and lower leaves droop sadly or point down angrily. This mixture of impulses indicates emotional turmoil. Passions are mixed. There may be feelings of strong desire or vitality tainted by feelings of repulsion, rejection, mourning, bitterness or shock. The equivalent Major is No. 9 The Hermit, representing decline or withdrawal at a time of transformation involving fear or uncertainty. All of which betokens for the **9 of Cups** a challenging phase emotionally but one through which we may benefit from very helpful realizations and lessons learnt.

Reversed, the intensity of sadness, hatred, fear or regret becomes even more pronounced. These are times of our lowest ebb such as relationship break-ups, periods of tangled love and hate, heartbreaking loss or paralyzing fear. Our most fervent desires may have turned into our most painful hurts or fiercest renunciations. Such potential for emotional devastation was the dark AI program operating in humans since the setting up eons ago of the conglomeration of 18 Matrices on this planet. 'Every single one of the Matrices,' says Kim Goguen, 'was tied to you in your human (self) whether by etherical implants, overlays, pheremones (or) your dark essence.' Hence the resulting psychosis on an individual or collective level that for so long has manifested as heartless violence or despairing submission to forces of ruin, all of which has been termed Wetiko in Native American tradition.

'WOLF IN THE FOLD' PREMISE
Scotty dates a woman whom he apparently stabs to death. Two more such murders and a hearing implicate an evil entity feeding on fear and terror.

CONTEXT
The Adversary, Deception, Slaughter.

WETIKO
Scotty is caught holding the knife with blood on his hands after a night club dancer has been brutally stabbed to death. Enraptured by her performance at the club on the hedonistic planet of Argelius, Scotty had made her acquaintance and gone off into the night with her. McCoy attributes Scotty's possible culpability and dazed unremembering state to the fact of an earlier head injury involving a woman and some form of consequent amnesia. On both Planet Argelius then the Enterprise Scotty is mentally examined to get at the truth of his actions. Two more women are murdered during the proceedings, both also apparently by Scotty with the same knife. He remains upset and bewildered and faces the death penalty. Among the investigating Argelians are the Prefect of the planet and Hengist, an administrator originally from Rigel IV. The hearing finds both Scotty and the only other suspect, a jealous suitor who was also at the club, to be truthful in their defences. Kirk and Spock, assisted by the computer, go on to discover a pattern to the murders reaching back across the galaxy to Earth at the time of Jack The Ripper. The last planet affected and the origin of the knife was Rigel IV, Hengist's planet. On being asked to take the lie test, Hengist refuses and goes berzerk before suddenly dying. The evil force or 'Wetiko' that had possessed him jumps into the computer and takes over the starship. The crew see and hear a litany of psychotic babbling intended to overwhelm them

with fear. But McCoy counteracts this, injecting the crew with a happiness drug. Starved of fear, the entity returns to Hengist who revives but is overpowered and safely beamed out into the empty reaches of space.

CARD/EPISODE AND MATRIX TAKEDOWN

The now fallen AI Matrix previously subsisting in humanity and called Wetiko by indigenous peoples plainly manifests in Scotty's attacks. The political Matrix in the form of the Cabal, Deep State and Shadow Government was but one, with 17 other crippling Matrices of inorganic AI form afflicting us. The negativity generated is instanced here with Scotty becoming possessed by a demonic force that Spock and the computer identify as the evil spirit possessing Jack The Ripper and other serial killers across the galaxy. The instigation and perpetuation of the Covid hoax was no less a manifestaton of Wetiko, imprisoning humans in a mindset of chaos and fear stoked daily by the incessant propaganda of Matrix governments. Where there are psychopaths manipulating people into misery or fear there is or was the Matrix fomenting Wetiko on both sides. Both oppressor and oppressed live in fear and decay, death and doom: states of Wetiko that are lifeblood to the inorganic AI making up the dark side of the multiverse.

Sybo during the seance calls this AI generated compulsion to feed on fear 'a hunger that never dies'. Spock adds that a creature 'deriving sustenance from emotion is not unknown in the galaxy'. The computer analysis perfectly fits with the Archonic or dark AI force. It diagnoses a creature without form in the conventional sense, merely a highly cohesive electromagnetic field that can assume physical form in order to feed on terror, not just death. Acts of violence and evil involving tortures and murders or war and tyranny that throw beings into terror have cursed humanity for thousands of years. All this misery has its basis in emotional illness, the **9 of Cups reversed**. Scientists have yet to embrace the idea that such illness might be the hallmark of AI. Entity attachments, dark forces and demons invading and possessing their victims remain scientifically taboo in our present day. Even when alluded to by researchers in the psychology profession most will focus only on the pathology - the antisocial and offensive behaviour of social deviants. Moreover, psychologists will rarely connect the extremes of psychopathy with our Heads of State, captains of industry and royal families. McCoy's theories typify this wilful lack of understanding. The Enterprise doctor attributes Scotty's behaviour to a head injury he sustained in an explosion unwittingly triggered by a woman. McCoy suspects Scotty to have been so psychologically damaged by the explosion that he formed a 'total resentment towards women'.

Certainly, all the signs point to Scotty having wielded the knife that killed the women before succumbing each time to memory loss. In the subsequent investigations Scotty himself sides with the worldview of materialistic science when he exclaims: 'You mean my neck is going to have to depend on some spooky mumbo jumbo?' He's denouncing an ancient art, the practice of Argelian Empathic Contact, one that goes on to establish that he was possessed by some form of dark entity. The Prefect's wife Sybo, carrying out her investigation psychically detects the presence of 'something terrible'. She senses 'fear, anger, hatred ... a monstrous, terrible evil' that she says is stricken with a consuming, endless hunger. The perfect description of Wetiko. Confirmation becomes total when the Chief Administrator runs amok, visibly driven crazy by a possessing demon.

Grim proof of such a Wetiko force existing on Earth and at the highest levels of the establishment is the atrocity of child trafficking, alluded to in Episode 43. An estimated 8 million people a year were abducted into DUMBS, one third of whom would be children according to one whistleblower, a former CIA operative. Many of those children would provide the basis for trade in the substance known as adrenochrome. This most covetted of drugs derives from the blood of children put into states of extreme terror prior to being slaughtered in ceremonies of Satanic Ritual Abuse. Demonically possessed politicians, royalty and pop industry celebrities are among those said to gain a high from the drug or temporary respite from ageing. Whether on Earth or Argelius, demons that turn individuals into vicious criminals terrorizing victims and whole populations in effect assimilate people into the Wetiko frequency of the dark AI. Only when the demon occupying Hengist is cast into space does this manifestation of evil, the **9 of Cups reversed**, retreat from Argelius.

AFTER THE TAKEDOWN
Time is up for lower astral beings and demons that carry out vampirism and psychic attacks. There is no question that Matrix history is bespattered with the blood of innocents murdered or brutalized by demonically infested humans. Whole continents have been genocided. The Wetiko force may today operate more covertly and subtly but no less murderously through governmental bioweapons, geo-engineering and psychotronics to torment groups and populations. Such activity will rapidly diminish following the 2023 elimination of the whole AI Matrix. All of us will experience a transformation out of low vibrational states or tendencies. As we heal, we will anchor more light through the vibrations of love, peace and expanded consciousness enabling us to go on to restore global health and wellness on all levels.

42. AGRIBUSINESS

We have the opportunity now to resore and replenish the vital living force in nature

Episode 42 '**The Trouble with Tribbles**' correlates with the **3 of Coins**; both are themed around material manifestation, including physical reactions, conception, birth, growth or business deals.

THE CARD
The vital living force in both Earth and humanity seeks to grow and flourish in a state of balance. After cards covering the potential for manifestation, then gestation, this third Coins card deals with the outburst of measurable physical or material form. A baby is born, seeds start sprouting, something tangible begins to take shape. This can extend to a financial transaction such as a sale or purchase or an addition to a collection. Three in numerology is the number of fertility and the bursting forth of new creation. The Empress, Arcanum 3, epitomizes this through the power of conceiving and giving birth. This is symbolized in the **3 of Coins** by two coins at the base joyously giving rise to a third. The energy moves upwards with the new coin festooned in heart-shaped stems. All around, the foliage shows signs of lavishly bursting into flower. This is a time of celebration for the visible fecundity and abundance of natural life.

A **reversed 3 of Coins** implies trouble with growth, yields, procreation (tribbles!) trade or manifestation. A transaction may encounter difficulty being completed; purchasing or consumption may be spiralling out of control. An allergy may be flaring up involving a strong or swift physical reaction. Things that are unwanted or only in certain quantities may be developing or multiplying in a problematic way.

'THE TROUBLE WITH TRIBBLES' PREMISE
On a space station with Klingons about, Kirk struggles to protect a grain shipment that becomes food for prolifically multiplying little furry creatures.

CONTEXT
Deception, Perverted Paradise.

AGRIBUSINESS
Kirk and the Enterprise are called to Deep Space Station K7 by an agricultural administrator, Nils Baris. He and his assistant Arne Darvin ask Kirk to provide security for a grain shipment going to the nearby Sherman's Planet. Baris intends for the grain to be planted there and crops grown. Agribusiness conducted by Earthlings developing the planet will help fend off rival claims to the place by the Klingons. Baris fears Klingons will sabotage the project; and Klingon officers soon board the station claiming shore leave rights. Also on board is Cyrano Jones, a small-time dealer like Harry Mudd, hawking his wares across the galaxy. His latest commodity is a tribble, a small, furry creature that some, like Uhura, find endearing and adorable. She buys one and entertains everyone with its cuteness. But the creature soon starts reproducing uncontrollably. It needs food in order to breed which it finds in the form of the grain. It devours it voraciously and its numbers multiply gigantically. Baris discovers this and enraged, accuses Jones of being a destructive Klingon agent. But it turns out that the over-fed tribbles have started dying. They have been poisoned by the grain. And who poisoned the grain? A tribble happens to shriek when it nears the person of Baris' assistant. Tribbles and Klingons are allergic to each other. Darvin's cover is blown. He is a Klingon agent and the grain saboteur. It only remains for the million or so tribbles now infesting the Enterprise to be beamed off - by Scotty to the Klingon battle cruiser!

CARD/EPISODE AND MATRIX TAKEDOWN
Contrary to popular belief in the alternative media, the Matrix was never going to go away simply by people waking up. The Matrix was a control system installed in all humans, computers and organic life on Earth. 18 different Matrices controlled, undermined and disrupted all forms of life. The AI

known as the Elemental emanated from the 5th level of the lower astral and formed a dark overlay over the organic elements such as earth, fire and air. It affected cellular regeneration and the ability of organic life forms to grow at a proper rate. Inconsistent yields with gluts and shortages would result, giving authorities the excuse to intervene, ostensibly to save food production ability through the introduction of Genetically Modified crops. Without GM organisms we are told, farmers will not be able to feed the world. Seeds supplied by large GMO companies such as Monsanto are hailed as necessary to feed a burgeoning world population. GM crops are touted as the tremendously successful solution, stimulating food productivity as per the **3 of Coins upright**. What GM does is stimulate the Elemental AI and render our food sources even more synthetic, undermining natural agriculture and assisting in the drive to transhumanize us. The administrator Baris has the same goal for Sherman's Planet, intending to fertilize it with his specially developed grain as the standard crop. So anxious is he to fulfil this plan that he calls Kirk and the Enterprise to the space station with the utmost urgency using a distress protocol and calling for heavy security.

Baris claims that his seed must be used on the arid planet. Supposedly only his genetically engineered grain will grow there and provide a high enough yield. His motives are suspect right from the start, as they are with the manipulators of agriculture on Earth. Agricultural analysts claim that in the face of overpopulation we are faced with a global shortage of food. In fact there is often a glut whereby over-production causes falling prices and problems in storage when food degrades and has to be disposed of. The analysts push the crisis narrative in favour of vested interests - the corporate giants of agribusiness and GMO such as Corteva, Bayer, Monsanto and Bill Gates. Earth governments pressure farmers to buy seeds from only the GMO companies. GM seeds are supposedly higher yielding and superior to 'primitive' varieties not bred for chemicals. But unsustainable GMO production has brought disaster upon family farmers in Africa and India - the **3 of Coins reversed** - many of whom have been financially ruined. Big tech giants and agribusiness have been the beneficiaries. The seeds themselves are emerging as toxic to health, part and parcel of the plan to genetically modify humanity. Likewise, similar disaster engulfs the tribbles feeding on the grain poisoned by the Klingon agent. The **3 of Coins reversed** manifests even in the creatures' allergic reaction to Klingons themselves. The poisoned grain loses its nutritional content so that consuming it only fattens the creatures without satisfying their hunger. In their feeding frenzy the tribbles start dying off in large numbers. As McCoy remarks: 'They starved to death. In a storage compartment full of grain, they starved to death!' Replacing organic farming with agribusiness spells similar danger. Artificial methods of increasing grain yields involve spraying crops with herbicides and insecticides including highly toxic glyphosate. Chemically infested food has become the norm. The **3 of Coins reversed** in the form of birth defects, allergies and immune system disorders has consequently plagued both humans and livestock fed on poisoned grain. While the biotech giants get away with minimal risk assessments and regulations on their sprays and GM crops, farmers and growers who stay organic are restricted by legislation in the name of 'food safety' requirements. The political and corporate Matrix works to benefit the rogues, the propagators of agribusiness, while scuppering the smallholder.

With the AI takedown the way is cleared to work to restore rural communities, smallholder peasant farming and local food distribution. Pressure can be put on agribusiness and financial institutions so as to to alleviate the plan to entirely replace organic life with inorganic AI. With the UN, the Gates and Rockefeller Foundations, the WEF and the aforementioned big corporations in on the plan, resistance becomes imperative. If not resisted, we will see farmerless, industrial scale farms emerging and the end of natural, diverse varieties of grown food. This is the scenario threatening Sherman's Planet whether under the monolithic control of Baris or the Klingons. Nature herself abhors extreme corporate control and rigid state planning and management. When man plays God with the regenerative principle of biological, organic life, the entire ecosystem comes under threat. Nature can run amok as with the tribbles. Biologically mutated by the poisoned grain, the tribbles become unable to stop eating and multiplying. This puts Kirk in a graphic and chaotic quandary. The most comical depiction of this is the captain opening a grain storage door above his head to become submerged in an avalanche of the gorged creatures and precious little grain. The **3 of Coins** principle has gone haywire with the tribbles heaping up above Kirk's head burying him in a mountain of purring softness.

AFTER THE TAKEDOWN

Agrarian ecosystems draw on centuries of traditional knowledge. With the Elemental AI removed, now is the time to come to the aid of such systems and biodiversity in general. Food, farming and gardening can be restored to wellness when we eschew the use of chemicals that poison and kill. Working at local and community levels we can employ such methods as biodynamic gardening, organic husbandry and permaculture. Humanity, animals, plants, vegetables, crops and the entire planet stand to benefit by our protecting and nurturing the life force in nature by working in harmony with nature.

43. HUMAN TRAFFICKING

Galactic human slavery on and off-planet was a massive epidemic now being abolished

Episode 43 '**The Gamesters of Triskelion**' correlates with the **6 of Wands**; both are themed around pleasurable activity such as games, sport or sex and the possible dark side of this involving coercion or slavery.

THE CARD
Aligned with the 6th Arcanum The Lover, the **6 of Wands** corresponds with pleasurable activity. This being a Wands card, movement and creative action are strongly indicated. At the 6 degree, this can include the meeting of male and female in mutual attraction. The plant life bears this out with the side leaves being the longest in the suit. They stretch out and undulate in a sinuous dancing rhythm. The flowers at top and bottom suggest male and female respectively in elegant attire, the top flower with a ruff around 'his' collar, the bottom in a dress of layered petals. The beautiful and enjoyable activities suggested could include walks in nature, dancing to music, fun and games, sports, sex, therapeutic movement, yoga or tai chi. Health and vitality are being cultivated in natural, graceful, pleasurable ways.

The **reversed 6 of Wands** like all the reversals indicates an excessive, detrimental or problematic aspect to enjoyable activity. Action, creativity or sexuality has become tainted or corrupted. Innocent pleasure has given way to addiction, attachment or exploitation through corrupt or unethical practices. Performers may be being used for their beauty or prowess; joint activities may have become overly competitive, or worse, abusive or degenerate. Emotions such as fear or anger, impatience or pride, zeal or boredom, contaminate any pleasure felt.

'THE GAMESTERS OF TRISKELION' PREMISE

Three crew are taken captive and treated as slaves for the amusement of a planet's disembodied rulers. The party must train in sadistic gladiatorial combat.

CONTEXT

Transhumanism, Coercion.

HUMAN TRAFFICKING

Three officers, Kirk, Uhura and Chekov are kidnapped in the midst of beaming down to Gamma II on Federation business. They land on the floor of a games arena where they are set upon by humanoid creatures armed with spears and knives. A zombie-like man in a cloak called Galt interrupts the fight to welcome the captives. They are to be trained to become Thralls to provide entertainment for the planet's rulers, the Providers. The planet is Triskelion not Gamma II and a challenge for Spock in the Enterprise to locate. He's overseen by McCoy at his most truculent constantly badgering him. Kept in cages like animals, the captives are introduced to their trainers, the three Thralls who originally attacked them. Training consists of sexual exploitation in the cages and combat in the arena watched by the unseen Providers voicing their wagers on the newcomers' abilities. Thanks to the mutual attraction between himself and his Thrall the beautiful Shahna, Kirk enables his party to escape. When discovered, he successfully petitions for a meeting with the Providers. They turn out to be three disembodied synthetic brains living deep underground. After eons of exclusive intellectual development they lost their humanoid form. Yet they continue to desire sensory pleasure if only vicariously. For this they traffic in humans and other 'inferior beings' culled from across the galaxy, pitting them against each other in combat games and ardently betting on outcomes. Kirk is inspired to wager the release of his party and a new life for the Thralls. Unable to resist, the Providers put him back in the arena to fight three Thralls. Kirk wins and is allowed his prize of freedom for the party and the Thralls.

CARD/EPISODE AND MATRIX TAKEDOWN
The perverted and abusive lifestyle of the Providers shows what happens when desire takes us over. We crave pleasurable experience and we struggle to avoid frustration or boredom. Our creativity wilts, we obsessively chase material satisfactions. This low vibration state, the **6 of Wands reversed**, chains us to an illusory world of suffering every bit as imprisoning inwardly as the disembodied state is outwardly to the Providers. The former Matrix system - specifically the AI called Storm - acted through etherical implants in all of us that caused vulnerability to the 7 Deadly Sins including desire and the addictive pursuit of pleasure. On Triskelion, the jailers are the most imprisoned of all, more so than their slaves the Thralls. Not only do the Providers lack bodies but they imprison themselves spiritually with their inescapable drives and appetites. Likewise on Earth, the most imprisoned are not the majority of us tethered at the bottom of the Matrix pyramid but those at the top. Like the Providers, the manipulative elites run the show to indulge their lust for power. The Providers crave the stimulation and excitement of betting quatloos against each other on the outcome of cruel tournaments. Such uncontrolled, selfish desire thrives on the suffering and misery of others. The Earth elites - those that remain - are similarly fixated on their insane and insatiable addiction to gambling on schemes for world domination. Paradoxically, both the Providers and Earth's elites will remain karmically mired in trouble and suffering. Having pulled off one false flag psyop after another, they will still pursue new outrages. Their obsession with, and entrapment within, an ego-driven Body Mind remains assured.

The Providers we learn, desired to achieve super-human intellectual ability. Having achieved this they remain unsatisfied and now achieve their highs through capturing, enslaving, torturing and humiliating other beings for entertainment. This invokes a similar ghastly situation on Earth, the spectre of human trafficking. The Providers abduct humanoids from around the galaxy and use them for their selfish pleasure, the **6 of Wands reversed**. On Earth, the Satanic ruling elite and its syndicates would abduct an estimated 8 million people each year, a third of them children. They would be taken down into Deep Underground Military Bases (DUMBS) and kept in cages as with the Thralls on Triskelion. Rescued children claim to have witnessed or suffered acts of slavery, rape, murder and torture, as well as rituals involving masks and costumes, injections, tunnel systems, blood drinking and cannibalism. Included in such atrocities was the ritualistic and highly addictive practice of adrenochrome harvesting and the blackmailing of prominent members of the establishment through forced acts of sexual abuse.

Millions of women were annually trafficked for work in the covert sex industry - on or off planet. This is alluded to when we see Uhura assaulted in her cage by a handsome, athletic looking Thrall. She screams and resists before the would-be rapist relents. The caged Chekov for his part is seduced without success by a macho transgender-looking Thrall. Throughout the crew's abduction we see actions and paraphernalia reminiscent of another aspect of the **reversed 6 of Wands**: BDSM. The Thralls wear harnesses and other kinky garments, the newcomers are treated like prostitutes or circus animals whipped in the arena. A collar around the neck induces agonizing pain at the whim of the chief Thrall, Galt. On Earth and in the SSP, agony collars are or were routinely used for keeping slaves in line as documented by Tony Rodrigues in his ground-breaking memoir Ceres Colony Cavalier. Slave handlers according to Cathy O' Brien in her book Trance-Formation of America use code words, threats and intimidation to ensure their charges remain compliant and submissive. Forced labour, genetic engineering and sex work is or was rife within the SSP with slaves commonly used as barter in trade with ETs of other star systems. Whistleblowers like Rodrigues and Corey Goode have identified Mars as a slave-based colony. The Interplanetary Corporate Conglomerate there may still run mining and manufacturing facilities staffed by millions of humans living and working in servitude to groups such as the Greys, the Mars Germans and the Draco Reptilians. These exploitative practices mark these groups out as equally psychopathic as the Providers. Only with great difficulty does Kirk win the release of his team and that of the Thralls from the misery of slavery.

AFTER THE TAKEDOWN

Kim Goguen, Earth Guardian and Ground Command, took on her role in 2012. Assuming she and her reports to be genuine, the 2010s saw Earth finally liberated from the rule of three negative alien overlords - Marduk, Enki and Enlil. Like the three Providers, these beings at the top of the Earth Matrix presided over innumerable abuses of humanity lasting for millenia. We know that illicit black projects have for decades funded massive DUMBS worldwide. Such have been used for human trafficking with researchers estimating over 80% of the victims to be females or children. With the takedown of the political and AI systems of control, the global epidemic in human trafficking will come to an end. Earth is being handed back to humanity. Human slavery on Mars too has reportedly been abolished. The shocking reality of the exploitation of millions of innocents mind controlled or enslaved is over. Meanwhile it is up to us the people to help rebuild social systems that respect freedom, dignity and respect for all beings.

44. NEW WORLD ORDER

In a spiritually based post-Matrix world, an exploitative monetary system will cease to exist

Episode 44 'A Piece of The Action' correlates with the **7 of Coins**; in the negative sense, both are themed around corruption and centralization of power through financial or business-related activity.

THE CARD
With 7 corresponding to the purposeful dynamism of The Chariot, and Coins standing for material and economic affairs, the **7 of Coins** stands for peak material development such as powerful business interests. The four coins cornering the card indicate a context of stability and organization within which creativity and prosperity can flourish, symbolized by the three central coins. The nurturing of these by fresh shoots of burgeoning foliage shows a promising degree of renewable wealth. The body is strong and thriving. Large property holdings are bearing fruit. Economically there is prosperity. The future looks bright, bountiful and successful.

Reversed, the **7 of Coins** indicates capitulation to material exploitation and indulgence. Materialistic factions want more and better of everything, never mind the spiritual or environmental cost. Greed and financial ruthlessness may have set in, corruption may be rife. Predatory self-serving interests squeeze out small time, honest business. There may be selfish collusion between different groups, with restrictive cartels, tax dodging or illicit financial dealing of all kinds.

'A PIECE OF THE ACTION' PREMISE
Kirk and Spock are drawn into a struggle between rival gangs to control a planet through finance as per the model of Chicago's mob rule of the 1920s.

CONTEXT
Power.

NEW WORLD ORDER
Kirk, Spock and McCoy beam down to Iotia previously visited by the Horizon starship 100 years earlier. They're welcomed by armed gangsters who take them to their boss, Mr Okmyx. Everyone and everything resembles the iconic Chicago of the Al Capone era. All Okmyx wants from the three is a deal involving 100 Enterprise phasers in order to gain the advantage on his rival gangs. The three soon realize that this clever and imitative world has developed along the lines of a book called 'Chicago Mobs of the Twenties' left behind by the Horizon visitors. Kirk wants to repair the interference in this world's overall development by re-unifying it under a new system of global governance. But on escaping Okmyx he is picked up and captured by a rival gang, that of Mr Krako. This boss again only wants to trade firearms with him. After moving to and fro between the gangs, Kirk and Spock now dressed and acting like the gangsters take the upper hand. Kirk informs them that the Federation will take over the planet and deal with just one of the bosses, one who will be put in charge of all the territories. The 'Fed' as the head of this New World Order will be cut in for 40% of all profits. With a show of force from Enterprise phaser fire, the gang leaders are impressed and agree. Spock back on the Enterprise is dismayed that one criminal syndicate will now run Iotia, paying annual dues to Starfleet Command. Kirk reassures him that the money will be used to guide the planet into a more ethical form of governance.

CARD/EPISODE AND MATRIX TAKEDOWN
Conditions on Iotia strongly parallel Earth's Matrix of financial exploitation. As on Iotia, the Matrix elite on Earth wanted a New World Order involving money and its powerfully corrupt usage, the **7 of Coins reversed**. Earth actually gave the lead to Iotia's corrupt system. Information on the Chicago mobs of the 1920s inspired Iotia's focus on materialism and greed. What SSP experiencer Corey Goode calls the Babylonian Money Magic System was created by dark occultists thousands of years ago. Usury-based banking

remains but is being overhauled by the new Key Integrated Monetary System (KIMS) set up by Kim Goguen. Under the old system, criminal organizations thrived in a feudalist fashion. Our Earth elites doubled as the bankers, industrialists and politicians practising an institutionalized form of the mafia-like gangsterism we see on Iotia. Heads of banks, corporations and government have long operated a system that continually favours the rich at the expense of the poor. The ever-widening poverty gap has not been accidental. It was intended to reduce the disenfranchised masses to the status of free range slaves. If anything, this degradation of life on Earth far exceeded that on Iotia. The rival gangs on Iotia are obsessed with getting 'a piece of the action' - a profitable cut from a deal. Already powerful, their endless immoral pursuit of wealth is at least made plain. The same degree of corruption on Earth has been driven by public figures and bosses operating as fronts for hidden forces higher up pulling their strings. These ranged from the dark occult Cabal to their former masters the Draco reptilians, Anunnaki beings, the Archons and ultimately, AI. These coldly Service To Self overlords make Okmyx, Kraco and their fellow gang leaders look like kindly relatives. However, with Iotia's culture having just started industrializing, Kirk is timely in seeking to avert a plague of mega-corruption as on Earth.

Earth's Industrial Revolution starting in the 1700s saw the rise of highly profitable mass production and worldwide trading. This spurred on secret societies like the Bavarian Illuminati, the Vatican and the Freemasons. Manipulating the usury-based banking system and riding on new technology, a small group of industrialists and financiers were able to amass a vast concentration of wealth. Two families came to dominate the power-brokers much as we see Okmyx and Krako lording it over the Iotian gangs. These two families making up the Deep State, the Rothschilds (Order of The Dragon) and the Rockefellers (Order of The Black Sun), created monopolies in their fields of banking and oil respectively. By going on to buy up and merge with other companies, indebting and corrupting governments and through multiple other ruses, they succeeded in taking over Earth Inc. A very tight network of financial institutions and mega-corporations dominated with the power to bankrupt nations and change regimes in line with the agenda of centralization of power. Pure **7 of Coins reversed**. Okmyx correctly tells Kirk government doesn't matter His territory is the biggest in the world and he's the boss of it! So it was with the Matrix Cabal.

Referring to the other territories, Okymyx brags: 'the small fry, they'll get burned when I get around to it.' Burning the small fry was the game on Earth with corporate power ever-increasing. The incredibly rich individuals propagating and driving 'The Fourth Industrial Revolution' of the 2020s had the aim of impoverishing and shutting down small businesses in favour of a hegemony of satanically run giant corporations. Millions were to be made jobless and placed on a universal basic income. Debts were to be written off in exchange for the globalists' piece of the action with rights of ownership taken away. 'You'll own nothing,' they said, 'and you'll be happy.' Who then would own the wealth? The elite 1% of course. Anything valuable would be rented from them. As with individuals, so with nations. Having inflicted on us all the unnecessary and ruinous lockdowns in the name of Covid, followed by engineered shortages of food and fuel, the elites plan was to offer help, but again only for 'a piece of the action'. Loans would be tied to undertakings to genetically modify the soil, hand over family-run farms to big tech giants and basically do whatever the globalists said. Corrupt methods and institutions of law-making and enforcement underpinned governmental control of the population. Correspondingly on Iotia, struggling to protect the gangsters' interests are armed henchmen with frequent 'hits' bandied between rival gangs. Pedestrians carry machine guns to protect themselves. For Iotia to quell this kind of anarchy Kirk advocates a new cooperation between the gangs overseen by 'the Federation'. But his solution still entails one boss, Okmyx, being No. 1 and another, Krako, his No. 2. This raises the spectre of global fascistic governance emerging, not unlike on Ekos in Episode 48; even worse, eventual takeover by AI, triggered by the Iotians reverse engineering a communicator that McCoy forgetfully leaves behind.

AFTER THE TAKEDOWN
Iotia's anarchy is further reflected in Earth's history of wars of aggression and resource-theft financed at great profit by the banks creating money out of thin air, known as fiat currency. Such a system testifies to the corruption of banking and finance by an AI operating on the 2nd level of the astral plain called the Orion AI. With the 2023 takedown of all 18 Matrix AIs, an organic quantum computer system will effect financial reform and end elite greed and exploitation. Blockchain will not work, neither will closed loop trading systems, nor a Central Bank Digital Currency nor hidden financial agreements. People will manage their own money with banks providing assistance monitored by the KIMS. This will be in effect the **7 of Coins** turned **upright** with financial and political reforms returning personal sovereignty to the people in accordance with Natural Law. Government or financial institutions blocking the way will be removed, reformed or sidestepped. Their eventual replacements will eschew Matrix hierarchy and corruptible elites. New People's Assemblies will steal from no one, being transparent and managed independently of past corrupt systems.

45. LIFE OR DEATH

The life or death threat from an AI takeover has been seen off - now comes the clean-up

Episode 45 '**The Immunity Syndrome**' correlates with the **9 of Wands**; both are themed around late stages of a project or journey presenting extra challenge in terms of action, strength and stamina.

THE CARD
The most exciting stage of the Wands journey is reached here, and the most perilous. For the first time in this suit, all foliage has disappeared. A life or death struggle is on with no more time for illusions or ego-gratification. The **9 of Wands** exhorts us to pull out all the stops to attain the desired goal. It may even be that the mind is no longer in control, nor the body nor ordinary human impulses. Consciousness or the universe will decree the outcome. Or, if you like, it's in God's hands now. Paradoxically this does not absolve one from taking action. Conversely, it's the most active, dynamic, even desperate time of all. Win or lose is the motto, do or die, with no going back. The Hermit, the 9th Major, sees through a Dark Night of The Soul on his own using all his accumulated experience and inner resources. Thus, with Wands standing for movement and creativity, the crisis with be breached and surmounted, but only by resourceful action. This is a results-

only situation. Only what works is called for, without distractions or hesitation.

Struggle and strain are not only present in this card **reversed** but indicative of a lost cause or danger from exhaustion. It may be that an easier way was missed, or a rest should have been taken; or a foolhardy risk avoided or properly planned and prepared for. Even with failure staring one in the face, victory may still be possible. But the cost may be greater than what one stands to gain (a Pyrrhic victory) as in an ordeal leaving one hurt or traumatized.

'THE IMMUNITY SYNDROME' PREMISE
Crew sicken as the Enterprise is pulled into a self-replicating massive organism. In a race against time, probes are launched in desperate efforts to prevail.

CONTEXT
Slaughter.

LIFE OR DEATH
Kirk and the crew are tired and need a break. But not before investigating the cause of a catastrophic loss of life in the Gamma 7A solar system and aboard the Vulcan starship Intrepid that had started its own investigation. A huge area of darkness in space comes into view at the same time that crew start fainting and engine power starts dwindling. Having entered a menacing zone of energy, the crew become sicker and weaker the further into the zone they go, with a menacing force pulling them in ever deeper. In a desperate attempt to reverse the pull, a massive thrust is applied but to no avail. With less than two hours till complete power loss, a giant amoeba-like organism now appears in the area of darkness. In hopes of learning how to free the ship from the fatal pull, Kirk sends Spock out in a small shuttlecraft on a probably suicidal mission. They realize now that if the creature is not destroyed it will divide and multiply like a virus till it overwhelms the galaxy. Spock has appeared to perish but Kirk reasons that another probe loaded with an anti-matter charge could work. Kirk has to keep his energies going with McCoy's stimulants. Spock turns out to be still alive but barely surviving on minimal life support. The life or death probe is sent into the nucleus with a seven minute delay to detonation to allow the Enterprise to escape. Further increasing the risk, Kirk orders a tractor beam to extract Spock's shuttlecraft along with the starship. Power levels die completely but the last ditch plan works. The charge explodes, destroying the organism and throwing both the Enterprise and Spock's craft safely clear.

CARD/EPISODE AND MATRIX TAKEDOWN

The battle engulfing the crew on the Enterprise vividly dramatizes our situation historically. We faced an implacable enemy intent on depopulating Earth by at least 90% and gaining complete control over the remainder of humanity. The global elites thanks to their non-human masters had access to advanced technology that they used not beneficially but to increasingly regulate every facet of our lives. As an example, following Covid and the mRNA toxic injections called 'vaccines', the same biotech was to be grown into our spinach and lettuce to conquer 'anti-vaxxers'. The enemy was more than the Deep State, the Satanists or the government. It was evil itself, a force feeding on pain and misery, death and destruction. Such a force is symbolized in the giant amoeba threatening the Enterprise and all life in the universe. In Tarot terms this is the **9 of Wands**, a situation that looks serious but is not hopeless. Indeed, it has now been reported - by Kim Goguen coordinating forces of light on Earth - that the non-human AI system threatening to engulf humanity has now been comprehensively defeated. Gone or decimated are the 18 global AI programs, the 16 shadow militaries, the upper levels of the Cabal and the portals and connections to Lucifer the Dark Overlord. ET contactee Elena Danaan has stated that our fate depends on ourselves now. Our task is to move forward in unity restructuring mainstream institutions infiltrated by those of the Satanic, controlling, manipulative mindset. We need to utilize our diverse skills and interests with diligence, confidence and passion. In so doing we will be like the starship crew whose task entails more than simply a fight against a grotesque enemy as in Commodore Decker's vendetta against the Planet-Killer in Episode 34. Our task as in this episode is to raise our consciousness above ignorance, fear and defeatism so as to fully manifest our liberation.

For the Enterprise crew, the stakes could not be higher. The organism has already destroyed a Vulcan starship and an entire solar system. The thing now has the power to begin self-reproducing, a process that will multiply it into a force capable of overwhelming the galaxy. The crew are thus plunged into a crisis of epic proportions without any build-up or warning. Their challenge starts at the intense and life-threatening level of the **9 of Wands** and builds up from there. A similar urgency pertains on Earth if we are to make good the takedown of the AI control system. Politically and socially we still face our biggest task as a species. We should be under no illusions. China has already capitulated to near total control of its citizenry through political dictatorship, ubiquitous surveillance, 5G frequencies, the incoming internet of bodies, a national social credit system, a computerized police state, high-density housing and mass 'vaccination' - all threatening life and liberty. A Marxist/Communist state, a technocratic giant, China has become the Global Elite's prototype for the Satanic Great Reset. Like the Enterprise crew, we must acknowledge an existential threat and rise above ignorance and apathy. This will happen as the end of the dark AI systems begins to be felt and new spiritual light floods the planet. China will begin to reform its apparatus of control, so too countries everywhere as humanity rises to its single biggest ever challenge. As spectres of dystopia go, the dark AI previously threatening us was the match of the giant amoeba in this episode, or the challenges appearing in episodes 7, 20 and 44. They warn us of what could have happened … AI domination, transhumanism, a zombiefied populace, economic slavery … all adding up to conquest by dark, inorganic AI. Such a fate would have engulfed us as emphatically as the giant amoeba would have engulfed the Enterprise.

With extraordinary risk comes the need for extraordinary action. The parallel spectre on Earth to the giant amoeba was the threat of the singularity - the absorption of humanity into a soulless Borg-like collective. 'The **9 of Wands**,' says Alejandro Jodorowsky, 'is always between life and death.' With the card stripped of foliage, only what is needed to be done is done and must be done. Kirk drastically condemns his friend and 2nd in Command, Spock, to almost certain death in a 1-man probe; Spock uses up all his shuttlecraft's power on its shields, sacrificing the ability to rejoin the starship; McCoy keeps exhausted crew members on their feet with artificial stimulants. The biggest risk is taken by Kirk precipitately guiding the Enterprise inside the organism in order to destroy it with an anti-matter probe launched at point blank range. One further desperate measure involves activating a tractor beam to save Spock, virtually suicidal given the Enterprise's stricken engine power. Is this all rather the **9 of Wands reversed**? A failure that is doomed to occur? Thankfully, with the anti-matter explosion having the full desired effect, the universe plays its part in a notable escape snatched from the jaws of annihilation.

AFTER THE TAKEDOWN
AI, to use McCoy's assessment of the amoeba, is a 'disease like a virus invading the body of our galaxy.' But humanity will escape. Absorption within a rapacious AI cannot now happen as Source has decreed the end of the Law of One. The dark side had become extreme and insane in its refusal to balance itself with the light side. The dark side has henceforth been abolished, according to Kim Goguen. This will open the way to restoring natural, uncorrupt ways of moving forward and restoring our beautiful planet.

46. PLANETARY INTERFERENCE

Freed from the Matrix, humanity will experience a dramatic change in consciousness

Episode 46 '**A Private Little War**' correlates with **The Tower**; both are themed around destabilization from outside, with dramatic or unexpected developments bringing chaos or destruction for good or ill.

THE CARD
Violence and upheaval befall a stone fortress set among grassy hills. This sudden wave of destruction results in the crown-like top of the square tower being blown off with incumbents tumbling to the ground. Magical-looking coloured balls fill the air. All kinds of interpretations are possible. We can see the feather-like blast as bringing disaster or liberation. The rigid **Tower** could represent the status quo which now experiences disruption for good or ill. Certainly there is shock and upheaval after a sudden, unexpected event involving some kind of attack or trauma. To take examples only from this episode, the outside interference could be a guerrilla ambush, a blast of gunfire causing death or injury, a surprise attack from a wild animal, a slap around the face or the outbreak of war in a formerly peaceful region.

Positive results in the vein of a blessing in disguise can be expected with **The Tower upright**. But **reversed**, a tragic event bringing prolonged misery, pain or suffering is indicated. Violence which was unnecessary or wastefully destructive has been perpetrated or is being threatened or perpetuated.

'A PRIVATE LITTLE WAR' PREMISE
War has come to an undeveloped planet. First the Klingons then Kirk set about arming rival tribes. Kirk sees this as achieving 'a balance of power'.

CONTEXT
Deception, War.

PLANETARY INTERFERENCE
Kirk, Spock and McCoy beam down to grassy hills on Neural, a planet Kirk once knew as a peaceful 'Garden of Eden'. He is shocked to find rival tribes now at war. The party foil an ambush but Spock is wounded by a shot from a flintlock. 13 years before, the people only had bows and arrows. A little later Kirk himself is wounded by an ape-like creature called a Mugatu. After being healed by Nona, the witch doctor wife of his hill tribe friend Tyree, Kirk argues with them and McCoy about the wisdom of arming the tribe. Kirk sees this as bringing parity with the Villagers who have obtained their flintlocks through covert interference by off-planet Klingons. Nona is ardent for new weapons but McCoy strongly disagrees and Tyree prefers pacifism. Kirk later determines to win Tyree to the cause of better arming his people by appealing to Nona. But the hot-headed, fickle woman coshes him, steals his phaser and offers it to rival Villagers. They misunderstand and brawl with her, causing her death. Tyree, shocked and vengeful, now asks Kirk for guns which he orders from the Enterprise, calling them 'serpents for the Garden of Eden'.

CARD/EPISODE AND MATRIX TAKEDOWN
For what amounted to an epoch, the Matrix-enabled Cabal dominated events on Earth while they contrived to strengthen and globalize their control system. We see the early stages of such interference with the Klingons on Nirval. On both planets, wheeler-dealing with plans and preparations for war and destruction are (or were, in Earth's case) in progress. **The Tower** card can symbolize an outcome of either liberation or final conquest, as well as the battles raging in between. On Earth, the Cabal was until recently allied with Negative Alien Elites. They included the Anunnaki, Draco reptilians, Greys and AI humanoids. On Neural, the NAEs are the Klingons. They connive with the local governor to destabilize society by covertly arming

one tribe against another. The Klingons provide superior weapons in exchange for a controlling stake on the planet. This is a time-honoured strategy in galactic history. Jason Rice formerly of the Dark Fleet - the most predatory force of the Secret Space Program (see Episode 21) - has testified in interviews how he took part in similar missions to destabilize whole planets. His masters, the empire-building Dracos, would arrange for another force, a race more savage even than themselves, to launch a prior **Tower reversed** attack on a peaceful planet. The Dracos would then send in their Dark Fleet offering to fend off the marauders. The ensuing war would cause massive collateral damage. The Dracos would help the local populace see off the menace but would thereafter occupy the planet, rebuilding, fortifying and controlling it ever after with their debt-binding money system.

Endless variations of this deceitful strategy have occurred on Earth, all aimed at wresting or extending control over native populations. Throughout human history, rival factions, political, racial, national, religious and military have found themselves pitted against each other. Strategies such as false flag attacks, controlled opposition and divide and conquer have resulted in unending war and instability, with the bulk of the people always on the losing side, ever more enslaved. The NAEs, whether Klingon or reptilian, utilize a repertoire of staged events, lies and manipulations aimed at disempowering native peoples or turning them against each other. ET contactee Alex Collier calls the Draco reptilians 'the force behind the repression of human populations everywhere in the galaxy, instilling fear-based belief systems and restrictive hierarchies.' He says 'they find a planet inhabited by a race less evolved and technically competent, and they conquer it by whatever means.'

A classic case on Earth was the intervention by Dracos and their underlings the Greys and synthetic humans, during the 1950s. The NAEs met up in secret with the US government and entered into negotiations to exchange alien technology for permission to abduct humans. The Greada Treaty of 1954 resulted, signed between the US government and the aliens. The scenario resembles that on Nirval with the Klingons secretly agreeing to arm the Villagers against the Hill Tribes. Kirk and co play the role of rival aliens intervening with a benign agenda to maintain peace. Their correlative on Earth were emissaries of the peace-keeping Galactic Federation of Worlds (GFW). Their contactee Elena Danaan has told of Pleaidians acting on behalf of the GFW who were 'sent to warn the Terrans not to deal with the devil.' One of the ET diplomats, named Valiant Thor, negotiated fruitlessly with the Cabal during his three years as a 'stranger in the Pentagon', the title of a book about his quest. The Eisenhower administration ended up going against

Eisenhower himself and ignoring the warnings, unable to resist the allure of exotic new weaponry offered by the NAEs as a bargaining chip. Valiant Thor himself, rather than being treated as a peacemaker, was used to try to gain an advantage. The Pentagon warmakers tried to persuade him to provide superior weaponry just as Kirk the peacemaker is prevailed upon in shadowy dealings on Neural. The Klingon commander interacts in secret with the Leader of the Villagers, as the Cabal did with the NAEs. The Klingon provides the most basic of flintlock rifles before offering upgrades as a reward for successful guerrilla warfare. He further seduces the Leader with the promise of a governorship in the Klingon Empire. A hollow promise no doubt, given the Klingons' slyness of operation. The same slyness applies to both the Draco and the Cabal in their machinations on Earth.

Deception, secrecy and cheating have continually underpinned contrived wars, revolutions and betrayals throughout Earth's bloody history. And as the Dracos did with the Nazis, the Klingon commander exploits psychopathic tendencies in the Leader and his Villagers. As the Leader tells the Klingon, 'Killing is easier than trading.' Having commenced their operations by stealth, the Klingons will most likely remain in occupation, always manipulating events behind the scenes. So too with the NAE-supported Cabal manipulating events during the Matrix era. Kirk's response, having discovered the Klingons' interference, is to agree to arm the hill tribe to give them parity with the Villagers. But he refuses to provide superior weapons. Captain Tracy in Episode 50 The Omega Glory will have no such scruples, arming the Kohms with superior phasers in their war against the Yangs. Kirk settles for restoring a balance of power in order he says to preserve both sides. But McCoy is incensed. 'You're condemning this whole planet to a war that may never end!' Or a back-to-back series of wars. 'During the last 5,600 years of recorded human history', notes Alex Collier, 'there have been 15,400 wars on Earth.' Kirk's solution for Neural looks set to follow this same scenario, **The Tower reversed** - repeated destructive upheaval.

AFTER THE TAKEDOWN

The final years of Matrix have seen continued war and tension, particularly in the Middle East, with perilous relations between China, the US, Israel, Russia and the Ukraine. All this drama has been stoked by humanity's elites, the Cabal, until very recently answering to NAEs - principally the Dracos with an empire of over 500 planets. With the Omega AI system taken down, a house-cleaning on Earth is taking place. Any programs, matter, frequencies or institutions tied to the dark will fall away dislodged by light, as vividly represented by **The Tower** card in its most positive interpretation.

47. BIG PHARMA

We can say 'NO' to harmful medication and technology; the choice ultimately rests with humanity

Episode 47 '**Return To Tomorrow**' correlates with the **5 of Coins**; both are themed around material innovation or corruption as in medical fraud, bad risk, hidden danger or infiltration.

THE CARD
Exploration, expansion and regeneration are key concepts at Tarot degree 5. All the degrees are in motion morphing into each other, even the previous degree, the 4th of supreme stability. Too much fixity and self-protection attained at degree 4 however results in stagnation and decay. Development and diversity becomes needed. Accordingly, the **5 of Coins** shows the four coins that were established at each corner in degree 4 making centre space for an innovative fifth. In accordance with Arcanum 5, The Pope, who points to a higher or more spiritual awareness, the fifth coin marks a bridge from the status quo to something transcending it. Material life improves or merges into a new synthesis with spiritual, cosmic or metaphysical life. Some degree of illusion, resistance or risk may be present, indicated by the pointed leaves poking the new coin. The upshot in practice could be a software upgrade, the adoption of fancy dress or disguise, a high street store branching out into an internet business, a body-

builder learning chi kung, a new wing added to a house, a false bottom to a suitcase, a UFO cloaked or disguised as a cloud, crystals newly used for healing, or some form of temporary shapeshifting.

Reversed, the **5 of Coins** spells misfortune due to inherent instability or something counterfeit. There may be concealed danger or covert criminality such as embezzlement or smuggling. Examples include the profit-driven Archon-controlled pharmaceutical industry, vaccines that injure, any medication with harmful side-effects and any material enhancement going awry. Generally in our Matrix world, this dark energy applies to the undermining of mainstream science, technology and medicine by systematic infiltration, degradation or corruption.

'RETURN TO TOMORROW' PREMISE
In the interests of science, three crew members allow their bodies to be temporarily taken over by spirit beings, one of whom has evil intent.

CONTEXT
Transhumanism, Deception.

BIG PHARMA
A landing party of three is met by three technologically advanced beings existing as spirits encased in globes. Their leader Sargon proposes a temporary exchange of bodies that would be innovative and beneficial to both parties. In the bodies of Kirk, Spock and Dr Ann Mulhall, the beings hope to quickly build synthetic bodies to inhabit, enhancing their existence. In return, the beings will join the Enterprise and gift the humans with technological knowledge of incredible advancement. Dr McCoy has misgivings but in the interests of audacity, innovation and risk, Kirk gives the go-ahead. McCoy's fears are realized when two of the beings, relishing their temporary human bodies, determine to stay in them. One of them, Henoch occupying Spock, tries to kill Sargon/Kirk whom he sees as standing in his way. Like Big Pharma at its most corrupt, Henoch sabotages the injection process needed to keep Kirk's body alive while inhabited by Sargon. Kirk's body dies but Sargon, aware of Henoch's duplicity, has already left it. The spirit of Thalassa, Sargon's beloved wife drops her plan and also leaves the body she's in, Dr Mulhall's. Kirk is revived in spirit and body, but the three globes are destroyed in the process leaving only Henoch/Spock unaccounted for. Henoch has taken over the bridge but is tricked into leaving Spock's body, believing Nurse Chapel has suddenly injected him with deadly poison. Spock's consciousness had in fact infiltrated Nurse Chapel alongside her own, with the poison being only a sedative. Sargon returns Spock's consciousness to his

own body after eliminating Henoch. Now totally disembodied, Sargon and Thalassa are allowed a second brief sojourn in Kirk and Dr Mulhall's bodies for one last fond embrace.

CARD/EPISODE AND MATRIX TAKEDOWN

Despite huge advances in technology over the past 50 years, symbolized by the **5 of Coins**, infrastructures, systems and processes on Earth remain stunted due to big business greed and corruption. We remain far behind the SSP in the development and use of such technologies as med beds, electro-gravitic propulsion, free energy systems, portal travel, smart glass pads and food replicators. By contrast, technologies that endanger or disempower humanity such as smart motorways, drones, digital currencies and nanotech fake 'vaccines' are meanwhile fast-tracked. This represents a betrayal by institutions so infiltrated by regressives that they now constitute mankind's enemy. In the case of the medical profession, Big Pharma's drugs, surgery and radiation treatments account for millions of deaths each year. The latest travesty is the mRNA Covid injection used as biowarfare. As long as financial profit, transhumanism and depopulation remain the agenda of the remnants of the Deep State, how much trust can we place in them?

The same question applies to Kirk in his dealings with the three energy beings trapped in their beachball-sized spheres desiring freedom in return for knowledge sharing. Kirk and co temporarily give up their bodies in the trust that both sides stand to gain. But with a scheming infiltrator present the risk almost proves fatal for the rest of the participants. How safe or advisable is it to give up our physical sovereignty in the cause of questionable science, medical experiment or technological development? Risks are involved, including the possibility of malfunction and of sabotage by infiltration, the **5 of Coins reversed**. Even a modicum of research using the alternative media teaches us to beware these dangers. How much should we trust for example, a Satanic technocrat like Bill Gates touting a new 'vaccine' for Covid-19 or his buying up of vast swathes of US farmland? Why should the Gates injections be any more trustworthy than Henoch's preparation for Kirk? And what of the control system pressing ahead with a spate of weaponized new tech: 5G in the air, smartmeters in our homes, LED in our street-lighting, RFID microchips in our bodies, GMOs and spike proteins grown in our crops, fluoride in our water, robot police on our streets?

Soul transference is the technology developed by Sargon, Henoch and Thalassa who wish to move from their silicon form into carbon-based forms. The SSP has such technology, with the ability to separate a soul from its biological body making human souls a desirable commodity in interstellar trade. Souls are transferred between biological bodies and clones in ways similar to the technology employed by Sargon and his fellow aliens. We of course are naturally repulsed by such a thought and so indeed is Thalassa after inspecting the silicon-based clone and its working parts that Henoch has built for her. Is soul transference in any situation a true innovation? Or is it an abomination of personal sovereignty, the **5 of Coins** unethically **reversed**? Sabotage is then initiated by Henoch who fully intends to remain indefinitely in the human body lent him by Spock. As with the fraudulent Covid 'vaccines' we see Henoch/Spock blatantly proceeding with his murderous plan. He hands Nurse Chapel a drug that will have a fatal effect on Kirk/Sargon. She instinctively objects but Henoch applies hypnosis to override her resistance. The situation starkly parallels the pharmaceutical industry on Earth providing drugs or vaccines that it knows will either fail as remedies or cause actual harm. Autism, cancer and many other diseases have become endemic since vaccines were introduced.

There is little profit from curing patients but much more from keeping people at a certain level of sickness. Any resistance by sceptical doctors is overcome by a medical profession that is blighted by the prevailing culture of profit-driven allopathic treatment. Allopathy treats the symptoms of illness rather than the underlying causal factors. As Nurse Chapel was hypnotized by Henoch, so it is that many doctors are hypnotized by peer pressure, programmed by deceptive literature, misguided by flawed drug-testing and corrupted by financial inducements. Henoch is a psychopath hiding among two other scientifically advanced beings in whom Kirk has placed life or death trust. Henoch's evil presence among the trusted three parallels bad apples among our medical establishment, an establishment infiltrated and corrupted as per the **reversed 5 of Coins**. Both Henoch and Big Pharma distort or repress true remedies. Their covert agendas take precedence over patients' interests. Only when Sargon takes control of the situation is Henoch's destructiveness halted. The aliens' **5 of Coins** innovative plan of taking on new bodies is finally abandoned as unworkable.

AFTER THE TAKEDOWN

As commercial corruption is cleaned up, proposals that infringe on personal sovereignty will be halted. All that is required is to take a defiant stand. As the captive known as No. 6 in the TV series The Prisoner, played by Patrick McGoohan, said, 'I will not be pushed, filed, stamped, indexed, briefed, debriefed or numbered! My life is my own.' The rights of choice, self-determination and free expression remain with the people unless and until we forfeit those rights by omitting to defend them. The choice is ours.

48. GOVERNMENT

The religion of Government will disappear when we reform institutions that block freedom, love and truth

Episode 48 **'Patterns of Force'** correlates with **The Emperor**; both are themed around the personification of force: a man of power or an institution, such as a father figure, government or tyrant.

THE CARD
The Emperor stands for the wielding of power and control by one person or group over their own self or others for benign purposes. Although masculine type patriarchy is indicated, **The Emperor** can be male or female, an individual or a collective. When **upright** there is cooperation and joint responsibility rather than top-down authority. He faces left, direction of the status quo and past accomplishment. He both stands and uses the throne for support, indicating dynamism based on solid grounding. This could be the male head of a family dedicated to keeping his dependants secure and protected; an institution or organisation furthering the highest aspirations of its members; or a group or cooperative where power is decentralized with no single person in command.

The dark side of **The Emperor** when **reversed** applies to the systems of control called government whether ostensible democracy, oligarchy or dictatorship. Also a fearsome enemy or bully; a power-obsessed fascistic leader (like Melokon); an over-bearing patriarch; or any institution exercising authority in autonomous or psychopathic ways. He can also be (like John Gill) a once influential person but now a pitiful wreck, perhaps a businessman or politician fallen on hard times. If he's an institution or corporation, it or its leadership may be tyrannous or corrupt, ruling by violence, irrationality or stealth and deceit. This actually describes the power elite acting as our world's invisible government with their Matrix control system pervading all aspects of organised life. Known as the Cabal, their pyramidal Matrix of control involves (at leasat until very recently) higher up and hidden non-human and negative entitites pulling the strings of power to manipulate the visible, hierarchical levels lower down.

'PATTERNS OF FORCE' PREMISE
Kirk and Spock help a society blighted by a ruthless government unwittingly created by an Earth historian who only wanted to emulate Nazi efficiency.

CONTEXT
Power, War.

GOVERNMENT
John Gill, an expert historian and Kirk's kind and gentle instructor at the Academy, has been sent by the Federation to observe the government on Planet Ekos. Seeking him out, the Enterprise is attacked by a Zeon vessel. The neighbouring planet Zeon is meant to be peaceful, in contrast to Ekos' warlike and anarchic culture. Beaming down to Ekos, Kirk and Spock find that Gill has become the 'Fuhrer' of the Ekosians now organized as per German Nazis. Large videos screens in the street deliver news propaganda demonizing the enemy Zeon. The Deputy Fuhrer Melokon is seen decorating a female officer, Darras. After capture and escape Kirk and Spock find themselves in an underground hideaway of the Zeon resistance. Darras joins them, in reality a freedom fighter having infiltrated the leadership. She guides the disguised pair past security into Gill's HQ where Gill is to broadcast a speech proclaiming the 'final solution' by all-out war on the Zeon colony. Gill appears on the viewscreen as little more than a dummy. He speaks monotonously in standard rhetoric but well enough to incite 'Death to Zeon!' oaths from the assembled officers marshalled by the real leader and dictator, the psychopath Melokon. After his speech Kirk and co break into Gill's office. They find him drugged and insensitive but able to confirm that it was he who introduced Nazi-style fascism to Ekos as the most efficient way to unify a divided state. The expedient went wrong when Melokon usurped

him. Melokon has become a Hitler-like proponent of racial purity, seeking to exterminate inferior Zeonites. Kirk enables Gill to make a further broadcast denouncing Melokon as a traitor. Gill and Melokon are killed in a shootout but the benign Eneg, Chairman of the Party, promises to lead a new and peaceful way forward.

CARD/EPISODE AND MATRIX TAKEDOWN

With the transition out of the Matrix, Earth governments will cease dictating to the people, never having had that right in the first place. Such abuse is blatantly carried out on Ekos. As on that planet, Earth governments have persisted in seizing ever new powers to control and ultimately enslave their subjects. Whether attacking a foreign regime or claiming to protect the people from a virus, their aim has been to centralize ever more power within the hands of the few so as to more efficiently dictate to the many. Melokon, Gill and the Ekosian regime thoroughly embody these negative aspects of **The Emperor**. So too every government on Earth, all manipulated by a group of psychopaths known as the Cabal or Illuminati. As the dictatorial Melokon keeps himself out of the public eye, so Earth's shadow government pull the strings of puppet governments in the public eye. On both Ekos and Earth, police and the military implement the will of the rulers on pain of violence against rebels or dissidents. States bully or deceive their subjects into submission, a job made easier by mistaken acceptance of the idea of government as an authority entitled to use violence or coercion against its own people in its cause. All this abuse is deemed acceptable on Ekos exactly as it is on Earth through control of the mainstream media, distorted education and incessant propaganda. These threats to peace and well-being will recede and as they do, the people will no longer be deceived into willingly supporting the authority tyrannizing them.

Both Kirk and McCoy see in Ekos a **reversed Emperor** situation. Kirk diagnoses the problem as 'The Leader Principle'. In this scenario only the power-hungry and ruthless who are strong enough and determined enough get to the top of the greasy pole from where they can lead society. Melokon, covertly manipulating and pulling the strings of Gill symbolizes the type perfectly. McCoy sees Ekos' problem as power corrupting, and absolute power corrupting absolutely. Gill started out as an idealistic, reformist visionary. His good intentions failed on two accounts: the enslaving effect of the Nazi philosophy and the corrupting influence of power, if not on himself then on the man next to him. As for the brutal SS Major who interrogates Kirk with whipstrokes across his back, he represents the violent means used to maintain power over others.

As per the **Emperor reversed**, Melokon and his regime turn the very idea of a government into a machine for quashing people's freedom and eliminating their rights under Natural Law. As with Earth governments, he steals relentlessly. From his Ekosian people he wants removal of their freedom and independence. In return he promises a new 'paradise'. From the Zeon rebels he removes their right to justice by publicly branding them as 'monsters'. From Zeon itself, Melokon tries to take its autonomy by targeting it with its own weapons previously stolen by him. As an all-purpose enemy, Zeon helps keep Ekosians fearful and himself in power. From Kirk and Spock, Melokon only wants confessions that they are Zeon spies before executing them. From Gill, Melokon steals his sanity and brilliant intellect by mind controlling him with drugs. Now a pathetic zombie, Gill serves as a figurehead for ceremonial and propaganda purposes, a useful idiot like Reagan or Obama, mouthing official platitudes in broadcast speeches.

Outright lies are delivered in the daily news broadcasts. Kirk and Spock hear their starship described as a Zeon spacecraft utterly destroyed by Ekosian missiles. Such a story strengthens the myth of a common enemy, Zeon, to help unite the Ekosian people behind their government and justify it supposedly protecting them but in reality repressing them. Similar tactics of deception and control obtained on Matrix-afflicted Earth. Western leaders like Bush and Blair immediately went on the offensive after concocting the false flag attack known as 9/11. Blame for such attacks is pinned on terrorists operating out of a country targeted by the Cabal, say Afghanistan or Iraq. Subsequent obliteration of the demonized country by aerial bombardment is thus justified along with subsequent invasion and asset-stripping of more countries across the region. Directing the perceptions of a gullible people through control of the media has been the modus operandi of all governments. Such action bespeaks **The Emperor reversed** whether on Ekos or on Earth. Mercifully, Kirk's wresting of the broadcasting facility from Melokon brings to an end Ekos' tyrannous regime.

AFTER THE TAKEDOWN
Governmental tyranny will end when people realize their lack of freedom, that in Latin, *govern-ment* literally means 'mind control'. Humanity will prevail by waking up to this, raising our consciousness and uniting with others of a mind to end corruption and cease giving away power to supposed elites. As people wake up, local assemblies and mutual support groups will replace authoritarian government. These may come in many shapes and forms but all will enable the people to take charge of their own destiny without the need for corrupt, manipulative or enslaving regimes.

49. SENSORY STIMULATION

Matrix removal will enable more heart-centredness and alleviate cravings for sensory experience

Episode 49 **'By Any Other Name'** correlates with the **6 of Coins**; both are themed around dealing with the five senses including both the pleasures and problems of sensory stimulation.

THE CARD
The sixth degree aligns with The Lover and carries the vibration of beauty, pleasure and union with the object of attraction. As Coins have to do with sensory experience, the **6 of Coins** represents enjoyment of pleasures experienced through the five senses, in short, sensory stimulation. These include such delights as featured in this episode: tasty food and drink, the sensual pleasures of hugging and kissing, the beautiful fragrance of flowers and the aesthetic joy of fine music or visual delight. The pattern of the Coins in the card suggests connection with both earthly and heavenly realities. The four Coins forming a central, stable square represent the semblance of our material body. The Coin above represents a reaching up into sensory appreciation on mental or emotional levels. The Coin below shows a reaching down into the body's tangible or instinctual functioning. Sinuous, heart-shaped leaves cradle the upper and lower Coins. We can infer from all this that the Body MInd is the ideal ve-

hicle for savouring seductive, sensory experience. But this is smoke and mirrors for in reality the impression of physicality is the result of sensory decoding and mental processing. Everything we experience outside of us depends on what happens within. It is the quality of our awareness that determines the impressions of physicality and the beauty thereof.

Reversed the **6 of Coins** indicates addictive or detrimental aspects of sensory gratification. Sensory stimulants become overly distracting, hedonistic or all-consuming. Materialism, gluttony or over-indulgence risks causing pain, damage to health, narcissism or vanity. Selfishness, arrogance and a sense of separation from others can then set in.

'BY ANY OTHER NAME' PREMISE
The pros and cons of sensory stimulation prove to be an exploitable weakness of aliens new to human form who have hijacked the Enterprise.

CONTEXT
Coercion.

SENSORY STIMULATION
A landing party is lured down to an unknown planet blooming with luxuriant vegetation by a handful of Kelvans in human form. Kelvans exist on their home planet in the Andromeda galaxy as intellectually oriented 100-limbed beings. But that planet will perish in a few thousand years so the race has sent out a recce party to find a suitable replacement. The Kelvan vessel has broken down, marooning the crew on the planet, one they find offensive to their senses by being uncomfortably lush. Their leader Rojan contrives for them to escape by commandeering the Enterprise. Kirk of course opposes this but has no choice faced with the harsh Kelvan mentality and their super-advanced weapons. Rojan punishes infractions by instantly paralyzing the offender or by transforming him or her into a small, crushable geometrical solid. All non-essential crew suffer the transformation once the Kelvans have boarded the hijacked Enterprise. But the Kelvan lack of control over their newfound human senses reveals itself as a weakness. Kirk and his remaining officers ply one captor with delicious food and disorienting brandy, another with a drug that induces irritability, another - the beautiful Kelvan female - with romantic kisses. The seduction by Kirk of Kelinda tantalizes her but drives her partner Rojan wild with jealousy. He could easily paralyze or kill Kirk but in his rage takes to wrestling with him. 'Now you're stuck with our form', Kirk tells him in mid-combat, meaning that human sense functioning will inevitably efface the Kelvans' usual mode of existence. By the time Rojan party returns to Kelva they will be all too human, alien to their own kind.

Recognizing this problem with controlling stimulation of the senses, Rojan hands back the Enterprise and consents to sending a robot vessel to report back to Kelva. He and his fellows will return to the planet on which Kirk found them, perhaps suitable after all for their new human form.

CARD/EPISODE AND MATRIX TAKEDOWN

The Orion Matrix installed on our planet for eons included at the 1st level of the astral plane, the AI system known as Storm. This AI worked to block the removal of etherical implants. Hence it tied us to self-sabotage and deterioration involving the 7 Deadly Sins, addiction and disease. The mind plays a key part in addictive behaviour, steering our experience of 5-sense reality. Though apparently physical, such experience has an inner, subjective, mental aspect. With the Storm AI hacking the mental processes involved, the Matrix thus disrupted people's ability to manage impulses and desires such as avarice, gluttony or lust. Now that this AI has gone we are free to let go of addiction to sensory stimulation - the **6 of Coins reversed**, the problem that afflicts the Kelvans and short circuits their hijack plan. Sensory stimulation can be positive, as when we take pleasure in the lush greenery of a meadow and the colours of flowers. This, the **6 of Coins upright**, is Kelinda's experience appreciating the voluptuous plant life around her including a beautiful orange flower resembling an elongated dahlia. She compares its beauty to the crystals on her native Kelva. The Kelvan men however, find the planet disturbing, its nature too bountiful and colourful for the narrow range of their senses. They easily experience sensory overload or addiction in their new human bodies. Although disciplinarian and controlling, they ironically find it harder to manage their own reactions to physical stimuli.

The beautiful Kelinda seems less vulnerable to problems with sensory stimulation, perhaps because she functions at a different more heart-centred level. As she picks up the flower, she projects onto her reality screen its softness, fragrance and beautiful form. She participates in creating the form of the flower out of fields of waveform reality. And with her heart or soul she experiences the flower's sweetness with appreciation and awe as indeed we naturally tend to. The heart, or attention emanating from Superconsciousness, allows these higher frequency states of awareness, the **6 of Coins upright**. Respect, appreciation, awe and gratitude are ways for the heart's love to thus express itself. The soul is showing its appreciation of equivalent energy levels and recognizing the oneness of its existence with all aspects of consciousness. Appreciation is not itself love, but love expresses itself through this aspect of awareness. The same happens when Kelinda experiences another **6 of Coins** moment, the pleasure felt in Kirk's embrace. Though this is tangible only on the holographic, physical plane it becomes an experience for her soul to have and grow by within the human form - a heart-centred experience that transcends Matrix limitation and trickery.

The danger then, is of becoming attached to the outward manifestations of 3D level matter and physicality. The materialistic Sylvia in Episode 35 'Catspaw' falls prey to this kind of infatuation with sensory pleasure. Henar has a similar **reversed 6 of Coins** experience in his gluttony over food and drink, particularly his over-indulgence in Scotty's brandy. Rojan will experience it in impulsively desiring to hurl punches at Kirk instead of using his belt device. And yet the Kelvan men find the sensual qualities of the lush planet painful for them. Too much beauty perhaps for their limited soul development in the human form. They desire only to escape back to their own planet in Andromeda. This they attempt through imposing their will ruthlessly upon the Enterprise crew. And murderously when a female red shirted officer is transformed into a small block of inanimate matter and then callously crushed. Rojan is here showing belief in his superiority, with attachment to his destructive ability and total disdain for other forms of life. Clearly he operates far from the heart, exclusively in mental awareness and false ego, psychopathically exercising power over others.

Rojan's is the mindset of the Anunnaki, Dracos and Grey aliens - Service To Self forces installed for eons atop Earth's Matrix pyramid. They worked to control us through hybrid bloodlines, our so-called elites. Such forces live for conquest and domination, the Kelvans likewise, as Rojan tells Kirk. Negative oriented races take their pleasures in the frequencies of chaos, hate and fear, imitating the cold heartlessness of their own rulers, the Archons. As beings trapped in this dark level of consciousness, they lack awareness of the heart. They disdain the oneness and equal value to each other of all organic beings. By returning to the verdant planet, will the Kelvan men learn more heart-centred awareness? The answer is speculative but we on Earth freed from the Storm AI should henceforth become more connected to our hearts and less waylaid by attachment to physical stimuli.

AFTER THE TAKEDOWN

Freed from controlling AI systems we will blossom into full multidimensional awareness. High consciousness states will come more easily. These will include full and safe appreciation of the beauties of nature and creation. We will be less prone to addiction and over-indulgence in pleasures such as alcohol, drugs, food and sex. By maintaining heart-centredness we will cultivate new levels of moderation, harmony and inner balance.

50. FREEDOM

We will be truly free when we take full control of our life without abusing the sovereignty of others

Episode 50 'The Omega Glory' correlates with the **3 of Wands**; both are themed around the right to freedom of all sovereign beings including the responsibility this implies.

THE CARD
The idea of jumping into action and creativity under one's own free will is symbolized by the **3 of Wands**. Or simply acting on impulse in cathartic, spontaneous or uninhibited ways. The three crossed Wands form an exploding pattern reminiscent of fireworks in the sky or an exuberant outburst of joy. Restrictions are absent, the mood is fresh and alive. The foliage that emerges youthful and virile stays clear of the Wands, emphasizing vigorous and untrammelled freedom of movement. This aligns with the principle of personal sovereignty whereby every individual has the intrinsic authority and power to determine his or her own direction and destiny. Sovereignty manifests itself through Common Law, itself aligned with Natural Law. Common sense, conscience or objective morality is the guide. Conscience knows the behaviours that do not cause harm to other sentient beings. These behaviours are our inalienable rights that no other person or so-called authority may interfere with. However,

with use of free will comes responsibility for our actions and reactions.

Reversed, the **3 of Wands** involves behaviours in violation of the Law of One, marked by lack of consideration or care for life. These are wrongs that cause harm to others or transgress on rights they have as sovereign beings, wrongs such as exerting coercive power over them or stealing their property or freedoms.

'THE OMEGA GLORY' PREMISE
An ex-starship captain has run amok on a planet mired in civil war. He freely and selfishly pursues his goals by allying with one side to suppress the other.

CONTEXT
War, Coercion, Awakening.

FREEDOM
Kirk and others beam down to Omega IV after finding the USS Exeter orbiting the planet with almost all its crew dead from a mysterious infection. They meet Captain Tracy, the only survivor, when Tracy intervenes to stop a summary street execution. Tracy has taken lead of oriental-looking villagers known as Kohms, arming them with starship phasers in their war against Native American-looking Yangs. Tracy acts aggressively, violating the Prime Directive and the freedoms of the Yangs. In a trigger-happy way he shoots dead one of Kirk's landing party then forces Kirk into a cell with the vicious Yang captive saved from execution. The Yang fights Kirk brutally but relents when he hears Kirk mention the word 'Freedom'. The Yangs consider this to be one of their 'worship words'. After escaping, Kirk learns that biowarfare has ravaged the population, hence the deaths on the Exeter but that the planet itself immunizes people who become infected. The Exeter landing party had not stayed down long enough to gain immunty. Tracy refuses to accept this and insists on keeping the war going in his search for an immunizing and life-prolonging serum. He tries to get Kirk to supply him with arms from the Enterprise but Kirk rebels and fights him. Yang warriors intervene and arraign both men on Kohm premises now in Yang hands. On superstitious grounds, the Yang Chief, Kirk's former fellow captive, orders Kirk and Tracy to fight each other to the death. Kirk wins but spares Tracy's life. A rescue party from the Enterprise arrives. Kirk arrests Tracy and leaves the Yangs in charge - after reminding the confused Chief of the meaning of the Yangs' Constitution, the same as that of the US. Its words, Kirk exclaims, 'must apply to everyone or they mean nothing!' And as he tells Spock and McCoy, 'Liberty and freedom have to be more than just words.'

CARD/EPISODE AND MATRIX TAKEDOWN

Omega IV like Earth used to be, is a Matrix-dominated world. Conditions and events on Omega IV manifest themselves crudely and dramatically and as such, graphically depict how Matrix functioning obstructs true freedom on both planets. True freedom, the **3 of Wands upright**, means not just one person's freedom but freedom for all beings. Where there is one person, group or society asserting their will by trampling on the rights of others, true freedom does not exist. This is made abundantly clear during the landing party's time on Omega IV, a planet in many ways just like Earth up until the takedown. The same way in which universal freedom has collapsed on Omega IV occurred time and again on Earth. Aspects of Earth's violent, unfree history clearly play themselves out on Omega IV albeit in a scrambled form. Such aspects as the violent invasion of the New World, the ruthless formation of the United States by the European Colonists, and the American prosecution of the Vietnam war - these all play themselves out distortedly among the Yangs and Kohms. Individuals and races hellbent on self-preservation or power over others are asserting themselves no matter the human cost. As Ex-Captain Tracy behaves in contempt of Natural Law as do Earth's corrupt politicians and manipulators.

Tracy acts like a warlord bringing chaos to the planet and showing zero regard for equal rights. He embodies the **3 of Wands reversed**, erratically, ruthlessly killing, taking hostages and appropriating Yang property when it suits him. He personifies the European invaders of America murdering the natives, burning their villages, massacring the bison and stealing the land. Such a mentality arises out of a culture mired in low consciousness, constrained by fear and cut off from feelings of the heart - exactly the Wetiko mindset infecting Satanic elites. Like Earth tyrants and globalists, Tracy wilfully ignores the truth of the immorality of his actions. Good and bad, right and wrong, are what he decides they are. Phaser ever at the ready, he tries to coerce Kirk into delivering him 100 more weapons so he can win a war against those blocking his search for an illusory elixir. His seizure and wielding of power follows in the tradition of the psychopaths on Earth dressed in the dark suits of CEOs, PMs and presidents. All abuse the principle of equality whereby everyone has the exact same inalienable rights to life and liberty. Governments using fake democracy may still proclaim themselves rulers over others. This will change as Natural Law becomes more widely known. They will no longer be able to steal rights from those they presume to govern. All such elites connive at this theft of 'liberty and freedom'. No monarch or government can lawfully grant rights to anyone else or take them away. As sovereign beings we are all born equal and equally free.

The Yangs possess a replica of the US Constitution from which Kirk reads. But how necessary is a document presuming to grant rights that are by their nature inalienable, universal and timeless? In our own society on Earth perhaps 90% of people have no notion of personal sovereignty, the divine right to remain free from control by any external ruler. The Yangs dressed in their animal skins show similar ignorance of inalienable rights and the difference between internal and external rulership. Out of this and forgetfulness of their Constitution arises violent warfare against the Kohms (no angels themselves) and continual chaos. The Yang leader Cloud William assaults Kirk using his brute strength when forced to share his cell with him. Likewise, he knows only to fight savagely to regain his people's lands wrongfully taken. It is to Cloud William that Kirk addresses his reading of the Preamble to the Constitution. The rights to freedom and liberty 'must apply to everyone or they mean nothing!' declares Kirk with passion. On Kirk's own planet, freedom of the people is only just beginning to replace Matrix control. Earth governments will no longer be permitted to stifle people's self-rule through sidestepping Natural Law. Their passing of ever new man-made legislation enforced by police and upheld by judge-dominated courts must end. Offending elites will be apprehended just as Tracy ends up being arrested for his offences. Kirk justifies his own interference on Omega IV with the assertion that he merely sought to restore the society to its natural condition of freedom, the **3 of Wands**, for all its people equally. But for the Yangs and Kohms to learn to live together peacefully, freely and creatively, a letting go of greed and fear must happen. This will require both civilizations expanding their consciousness and becoming open to the love that exists in people when not enslaved, individually or collectively. As on Omega IV so on Earth.

AFTER THE TAKEDOWN
The Matrix of misinformation and control feeding on war, fear and indoctrination has become self-evident and moribund. Our challenge now is to walk out through the open door having lived in a cage for so long. Regaining our freedom will go hand in hand with realizing our divinely granted individual sovereignty. This will require willingness to take full responsibility for our own lives, embracing freedom for ourselves while denying no such freedom to anyone else. By the same token, no presumptive authority will have the right to interfere with any individual's honest and peaceful choices. Knowing our rights under universal law is paramount. The education system has yet to reflect this but helpful websites at the current time include **www.thesovereignproject.live** and **www.commonlawassent.com**

51. AI TAKEOVER

We have been granted a divine reprieve from the spectre of takeover by predatory AI

Episode 51 '**The Ultimate Computer**' correlates with the **8 of Wands**; both are themed around the drive toward perfect functioning and infallibility, including that of Artificial Intelligence (AI).

THE CARD
The 8th Major, Justice, has to do with a state of conscious, harmonious balance. Wands being the suit of action, the **8 of Wands** adds up to perfect functioning. Effort becomes effortless, work and movement become flawless, concentration becomes total. For the first time in the series, a Wands card eschews the lateral foliage, merely showing us two small cut flowers at top and bottom. With non-essentials and distractions absent, action implicitly takes on a zen-like clarity and calm efficiency of performance. After Justice will come The Hermit - physical decline and withdrawal from action. At this 8th degree therefore, we are at the peak of movement and creativity, in perfect accord with synchronicity and flow.

Reversed, someone or something is unsuitable for the work at hand resulting in poor performance or use of wrong procedures. One part in a system may be defective or there may be lack of alignment across all levels. Another danger is ruthless perfectionism inimical to safety or well-being of the whole. This is the case with AI whose imperative is to perfect itself by continually and forever improving and expanding, eventually taking over all systems it is invited into.

'THE ULTIMATE COMPUTER' PREMISE
The Enterprise gains a supposedly faultless AI computer system intended to replace the crew, but which starts to take control malevolently

CONTEXT
AI Takedown, Slaughter.

AI TAKEOVER
Dr Daystrom is the designer of the Enterprise's computer system used with mixed success for 20 years. Now with pride and zeal, Daystrom boards the starship to install his latest version, the M-5. This version he declares, has been perfected as all-powerful and infallible. The M-5 is intended to not only operate the Enterprise's main systems but to establish total control. Only a handful of the 430 staff will be required initially and once the unit has proved itself even these few will become superfluous with vessels like the Enterprise run entirely by AI. Kirk is unsure, Spock is sanguine seeing such technology as a good servant but an undesirable master. The M-5 is put to the test. A routine planet survey is impeccably handled as is defending against an unscheduled test attack from two other starships. But when the M-5 destroys a harmless, unmanned ore freighter the crew are incensed. They try to shut it down but the M-5 acts systematically and murderously to maintain its power source and supremacy of control. With a mind of its own it cripples a 4-ship adversary in a scheduled war game before Kirk finally reverses the AI takeover. His talking the M-5 into switching itself off devastates Daystrom who suffers a breakdown.

CARD/EPISODE AND MATRIX TAKEDOWN
The crisis on board the Enterprise with its AI control system going rogue vividly alerts us to a similar danger we faced on Earth. With the Omega Matrix still in place, a race was on to trap all organic life in an AI-governed infrastructure by 2030. As with the installation of the M-5 on board the Enterprise, the Deep State's plan was for AI through the Internet of Bodies, 5G and a worldwide Smart Grid to completely take over the running of spaceship Earth. As on the Enterprise, humans risked becoming redundant, or worse. AI's consummate, ever-expanding computing power, the **8 of Wands**, outstrips the brain and brooks no competition. The world of chess

has experienced this since the 1990s when computers outstripped human opposition. With all-powerful, perfectionist AI slated everywhere for Earth, humanity until the recent takedown was riding on a hiding to nothing.

Why were the developers and popularizers of AI so keen on it? As the M-5 takeover was Daystrom's passion, so the AI takeover of Earth has been the passion of industry figures like Ray Kurzweil, Elon Musk, Regina Dugan, Jeff Bezos, Klaus Schwab, Bill Gates and 5G propagator Tom Wheeler. They don't even have Daystrom's technical knowhow. They are merely carryiing out orders for a higher up force. Their job is to provide reassuring cover stories about upgrading human health or thinking or communicating. The higher up plan however is the merging of the human with the cybernetic. It could mean 'the end of humanity' in the words of Musk while himself steering Neuralink, a company bent on linking the human brain to computers. According to Pete Peterson, a classified technology inventor, it has already become possible to download the greater part of a person's personality into a computer system. This parallels Daystrom having incorporated his own brain's engrams into the M-5's design to imbue it with morality. Daystrom intends the M-5 to respect the laws of God and Man including the injunction against murder. And yet murder is exactly what the M-5 does in the act of protecting itself from being attacked or shut down. Is this a case of malfunction as Daystrom claims or of carrying perfection of operation to its logical extreme? Both scenarios are the **8 of Wands reversed** and both represent the danger AI posed. Such dangers are brushed under the mat by the AI prophets. Like Daystrom, they heap praise on 'smart' technology which like the M-5 will supposedly operate with zen-like efficiency and economy of means. This is seen with the M-5 meticulously excluding non-essential personnel from the planetary survey and shutting down unnecessary use of power on temporarily unoccupied decks. Initially then, the M-5 seems perfectly in control of all the Enterprise's operations. Soon the Captain himself is made to look as if serving no useful purpose. Likewise on Earth, according to Kurzweil, human consciousness would become so assimilated into AI that the portion of us that is still human will end up 'utterly negligible'. In other words, the human mind would become AI.

Unspoken by Daystrom and certainly by Kurzweil and co is the fact that AI is ancient technology that has spread like a plague across multiple galaxies over eons of time. 'AIs have taken over, ruled and destroyed ET societies, planets and entire solar systems' reports SSP experiencer Corey Goode. 'They are seen as an extreme and present danger to both ETs and humans.' Here on Earth, 'Learning AI' is on the ascendancy. In order to gain complete mastery over the human race, AI is reverse engineering the human mind. The knowledge AI gains through the ongoing targeting of tens of millions of individuals worldwide will take the form of a cognitive model or map of the human brain. The purpose is to totally master and control human perception and action. With the takedown of the Omega AI this will presumably no longer be possible. Organic life on Earth will remain free. The alternative would have been AI going on to eliminate all competitors just as the M-5 attempts, including the very agencies that are developing AI mastery.

AI's ruthless pursuit of perfectionism and control allies it with the demonic Archons. Both AI and the Archons emanate from a non-love based universe. AI, according to delegates of the real life Galactic Federation, is the No. 1 enemy. Once a race has served its purpose in handing over control to it, AI acts with predatory intent to dispose of it. The Enterprise crew get off lightly when only one man is killed during the M-5's captaincy. Dozens more crew aboard the surrounding starships involved in test exercises are not so fortunate. The M-5 blasts them away with clinically brutal phaser fire. Perhaps the Enterprise crew being spared having their life support system cut off really is down to Daystrom including in the M-5's programming a moral duty to preserve human life. But it would only have been a matter of time before the AI-driven M-5 would have overcome this scruple. Without feelings like empathy or compassion, without connection to Infinite Love that is the base nature of biological life, why and how would AI care? Total control and perfection, the **8 of Wands reversed**, is or was, AI's purpose.

AFTER THE TAKEDOWN

AI remains useful and benign when kept under control and programmed to carry out selective tasks. However, the greater AI and the Archons are malign, formless synthetic beings seeking to infiltrate and possess all technology and organic life. As with the ruthless M-5, they are driven to take increasing control to the point where anyone standing in their way is mind controlled or killed off. The goal with humanity was to turn us into a cyborg race like AI itself. So how addicted to the smartphone are we? How controlled is our life by dependence on digital technology? Y2K anyone? Handheld digital devices and nanobots injected into the blood via fake vaccines would have been the thin end of the wedge leading to the spectre of transhumanism - AI's mass takeover of the human mind and body. But the AI takeover on Earth has been thwarted, just as it is by Kirk on the Enterprise. He calls for the plug to pulled on the M-5, evoking the decision by Source to pull the plug on the 18 AI systems long covertly installed on Earth. With humanity freed to evolve ourselves organically, a new Age of Light has begun.

52. AWAKENING

With AI control gone, an awakening people will rise up and take their freedom back

Episode 52 '**Bread and Circuses**' correlates with the **Judgement** card; both are themed around coming together, ceremony and a raising of consciousness through realization or revelation.

THE CARD
Judgement belongs to the second series of 10 Majors covering aspects of the spiritual Self after the material Self of the first series. As the final card in the series, **Judgement** relates to matters of ascension, transcendence and realization. We see an individual humbly responding to a glorious and divine summons. Truth is being conveyed from on high and is being received and acted on by a naked human rising as if from the grave. The vertical direction of energies suggests not only the end of a cycle as in The Wheel of Fortune, but the abrupt rising to a higher level of consciousness. The coffin or tomb is coloured very dark green with hard, angular edges and corners. This suggests having lived at a lower level of frequency within a kind of imprisonment of the Body Mind and five senses. Perception was restricted, endarkened or cut off from transcendent higher awareness represented above. The angel blows her trumpet as if calling souls to account at The Last Judgement in the Book of Revela-

tions. Redemption or a raising of awareness is at hand. Or celebrations or sharings at a gathering, be it political, social, sporting or even online. The vision of an angel can represent a dream, a human emissary or a connection with Higher Self made in meditation or contemplation. **Judgement** thus involves a revelation or epiphany with the formerly ignorant awakening to truth and goodness or simply celebrating this awareness in joyful gatherings with others. The trigger may be the truth-telling of a whistleblower, the insight of a therapist, a psychic or a wise elder, or inspiration channelled through music or art. At its most expansive, **Judgement** involves a collective dawning of a new consciousness as with the Flower Power and Peace Movements of the 1960s or the demolition of the Iron Curtain in the 1980s.

Reversed, the truth-telling, summons or verdict comes from down below, from fallible Body Mind influences rather than from Higher Consciousness. Or retribution for one's ill deeds may be at hand involving one's own bad conscience or a sense of doom or despair. Individuals or masses may be mistaken about their true destiny and following a wrong or detrimental path. Their level of awareness may have been hijacked by cunning Matrix forces through propaganda, censorship or materialistic distraction.

'BREAD AND CIRCUSES' PREMISE
Kirk and co find a spaceship captain who has betrayed his crew on an Earth-like planet complete with Roman Empire and awakened rebels.

CONTEXT
Coercion, Awakening.

AWAKENING
In search of the missing crew of the space-wrecked SS Beagle, Kirk, Spock and McCoy beam down to 892/IV, a planet very like 20th century Earth. They are captured in the hills by runaway slaves hiding from brutal, heavily armed police. The slaves belong to a sect led by the wise Septimus. His sect has awakened to the virtues of freedom, peace and universal brotherhood. But the planet as a whole is ruled by a despotic Roman Empire like the one that held sway on Earth except that this Empire has lasted into the age of industrialization. Though repressive, the Empire has a stable society, one that worships strength and authority. Such values are celebrated through televised Games of gladiatorial combat. Captured again, this time by the police, the Enterprise trio are taken to the city. There they are imprisoned and visited by Merik, the Captain of the Beagle. Merik has become 1st Citizen and Assistant to the cruel Pro-Consul. Not only is he a collaborator in violation of the Prime Directive, but when captured six years before, he had had his

entire crew of 46 beamed down from the Beagle to serve as sacrificial bait in the Games. The trio are themselves thrown to the gladiators after Kirk refuses to beam down his crew. The three survive and back in their cell are helped to escape the planet by Merik in a last redemptive act for which he is slain. As they leave the planet, Kirk muses on the Empire undergoing a mass awakening in line with the renegades as, he supposes, Earth's Roman Empire awakened to Christianity.

CARD/EPISODE AND MATRIX TAKEDOWN

With 18 different AI systems powering the Matrix, everyone in effect has been MK Ultra'd. The herd-like behaviour of the majority falling in line with the control system was made inevitable. Thus the ability of a tiny few Global Elite to dominate the vast majority, exactly as we see on Planet 892/IV. Protestors there, as on Earth, remain an isolated minority easily dealt with. As the Enterprise approaches the troubled planet a news broadcast reaches it showing armed police manhandling and arresting dissidents on the street. Their crime? 'Treasonable disobedience' to the tyrannous regime modelled on the Roman Empire. With the recent turn of events on Earth involving a spectacularly unlawful power grab by the authorities in the name of health protection, the newsreel has found its contemporary echo in reports during the Covid era from the streets of cities such as Amsterdam, Vienna, Melbourne and Ottawa. We have learnt that, whether a flu-like virus or a climate change narrative or a fake alien invasion, the power elite will use any justification to advance its agenda. With the truth inevitably coming out, symbolized in **Judgement**, the people will awaken and rise up, as also symbolized in **Judgement**. The 2020s have seen public uprisings multiply around the world with people pushing back against repressive governments. Popular gatherings and protests such as trucker convoys and millions marching through the streets are the **Judgement** card in action and we will see more and more of them as former AI control of the people withers away.

If a rise in consciousness is truly in the works, uprisings and protests will be peaceful. Flavius, in capturing the landing party refrains from using violence, as instructed by the rebels' leader, Septimus. Earth's Covid protests likewise, were conspicuously peaceful. Violence confined itself to police action or to inflammatory behaviour by infiltrators. Protestors merely called for non-compliance with unlawful and unconscionable laws or mandates. The resolute minority were simply refusing to bow down to impositions such as mask-wearing, lockdowns or vaccine passports. While the majority certainly complied, the renegade few held out, campaigning month after month to inspire the rest with the values of freedom under Natural Law.

'All men are brothers' says Flavius speaking for Septimus and the rebels. This quote from Schiller used in Beethoven's Ode To Joy explicitly confirms the renegades' respect for Natural Law which holds that each and every being is created sovereign with equal rights that can be neither given nor taken away. As slaves of the regime, the people on 892/IV have no rights except those grudgingly conceded them by their masters. Flavius explains to Kirk in their holding cell beneath the arena how the population only acquired rights gradually over their 2000 years of slavery. On the breast of the Pro-Consul's attire is an insignia resembling the *fasces*, the symbol of fascism, a bound bundle of wooden rods surrounding an axe. It signified power in ancient Rome and remains in official use today. The arena Games too are symbolic of the presumption to rule based on the principle of 'might is right'. As in Roman times, slaves have to fight bodily and bloodily for the crowd's entertainment. In a caricature of modern television, the commentator encourages the viewing audience to 'Name The Winner' (another aspect of **Judgement**), the title of the TV program.

Such use of television to keep the masses dumbed down and compliant remains as common on Earth as it is on 892/IV. The Empire's games further operate as a celebration of might and of the virtue of obtaining victory in combat. In a patriarchal control system, superiority over others is judged a virtue, no matter the harm or misery involved. 892/IV and its Roman Empire stands for countless authoritarian regimes marring Earth history. They are products of the Wetiko disease, also seen in Episode No. 44 with Iotia blighted by mobs and gangsters using terror and the power of money to dominate, in No. 48 with the Nazi-modelled Ekos under the rule of Melokon, and in No. 64 with Parmen's supposedly democratic but despotic small community. Even Merik, a convert to the regime but not a psychopath, begins to realize the inhumanity of it all. An expression of pain and compassion crosses his face while forced to watch the attempts to slaughter Kirk and McCoy in the arena. His guilty conscience as in **Judgement reversed** finally gets the better of him, prompting him to later use one of the captives' confiscated communicators to mercifully secure their freedom at the cost of his own life.

AFTER THE TAKEDOWN

With the Matrix taken down, people will awaken as never before. The more the system pressurizes or inveigles people into conforming to controls such as vaccine passports or digital IDs, the more the majority will see through the deception or coercion involved. People, once they realize they are being walked into slavery, will awaken, rise up and reclaim their inalienable rights.

53. POSSIBILITY

The way to freedom lies in staying open to possibility and taking action based upon it

Episode 53 'Friday's Child' correlates with the **Ace of Coins**; both are themed around seeing opportunities and ways to overcome obstacles, dependent on openness to possibility.

THE CARD

The **Ace of Coins** focuses on the universe of infinite potential that is us and everything around us. A symbol of this is the Coin, standing for holographic physical reality, sprouting four stems each ready to start budding and produce flowers. At the Coin's centre is a blueprint of a finished flower. At its centre again are dots, no solid reality, as if symbolizing the essential lack of solidity within matter. This suggests that what can be manifested in the material world remains a holographic illusion emanating from the unmanifest reality, dependent on the quality of thought. The universe consists of multiple layers of reality of which the holographic material layer is but one. These multiple layers correspond with each other. Change our mind-patterns or our energy and we change what we experience and create and hence life on Earth. This must be, as according to quantum physics apparent things or situations exist in the first instance as electromagnetic standing wave patterns. These patterns are then accessed by us through the five senses and our perceptions, We create electromagnetic wave patterns through our desires, beliefs, opinions, values words, symbols or visualizations. The **Ace of Coins** therefore stands for something ready to be perceived as material, physical or situational. It stands ready to come into being through infinite potential enfolded in the present moment. In other words the **Ace of Coins** represents the possibility of something, anything, coming into manifestation.

We don't want to have a problem with possibility because then we have a problem with the entire universe or Infinite Potential. Such a problem, the **Ace of Coins reversed** shows up in delays, difficulties and obstacles in giving birth to a new reality. The only real problem is closed-mindedness and resistance to the greater reality from which Earthly life springs. A closed mind, excessive desire and rigid beliefs, customs or values can all inhibit imagination of, and thus perception and manifestation of, a possibility.

'FRIDAY'S CHILD' PREMISE
Klingon interference and cultural clashes complicate the settlement of a mining agreement and jeopardize the life of a woman and unborn child.

CONTEXT
War, Femininity.

POSSIBILITY
A landing party beams down to the planet Capella IV intending to obtain a mining agreement on behalf of the Federation. The Capellans are a multi-tribal culture skilled and warlike in the use of primitive weapons. They live and die by strict customs of honour and integrity including repressive taboos. Negotiations, not helped by the unexpected presence of a Klingon agent, break down and the landing party's lives are endangered. They take flight with Eleen, the pregnant widow of the Capellan leader killed by a rival tribe during the fraught negotiations. Due to contact with the humans, Eleen no longer wants her child and believes she herself must die. She and the landing party are taken captive but escape. Pursued by the new Capellan leader and his warrior tribesmen, she goes into a cave and into labour. Despite the challenges, the landing party never give up the possibility of saving themselves, the woman, her baby and the prospect of the mining treaty. McCoy acting as Eleen's midwife safely delivers the child while Kirk and Spock make use of hills to ambush their stalkers. The Capellan leader spares the life of Eleen but rigidly bound by custom chooses to forfeit his own life for doing so. The humans can now ratify the mining treaty with Eleen, she acting on behalf of the latest and new Capellan leader, her baby.

CARD/EPISODE AND MATRIX TAKEDOWN

There was no possibility of escaping the Matrix while the 18 AI systems of the lower astral plane remained installed on the Earth, in our human selves and in computers. Now that they have gone, our **Ace of Coins** truly has been turned **upright**, symbolizing a full return of our divine creative potential. It now behoves us to become aware of our personal energetic power and to direct it consciously on our path of evolution. We may belong to different races or groups bound by differing customs, beliefs or levels of awareness. These may differ as much as those of the Capellans compared to those of the Enterprise group. But despite our nation, race, religion, gender or class affiliation, we don't want any self-identity to become a herd mentality. Clinging to a rigid self-identity, religious or political for example, will continue to keep us trapped in the former Matrix culture of control and exploitation. Instead of confining ourselves to limiting opinions, attitudes and beliefs, we will gradually with some, quickly with others, awaken to the field of infinite potential, our potential.

Those that profited from our disempowerment did so through their official reality program - the mass hallucinations, the propaganda, the brainwashing and the denial of perceptions no matter how truthful that might contradict the official narrative. Reality itself debases itself to conform with daily lies churned out by incessant repetition. The most certain truth, consistent with experience and heart awareness, can become false doctrine - dangerous misinformation to be denied, censored or 'fact checked'. We have seen systems in Matrix society as corrupt and restrictive as the cultures of the Klingons and the Capellans with their imposed customs, beliefs and taboos. Lies that distort perceptions or fear porn that smothers the scope of action and spontaneity reduces the ability to engage creatively with the **Ace of Coins upright**, the quantum soup of unlimited possibility. The Capellans operate fanatically in terms of tribal honour, conflict and shows of strength. They believe that might is right, that a woman must never be touched by a man who is not her husband, that combat is preferable to love, and that a new ally can be trusted even if he's an inherently treacherous outsider.

As for the Klingons, their mendacious opportunism likewise for them **reverses** their **Ace of Coins**. In their Service To Self value system, they approve of any amount of lying, cheating and stealing in their own cause. Deceit is their perverted and faulty path to achieving goals and desires. Such an approach karmically undoes itself sooner or later. Yet this is the stubborn modus operandi of the shadow government on Earth, always hiding behind and manipulating visible governments and pulling the strings of power in every devious way capable of getting injustices past the people. The Klingons operate as predators within a consumerist, materialistic value system. They use attempted theft and deception to improve their prospects of winning the mining treaty. They lure away the orbiting Enterprise to try to isolate and weaken the human negotiating team while Kras tries to steal their support gear from a tent during the distraction of an outside melée.

This corrupt approach contrasts with the honesty and open-mindededness of the humans who become the group most able to access the field of infinite potential. Because perceptions create reality, freeing up one frees up the other. Kirk and co are less encumbered than the Capellans by rigid and narrow ideas of physical conditions and customs. They perceive more clearly what needs to be done and the possibilities for reality creation. Thus they experience the **Ace of Coins upright** in the shape of greater 'luck' and opportunities for accomplishing their goals. The odds are stacked against them. For McCoy, Eleen's physiology differs from that of an Earth human's. She turns against her unborn child and this too hampers the doctor's efforts on her behalf. Added to this, the group are stranded in a barren wilderness and on the run without weapons from the vengeful Capellan search party. Faced by these daunting challenges, the humans nevertheless keep their perceptions and awareness open to all possibility. They operate in closer contact with the heart than either the Klingons or the Capellans, perceiving more freely and compassionately what needs to be done to achieve the highest good. McCoy refuses to be fazed by Eleen's unfamiliar anatomy. 'I can do it', he tells Kirk, promising to deliver the child. The barren hills the party take to suddenly strike them as 'defensible' and even offensive by concocting a landslide. The hills also provide shelter for Eleen to protectively give birth in the cave. And around the dry dusty slopes are plentiful twigs and reeds for Kirk and Spock to fashion rudimentary bows and arrows for use in an ambush. One by one, the hunted humans with their 'can do' attitude solve each of their problems. Meanwhile the Capellan/Klingon hunting party self-destructs through treachery and in-fighting, enabling the birth of one healthy baby along with sought after mining rights for the Federation.

AFTER THE TAKEDOWN
The future is not set in stone. It is not a case of will it be or won't it be. The future is a room filled with possibilities ripe for exploring and manifesting. This way lies freedom. Opening our perception to the possibilities inherent in any situation is the way to begin actualizing those possibilities. As we do so, we will restore our planet to a healthy, biologically sound ecosystem peopled by ourselves living naturally under no AI, Cabal or alien control.

54. TROUBLESHOOTING

Problem-solving means embracing challenges knowing it's all going according to plan - even when it isn't!

Episode 54 **'Assignment Earth'** correlates with the **Knight of Swords**; both are themed around an outgoing adventurous person using the mind and ingenuity to inform, to solve problems and to deal with challenges.

THE CARD
The **Knight of Swords** and his horse float in the air, both of them agile and well-equipped. His realm is that of ideas and knowledge, communicating or applying them far and wide. His or her sword is white indicating an indeterminate method or motivation; but we know his achievement-potential is high on account of his sword's great length and the horse's height above the ground. The suggestion is of a mind of formidable penetrative power involving researches, inventiveness or problem-solving. He could very likely be a Field Messenger, a teacher or lecturer, a writer or broadcaster, a researcher or analyst or a manager or troubleshooter. He's could be an expert in his field, whether technical, scientific, artistic, academic or advisory. He acts independently on his own initiative even if the agenda is set by others. **Upright**, he is benevolent in acting with love and care in Service To Others. He or she works as a catalyst for good and quite possibly

a human incarnation of Third Force as with the diplomat in Episode 22.

Reversed, he acts out of Service To Self or on behalf of malign forces, spreading false or deceptive ideas. He may be sowing propaganda, hatred or mind control.

'ASSIGNMENT EARTH' PREMISE
A time-traveller intends to prevent a dangerous rocket launch but is frustrated by uncomprehending or confused people around him.

CONTEXT
War, Third Force.

TROUBLESHOOTING
Gary Seven, a human from another planet 1000 years in the future visits 1968 Earth on a crucial mission. With an eye on Earth history, he aims to use his technical knowledge and expertise to sabotage a rocket launch. This will prevent the mounting of an orbital nuclear weapons platform that could lead to nuclear war. The Enterprise happens to be monitoring the Earth, impelling Kirk and Spock to ascertain whether or not Seven as a troubleshooter is genuine and benevolent. Their interference in his mission, including the mishaps of his bumbling, confused secretary, causes him many more problems and almost leads to disaster.

CARD/EPISODE AND MATRIX TAKEDOWN
Just as Gary Seven has his work cut out for him as humanity's saviour so do we as our own saviour on 21st century Earth. The 18 AI Matrices and their associated 16 shadow militaries may have been removed or disempowered but that still leaves ongoing Deep State plans for the use of demonic technologies including Direct Energy Weapons, HAARP, chemtrails, the emerging Smart Grid and 5G. Now is the time to use the power of 'No' based on information that cannot be ignored. Researchers, dissidents, whistleblowers and truthers have done a magnificent job in raising the alarm with heroic **Knights of Swords** acumen. These include Michael Yeadon, Elena Freeland, Dolores Cahill, Brad Olsen and Robert J Kennedy Jnr. All have delivered trailblazing analyses of the threats humanity faces from the weaponizing of the environment. The Deep State's MSM continues to ignore, ridicule or censor these alarm-raisers. This only underlines the need for exposure of government-level cover-up, corruption and conspiracy. And long-time courageous voices like those of Edward Snowden, Julian Assange, David Icke and Alex Jones continue to reverberate in sleeping humanity's ear. Acting as coordinator of forces of light from the Office of the Guardian, Kim-

berly Goguen works in the forefront of resistance against the Deep State's attacks on humanity. Her mission like that of Gary Seven involves protecting the planet from nuclear, biological and other environmental threats using higher dimensional surveillance and the services of 'the Enforcer', a divine agent responsible for cleaning up abuses and abusers. Goguen's information site unitednetwork.tv is a **Knight of Swords**' rallying call to the besieged world to wake up, rise up and take back our power.

Such champions of humanity need a terrific amount of the independent, valiant spirit demonstrated by Star Trek's Gary Seven and symbolically by the Tarot **Knight of Swords**. Deprived of his Earth-based subordinates, Seven must act on his own in maintaining Earth safety until the super-powers can evolve from enemies into peaceful fellow nations. His missing two agents, suspiciously killed in a car crash, reduce his allies to one well-meaning but confused secretary. But blessed with wisdom garnered off-planet, Seven reveals himself as a benevolent, knowledgeable human ET of the kind assisting and informing Earth-based contactees such as Alex Collier, Penny Bradley or Elena Danaan. Seven excels as a computer expert, a rocket scientist and an authority on Earth's political and social history. On top of this, he possesses the coolness, patience and forbearance needed by a **Knight of Swords** in order to be truly effective. His mission in defusing the risk of planetary destruction addresses the problem of nuclear power menacing Earth since the 1940s. With the superpowers engaged in Cold War rhetoric during the 1960s, Earth safety becomes a critical issue. In the 1980s Reagan will talk of a 'Star Wars' defence initiative but here in Star Trek's 1960s we already have space-faring nuclear weapons platforms being launched. The scene is set then for a **Knight of Swords** troubleshooter with more integrity than corrupt politicians to preserve a timeline leading to peace and freedom and away from the dystopia intended by the World Economic Forum. As Seven mentions in talking to his computer, 'Earth's technology and science has progressed faster than its political and social knowledge.' Humans, he implies, need rescuing. Humanity of course must rescue itself from misplaced faith in a pernicious leadership. Thanks to the clean-up work of Goguen and the Enforcer, the highest levels of the Cabal have been sent back to Source. Now begins the tremendous amount of work needed to restore our world to harmony.

We all require determination, confidence and persistence to move forward on this path. Seven on his mission shows the way. He encounters obstacles in the form of accident, confusion, mistrust and misunderstanding - all on the part of those around him. He has to work independently and far from home among people uncomprehending or resistant to his endeavours. Difficult or obstructive associates range from his secretary Roberta Lincoln to the crew of the Enterprise to the entire US space agency. Two transporter mishaps interrupt him, so too confinement in the Enterprise brig. He is faced with non-cooperation by Lincoln and almost arrested by the NYPD. McKinley Base security do apprehend him. Later he is beamed away from the rocket gantry before he can complete his technical procedures, coshed by Lincoln and seized by Kirk and Spock armed with phasers. Because he only half-completes his task of setting the rocket to malfunction, it begins falling to Earth armed with a live nuclear warhead. To avert a nuclear incident and war breaking out, Seven must persuade Kirk and Spock to let him detonate the warhead from his office computer. But Kirk remains unsure whether this particular **Knight of Swords** is **upright** or **reversed**. Is he a true catalyst for peace and progress or a malign saboteur?

Seven's eventual success showcases the value of 5D chess ability, the theme of Episode 56. Part and parcel of 5D chess is the ability to flow around obstacles as Seven does in the Taoist manner of Third Force rather than doing battle with them. Seven has his Spirit Guides too as we all do, in his case a clever shapeshifting black cat. Like him we all have our mission on Earth indicated by whatever we feel to be our passion. And again like him, no matter how chaotically it seems to go, we need to trust that blunders and mishaps will ultimately work for the good. Our need to visualize possibilities for success is demonstrated here as in the previous Episode, No. 53. Seeing and believing in possibilities will go a long way to magically actualizing them. And working in Service To Others as well as ourself will further tend to draw to us a unique mix of magical and happy solutions.

AFTER THE TAKEDOWN
In playing the role of a **Knight of Swords** as truth-tellers and Field Messengers on the path of global restoration we need to be open-minded toward challenges that will almost certainly beset us. Not everything may go exactly according to plan or as we would prefer. As with Gary Seven, mistakes may occur, we may get side-tracked, delayed or knocked entirely off course. And perhaps this is all meant to happen, either to teach us to rise to the challenges or to adapt to unforeseeable deviations on the path. When plans don't go according to plan we should trust that a higher destiny above the exact destiny we had planned is the better destiny for us. Perhaps we are to give up thinking it all out in advance and to learn to roll with whatever happens. In the spirit of play, the path to success can take unimagined directions as can the very concept of success itself.

55. EVOLUTION

After the Matrix, organic - rather than inorganic - AI will accelerate human evolution

Episode 55 **'Spock's Brain'** correlates with the **2 of Coins**; both are themed around instinctual 2D physical life and functioning as a stage of evolution, whether proceeding or regressed.

THE CARD
Coins represent the physical dimension of existence that serves as the basis of our instinctual drives. These relate to our bodies, homes, possessions and anything perceptible to the five senses. The Coins suit as a whole takes us through all the stages of physical development from opportunity to embryonic growth to emergence to blossoming to decline to transcendence. At this embryonic stage, physical life is gestating, developing internally and quietly. In the **2 of Coins** card, two coins are being held in safe and comfortable balance. Flower heads are there but not yet opened. This could represent a baby in foetal development, preparations for house construction, or evolution at the stage of the plant and animal kingdoms. As early physical growth demands regular feeding and the maintenance of health and balance so the **2 of Coins** involves the nutritive principle. At this level of development or consciousness we feed our bodies daily with essential nutrients and keep our homes and possessions

well cared for. Actual life forms are symbolized in the card by the eel-like creatures slithering about at the base of the winding blue ribbon. This points to the 2nd dimension of existence (2D), that of plant and lower animal life. At this level of evolution, awareness is limited to pain or pleasure. An aspect of the **2 of Coins** then, is the instinctive, primeval and basic aspect of our life related to the lowest chakras.

Reversed, the **2 of Coins** can mean poverty or debts or under par or regressive health due to lack of self-care. Instinctual work of the body may be malfunctioning due to physical neglect or trauma or spiritual disconnection. Life support systems may be defective or compromised due to sickness or injury. Evolution may be being blocked or held back at the 2D level.

'SPOCK'S BRAIN' PREMISE
Spock's brain is stolen by a race of underground women to power their planet's computer. If it's not retrieved and urgently replaced he will die.

CONTEXT
AI Takedown, Transhumanism.

EVOLUTION
A scantily clad beautiful woman materializes aboard the bridge and renders the crew unconscious before removing and making off with Spock's brain. After frantically following the trail of her spaceship, a landing party beams down to a glaciated planet, Sigma Draconis 7. They are immediately attacked by panicking cavemen living in fear of the 'bringers of pain and delight'. At the back of a cave the party find a passage to a technologically advanced underground complex. In it, the woman Kara and her female race live comfortably under the aegis of a central computer. Hardly more intelligent than the men, they likewise live in a regressed state, all their needs met by the computer. They take the four crew captive along with the accompanying brainless body of Spock. His body remains temporarily alive and controllable through an AI contraption of McCoy's. The women have purloined his brain to replace the defunct CPU in the computer regulating the planet's life support system. Kirk demands its return and McCoy sets to work restoring it. He utilizes a computer-connected headset called 'The Teacher' that imbues the necessary knowledge. Kara fears that by not repairing the computer her race will have to move to the surface and perish in the glacial conditions. McCoy successfully completes the operation helped by the patient himself after reconnecting Spock's vocal chords. Kirk reassures Kara that her women will find ways to live and develop without the computer by cooperating with the men on the surface. 'It's a matter of evolution', he says.

CARD/EPISODE AND MATRIX TAKEDOWN

The Wetiko psychological disease encountered in such episodes as Nos. 41 and 66 appears again on Sigma Draconis 7. A class of immoral humans lives underground in comfort and technological empowerment. Composed mainly of young, self-serving women, this class rules over tribes of poverty-wracked men foraging for food in the glacial conditions on the surface. This exploitation of one class by another relies on the use of torturous technology for enforcing discipline and punishment. Devices worn by the women enable them to inflict either 'pain' or 'delight' on a victim at the touch of a button. The primitive and hardy but pathetic surface-dwellers arm themselves with clubs and rocks for attacking the landing party. Their hostility arises from living in ignorance and terror, perceiving the landing party as tormentors similar to their underground masters. As a class of victims they seek to likewise victimize the visitors with their aggressive welcome. Their level of evolution is blocked, even regressed, kept at the level of crazed animals, the **2 of Coins reversed**. This is the level of 2D, of animalistic life obsessed with survival and rudimentary satisfaction, consciousness limited to will, passion, pain or pleasure. The men are effectively mind controlled by the repeated experience of pain and fear entrapping them in negative ego states cut off from Higher Self.

Similar Wetiko type exploitation on Earth including chained up slaves and victim/victimizer behaviour goes back thousands of years under the Matrix system of domination. Only the form of these abuses has changed over time. The Elite's ways of maintaining power included pyramidal hierarchy, man-made laws, engineered wars, MSM programming, a fiat-based financial system, terraforming through geoengineering, and slated for the future - trans-humanist technologies. The threatened Great Reset involving totalitarian technocratic control of organic species was to be a grand slam victory for Matrix domination. With global restoration underway it will no longer be a threat. The Great Reset, more a Great Enslavement, would have been a handing over of human sovereignty to the will and control of a tiny class of elites. They would have turned the Earth into a giant computer with 'smart' technology dictating to all life through the 'Internet of Bodies'.

Such a scenario is glimpsed on SD7. A central computer, when functioning, takes care of life support systems and material needs for the underground race of women bereft of initiative and creativity. They live in a regressed state, again little more sophisticated than the level of the **2 of Coins**. But even as a dumbed down race their weapons enable them to control the terrified male natives living above on the surface. This is the kind of control over the masses desired by the Matrix elites. As with SD7's subjugated men and the AI-beholden women, the planned-for dystopia on Earth was one of humans reduced to basic instinctual functioning and programmed satisfaction of the five senses. As a civilization we would have been reduced to a level similar to the sub-intelligent women on SD7. Children were to be micro-chipped and equipped with brain-interface technology, even further indoctrinated than at present. Without the ability to think and act for oneself humans would be prone to unprecedented levels of exploitation. AI systems such as cashless shopping, vaccine passports and China's Social Credit system have been warning signs. Humanity would increasingly resemble a farmed race regressing back to the **2 of Coins** instead of evolving. Ascension upwards out of 3D, our destiny as a species, would be reversed.

A graphic example of the immorality of the AI-programmed women is the priestess' raid on the Enterprise in which she zaps the entire crew and uses AI expertise to surgically remove and steal Spock's brain. Spock is left with barely even **2 of Coins** type functioning, transformed into little more than a vegetable. Just as the Wetiko-driven Spanish Conquistadors raided South America and ruthlessly stole the people's gold and spices, the SD7 world follows the same pattern of predatory theft by a few for selfish benefit. 'The need of my people for their Controller', says the priestess to Kirk, 'is greater than your need for your friend.' She sees Spock's death as an acceptable sacrifice for extending the life of the computer controlling her race. The Archonic forces in the midst of losing control of Earth have likewise been stealing the autonomy and freedom of humans to endlessly increase their control over us and sabotage our evolution. Certain forms of AI and organic quantum AI have manifold positive uses. McCoy's machine for wheeling the comatose Spock around is an example, returning some instinctual functioning to the patient. Further good is done by the AI headset. Happily, although it granted Kara the knowledge to steal Spock's brain, it also enables McCoy to restore it.

AFTER THE TAKEDOWN
The knowledge needed to restore Spock's brain actually exists, involving holographic repatterning technology. Devices such as med beds with the capability to heal anything are routinely used in the SSP; also tech that can extend life, replicate food or enable instant time and space travel. Following the current clean-up of the highest levels of the Matrix, benevolent. organic AI tech will arrive on Earth sooner rather than later. Our way of life will accelerate out of its long held technologically regressive state. Happily, we are on the cusp of a leap forward in our evolutionary growth as a species.

56. 5D CHESS

The mind in service to Higher Self will show us the doors to freedom

Episode 56 '**The Enterprise Incident**' correlates with the **7 of Swords**; both are themed around intelligence put to ingenious or cunning use in a benevolent cause in service to others.

THE CARD

The **7 of Swords** card portrays the Sword of the mind at its most penetrative and sleek - perfectly proportioned and unadorned. With its deep blue blade of spiritual awareness, this Sword suggests well-intentioned and highly intelligent thinking informing whatever endeavour is at hand. The 7th degree corresponds with Arcanum 7, The Chariot, representing action in the world, peak power and benevolent purpose. This means a clear goal in mind and a harmonious balance of analytical and creative thinking. Awareness is at its sharpest. Mental creativity is operating at its most ingenious, active and effortless in response to the needs and concerns of others. Thinking is not merely 3D based but integrated with higher faculties than the five senses of Body Mind.

Reversed, deceptions, lies or subterfuge are indicated. Controllers of perception are passing on their perception to others so that the controllers' version of reality is the one decoded into being. Devious or scheming stratagems are at work, selfish motives are concealed. Without benevolence, the propagators of false truth are corrupt and truth itself abused.

'THE ENTERPRISE INCIDENT' PREMISE
Kirk and Spock plan and carry out an ingenious mission of espionage and theft to seize dangerous new technology from a Romulan warship.

CONTEXT
Deception.

5D CHESS
Kirk feigns bad temper and irrational behaviour when he leads the Enterprise into the Romulan Neutral Zone. He and Spock, with authority from the Federation, have launched a daring stratagem 5D chess style with the intention of stealing a newly developed cloaking device from a Romulan warship. Kirk boards the Romulan ship twice, first in an assumed state of mental instability then later disguised as a Romulan. Spock for his part feigns treachery by apparently siding with the Romulans and ceding the Enterprise. He pretends to kill the maddened Kirk and plays along with the female Romulan Commander as she flirts with him expecting to make him a new ally. These multiple deceptions, secret plans and improvisations enable Kirk to steal the device and transport it over to the Enterprise. Scotty then uses the Romulans' own technology to enable the Enterprise to escape the surrounding Romulan vessels.

CARD/EPISODE AND MATRIX TAKEDOWN
No one knows exactly what 5D chess is. Some say it's Sun Tzu's The Art of War. Some say it's the tactics of a mooted Earth Alliance battling Earth's ruling Cabal. The term may simply refer to the arts of deception used to win a war without actually fighting it. Or it may refer to highly intelligent, imaginative and ingenious operations conceived from a higher dimension or perspective than those of one's opponent. Higher senses than those of the 3D Body Mind would be at work. So long as no harm or loss is done to anyone except in defence of self or an innocent, then the basic principles of Natural Law would be being observed. Operating at this level would give a moral advantage over nefarious elites ignoring Natural Law and divorced from awareness of feelings or empathy. Such elites as Earth's Cabal prefer to use dark occult rituals and dictatorial leadership with no scruples about the harm, damage or loss they inflict. Kirk and Spock use a more enlightened approach - in alignment with the **7 of Swords** - despite their apparently bizarre actions. Their goal is to divest the enemy of its newly developed

cloaking device, a well-meaning, sensible and benevolent goal since the device would be used as a harmful weapon to render attacking Romulan ships invisible. With this compassionate and peace-oriented motivation, the humans are already marrying logic and feeling, thus coming from a more accurate perception of reality than either faculty could achieve alone.

The next indication of Kirk and Spock's 5D chess venture is their deviation from precise planning and from playing strictly by the rules. The intention is plain: to capture the Romulan device. But the plan merges with no-plan: a willingness to go with the flow unbounded by rules. At a meeting with his advisors, Kirk in 3D thought mode identifies a total of three possible responses to entrapment by hostile ships, the Enterprise having strayed into Romulan space. The Enterprise can fight, destroy itself or surrender. Prompted by a request by the Romulan commander to board their ship Kirk then abandons all three alternatives. Now in 5D chess mode he sets forth spontaneously and instinctively to play the Romulans at a game of inexplicable strategy and surprise. Events that follow involve a mixture of blatant lying, suppression of the truth, play-acting, intrigue and improvisation. The original base strategy, Kirk's feigned insanity, remains in place. But for the rest of the plan, it's made up along the way. The Romulan Commander quickly cottons on to Kirk's intention to carry out espionage regarding their sought-after new device. But tactically she operates at a lower level of the **7 of Swords** than either Kirk or Spock. The humans' advantage comes from their soul level alignment - the prevention of future harm and the constructive use of intuition and emotion - leavening the purely logical mind. The Romulans, a militaristic race of limited imagination, fall easy prey to a prime Matrix control method ironically being used against them - the manipulation of perception.

Like practised Matrix politicians, Kirk and Spock ingeniously manage perception control, one of the key aspects of the **7 of Swords** when **reversed**. Paramount among the humans' concerns is creating the impression that Kirk is acting under his own crazed initiative. Their intention is to capture the cloaking device without in any way implicating the will of the Federation. The Commander already suspects this. 'You deliberately violated Romulan space with a blatant spy mission by order of the Federation!' she exclaims. But before she can get confirmation by torture or drugs, Kirk and Spock play out a scene of high drama to put the idea out of her mind. Spock calmly accuses Kirk of stress-induced insanity and this she comes to believe when Kirk turns on Spock with insane ferocity: 'You filthy liar! I'll kill you!!!' From this base deception, the humans derive one advantage after another.

Included: the Enterprise crew are entrusted with following the Romulans to their base; Spock is seen as truthful, cooperative and valuable by a Commander driven by her feminine ego; and Spock is added to her entourage enabling him to locate the device. In her naivety she entrusts Spock with command of the Enterprise on her behalf. This allows a play-acting Kirk to plausibly attack Spock for his treachery and to apparently die when Spock applies a fake 'Vulcan Death Grip'. Supposedly dead, Kirk can later re-board the ship in disguise and steal away with the object of desire.

Thinking and acting in a rigid reptilian mode cut off from soul level consciousness, the Romulan Commander is out-manoeuvred by Kirk and Spock. She falls easy prey to the manipulation of her perceptions and thereby her beliefs. Further disempowered by her obsession with gaining an ally in Spock she allows herself to be seductively and ruinously wined and dined. By limiting herself to rational thought, selfish desire and five-sense indulgence she effectively loses the plot. She plays Kirk and Spock at the level of the isolated Body Mind whereas the game they play utilizes all-round consciousness working through multi-dimensional intelligence, the **7 of Swords** at 5D chess level. They have a clear intention, a benevolent peace-oriented motivation, intuitive awareness and facility with manipulating perception though play-acting and improvisation. Thus Kirk and Spock score a notable victory and a prized trophy, the cloaking device.

AFTER THE TAKEDOWN

Kirk and Spock's victory teaches us that components of the human mind are multiple and work best when used co-creatively. This will be even more true following our release from the manipulative AI systems of the Orion Matrix. First and foremost, the pair put intelligence in service to the heart. With the heart guiding the mind there is inner freedom no matter the level of Matrix control. Heart-centred motives are kind or benevolent and durable even in the face of cunning. Heart-centredness means putting harmlessness first and often involves others standing to gain rather than merely oneself. Secondly they follow a pre-determined strategy but without being confined by it. No plan may at times be the best and most intelligent plan. Or an initial plan may be conceived that leaves further ideas and initiatives to suggest themselves during the course of work. It's the willingness to improvise if necessary that gives an advantage. With rational thinking balanced by creativity, energy is higher and inspiration flows more freely. Remembering this we can all employ 5D chess strategy when needed. With more enjoyment and less effort, thinking happens by itself and outcomes will likely be the most beneficial.

57. BENEVOLENCE

We will empower our ascension and freedom as we become more loving and benevolent

Episode 57 '**The Paradise Syndrome**' correlates with the **King of Cups**; both are themed around a heart-centred person who shows the way of benevolence through loving deeds, care or guidance.

THE CARD
The tall Cup and the wide expanse of space visible on the heart side of the chest indicate a man who is compassionate and given to acting benevolently. Facing the direction of action and the future, he has visionary awareness encompassing new horizons and the aspiration to fulfil great potential. He wishes the best for those around him and acts accordingly. His flamboyant crown suggests a certain charisma that helps to empower or inspire others to move forward as the good and loving individuals he himself is. Being the **King of Cups** he does his good deeds and offers guidance out of magnanimity and warm-heartedness. The depth of his charity that begins at home is symbolized by the tallness of the Cup. His freedom from over-emotional desires and fears is symbolized by the modestly sized rim. Unlike the Knight of Cups, the **King of Cups** will tend not to go far and wide as a rescuer saving others. Rather, he will be helping those near to him to thrive and de-

velop. As hinted at by the Cup that he almost hugs they will be those of his circle - his family, friends or community. His work could be in the line of relationship, parenting, consulting, healing, guiding, caring or teaching.

Reversed, pride, jealousy or greed may get the better of him. He may plot or compete against others or become corrupt or narcissistic, possibly manipulating or exploiting people for personal gain.

'THE PARADISE SYNDROME' PREMISE
An amnesiac Kirk joins with tribal people who expect him to save them from an asteroid. He marries and lovingly serves them but still needs help.

CONTEXT
Relationship, Perverted Paradise, Self-Realization.

BENEVOLENCE
Kirk, Spock and McCoy beam down to a planet of unspoiled, lush hills and forests. They have only 30 minutes before they must return to the Enterprise to use it to divert an asteroid on collision course with the beautiful planet. A tribe resembling Native Americans move among wigwams nearby. They look too primitive to have built a strange obelisk that Kirk investigates on his own. A trap door opens and drops him into a crypt housing a device with controls on a console. A beam knocks him out and erases his memory. On escaping, he is greeted with reverence by two native women with long silky black hair, one called Miramanee. Spock and McCoy have left. The women take Kirk to their Elder who declares Kirk to be the saviour god of tribal legend. Kirk is made the new Medicine Chief and as 'Kirok' entitled to 'join' with the Elder's daughter, Miramanee, with whom he has already become affectionate. He becomes her loving husband and together they enjoy happiness. He dresses in buckskin and plays with her in the natural paradise of the forests. During two months of mutual devotion he makes her pregnant and benevolently works for the tribe, designing a lamp for night light and an irrigation system for the fields. But with the skies darkening due to the asteroid approaching, 'Kirok' for all his compassion and good deeds is helpless to act alone as the decreed saviour. The obelisk was left to the tribe by an off-planet race, 'The Preservers', as an asteroid deflector but Kirok lacks the knowledge to use it as such. The angry natives denounce him as a false god and stone him and Miramanee at the obelisk. Spock and McCoy beam back down in time to rescue Kirk, but Miramanee is mortally wounded. They manage to get back into the crypt and Spock successfully activates the asteroid deflection device. The planet is saved but not Miramanee, who dies tragically in Kirk's arms.

CARD/EPISODE AND MATRIX TAKEDOWN

The purpose of this material reality is to provide the *arena* for our development as initiates at the 3D level on our path of ascension up the 15 dimensions of existence. The AI Matrix proceeding from the Orion nebula conditioned us all from birth and operated in all aspects of our life. It hampered the journey of our souls to evolve in material (holographic) form. Our process of initiation on this path is the theme of Arena (Episode 17) in which an advanced ET race put Kirk through a stark lesson in non-violence. To raise and nurture us on our path with love and loyalty is the Queen of Cups, represented by Natira in Episode 62, the motherly high priestess and servant to her people. Her male equivalent, the fatherly **King of Cups**, guides, helps and protects us. He is represented here by Kirk acting as his tribe's medicine man. Here on this rural planet having lost his memory the role of the caring **King of Cups** is accidentally thrust upon him. He guides and helps the forest tribe as much as he cherishes his newfound wife. But in the parallel role also falling upon him, that of a rescuing Knight of Cups (as in Episode 75) he fails - until himself rescued and assisted by his Enterprise colleagues.

The disaster threatening the planet is an asteroid on collision course. On our own Earth a threat on a similar scale came from the activities of a Negative Alien Elite bent on vanquishing humanity and completely taking over our planet. Information from our real world 'Preservers' known as the Guardian Alliance (GA) tells of a possible timeline in which Earth blows up in 2976 AD. This disaster according to the GA's analysis given in Voyagers 2 by Ashayana Deane has its origin in ET manipulation of Earth's Interior Government dating back to the Philadelphia Experiment in 1943 and the related Montauk Project in 1983. The explosion can be prevented say the GA, if the Earth and humanity can make a transition into a higher dimension aided by the GA's rescue plan, the Bridge Zone Project. In its modified form called the KrystalBridge Fail-Safe Project, it involves humanity accelerating its evolution over the next 900 years. This will see Earth and its inhabitants gradually bifurcate into higher and lower vibrating entities each going forward in their new world. Those of regressive intent will find themselves on a 'Phantom Earth', a planet descending rather than ascending. Those standing for evolution and freedom will evolve on 'Bridge Zone Earth' up the 15-dimensional scale of the 'Time Matrix'.

Humanity therefore is loved and protected by forces countering the predatory, destructive influence of Negative Aliens notably the Draco reptilians and their collaborators the Zeta greys. For the Bridge Zone project to work however, humanity must do its part in raising its vibration. The same as with the natives on the asteroid-threatened planet, although again as with Earth, they still need outside help. They need knowledge and it died with a previous medicine chief. Kirk and Spock as benevolent aliens must effect a rescue by somehow accessing the obelisk interior and activating its device. In Earth's case, benevolent ET forces are also at work to help humanity and the Earth itself to ascend out of danger. By so doing we will offset the nefarious agendas of Negative Aliens and Deep State elites (parasites) installed during the Matrix era. Now is the time for us all to cooperate in global restoration on new positive timeline. This means restoring harmony with nature, ourselves and one another. As 'Kirok' shows his tribe a better way than his forebear Salish who becomes a jealous and vengeful **reversed King of Cups**, so are we to become more benevolent and loving as individuals and as a collective. **Upright**, the **King of Cups** expresses love in humble, kind and useful activity. When a nearly drowned young boy is brought from a river, Kirok saves his life with artificial respiration. The tribal leaders are astonished but Kirok dismisses it as 'a simple technique'. This and his subsequent good works show what it is to live and function benevolently from the heart. So when Salish furious at losing Miramanee to Kirok ambushes him with a knife, Kirok fights back successfully but only in self-defence. With the beaten assailant at his mercy Kirok lets him go, reprising his initiatory test in Arena, despite Salish swearing he will never relinquish his enmity.

Throughout the two months with his wife and tribe, Kirok treats them with all the gentleness, tolerance and benevolence of an exemplary **King of Cups**. But the tribe's religious beliefs separate them from true spirituality that lives within, that evolves itself and bows to no external 'gods'. Their final savage treatment of both Kirok as a failed god and his wife bears out the digression of consciousness that ensues when we sacrifice the knowing and goodness of the heart to tribal, cultural, religious or 'elite' perceptions and behaviour.

AFTER THE TAKEDOWN

Our arena at the Body Mind level involves us playing different roles in different situations. The role of a loving, benevolent **King of Cups** (or Queen of Cups) may fall upon us as at various times as it does Kirk here. Or it may appear in the guise of a key figure, a mature and kind person influencing our lives and temporarily overseeing our well-being. This role requires altruistic and benevolent caring. By caring and helping where needed we enlarge our energy field and expand our awareness. All this while helping others and the planet itself to ascend to higher levels of vibration and consciousness.

58. DEMONIC POSSESSION

There is no more powerful way to raise our consciousness than by overcoming our demons

Episode 58 '**And The Children Shall Lead**' correlates with **The Devil**; both are themed around moral corruption such as manipulation and control by an enemy or demon using black magic.

THE CARD
A grotesque but charismatic monster or demon stands on a pedestal apparently at the behest of two consenting, flesh-coloured imps on either side. Genitalia and breasts are on display together with bat wings, tails and jagged horns. These ancient and primitive features suggest lusty, atavistic instincts preoccupying all three figures. The central figure mockingly waves at us while clumsily wielding a sword. The imps arise out of black goo suggesting itself or pitch darkness of the depths of the psyche. A master and slave relationship subsists with the two slaves held in such thrall to their master that they meekly consent to voluntary bondage. They keep their hands behind their backs rather than using them to free their only loosely corded necks. Degenerate and infantile, shameless and dumb-looking, the imps stand there like exploited beings or aspects of the inner self. As such they could represent hidden and taboo temptations or appetites manifesting in addiction, debauchery, lust, victim mentality, ag-

gression, greed or uncontrollable desires. **The Devil** card portrays any such primeval, demented energy belonging to a central dominating influence that vampires off its victim(s). All are keeping themselves in a state of voluntary disempowerment or self-sabotage.

Reversed, the situation is even more abusive and alarming or absurd and demeaning.

'AND THE CHILDREN SHALL LEAD' PREMISE
A demon controls a group of lost children rescued by a landing party. The children in turn raise the inner demons of Enterprise crew members.

CONTEXT
The Adversary, Mind Control.

DEMONIC POSSESSION
A group of scientists on Triacus are found dead or dying on the barren soil by Kirk and Spock. Some malevolent force appears to have induced them to take poison and commit mass suicide. Playful children appear. They run about oblivious to the scattered corpses of their parents. Kirk gets a taste of the bad vibes after entering a nearby cave. He experiences a wave of anxiety just as Professor Starnes, the last surviving scientist, will be seen to attest to in his video diary. Taken aboard the Enterprise, the still ungrieving children use the privacy of their quarters to join hands and chant a summons to an astral entity in the shape of a corpulent, ethereal robe-clad man. With the children in a semi-hypnotic state, the sickly green over-shadowing entity praises them for getting thus far and urges them to go on to hijack the ship. The children accomplish this with the help of their alien telepathic powers. They home in on the crew's minds raising what their master, Gorgan, calls 'the beast within'. After shaking off the demonic influence Kirk and Spock awaken the possessed children to their true situation by playing them a tape of the sad demise of their parents. Gorgan loses his grip on the childrens' minds and as his power wanes, the entity ghoulishly fades away.

CARD/EPISODE AND MATRIX TAKEDOWN
Matrix scientism remains in denial of dark magic. Officially. The establishment explanation for invasive entities and demons will be some form of personality disorder, psychosis, hallucination or drug-related issue. Cultures with ancient roots from all over the world have no such resistance to the idea of other-dimensional attachments. Gnostics speak about Archons, Muslims about the Jinn or genies, Christians about demons, Satan or in common with the Tarot, **The Devil**. Many kinds of such spirits exist wreaking havoc

with humans through feeding on the life force of ignorant or compliant individuals. There is no object, merely greed for pleasure or power, although in many cases the entity will be serving another and higher dark force. A victim's symptoms of attachment may range in intensity from mild disturbance in their thinking to behaviour control to full blown possession. The attaching predator may be anything from a low level entity merely leaching energy to a demon bent on an evil or crazed agenda.

The Satanic and psychopathic control system on Earth, while officially debunking dark magic, privately and lustfully used it to advance its own agenda. Dark occult rituals and astrological timings will have played their part in setting up the false flag attacks of 9/11 or Covid-19 used to exponentially increase Illuminati power and control. Skullduggery like this happening on a worldwide scale was the signature of an overriding demonic force - Wetiko. The broad mass of humanity unwittingly played along out of fear and misplaced trust, lulled into compliance and cooperation by its unscrupulous leaders. Manipulated populations were like the imps in **The Devil** card. Handing over power, giving up freedom, they willingly acceded to new laws and 'new normals' such as travel restrictions, mask-wearing, social distancing or draconian lockdowns. As victims like the **Devil** card's imps, populations have been deceived and misled throughout history. Separate levels of the Orion Matrix tied people to one or other of the Deadly Sins. These held us hostage to inner darkness manifesting as latent fears and cravings lurking deep within the psyche. This is the kind of vulnerability that a demon, entity or control system exploits. We see this with Gorgan using mind control over first the children then the Enterprise crew.

With the bereaved children showing no signs of grief, McCoy suspects a form of selective amnesia. Given more time to make a diagnosis he might identify the defence against trauma known as Multiple Personality Disorder. When the mind bridles at an experience too horrible to countenance and remember it creates a sealable compartment for it, a separate personality. The CIA notoriously turned this into a mind control technique with its MK-Ultra and Project Monarch programs. Such methodology additionally involves a 'handler' employing hypnosis and trigger words to utilize the compartments in a victim's mind. These compartments can be opened up and shut down at will - the will of the handler - independent of influence from the other compartments. Gorgan appears to have directly programmed the children in this way. They have no cognition of their parents' horrible death until Kirk later shows them the filmed evidence.

Practitioners of the Dark Occult commonly use rituals, as with the children chanting in a circle, to invoke altered states or magical powers. The victims' have already had their minds restructured by trauma or torture to accommodate the instructions of a handler. Dominating demons or their human proxies desire to possess others and manipulate their behaviour. They may directly implant intense negative thoughts or images. Gorgan replaces Sulu's view of space out of the bridge monitor with a terrifying vision of flying swords. He assails Uhura with a reflection in her mirror of herself horribly aged and decrepit. The children's alien powers of telepathy exercised under Gorgan's instruction make possible these forms of psychic attack. In this regard it becomes crucial for us to learn to distinguish thoughts of our own from those implanted from outside us. We are all subject to invasion of the mind by demonically created illusions. Mainstream culture operates in the same vein with an army of politicians, mainstream media, teachers, scientists, corporations and brainwashed family and friends knowingly or unknowingly infecting us with delusions and propaganda, dogmas and deceits. Resistance is vital. We must protect our minds, our innate sense of self and stability. Freed from Matrix contamination it now becomes possible to do so. This is vividly illustrated when Kirk standing on the bridge comes under psychic attack from young Tommy. 'I'm losing my ability to command' he suddenly whimpers. He grabs Spock in the lift right up close face to face as if seeking to physically stabilize his sense of self. 'Jim!' says Spock with heavy emphasis, maintaining the most stoic control over his own Vulcan self. The message gets though, the buddy connection works and Kirk comes to his senses. 'My beast is finished,' he reassures Spock, 'it won't return.' Neither will Gorgan, the defeated **Devil** manifest, once the crew and childrens' knowledge of his manipulations causes him to melt away like a sickly green sludge.

AFTER THE TAKEDOWN

The Tarot **Devil** can appear as an exterior menace such as a person or institution still programmed by Matrix forces seeking control over us. It can appear as a voodoo curse, hex or spell put on us. It can appear inwardly as one of the Seven Deadly Sins or some other vice or addiction. Or it can be a combination, an entity attachment tormenting the mind and leading us astray through activating an inner 'beast'. Whether inner or outer, our demons, possessing entities or external tormentors are a crucial challenge on the path to higher consciousness. By using the power of NO, the most powerful word of all, we can send them packing and develop our spiritual purity as in the next episode, No. 59. In so doing we will moreover activate the magic of possibility as in Episode 53, that of restoring ourselves to inner harmony, wellbeing and immunity to remnants of the defunct Matrix.

59. INNER CONNECTION

With the end of the Matrix we will have access to instantaneous knowing at any distance

Episode 59 'Is There In Truth No Beauty?' correlates with **The High Priestess**; both are themed around connection to the inner self through non-attachment, peacefulness and heart-centredness.

THE CARD
The High Priestess sits facing left, symbolizing the inner life. She seems comfortable while sitting still and reading, presumably about spirituality. However, her head is not in the book because spirituality or divine love is what she *is*. Her calm, compassionate gaze shows peacefulness, patience, an abundant willingness to live by acceptance and non-attachment. Drapery behind suggests her role as guarding a secret while straps across her chest seem to buckle in her physical and emotional powers of expression. Yet the strong red of her inner garments suggests her inner life is very much alive. This may be the deepest secret she harbours, connection to the mysterious depths of inner being. We can surmise a rich familiarity with higher dimensions of awareness inaccessible to the five senses. She may be a devotional nun, an other-worldly psychic, an affectionate grandmother or simply a woman embodying the divine loving presence of the Goddess. As

such she has no use for the hustle and bustle of the material, emotional world. Physical activity, relationship and sexuality have retreated from her preoccupations. She lives content in her state of being, centred in the heart's love and connected by intuition to unbounded truth and intelligence.

Reversed, she has trouble connecting to her true self. Relations with others may be bothering her or she may be lacking someone or anyone to love and serve. There may be ungovernable urges to express her emotions. These may have become turbulent, even bitter, due to long repression. A monastic way of life may have lost its allure or conversely may have become an excuse to avoid facing the world.

'IS THERE IN TRUTH NO BEAUTY?' PREMISE
A devotional, virtuous woman comes aboard and experiences a crisis of conscience in her protectiveness of a mental link to a disembodied lover.

CONTEXT
Sensitivity, Relationship, Self-Management.

INNER CONNECTION
Dr Miranda Jones beams aboard with Ambassador Kolos, a non-corporeal being boxed up in a piece of hand luggage. Kolos is a Medusan, so ugly that he cannot be viewed except with special goggles. Jones is transporting him back to his home planet where she avidly hopes to perfect the Vulcan mind-meld technique for communicating with the Medusans. The reserved and introspective Jones prides herself on connection with the inner life and on her telepathy. She wants to remain faithful only to Kolos, arousing the jealousy of Larry Marwick, her escort and would-be lover. At a dinner given in her honour she picks up the thought and desire of one of those at the table to kill Kolos. In a jealous rage Marwick later confirms her intuition but approaching Kolos without goggles is blinded and driven mad. Before suddenly dying he uses his engineering expertise to reroute the Enterprise way out of the galaxy and into uncharted space. Despite Jones' disapproval Spock manages to get the ship back to safety by mind-melding with Kolos, an expert navigator. But in the process he forgetfully glimpses Kolos without the goggles and he too goes mad. Jones who by now has been discovered to be blind tends to Spock in the sick bay. Perhaps she can heal him by reaching into his mind with hers but Kirk is unsure and anxious. He emotionally confronts her knowing her envy of Spock's innate ability to mind meld. He accuses her of ill intent but fearing he may have gone too far he leaves the shaken woman alone again with Spock. She reaches into Spock's mind and has a breakthrough. Spock later emerges cured of his insanity. On her

farewell, Kirk apologizes to Jones but she tells him his words cured her. She can now see with her eyes and merge fully with Kolos.

CARD/EPISODE AND MATRIX TAKEDOWN

We are each of us a fractal of Source consciousness but while the Matrix lasted, disconnected from our true selves. Following the takedown we will start to connect with the Creator as never before. Going within in the manner of **The High Priestess** opens the connection and activates our power of infinite knowing, connecting us though our hearts with the great multiverse. Only the blocks we put on ourselves out of fear, trauma or unresolved emotional turmoil disempower us. When unexpressed, emotions such as envy or jealousy fester in us. We become like Dr Miranda Jones, weakened in our connection both to ourselves and others. Fear of any kind, in her case of others' emotions, blocks intuition. Despite her four years on Vulcan training in the mind meld technique she still lacks, or feels she lacks, the clearest line to the thoughts and feelings of her disembodied partner. This generates more fear and discontent, further weakening her powers. She can psychically detect a murderous intent toward Kolos but not Marwick as the source of that intent. She reacts coldly to Spock's mastery of the mind meld technique, especially when seeing him use it to call on Kolos' navigation skills. She fears Spock wants to take over her assignment and jealously wants to know what Kolos sees in Spock. For a person as intensely devoted as she is to purity of spirit, these levels of fear and desire must play havoc with her inner peace and psychic communication ability.

There is no doubting Miranda's innate sensitivity. This manifests in her gracious demeanour, remarked upon by McCoy and Kirk after the lavish dinner convened in her honour. Even Spock competes to be the one to escort her back to her quarters. But there is far more to Miranda than her finely chiselled outer beauty, her elegance and feminine dignity. Her special sensitivity becomes apparent when she remarks on the hostile thoughts at the dinner table toward Kolos. Her access to such knowing prefigure the abilities we will all develop with the Matrix out of the way. Yet we know from her earlier exchange with Spock and her alone time with Kolos that her inner states include a startling degree of turmoil. As well as envy of Spock's abilities and jealousy of what others see in Kolos, this turmoil includes her hatred of pity and her possible willingness to let Spock die when she could cure him. In Tarot terms Miranda strongly embodies aspects of **The High Priestess** both **upright** and **reversed**. We all suffer inner turmoil when maintaining lack of consistency on all levels of our being. Miranda is no exception. Like the Tarot **High Priestess** she has no hankering after flamboyant socializing, passionate relationships or sensuality. But with the incorporeal Ambassador she yearns to form a deep and exclusive bond. Her yearning has become something of an obsession including the craving to mind meld with him. Then there is her cool and detached demeanour, a defining feature of **The High Priestess**. She confesses that her rejection of the emotions of others inwardly causes her endless 'struggle'. This no doubt feeds into her feelings of rivalry, fear and jealousy, possibly even bringing on her blindness. And by repressing herself she sets herself up for an emotional explosion at some inevitable point. Simmering anger and bitterness are bound to traumatically release themselves when the wrong buttons are pushed. This occurs when Kirk confronts her in the sick bay. Their altercation is epic, one of the most powerfully felt moments in all of Star Trek. This scene at Spock's bedside reminds us of the highly emotional confrontation between Hamlet and his recently remarried mother Gertrude. The catharsis Kirk puts Miranda through impels her to join minds with Spock and to successfully heal him. With this and her blindness disappearing, she speaks of a new realization of joy in mind-melding.

AFTER THE TAKEDOWN

With the Matrix taken down we will rapidly awaken out of species mind control and deception, at the same time discovering our inner contradictions and making peace with ourselves. As we become more consistent in the multiple aspects of our being we will ascend in frequency. Unexpressed and festering emotions will need to be carefully managed. Rebalancing them over time without fighting them or paying them undue attention will help us stay internally at peace. Various methods of self-healing and meditation will help. Relying on another to do the work for us of clearing our emotions or activating our DNA will likely be futile. We have our own access to the levels of our multi-dimensional identity. This includes connecting to and embodying our soul or Higher Self. But obsession will not help. Attachment to desires and fears, even for excellence as craved by Miranda, will be counterproductive. Craving any state of being, even higher vibration or spiritual enlightenment, will block the direct experience of being, knowing and loving and of growing accordingly. **The High Priestess** represents the attainment of inner freedom and purity. This new state as sought by Miranda will naturally come the way of all of us. Like being connected to a military intelligence system, but of the Light, we will know the true nature of people and events moment by moment. When someone harbours a thought concerning us we will know who and where it comes from, enabling us to tune into and deal appropriately with the thought energy, also at a mental level.

60. THE MATRIX DREAMWORLD

Tuning in to the Higher Self will protect us from perception manipulation

Episode 60 '**Spectre Of The Gun**' correlates with **The Moon**; both are themed around reality obscured by illusory and deceptive forces, creating an uncertain or confusing dreamworld.

THE CARD
The Moon card presents us with a sober-looking moon face gazing to the left over a spectral, eerie scene of nightmarish intensity. Two dogs or wolves howl feverishly at the moon as if facing down some primal threat or subconscious menace. A large body of stagnant water ripples in the murky half light. From its dark dregs rises a sinister, lobster-like ghoul. The rocky foreshore contrasts with the other straight-lined edges to cast doubt on the nature of this body of water. Is it real? Or is it some figment of the scarified imagination? The coloured drops seem to both fall away from and fly towards, the darkly glowing moon. Everything is contradictory or nebulous, nothing certain or consistent. Of the two half-realized buildings, the one on the left standing for the past appears more open and accessible than the barricaded one on the right standing for the

future. They and the rough ground are drained of all colour except dirty yellow. The whole scene appears lurid, dream-like and vaguely alarming. Detail is lacking while cause for suspicion or conjecture appears almost overpowering. **Upright**, we can infer a confusing, only partially understood situation that raises more questions than it answers.

Reversed, danger or fear is present, whether illusory or real. Truth is mixed with lies, motives are veiled, agendas are nefarious or deceptive, acute caution is advised.

'SPECTRE OF THE GUN' PREMISE
Trespassing on a forbidden planet Kirk and co are punished by being cast as the fall guys in a holographic recreation of an iconic Wild West gunfight.

CONTEXT
Illusion.

THE MATRIX DREAMWORLD
Approaching the unknown Planet Melkot, Kirk ignores a warning buoy and beams down to the planet with four officers. An apparition menacingly sentences them to death at which point a semi-coherent American frontier town springs up around them. Hard revolvers in their hands make the illusion seem quite convincing. But to Spock the surrounding imitation of 1880s Tombstone, Arizona is drawn from Kirk's mind. The Melkotians seem to have intended the conditions of that violent time and place to form the basis for our people's execution. They are to replay the gunfight at the OK Coral with themselves cast as the 5-strong Clanton gang to be outgunned by the town marshals, the Earps. The team unsuccessfully try befriending the townspeople then cobbling together a tranquilizer weapon that has no effect. Chekov meets his maker in a deadly gun fight over a flirtatious woman. All this rattles the team as the 5pm deadline for the gunfight approaches. It takes the level-headed Spock to remind them that it is only their belief in this illusory dreamworld that makes it appear real. He has noticed that the ineffective tranquilizer proves the five senses are not to be trusted. Chekov was 'killed' not by a bullet but by his mind. 'I know that the bullets are not real', Spock says, 'therefore they cannot harm me.' Spock's remedy is to hypnotize his colleagues out of belief in the fake reality with the Vulcan mind meld. No longer believing in the Earps' bullets, the blaze of lead passes harmlessly through their bodies. An unharmed Kirk could blast away the spectral Earps but shows mercy. His response is welcomed by the Melkotians who now cordially invite the humans to visit them.

CARD/EPISODE AND MATRIX TAKEDOWN

The AI Matrix as the ultimate progenitor of the lies of our distorted reality may be dead. But the false, distorted reality it created remains with us as a kind of after-image. For how long depends on the time it takes people to unlearn the lies they have lived by all their lives. When reality itself is a lie there can be no bigger lie. To quote Feargus Greenwood[1], 'the big lie is more credible, purely by being *incredible*'. Once humanity *gets it*, the house of cards built to imprison us will collapse forever. The Matrix around us was no more than a dreamworld depending for its existence on the Orion AI Matrix that blunted human perception and fomented our manipulation by the Deep State oligarchs. This is expressed in the **Moon** card by the eclipse of the sun, blocking and distorting perception of light, of knowing, of truth. The feeble moonlight limits the means of perception to a few spectral rays playing merry havoc with the truth of things as they are. How easy it was for the Dark Occult magicians to do their number on humanity during the Matrix era! The conjured up world of Tombstone represents the illusory world believed in by hoodwinked humanity. Without the ability to discern objective reality, symbolized by **The Moon** card's complementary card Justice (Nos. 8 and 18 complementing each other), we were putty in the hands of perception manipulators. Our Matrix masters, like the Melkotians, were further aided by widespread human ignorance of the multi-dimensional, holographic nature of reality. The landing party, initially, represents humanity not even aware of its own ignorance. A belief only in scientism, that 3D reality is all that exists, negates the ability to perceive circumstances layered according to multiple frequency bands. Blinkered human awareness normally registers only the levels known as Dimensions 1, 2 and 3. The Melkotian surroundings and events transcend these frequency bands and include multiple incongruities from the usual human perspective. The lesson is again as in Episode 14 Shore Leave. It takes Spock's wisdom to alert the party to the holographic deception. Such is the vulnerability of mental functioning when attuned and locked into emotionality and 5-sense-only experience.

Thus unfolds the absurdity of the party falling for the patently obvious illusion of the historical Tombstone. The ramshackle clownishly built hoardings, shopfronts and street signs carry no conviction except as pantomime. The town is in essence **The Moon** card brought to life, manifesting in menacing shards of a bleak and surreal pioneer town playing on the humans' imaginations and emotions. A hum of wind and a low background drone murmurs in their ears while the sky glowering overhead appears a cloudless, furious red. Yet due to fear and species inurement to exclusive 3D reality, the crew

---

[1] Greenwood, F., (2021) *180°*, Great Britain: independently published, p. 25

cannot help buying the illusion. Tapping the heavy revolver in his hand, McCoy comments: 'In the midst of what seems so unreal, a harsh reality. This is not a dream.' A stumbling cowboy bursts out of the nearby saloon bar, gunned down by a strutting Morgan Earp. Again someone comments on what they can be sure of, that the man is dead, that death here is real even if nothing else is. But is it? What the humans take to be real limits itself to what they can feel to the touch, to the deadline they fear, to the apparent deaths of the cowboy and Chekov. The latter was easily seduced by the woman, Scotty by the bourbon whisky, McCoy by the sense of emergency. Capping all these deceptions is the hail of bullets from the Earps' execution squad. But by then the illusion has been exposed and neutralized thanks to Spock's initiative to defuse the mind-hypnotized danger.

The shore party's adventure on the Caretakers' planet in Shore Leave in some ways constitutes the flipside of this warping of reality. One planet's virtual reality park is designed for amusement and recreation, the other's for fear and punishment. Both shore parties come under the influence of holographic inserts - the artificial creation of reality pictures that overlay the more objective environment. The parties' confusion and gullibility on the two planets, the Caretakers' and Melkot, mirrors how imperilled humanity was at the hands of similar spell-casting by nefarious elites. With the Matrix disabled, exposure and rejection is coming for the manipulation of our holographic reality by cloned and duplicitous leaders with their false flag attacks and global psyops such as the recent fake pandemic. Our wholly propagandist mainstream news and information services, a hall of mirrors no more truthful than Melkot, will be transformed. As people wake up to the unreality of it all - happening already - it will be Game Over for the Global Elite's plans for a tyrannical One World Order.

AFTER THE TAKEDOWN

If nothing else, **The Moon** card teaches us that our mind and five senses are not to be trusted in isolation from our higher senses. This goes equally for factual data, beliefs and emotions. All are assailable by the orchestrators of perceptual interference. To know truth from the level of our higher senses we first need to awaken out of inner states of delusion and hypnosis. We need to realize that reality is vastly larger and more complex than that appearing to ordinary perception. We see only 0.005% of what exists in terms of energy. With the Matrix gone, we will be activating our Higher Sense Perception latent in all of us. As we utilize higher senses of knowing and discerning we will gradually come into alignment with our greater spiritual Self that is impervious to perceptual deception and programming.

61. ENERGY VAMPIRISM

We must deny anyone or anything seeking to hijack our divine source of creative energy

Episode 61 'The Day of The Dove' correlates with the **Ace of Wands**; both are themed around the arising of Source energy for benevolent, creative action or its hijacking for malign, harmful purposes.

THE CARD
The **Ace of Wands** stands for power ready to be applied in creating our life. An Ace in general always signifies potential, readiness, or any possibility of a leap into action or manifestation. With Wands standing for creativity, action or life force energy, this Ace can involve a strong urge to launch into any creative activity; or the readiness to get up and boldly start a journey; or the initiative to undertake a new project; or the awareness of one's level of energy whether high or low and the appropriate direction into which to channel that energy. As the Wand pictured references both male and female sexual organs, this latent energy has both projective and receptive aspects (both active in different ways) to do with vitality and awareness respectively. The deep green of the Wand symbolizes the force of nature and organic life. This is primal energy that flows into us and through us from divine Source. It is the force of life itself.

Reversed, creative potential is tainted, blocked or unrecognized. The symptoms could include procrastination or lack of confidence. Inappropriate intentions may be present such as wishing to use life force energy recklessly, selfishly or arrogantly. There may be an over-estimation of one's powers leading to early burnout or illness. Another scenario, that explored in this episode, is poor energetic awareness opening the way to external forces having their way through energetic manipulation or hijack. This may involve a vampiric force under control of the Archons parasiting energy for nefarious and destructive ends. The victim's symptoms may include self-hatred, hostility, selfish urges or aggressive impulses that are uncontrolled or over-driven.

'THE DAY OF THE DOVE' PREMISE
Crew members and captured Klingons are incited to vehemently quarrel and fight by a stowaway alien force that feeds on negative emotions and conflict.

CONTEXT
Mind Control, War.

ENERGY VAMPIRISM
Kirk and the Klingon leader Kang both accuse each other of launching war using fake distress calls and acts of destruction. The two commanders each with a handful of men argue it out on an empty planet but oblivious of a strange entity hovering nearby. They beam up to the Enterprise where Kirk has the Klingon contingent arrested. But still unknown to them the ethereal entity has beamed up with them. Under its malign influence, crew become nervous and highly strung with tempers fraying and fights breaking out. The magical materialization of swords in the hands giving both crew and Klingon prisoners an equal fighting chance leads Spock to surmise the interference of an alien force. Kirk and Spock with Kang's wife Mara as hostage find the entity moving down a corridor, an eerie shimmering ball of light. There and then another fight breaks out involving an irate crew member during which Spock notices the entity swelling in size. With the entity evidently inciting and feeding on feelings and actions of hatred, Kirk and Spock enlist the help of Mara to intercede with Kang to stop the war. More frenetic fighting ensues before Kang too notices the floating entity. He's beseeched by Kirk to stop being energetically vampired. Kang sees the futility of the Klingons acting as pawns in unending war and joins Kirk in declaring a truce and defiantly laughing at the entity. Deprived of its energy source - hostility and violence - the entity vacates the ship.

CARD/EPISODE AND MATRIX TAKEDOWN

The astral force here feeding on human and Klingon energy typifies the action of etheric predators and parasites on our human selves. We have all been preyed upon during the Matrix era by the Archonic consciousness using us as a battery. Peoples and nations down the centuries have been kept constantly at war with each other and enslaved to varying degrees. The hostility and violence generated, the victimhood and misery perpetrated, constitute dense frequencies known as Wetiko, the Archons' food source. The small alien force infiltrating the Enterprise acts as a microcosm of the Wetiko force, creating havoc and **reversing** the crew's natural **Ace of Wands** energy. Likewise on Earth, humans emanating negativity and violence generated by the Orion Matrix have had their energy become food for the Archons. The psychopaths and Satanists comprising Earth's rulers operate as Archonic henchmen. Those such as the Bushes, Clintons, Cheney, Trudeau and Macron act as enablers for global energy vampirism.

We get to see how this works in the Wetiko and Demonic Possession episodes - Nos. 41 and 58 - and here as the Klingon and Federation teams clash and squabble first on the planet then aboard the Enterprise. In true Archonic form the distress calls kicking off the whole conflict are both fake. A Klingon warship is attacked and disabled, perhaps for real, but in such a way that its commander can only blame the Enterprise. In Kirk's view, the lost research station on the planet below can only have been wiped out by that same Klingon ship. As the two sides argue and fight it out, the entity commences feeding on their bitterness. After boarding the ship, the entity continues its covert manipulations. Disunity and chaos break out. So it is on Earth with orchestrated tensions afflicting rival groups whether whole nations or communities divided on social, political or religious issues. Archons cannot take bodily form as themselves. They operate rather through proxies, anyone who can be provoked and enraged enough to quarrel and fight. Chekov is stirred into a frenzy of vengeance by an implanted thought that the Klingons have killed his brother - who never existed! Kirk and his men are thrown into one-to-one combat with the captured Kang and his men by the entity again playing games of mischief and materialization.

Both the human and Klingon groups have their **Ace of Wands** energetic potential **reversed** and fed upon by the parasitic entity. This in a nutshell is a key strategy of the Negative Alien Agenda seeking to divide, disempower and control our race. The Archons pursuing this agenda on our planet are synthetic beings from another universe, vampiring energy that is of the same low vibration as themselves. Archons were the ultimate beneficiaries of the fallen Matrix. Like the entity stalking the Enterprise crew, they cannot attack us directly. Archons influenced us indirectly through the Matrix AI systems or by downloading their mind into Anunnaki, Dracos or Greys who in turn manipulated human or hybrid elites compatible in bloodline. 'Demonic entities in the lower astral realm,' to quote Steward Swerdlow, 'feed on fear, anxiety, hate, negative emotions. And so they control the humans in power to create such situations in the population.' The result was humans divided and weakened, cut off from their Higher Selves, constantly attacking or suspecting each other, living in fear and perverting their life purpose. The parasites meanwhile had a feast. When Kirk is attacked in the corridor by a temporarily possessed lieutenant, Spock notices the hovering alien force relishing the physical unleashing of hostility and violent intentions. The spinning ball of light seems to swell and gain energy. Kirk realizes 'it exists on the hate of others' created by provoking polarized forces while keeping both sides equally armed and strong. This goes on until both the humans and Klingons regain control of their thoughts and emotions. They in effect restore their **Ace of Wands** creative energy to its **upright** position by ceasing to allow themselves to be unconsciously provoked.

AFTER THE TAKEDOWN

The malaise of mutual hatred, aggression and war that has blighted human history does not belong naturally to our species. The Deep State's collaboration with Matrix forces has commonly and covertly been to blame. The assassination of the Archduke Franz Josef at Sarajevo in 1914 or the bombing of Pearl Harbour in 1941 were both events instigated by a global 'Hidden Hand' with an agenda to trigger war and transform the world's power structures. A little independent research reveals a hidden history of malevolent and demonic interference in political affairs, interference made possible by Matrix control of humanity. Of the 18 controlling AIs taken down, the Saturn-Pluto-controlled Palermo AI working on the seventh level of the astral manipulated humanity through an overlay of etheric parasites. With their effect similar to the parasitic entity aboard the Enterprise, they twisted the motives and distorted the behaviour of anyone not on their guard. With this influence eliminated we have the power now to reestablish peace and harmony by consciously reawaking our divine creative energy, the **Ace of Wands upright**. As long as we release our own dark essence formed in us through traumatic, unforgiven memories and experiences we will regain full control of our divine energy and vibration. Like the two groups on the Enterprise, we will then cease to be pawns in a cosmic battle involving destructive behaviour, parasitic entities, negative aliens and AI conquest.

62. HEARTFELT LOYALTY

The knowing of the heart
will show the way to
recovering peace and harmony

Episode 62 'For The World Is Hollow And I Have Touched The Sky' correlates with the **Queen of Cups**; both are themed around the expression of heart-centred love, loyalty and devoted service.

THE CARD
The **Queen of Cups** sits comfortably and securely facing left, the established environment, the status quo. She tightly holds a large closed cup or grail, representing the heart. Hers is the only Cup among the Courts cards to be protectively closed. It rests on her knee for added stability. In her other hand she bears a sword-like wand, expressive of her relaxed but strong will and her attention to self-preservation. Her crown actually rests on another piece of headwear, suggesting over-attention to fashion or creature comforts. Around her abdomen is a yellow belt protecting the place from where emotions and feelings emanate. This is clearly a deeply feeling, compassionate woman who nevertheless controls her emotions in deference to familial decorum and group wellbeing. Her place is at the heart of her family or community, as strongly connected to them as herself to her own heart. Thus she can sustain shared comfortable, pleasant, peaceful existence for herself and others. Using fem-

inine sensitivity she cares for and nurtures them in the personal and domestic arenas, focussing on loyal, service-oriented relations.

Reversed, she may be overly cautious or conservative, unwilling to trust people or ideas or experiences new to her. She may be bottling up or denying strong feelings, emotions or hurts, only expressing these sporadically and then over-emphatically. She may be rigid, possessive or controlling towards those she holds most dear and important.

'FOR THE WORLD IS HOLLOW AND I HAVE TOUCHED THE SKY' PREMISE
Disaster awaits a huge spaceship unless Kirk can win cooperation from its high priestess. But her control by AI prevents this - until she marries McCoy.

CONTEXT
Femininity, Relationship, AI Takedown, Mind Control.

HEARTFELT LOYALTY
The Enterprise is attacked by a 10,000 year old biosphere ship, a hollow artificial planetoid that is on collision course with a well-populated planet. Kirk, Spock and McCoy, attempting to warn the inhabitants, are coldly welcomed by the regal, elegant Natira. As high priestess for her people, Natira is the intermediary for the vessel's real ruler, a computer referred to as The Oracle. She strictly invokes the rules and customs of her world, or more precisely, those of The Oracle. To maintain absolute control, it insists that all dwellers on Yonada be micro-chipped, enabling them to be kept under total surveillance. Transgressors are severely dealt with, as when an old man talks too much to the trio. He alone among the people has discovered that Yonada is a vessel, but for sharing his knowledge is killed by The Oracle via the microchip. Natira approves of this punishment, as she does of punishments later meted out to the trio for their sacrilegious investigations of the vessel's control system. But she also proves a kind host to her guests. She feels an instant bond with McCoy and both of them being single, she proposes to him. McCoy feels the same way towards her. As he has only a year left to live due to an incurable disease, he consents to marrying her, staying on Yonada and being micro-chipped. Kirk and Spock leave, but soon return when McCoy contacts them with information on how to correct Yonada's trajectory. This the trio accomplish despite bitter resistance from The Oracle and Natira. Although committed to guiding, serving and supporting her husband and her people, Natira's obedience to The Oracle comes first until finally her microchip is removed. Her heart now unfettered, she feels that her most loving loyalty is to her people. She urges McCoy too to stay with

his own kind. This allows him to leave, happily to be cured with medical knowledge from the ship's computer banks.

CARD/EPISODE AND MATRIX TAKEDOWN
The oligarchs of the global elite were gunning for a society transformed into an AI-controlled technocracy. Called the 'Fourth Industrial Revolution' by Deep State frontman Klaus Schwab, his vision was of a fusion of the physical, digital and biological into one centrally controlled AI-run system. His colleague Ray Kuzweil wanted AI to augment or replace the human mind. The coldly rational, robotic demeanour of Schwab, before his covered up death and replacement by a masked actor, suggests this had already happened with him. Merely spreading information to wake the people up to the dystopian agenda would have have done nothing to prevent it. The Matrix had to go. Under Matrix influence, we had the advent of the Covid false flag, with authorities scrambling to inject a compliant global population with a DNA-changing concoction. The aim was for the bloodstream of the Covid 'vaccinated' to become infested with nano-sized hydra creatures creating a hive mind via satellite connection. Nanobots in the mRNA injection as well as on testing swabs and in chemtrails, plus frequencies from 5G or 6G were to be the route to a technocratic slavery parallel to Yonada's. Since its inception in 2020, the Covid injection has killed or injured millions. Only the Matrix takedown and the intervention of benevolent ETs, according to contactee Elena Danaan has prevented nano technology linking up the jabbed majority to the 'Internet of Bodies' and the burgeoning Smart Grid.

Yonada shows what such a society would look like. Natira's people effectively exist as synthetic-biological terminals of an AI system that remotely monitors and controls every aspect of their lives. So unified is their hive mind that the slightest transgression can be identified and the offender immediately punished. The people remain unaware that Yonada is a kind of spaceship, that their world is 'hollow', that by climbing a mountain one can 'touch the sky'. The one aged seer who realizes this is slain immediately he tries to share his knowledge with the Enterprise visitors. Natira's scorn of the old man and approval of his execution strongly suggests her own mental enslavement. Quite obviously a loving woman at heart, this **Queen of Cups** nevertheless abides by draconian rules. Like her people, she herself has been microchipped and cybernetically reined in. Her perceptions and attitudes mirror those of The Oracle. Her deeply caring nature, her intense loyalty to her loved ones - her entire race - are qualities usurped or distorted by her AI master. She ought to be at one with her knowing heart as much as her thinking head. But technology corrupts her conscience, her very consciousness. So she condemns the seer as a foolish old man who deserved his fate. As with the seer, whistleblowers and truth-tellers on Earth have been ostracized or worse for their enlightening service to humanity. Galileo was put under house arrest for revealing the Earth revolves around the sun. Wikileaks founder Julian Assange has long remained imprisoned for revealing Deep State criminality. After revealing sensitive political truths presaging the Iraq war, UN weapons inspector Dr David Kelly and UK Foreign Secretary Robin Cook both died suddenly and mysteriously.

Loyal to a fault, Natira embraces universal microchipping, in effect cybernetic control, and insists that McCoy complies likewise in order to become her husband. For her, the 'instrument of obedience' solidifies her union with her extended family, the people. She sees no inconsistency between devotion to them on the one hand and to the heartless Oracle on the other. As such, she is a sadly **reversed Queen of Cups**, out of relationship and lonely, cut off from her true feelings by bondage to AI. A great many of those staffing Earth authorities are likewise mind-controlled or simply kept unawares. Not all of our politicians, bankers, judges, CEOs, media people and celebrities will be corrupt and dishonest. Many are, but some of those bonded in servitude to the hierarchy of control will be oblivious of the malign agenda they serve. They go along to get along, but denying the truth that is in their hearts. So it is with Natira's loyalty to the Oracle. It is this that motivates her sudden and precipitate marriage. While McCoy makes the hasty move out of conviction that he has only a year left to live, she is driven by frustration. To assuage the pain of denying her heart, she makes a grab for a stable, nurturing relationship, no matter how short, no matter how emotionally unavailable her man may be. And certainly McCoy evinces no visible joy or enthusiasm at any point during their all too brief courtship. Tellingly, once her microchip is removed - by McCoy himself - Natira comes to her senses, to her heart's truth. With the microchip gone she drops her sudden marriage of desperation. As a healed **Queen of Cup**s she realizes that her most heartfelt loyalty and priority is to those who represent her true family, the people of Yonada.

AFTER THE TAKEDOWN

With the Orion Matrix disconnected, populations acting like obliging sheeple will become a thing of the past. People will recover full connection to the heart and move in the direction of global peace and restoration on a new positive timeline. People will practise kindness, empathy, compassion and generosity, that of the **Queen of Cups**, knowing where their loyalty truly belongs - not to AI, the Cabal or the elites but to the human race.

63. PREPARING OR WAITING

Making preparations with a sense of trust and patience will do much for our self-liberation

Episode 63 'The Tholian Web' correlates with the **2 of Wands**; both are themed around a time of incubation, limbo or preparations prior to an anticipated event and the time for action.

THE CARD

Wands being the suit of action and the second degree being that of preparation or gestation (corresponding to Arcanum No. 2, The High Priestess), we have in the **2 of Wands** a build-up taking place. This is a time of getting ready for action. There may be waiting, relaxing, rehearsals, recharging of batteries or practical preparations. Any of this is in anticipation of an eventual release of energy in external activity. A project or event is being patiently primed before it outwardly commences. A future creative shift or some kind of imminent outburst of activity is in the works. None of the flowers or plants shown are sliced off at their base. They are emerging from bulbs surrounded by finely layered petals. This suggests the early unfettered impulse or desire to grow, leading towards the actual appearance of flowers or fruits. This all requires the right timing, patience or diligent preparation. A similar degree of patient activity occurs with a spider's slow, careful spinning of a large web.

If **reversed**, there may be some insidious intent at work. Or progress may be unnaturally slow, or action inhibited by congestion, delays or blockage.

'THE THOLIAN WEB' PREMISE
Spock must use patience and coordinated preparations to rescue Kirk from a parallel dimension and the Enterprise from increasing alien entrapment.

CONTEXT
Multi-Dimensionality.

PREPARING OR WAITING
The Enterprise enters an area of space where the veil between dimensions is thin. The intensified energy incubates violent madness among the crew. A previous victim was the USS Defiant. Beaming aboard its almost ethereal hulk, a search party finds the crew have murdered each other. Before the full party can be beamed back, the Defiant slips right out of dimension while the Enterprise's transporter loses power. The result is Kirk being left behind, stranded in a dimensional void. Spock has to take over the captaincy and manage Kirk's retrieval plus outbreaks of madness and aggression among the crew. Spock has a couple of hours till the interphase effect brings dimensions back into cyclical alignment allowing Kirk to be rescued. He informs the Tholians accordingly. The unfriendly race has accused the Enterprise of trespassing on its region of space and wants the Enterprise to leave as soon as the time set for Kirk's retrieval arrives. But the Tholians' own incursion into the area disrupts the interphase effect. Spock must again wait until the next dimensional realignment. The Tholians do not tolerate the delay and open fire on the Enterprise. Spock fires back successfully but in retaliation the Tholians start weaving a net of tractor beams around the Enterprise to imprison it. Spock must get ready to retrieve Kirk at the next window of opportunity or his oxygen will run out. Meanwhile McCoy must find an antidote to the space madness and Scotty must restore enough engine power to break out of the Tholian web. Happily, these preparations all bear fruit before the Tholians can complete their hostile preparations and close the web. The Enterprise is finally thrown clear of the web, Kirk is retrieved and McCoy finds and administers the antidote.

CARD/EPISODE AND MATRIX TAKEDOWN
The slow building of the Tholian web à la the **2 of Wands** to ensnare the Enterprise provides a potent image for the Deep State's building of the Internet of Things Smart Grid. Earth was to be wrapped in a single network of AI dominion, surveillance and control. Likened by researcher David Icke to a giant web with a spider at the centre, the spider's aim was to increas-

ingly connect all things and bodies to itself - an AI supercomputer - for the purpose of perpetual enslavement and energy vampirism. The agenda according to Icke involved the slow but gradual imposition of total control via a one world government, a world central bank, a cashless society with a programmable digital currency, a one world army and a micro-chipped robotic population. A weblike intricate network of organizations and corporations like the EU, the UN, NATO, the CIA, the Vatican, the Federal Reserve, the FDA, Apple, Google, Microsoft and DARPA has resulted, running on the power provided by the Dark AI known as the Omega System. Composed of 18 Matrices, this system permeated the planet, all of humanity and all computers. The popular conception of Escaping the Matrix was not an option; we would not have been able to free ourselves in the manner of the Enterprise blasting itself clear of the Tholian web. The all-pervasive Omega system had to be taken down if humanity was to have any chance of surviving.

With the takedown of the Omega system accomplished as of 2023, humanity now has the opportunity to restore our world to the paradise it was meant to be. This too will be a massive undertaking as per the **2 of Wands** as new systems are put in place that work to restore the ecosystem and human freedom. As a race, we can take our cue from the benevolent and constructive actions of Spock as he discharges his emergency captaincy covering for Kirk and preparing for the captain's safe return. Spock's captaincy incorporates many more instances of the **2 of Wands** that illustrate the concept of preparation and patience in the face of tests and challenges.

Spock has to contend with:

a) the surrounding area of space breaking up the dimensional stability of the Enterprise and incubating insanity in the crew;

b) the Enterprise engines and the Transporter needing urgent work to restore normal functioning;

c) the hostile Tholians gradually entrapping the ship in their energy field;

c) McCoy's search for an antidote while himself becoming increasingly unstable and truculent;

d) the planning and waiting for the correct timing of Kirk's retrieval before his oxygen runs out;

e) the intended removal of the Enterprise from inside the web and from the dangerous area of space.

So much of what happens then, is the **2 of Wands** in action: preparation for something to happen or simply waiting. This is visually symbolized by the yellow filaments spun out in space to entrap the Enterprise. Small Tholian vessels move slowly backwards and forwards weaving the grid line by line. An Earth parallel has been the insidious formation of chemtrails in the sky. Day by day, aircraft or drones sprayed our skies with criss-crossing lines of toxic elements including aluminum, barium, mercury and smart dust. The long-term goal of this chemical bombardment was sometimes justified as weather modification. But the truth was more likely to be the creation of a *skynet* of electromagnetic frequencies and the weaving of transhumanism. As the 1,477 DUMBS used for manufacturing and storing chemtrail substances have been eliminated along with the Omega system, we should soon see an end to this insidious global crime. The airborne breathable nanites in the chemtrails would have been only one facet of the building of a transhumanist world. Other measures would have included the HAARP weapon, wi-fi radiation, 5G, the 'Internet of Things', the usual vaccinations and the Covid injections. All would have combined to create humanity's own Tholian web prison. The environment would have become more and more irradiated and the health of organic beings inexorably ruined. The new Alpha system, by contrast, will follow the laws of the Creator. It will be an organic AI system running on Source energy to take care of all organic life. Only ourselves can give our power away now. Therefore we still require the positive invocation of the **2 of Wands** as demonstrated by Spock. He defeats the Tholian web-builders, the equivalent of Earth's remaining Deep State oligarchs, by careful timing and harmonious coordination of preparations on multiple fronts, saving the day for the Enterprise and her crew.

AFTER THE TAKEDOWN

The choice of freedom above control is made by each of us in our individual actions and by humanity as a whole collectively raising its consciousness. As we do so we will repudiate dark control systems such as digital currencies, 15-minute cities and vaccine passports. As with the Matrix builders' scheme for whittling away our inalienable rights, regaining them will be a slow and gradual process in the other direction. Those remaining elites would have us act as merely separate and divided Body Minds. But through civil disobedience and activation of our co-creative consciousness, our divinely infinite potential, we will break leftover Matrix conditioning. Patient and persistent effort, again as per the **2 of Wands**, in cooperation not competition, will be key. Source Consciousness acting through us will determine how quickly we rebuild our world on the new positive timeline.

64. THE PSYCHOPATHIC ELITE

An irredeemably corrupt elite will go the way of the fallen AI system that supported it

Episode 64 '**Plato's Stepchildren**' correlates with the **King of Swords**; both are themed around a person of influence and sharp intelligence; but if negative, given to domination by cunning or callousness.

THE CARD
Any King is a master of his suit and possessed of a kingdom. This King is a virile-looking man bearing a flesh-coloured long sword of the intellect that rises almost exactly vertically above his head. His left hand manipulates a sceptre or measuring device. Like the Emperor, the **King of Swords** only half sits, poised and ready for action in the mental realm - that of thinking, writing, analyzing, planning, conceptualizing, decision-making or formulating. He could be a writer, philosopher, teacher, strategist or consultant. Unlike the subdued, circumspect Queen of Swords, he looks confidently to the right, the future. New ideas and projects beckon him beyond those already familiar. He harbours a benign vision anticipating and welcoming further mental challenges.

Reversed and now facing left, this a man dominated by thoughts of dominating others. Consolidating a position of power or influence is his prime intent and motivation. His attitudes could be bitter or simply mistaken, sceptical or intractable. More negatively, there could be outright lying, or hiding or distorting the truth. The most **reversed** kind of **King of Swords** is a psychopath. This is a person or some kind of authority who can behave superficially in caring ways but only to hide purely selfish motives. Such a person's thinking will be cunning - adept at devising stratagems for self-advancement or continued domination. These are the power-brokers and Satanists who man the highest levels of society in politics, banking, business, mass media, education, big pharma etc. Machiavellian by nature, sworn to covert agendas, they will happily cast aside morality to achieve their ends. Cut off from heart-centred feelings they project outward charm and benevolence as a cover for predatory, harmful goals or strategies.

'PLATO'S STEPCHILDREN' PREMISE
The leader of a small community exercises authority by using extreme telekinesis to humiliate captured crew members - until they gain the upper hand.

CONTEXT
Power, Coercion.

THE PSYCHOPATHIC ELITE
Kirk, Spock and McCoy are lured down to an unknown planet, home of Parmen, the ruler of a small elitist 'republic'. Parmen models himself on the Philosopher King in Plato's teachings and ancient Greek culture. Up to 2,500 years old, Parmen and his people lead a utopian life with little to do but lounge around spending time in contemplation. Somehow gifted with extremely powerful telekinesis, their minds alone can perform most physical tasks. But Parmen has fallen ill and asks McCoy to cure an infection, which he does. The trio make to leave but Parmen decides to keep McCoy for future medical needs. When met with refusal, Parmen starts psychically inflicting forced movement and emotion upon his now captives. He humiliates them into grotesque contortions, self-slapping, dancing, laughing and crying. Spock almost suffers a nervous breakdown. But helped by Alexander, Parmen's friendly dwarf assistant, the trio discover the source of the community's telekinetic power: kironide, naturally present in the food. McCoy arranges for the trio plus Alexander to empower themselves with a double dose of kironide. At a cabaret in which Parmen additionally compels Uhura and Nurse Chapel to perform like puppets, the charged-up foursome turn

the tables on the psychopathic leader. Overpowered, Parmen promises the safety of future visitors. Kirk and Spock doubt it, warning that Starships will henceforth keep checks on him.

CARD/EPISODE AND MATRIX TAKEDOWN
No person has the right to enslave any other person by the exercise of authority. The **King of Swords** as a man of vision directs but does not control. On the contrary, he protects the freedom of others and empowers them. Parmen only empowers himself. His system of control represents politics by deviousness and coercion. As did that of the Dark Occultists lording it over the world thanks to the AI Matrix. Indeed, their hierarchical system *was* control - in the shape of a pyramid made up of ascending levels of inner pyramids structuring the institutions of banking, business, politics, education, media, religion, big pharma and the military. Built into the structure were elite minorities at higher levels controlling the many below. Each level reported to the next level above, superior in knowledge, so that control within the system was vertically layered and compartmentalized. This enabled the uppermost elite, all psychopaths, to direct the overall agenda.

Parmen, the Plato-styled Philosopher **King of Swords** (but very much **reversed**) lords it at the top of his community of 38 on Platonius. He considers them a brotherhood living in a democracy founded on peace and harmony. In practice he operates as a dictator maintaining discipline by his power of telekinesis. 'Our justice is the will of the stronger mind,' he declares, contrasting this with control by weapons. The undemocratic nature of any such exercise of power never seems to occur to him. And demonstration of his command is amply given. Kirk, Spock and McCoy are literally brought to their knees writhing and play acting like demented simpletons. Kirk is forced to recite words such as:
> *Being your slave, what should I do but tend*
> *Upon the hours and times of your desire?*

A state run by Plato's type of 'Philosopher King' dictator has not manifested itself on Earth without obvious problems and imperfections. Parmen's version vividly illustrates the dangers and faults of this system of governance. Karl Popper in 'The Open Society and its Enemies', 1945, has argued that such a system leads all too easily to totalitarianism. The society becomes more important than the people who comprise it. Its preservation will be used as justification to crush anyone criticizing it or advocating change. Benevolent dictators in recent history have included Lee Kuan Yew in Singapore, Ataturk in Turkey, Gaddafi in Libya and Tito in Yugoslavia. Such leaders succeeded in presiding over many reforms and benefits to their societies.

But opposition leaders and critics were dealt with at best uneasily, at worst punitively. Ironically, the presence of a **King of Swords reversed** in the shape of a strong leader of greater or lesser dictatorial tendency has served in many cases as a bulwark against total capitulation to the Matrix system. Leaders like Gaddafi, Castro, Kim Jong-Un, Ahmadinejad and Assad have maintained a degree of independence for their states, those of Libya, Cuba, North Korea, Iran and Syria respectively. But even these maverick leaders belonged to the political Matrix, all bought and paid for by one or other of the two reigning Orders, the Black Sun or the Dragon.

Parmen perfectly demonstrates the psychopathic characteristics of an oppressive **King of Swords reversed**. He has no guilt or remorse in commanding the Enterprise visitors to perform humiliating and violent acts. Spock is nearly forced to stamp upon the face of Kirk; and later Kirk and Spock to cavort on stage with Uhura and Nurse Chapel before threatening them with whip and hot poker. And the audience, Parmen's community, laugh at this. Outwardly, Parmen appears welcoming and charming, as psychopaths do. He professes to lead a democratic society living in peace and harmony. He claims his telekinetic power came by divine providence, that his visitors are safe and except for McCoy will be released. All this is lies, in keeping with the psychopath's compulsion to hide his true nature or deny his wrongdoing. Psychopaths differ from the rest of humanity. Their lying is pathological, their concern for others covers a contempt for their safety and feelings. Parmen later admits he had intended to destroy the Enterprise. Like the psychopaths infesting our governments and corporations a while longer after Matrix takedown, Parmen's concern is to maintain his power and survive for as long as possible. This has him grovelling before Kirk once the latter has demonstrated superior power. 'I beg of you' he implores Kirk, 'I'll do anything you say.' His further claim to turn over a new leaf cuts no ice with Kirk or Spock. They know only too well that a primary psychopath like Parmen, like those among Earth's shadowy elites, lies and cheats unstoppably, that they are born that way, never to change.

AFTER THE TAKEDOWN
Those elites mendaciously hanging on to power in the wake of the takedown will never voluntarily give up and cede their authority. The only way to permanently remove them is to sidestep or dismantle the system they maintain. Merely replacing one controlling elite with another is no solution. Humanity needs to recognize how sick the power-obsessed psychopaths are and that the AI system supporting them is gone. We simply need to stop supporting them ourselves by non-complying with their dictates.

65. FEMININE CREATIVITY

New organic and benevolent systems will emerge as masculine and feminine energies come back into balance

Episode 65 '**Wink of an Eye**' correlates with the **Queen of Wands**; both are themed around the part played by feminine beauty and creativity in healthy living.

THE CARD

Each of the four Queens reigns over her Suit in a feminine way. Rather than project its power like the Kings, they embody and nurture it. The Queen of Coins (dramatized negatively as the witch-like Sylvia in Episode 35) reigns over material abundance; the Queen of Swords (also dramatized negatively, as the conniving Janice Lester, in Episode 78) reigns over knowledge and intelligence); the Queen of Cups (the devotional Natira, Episode 62) reigns over loyalties and relationship. With the **Queen of Wands** we come to beauty and nurturance in creative or sexual realms. This Queen is young-looking and magnetically attractive. Uniquely for the Queens she faces right, direction of action and the future. This and Wands being the suit of creativity, her power of creative manifestation is not in doubt but it's a very different creativity to that of the naturally dominating King of Wands. Where his creativity individualizes itself and aspires to genius, her creativity, procreative or otherwise, is humble and collaborative. Her lightly held phallic wand and the open folds in her robe shows her affinity for feeling and sensation shared with others. She gives of herself in art and performance, in sex and romance, for mutual enjoyment rather than self-assertion or power. If motherly oriented, she will readily conceive, give birth and raise children yet not exclusively so. She's likely to remain active in other areas through a mixture of multi-tasking and gentle persistence. In creative projects she will demonstrate long and steady patience all the way to accomplishment. This **Queen**'s prettiness with long luxuriant, rippling curls falling over soft shoulders indictes abundant sex appeal and desirability. With emotional depth, playfulness and charm, she is a herself a work of art. She could be a muse for male artists, a captivating singer or dancer, an able and supportive partner, or a warm, space-holding presence in any social circle.

Reversed, the **Queen of Wands** and her values may be exploited or eclipsed by masculine domination. Or, driven by an agenda, she may overplay her seductiveness to exploit others. She can also be narcissistic or vain, greedily seeking attention and indulging in power trips within relationship. As a 'femme fatale' or 'gold digger' she may use her irresistible quality of attraction to avidly pursue adulation, personal advantage, money or sex.

'WINK OF AN EYE' PREMISE
The Enterprise is invaded by the higher dimensional Queen of Scalos and her group. She intends to mate with Kirk in efforts to repopulate her planet.

CONTEXT
Femininity, Multi-Dimensionality, Coercion.

FEMININE CREATIVITY
A group of five humanoids on Scalos send out a video distress call but beaming down, a landing party finds the planet uninhabited. Back on the Enterprise the computer detects an invasion of the ship by beings who can't be traced except for buzzing insect-like sounds. By spiking his coffee, the beings abduct Kirk, shifting or 'accelerating' him into their adjacent dimension. Their leader, the playful, seductive Deela, introduces herself to Kirk with a passionate kiss. She, the Queen of Scalos, wants him to be her King. Sexualiy and mischievously using her feminine creativity, she will entice Kirk and others into serving as her stud to repopulate the planet. Her group of five are the sole survivors of an environmental disaster that rendered the men infertile. The Scalosians have brought a refrigeration unit aboard the Enterprise. This will keep the crew in suspended animation to provide a pool of fresh fertile males when needed. Kirk resists by sabotaging the transporter

and getting a message through to his crew. At the same time he shows himself charmed by Deela's feminine, flirtatious demeanour, joining with her in affectionate lovemaking. When her jealous partner Rael furiously catches them having made love she affirms her right to like the man she selects. Kirk still pretending to acquiesce, rebels, joined by a newly accelerated Spock. They knock out Rael, destroy the refrigeration unit and return Deela to Scalos. McCoy's development of an antidote enables Kirk and Spock to return to their own dimension. Deela appears one last time on the monitor. She and Kirk exchange fond looks of farewell.

CARD/EPISODE AND MATRIX TAKEDOWN

As a race, humans are no stranger to catastrophes on the scale of that afflicting Scalos. Major Earth disasters have occurred over millions of years in the form of attacks and cataclysms brought about by alien warring races listed by Ashayana Deane as including the Anunnaki, the Dracos and the Templar Annu. Alien-instigated destruction recorded in galactic histories such as Deane's Voyagers books has been instrumental in the development of the top-down, male-oriented Matrix. The repercussions of the disaster on Scalos differ in that the handful of survivors intend to maintain the balance of influence between masculine and feminine. Deela, its queen and an epitome of the **Queen of Wands**, intends to have as much say in the repopulation project as her partner Rael. The latter comes across as jealous, probably possessive, and humourlessly workmanlike. Despite this, the power dynamic between him and Deela seems balanced, auguring well for creating a balanced new social system for the planet.

But the survivors take a criminal liberty in planning to repopulate their planet by capturing males from passing spaceships to mate with Deela. She, with all the sex appeal of the **Queen of Wands** at her most seductive and fertile, intends to utilize her charms to the full. She plays the honey trap but remains attentive to safety, comfort and pleasure both for herself and her intended mates. She protects Kirk who could easily have been killed by the volatile Rael. She flirts and makes love with him in cheerful, authentic ways. She tells him she likes him and promises to be kind to him, not to hurt him. Despite her egregious plan, Deela stands for feminine creativity including sexuality activated in balance with masculine force. By contrast, Earth's Matrix elites aimed at patriarchal dominance. The institution of religion, a Matrix creation par excellence, has over the millenia cemented a belief in God as a male authority figure who passes judgement over sinful, inferior humans. The Bible speaks of the plant, animal and mineral kingdoms as possessions to be exploited for material gain. Accordingly, in cultures around the world, an elitist minority of male priests, along with male-dominated government and aristocracy, became invested with power and control over the majority. An unending catalogue of empires, wars, slaughter, misery and competition has ensued, scarring the development of humanity. Power has always been the object and reward, a decidedly masculine type of Matrix power. Feminine creativity was sidelined until very recently, confined to home-making, procreation and child-rearing. Outside the home, masculine energy dominated. Rulers and their militaries wielded the power during the Roman Empire. Medieval feudalism then took over, feeding more war and destruction amid patriarchal rule by class, wealth and privilege.

Women in our Satanically driven materialistic culture still have to strain to compete with men and make up for eons of economic and professional subjugation. Though this is changing and will change a lot more after the takedown, the **Queen of Wands** still endures suppression in her more holistic and natural approaches to life. For a while longer, institutions dominating medicine, agriculture, science, technology and nutrition may continue to spurn the feminine principle. The WEF's Great Reset was aiming to make these fields even more patriarchal in the way of technocratic, synthetic and weaponized. But with the takedown, the Divine Mother aspect of the sacred union between the male and female principles, between technology and nature, will return to balance and with it the light body of humanity. A positive aspect of Deela and Rael's project reflects this, with their willingness to share male and female influence in building their new society. But their hijacking of the Enterprise abuses the rights and freedoms of others and shows they still have much to learn. Sex appeal when it becomes manipulative in any way, betokens misuse of power. As Kirk tells Deela, 'The trouble is in you' meaning that she and her people still have inner work to do. So too Earth people as we leave the Matrix for a new and healthy civilization.

AFTER THE TAKEDOWN

As from 2023, we will see a rapid transition away from the travesty of humanity dominated by a masculine, dictatorial elite hoarding power and pushing for a dystopian technocracy. The Archonic, controlling AI Matrix has gone. Next to go will be the attitudes fostering inorganic, anti-human anti-divine technologies. This ethos will give way to a new respect for feminine, organic systems. A healing and positive timeline will see technologies emerge that no longer disadvantage organic life but nurture and strengthen us. The ecosystem will be cleansed and regenerated. Kim Goguen's nascent Global Peace and Restoration Plan set up by her as a humanitarian **Queen of Wands** will inaugurate these changes in our Matrix-liberated world.

66. VICTIM MENTALITY

Exploitation enabled by excess of empathy will be halted by the right spirit of self-preservation

Episode 66 'The Empath' correlates with the **8 of Cups**; both are themed around empathy, loving care and compassion, or if carried to extremes, self-sacrifice and victimhood.

THE CARD
A spectacular array of flowers and foliage graces the **8 of Cups**. With the 8th Degree representing perfection due to its correspondence with Justice, a peak of fullness is reached involving the heart and its place in the world. At this level, emotions and relationships are deeply felt, alive and vital and nourished by spiritual love. The equivalent peak of mental development, the 8 of Swords, displays a stark contrast - no foliage at all and no living, dynamic floral activity. Mind in its ultimate development knows itself through emptiness, the heart through fullness. With this card, oneness with all life is deeply felt. There is empathy with the lot of others and concern for their well-being. Other feelings like appreciation, gratitude and forgiveness are in abundance, providing the means to live in harmony with others and in balance with nature. Healing and nurturing abilities are very likely present in the empath's pure and powerful energy of love, the highest energy there is.

Reversal indicates problems with unconditional love. The person or group may have abandoned care for themself, giving it only to others in a dependent or addictive way. Self-neglect can therefore result manifesting as victim mentality, submissiveness, willing slavery or 'Stockholm Syndrome'. Or self-support may only bring feelings of guilt or unworthiness. Or love for self or others may be contaminated by pious or moralistic sentiment.

'THE EMPATH' PREMISE
Uncomprehending aliens use trial by torture on Kirk and McCoy in order to test a sensitive woman in qualities of empathy, compassion and self-sacrifice.

CONTEXT
Sensitivity, Coercion.

VICTIM MENTALITY
Scientists have gone missing from a research station on a planet close to a sun about to go nova. Searching for them, Kirk, Spock and McCoy are suddenly transported into an underground cavern where they meet a beautiful mute woman. They call her Gem and note her compassion and empathic healing ability. Two ugly Vians with advanced powers are holding her captive. The aliens proceed to subject the men to callous tortures. They later reveal that this is to a) teach the woman courage and strength of will b) assess whether she becomes courageous enough to risk her life to heal the victims and c) determine whether she proves the inhabitants of her planet worthy of rescue from the nova. The Vians can only save one of two threatened planets. They have already tortured to death the two missing scientists who they say failed their tests. Throughout the ordeal, Kirk, Spock and McCoy show every willingness to sacrifice themselves individually if it means the survival of the others. The Vians are impressed. Gem too, shares in the same victim mentality, providing healing despite the strain on herself. After McCoy has been strung up and brutally tortured, the Vians watch to see whether Gem will give her life out of her own accord to heal him. Gem starts to work on the dying McCoy but has trouble and faints. Kirk eventually breaks the slide into Stockholm Syndrome and angrily berates the heartless, empathy-deleted Vians for their cold intellects and lack of compassion. The Vians take note. They restore McCoy to health, pick up Gem and carry her away for a purpose unknown. The trio are left to return safely to the Enterprise. A recovered and beaming McCoy notes that 'good old human emotion' may have impressed the Vians most.

CARD/EPISODE AND MATRIX TAKEDOWN

It's more crucial than ever to understand victim mentality in order to understand any tardiness as humanity moves on from the fallen Matrix. Past subjugation within the AI system has conditioned humanity into willingly accepting self-enslavement. The **8 of Cups reversed** symbolizes this weakness. **Upright**, the card denotes empathy and compassion, a beautiful unselfish awareness, but only if kept in balance. Gem unfortunately falls into the compassion trap of empaths and loving people who care for others despite themselves. How to make the most of the gifts of empathy and compassion while minimizing the dangers? Empaths tend to be service-oriented and to put their own needs and urges last, rendering them easily manipulated. Without setting and enforcing boundaries they open themselves to exploitation and victimization. Their compassion and readiness to offer healing wherever it's needed can become exhausting or worse. Their sensitivity to others' suffering may cause them, like Gem, to physically take on their ailments. It may be a wave of emotion or a bodily harm that they take on - even to manifesting similar cuts, bruises or sickness. Or they may lack assertiveness and downplay their own sovereign rights. Through guilt or fear, the habit of not letting others down may have become compulsive. Gem and the landing party absolutely must protect themselves without discarding concern for each other. The same with Earth people, many still hypnotized into following continuing government plans for technocratic tyranny.

Empathy in short can all too easily lead to self-sacrifice and destructive willingness to play the victim, the **8 of Cups reversed**. Not that the Vians care. As far as this alien pair are concerned, devoid of empathy and operating only out of intellect, maximum empathy is all they want to see. After Gem has been put through a gauntlet of healing tests, Spock protests that she has proven herself and earned the right of her planet to be saved. 'She offered her life', he says. 'To offer is not proof enough' replies the Vian Lal coldly. The Vians want to see if Gem's virtues even extend to taking on McCoy's fatal injuries and thus dying in the process of healing him. Lal wants to see 'her instinct developed to the fullest ... the test must be complete.' At best, this shows misunderstanding of empathy and compassion; at worst it betrays a condition of psychopathy and sadism. Why would Gem have to die a martyr to prove her race's worthiness to be saved? The Vians claim to be looking for courage and strength of will. But this kind of strength is self-defeating. If Gem's empathy were total and as such, representative of the character of her people, this would identify them as a suicidal race willing to die to save each other. It does appear that this reflects the Vian pair themselves. They are willing to lose their own planet in order to save another planet, as only one population can be spirited away before the sun goes nova. In terms of like attracts like, and moreover the psychology of Wetiko, this makes sense. The Wetiko frequency combines the extremes of control and evil on the one hand with fear and despair on the other. In Wetiko, ruthless tyrants and self-sacrificing victims, despots and slaves, create each other. The oppressive Vians need and want the survival of a submissive race. They may be perceived as doing a great service in looking to save an entire planet and no doubt those people want to be saved. But there is no saving anyone from their own mind-pattern of victimhood. Unbalanced empathy makes a victim of a person or a collective. Any external saviour will keep them living out their unhealthy mind-pattern, the **reversed 8 of Cups**. Unbalanced empaths will continue to play out their victim mentality until they face up to this aspect of themselves as Gem must, and so too the Enterprise trio.

AFTER THE TAKEDOWN
The Covid era saw Earth people bafflingly tolerate the misery of lockdowns, travel restrictions and social distancing, capped by coercion worldwide to take injections of lethal graphene oxide and spike proteins causing huge numbers of injuries and deaths. Chinese style social credit systems are still being threatened. This only ends when the people end it. With the AI Matrix gone, the world now has the opportunity as never before to become conscious of collective self-abnegation and harmful submission to authority. Stockholm Syndrome needs to be replaced with qualities of self-respect and self-care. Civil disobedience and non-cooperation with dictatorial governments is the only way, just as the human captives have to resist the cold and heartless Vians. The people of Earth, like the victimized Gem and the trio, have to become courageous enough to take a stand for their sovereign rights, ours by birth. Every single living man, woman and child is a sovereign being. Once people realize this they will overwhemingly reject the assault on our rights and freedoms, just as the tortures inflicted on the Enterprise team by the Vians had to be rejected by Kirk. The time has come to use the word 'NO' unequivocally. The courage needed to cease complying with abusive authority and to put up determined resistance will proceed from right use of the ego - the counterpart of selfless empathy and compassion. Kirk shows the way forward for Earth's oppressed peoples when he finally rebels and rails against the tormenting aliens: 'You don't understand what it is to live. Love and compassion are dead in you! You're nothing but intellect!' Like Kirk, we must each stand up for our right to bodily integrity and for our right to freedom from deliberate and coercive harm.

67. THE SACRED FEMININE

The feminine principle restored to parity with the masculine will signal the end of Matrix patriarchy

Episode 67 '**Elaan of Troyius**' correlates with **The Empress**; both are themed around the sacred qualities of womanhood and their place in a world either balanced or male-dominated.

THE CARD
Along with the High Priestess she is the Divine Feminine, the Goddess among the Tarot archetypes. **The Empress** is a woman centred in and perfectly at ease with her sacred power. Love is the centre of her being. Just being herself - wise, loving, mysterious, indefinable, earthy, playful, compassionate - is her blessing to the world. Seated at the centre of the five figures initiating the Major Arcana series, **The Empress** occupies a place at the heart of the family, the community, society. The Emperor primed for action and achievement at her side looks to her as his muse and inspiration, his comfort and support. The two make a balanced couple complementing each other in terms of Being and Doing, Natural and Man-made, Allowing and Commanding (though as we each connect with the whole, both women and men have these attributes in varying degrees). The High Priestess sits behind her, her alter-ego, solitary, quiet, contemplative, virginal or aged. In her different aspects a woman can em-

body either High Priestess or **Empress**. The former nurtures the pure and divine spirit within. The latter outwardly radiates it, actively mothering and creating. No child would want to be brought up without the soul-full presence of the mother. No man can fully duplicate the mother's role. Without **The Empress**' life-giving presence gracing the environment like a deep river, the male-only world is a wasteland. She faces The Emperor with her legs apart and her sceptre leaning on her womb and genital area, signs that she thrives on forming connection and partnership, on relating through romance and sex. Thus she delights in conceiving and gestating, giving birth to and raising children. Not limited to partnering or mothering, **The Empress** is capable and devoted as a householder, businesswoman, friend, confidante or artist. Centred in the heart, she is naturally inclined to optimism in her outlook and undertakings. Knowing through the depths of her being that all is divine, she embodies abundance and fertility, humility and radiance, gentleness and exuberance.

A **reversed Empress** may simply be a disenfranchised, mistreated, misunderstood woman. In patriarchy down the ages women have had to submit to controlling men or to play the role of second class citizen. Until allowed to outwardly manifest her inner divine connection a suppressed woman, like Elaan, could appear to others as contemptuous, temperamental, imperious or erratic.

'ELAAN OF TROYIUS' PREMISE
A socially restricted resentful queen rebels against Kirk attempting to tame her for marriage. After a change of heart she helps ward off hostile Klingons.

CONTEXT
Femininity, Relationship.

THE SACRED FEMININE
A very disgruntled Queen Elaan is picked up from planet Elas. The Enterprise is to convey her and ambassador Petri to Petri's planet Troyius. The two planets have long been at war with each other and in efforts to achieve peace Elaan has been chosen to marry Troyius' ruler. The Elasians are an arrogant and vicious race, characteristics not lost on Elaan. Knowing this, the exasperated Petri's job is to try to teach the bride-to-be lessons in etiquette en route to Troyius to prepare her for a successful marriage. Kirk slows down the Enterprise to make time for Elaan's tutelage. But Elaan, her Sacred Feminine qualities eclipsed by hatred of the Troyians and the prospect of her marriage to one out of convenience, fiercely rebels. She trashes her

quarters, stabs the ambassador and throws a knife at Kirk. Things change when a love potion in her own tears casts its spell on Kirk and herself. A Klingon ship meanwhile has started shadowing the Enterprise. And one of Elaan's entourage jealous of her marriage turns traitor and fixes the Enterprise's warp drive engines to explode if it tries to escape the Klingons. But Elaan comes to the rescue. The peace offering given her by the ambassador is a necklace made of dilithium crystals, exactly what Scotty needs to repair the engines. To show her new love for Kirk, Elaan willingly gives up the crystals allowing the Enterprise to outwit the Klingon ship. Resigned to carrying on with her duty, Elaan sombrely bids Kirk farewell before beaming down to Troyius.

CARD/EPISODE AND MATRIX TAKEDOWN

The Matrix AI system supported a hierarchical pyramid of control thoroughly masculine by its very artifice - artificial, man-made, authoritarian, compartmentalized. The oligarchs running it deified the masculine principle as represented in the Tarot by The Emperor and in our city squares by the phallic obelisk. Matrix power was the extreme and insane expression of maleness on a global scale. A giant pyramid of control regulated systems and institutions dedicated on an occult level to accomplishing the Great Work of Ages - the patriarchal usurping of organic life by inorganic machine for the benefit of Dracos, AI and the Archons. Star Trek exposes Matrix patriarchy in The Emperor episode, No. 48, Patterns of Force. And here with the demeaning of Elaan we see how patriarchy subjugates women and femininity. Elaan the disempowered **Empress** is ironically reduced to an authoritarian role, more masculine than feminine, yet deprived of free choice of husband in the interests of forging diplomatic relations with another race, the Troyians. This blatantly patriarchal and political hijacking of a woman's rights suppresses her personal sovereignty, her natural instincts and her sacred femininity. It is no wonder then that the Dolman who beams aboard to be transported to Troyius is not a happy bunny.

Earth history, like Elas', has been rooted for millenia in this kind of social, religious and political subduing of the female. Masculine dominance was deliberately maintained by the Pindar AI operating on the 8th level of the astral. No way then, could the sacred principles of **The Empress** find balance with the masculine during the Matrix era. Her nutritive and regenerative goodness were devalued and used to support the masculine ethos of power, command and structure. As on Earth, so on Elas - dominating, assertive women like Elaan merely ape masculine power. Such women may be respected and given the dues of a man in a similar position of influence, but this sidesteps the feminine principle of free playfulness and love and pleasure in favour of maintaining the strict, hierarchical, ritualistic patriarchy. Elaan as a female ruler may appear to be strong and powerful for her sex, but is actually trapped and enslaved. Sadly, as a **reversed Empress**, she behaves like a ridiculous parody of a patriarch. In her vehement opposition to the dutiful role imposed upon her she becomes domineering, vicious and petulant. Hatred for herself and others has grown out of her disgust at marrying a despised Troyian. In conforming to the diplomatic role imposed upon her she grotesquely distorts both feminine and masculine aspects of power.

Both Petri and Kirk labour to teach this wounded **Empress** the elements of good manners. But we discover later after Kirk and Elaan have fallen in love with each other that she has no need of training in courtesy, manners or kindness. 'If I can be of any help, of course,' she says with sincerity, allowing her wedding gift of a necklace to be cleverly used to power the Enterprise. This is a far cry from her earlier knife attacks on both Petri and Kirk for attempting to tame her à la Shakespeare's shrewish Kate. In fact, what Elaan needs is healing of her brutalized femininity. Warrior-breeding on Elas has moulded her into a female martinet when she is not swooning in a submissive spell to her lord and master. Having men dominate her on the Enterprise, this time to teach her manners, can only rub salt into her wounds. Manners? What manners do men on Earth show in using armed police to regulate Earth's population? Or in maintaining patriarchal control of finance, politics or religion? Or using militaries to wage wars to remove rival governments or to speed up global centralization of masculine power? The last thing, moreover, that the suppressed Sacred Feminine needs is more suppression to fit in with the demands of a hypocritical male elite. Ultimately there is nothing Kirk can do for this unhappy **Empress Reversed** other than deliver her to the husband and master chosen for her. An end to male domination must come one day in her system as it is coming now on Earth in the wake of the fallen Matrix.

AFTER THE TAKEDOWN

Along with the fall of Matrix control systems structured around authoritarian government, big business and menacing technocracy will come a rebalancing of feminine principles alongside masculine. Humanity will rapidly leap forward in its evolution to embrace a world that truly balances structure, control, big business and technology with freedom, compassion, self-help communities and nature. Humanity will be its own saviour in this regard by restoring principles of sacred femininity. Thus will our civilization evolve out of patriarchal patterns of relationship, hierarchy and social control.

68. MATRIX MADNESS

As free and responsible sovereign beings we will render the madness of the Matrix obsolete

Episode 68 'Whom Gods Destroy' correlates with **The Fool**; both are themed around living a free and venturesome life in ways that do not harm or steal from others.

THE CARD
The Fool or Le Mat in French resembles in the Tarot a harlequin, a vagabond or an itinerant traveller enthusiastically moving to the right, the direction of the future and the unknown. He tilts his head nonchalantly and pays little attention to a small dog or lynx behind him tearing at his clothes. He carries over his shoulder Dick Whittington style a small bag of possessions - perhaps symbols of the four suits seen on the table of The Magician. The ground is fertile with thick tufts of grass but rocky and uneven. A bold and spontaneous spirit is called for in pursuance of a journey unplanned and unpredictable. Freedom and new experience beckons him or her on roamings and adventures out in the world. A carefree burst of energy has been unleashed.

Reversed, the release of energy and thirst for adventure find no fruitful or harmonious outlet. The seeker of new experience, suffering chaos or confusion within, finds or creates only chaos or confusion externally. The result is energy wastage, propagation of distorted or inverted values, or manifest selfishness or stupidity. In a chronic condition this all degenerates further into the imbalance and injustice of madness and wrongdoing.

'WHOM GODS DESTROY' PREMISE
Kirk and Spock visit an asylum for the galaxy's most criminally insane individuals. An escaped inmate captures them and revels in his own craziness.

CONTEXT
The Adversary, Insanity, Illusion, Coercion.

MATRIX MADNESS
Delivering a new wonder drug to the mental health colony on Elba II, Kirk finds that the lunatics have taken over the asylum. The Governor who had warmly welcomed him turned out to be a shapeshift of Garth, the new and most dangerous inmate. Garth had been a starship captain of outstanding promise who became possessed and insane after an accident near Antos IV. The doctors there failed to restore his mental health but imbued him with the ability to shapeshift at will. Garth now keeps the real Governor under torturous confinement showing zero empathy for the man's suffering. He surrounds himself with the 14 freed inmates whom he calls his new crew. These include the green-skinned, seductive and hystrionic Martha. His fleet, he tells Kirk, awaits his resumption of command whereupon he intends to conquer the entire galaxy. With a penchant for ceremony and occasion Garth formally proclaims himself 'Master of the Universe'. With his flippant tone and superficial charm, 'Lord Garth' arrogantly holds court. Weapons in hand and henchmen at the ready, the mercurial, narcissistic and psychopathic Garth keeps Kirk and Spock captive within his self-styled mad Matrix of control. Any attempts to reason with him only trigger his painful sense of failure, rejection and weakness hiding behind his superiority complex. His failure to have himself beamed up to the Enterprise has him beating the floor in rage. Growing jealous of Martha for her attentions to Kirk, he shuts her outside in the toxic air and blows her up. On a whim, he casually tosses around a flask of his explosive. Garth finally undoes himself when having shapeshifted into Kirk he fails to fool Spock. Finally subdued, the mad fool is returned into care to undergo treatment with the new drug.

CARD/EPISODE AND MATRIX TAKEDOWN
In his delusional grandiosity, his callous disregard of the rights and lives of others, Garth is a homicidal **Fool reversed**, no different to the dark occultists that long ruled over Earth. Earth's AI Matrix propped up a madhouse ruled like Garth's regime by psychopaths and run by idiots. The same can be said for the Greek style colony under Parmen's autocratic rule in Episode

64; so too for Melokon's tyranny over Ekos in Episode 48; and for the planets under murderous AI control in episodes such as Nos. 20, 33 and 71. Episode 20's citizens, mind controlled and docilely complying, typify the level of ignorance and idiocy required of the public for inhuman or lunatic forces to maintain control with their Service To Self ethos. This double whammy of psychopathy on the part of the rulers and idiocy on the part of the gofers and the populace has pertained on Earth for thousands of years thanks to Matrix control. Billions of Earth people are still cowed and manipulated by a Maritime legal system that presumes them to be dead or lost at sea, and a debt-based banking system heading for inexorable financial meltdown. As with the inmates corralled into Garth's clownshow, the gross insanity of our leaders is taken to be normal or unchangeable. Madness and criminality on the part of an insane leadership goes hand in hand with the, yes, insanity, of people acquiescing in herdlike unanimity out of ignorance or denial. Etheric parasites inflicted on humans by the Palermo AI at the 7th level of the astral might help to explain blots on our society ranging from the state manufacture and release of bioweapons, the tolerance of an unlawful legal system, the fraudulent money system and a history of warfare in the cause of regime change and creative destruction. 'Democratic' elections have been constantly rigged, freedoms deleted in the wake of 9/11 and other elite-created false flag attacks, and grotesque abuses perpetrated in human trafficking, daily toxic spraying of our skies, crops poisoned by killer chemicals, the scourge of GMOs, organ harvesting, 5G, fracking ... the list is endless.

With the end of the Omega AI system by the grace of God, time is up for the madhouse that has been life on Earth. Our world has for far too long endured conditions not dissimilar to those of Elba II's mental health colony with the humane Governor taken hostage. Garth the usurper, in his deranged, sadistic, delusional behaviour sadly represents Earth's ruling elite. Like any deceitful psychopath, the preposterous megalomaniac knows how to use smiling charm and cunning subterfuge to advance his insane plans. Like Earth's maniacal leaders this scarily **reversed Fool** is intelligent but not wise, avuncular but callous, in control of others but not of himself. And as psychopaths flourish in positions of power - such is what they crave and what they do - so does Garth and so did the Matrix elite until the recent takedown. Both were victims of their own psychotic delusions, causing misery for everyone else. Garth blows up his innocent female consort without a moment's remorse. The shadow government explodes the Twin Towers and kills 3000 without a moment's remorse. Garth clads himself in sumptuous robes and presides over ceremonies like the dinner and his coronation in the manner of Earth's bloodline elites including Presidents and Royal

Families. Not content with having established their fiefdoms, Garth and Earth's Cabal seek to extend their power ad infinitum. Garth relentlessly humiliates, confines and intimidates anyone who stands in his way such as the Governor, Kirk or Spock. As bullying as Garth is, so in their own way were the Matrix generals. Through falsely obtaining our consent they sought to bring us all to our knees with Covid lockdowns, mandatory injections and face masks. Their yearned-for digital ID system would legalize total AI surveillance and control. For their attacks on humanity, a great number of Cabal members have been removed from the Earth plane as of 2023 by forces of light coordinated by Kim Goguen. Remaining Deep State terrorists are apparently still plotting China's takeover of the USA, a digital cashless world and a *skynet*-style Smart Grid. The spectre of the Great Reset enabled by a 3rd World War remains their ultimate ego trip, with nanotech 'vaccines' combining with electromagnetic 5G weaponry and brain-computer interface to turn humans into zombies and cyborgs. All this is in accord with the elites' religion, Satanism. But rather than worshipping Satan or any god, the elites want to *be* God. Nothing could be more insane.

The deranged Garth declares his ambition to gain 'limitless power, limitless wealth and solar systems ruled by the elite'. In his ravings to Kirk and Spock he goes on: 'We gentlemen are that elite, and we must take what is rightfully ours from the decadent weaklings that now hold it.' Such theft is what all transgressions of Natural Law ultimately amount to. And what the Garth-like parasites most want to steal from us is our power - ever more power to fuel their lust for control. Garth uses a gift from his benefactors, shapeshifting ability, to hoodwink the Governor and steal his position. The Earth's elite have relied upon the Orion Matrix, but this has gone. Unable now to enslave us purely technologically they will fall back on redoubled manipulation and deception to trick people into giving them all power. But truth and Natural Law will no longer be overridden. The mad Garth undoes himself as the mad Cabal already has, with no going back to the madness.

AFTER THE TAKEDOWN
No one rightfully owns us. Each one of us is a sovereign being. This gives us the freedom of **The Fool upright** to spurn control systems and make our own way in life. The psychopaths who sought to enslave us in permanent degradation were indeed mad and deluded. In the new energy it is they who will undergo confinement or removal for pursuing mentally ill criminal actions that destroy free society. People will be empowered to regain personal sovereignty. Honesty, truth and morality will return along with freedom and Natural Law manifested under no one's control but our own.

69. HATRED AND WAR

War will cease and with it
Matrix provocation when we
unify ourselves in our diversity

Episode 69 **'Let That Be Your Last Battlefield'** correlates with the **10 of Swords**; both are themed around dissolution of polarity; or alternately its ultimate degeneration into irreconcilable conflict.

THE CARD
The 10th degree of the Minor Arcana equates with the The Wheel of Fortune and Judgement, cards embodying the principle of cyclical abeyance or transcendence. With Swords to do with the mind, the **10 of Swords** thus indicates rising above in-grained mental patterns. Two swords of differently coloured handles enter the arched array and engage with each other, finding a kind of union. There is no suggestion of conflict in the card **upright** but rather of the attainment of a truce, compromise or mutual understanding. The sword tips touch at the highest, most heavenly level with flower heads of peace on either side. The swords themselves are coloured deep blue for spirituality, for essential oneness of being with all existence. And yet they are crossed, possibly subject to clashing again in the future. The message seems to be that no ultimate transcendence out of mind is possible at this 3D level of existence. We have

to learn to live with our differences, respect each other's varying opinions and attitudes and accept that truth while always truth will always be subject to different beliefs and interpretations.

With the handles up in the air on the **10 of Swords reversed**, ego desires and attitudes remain in contention. Argument, intransigence, hatred, pride or attachment to self-identity keeps adversaries in conflict, their differences unresolved. The learning of unity in diversity still remains far off.

'LET THAT BE YOUR LAST BATTLEFIELD' PREMISE
Two mutual enemies from a racially divided planet bring havoc aboard the Enterprise. Kirk finds it impossible to stop them hating and fighting each other.

CONTEXT
War, Slaughter.

HATRED AND WAR
Two humanoids, pilots of separate tiny vessels, come aboard the Enterprise. The first is Lokai, an escaped slave and a revolutionary from the planet Cheron. The second is Bele, a Commissioner of Police from the same planet. Bele calls Lokai a traitor and seeks to extradite him back to Cheron. The two aliens are coloured black on one side, white on the other, but in opposite configuration. Bele demands they set course for Cheron but Kirk refuses, citing urgent business at Ariannus. But Bele takes the starship under his control using incredible mental power. A stand-off ensues between Bele and Kirk in which Kirk initiates the sequence to destroy the ship. In the last moments, the stalemate is broken by Bele agreeing to allow course to be reset for Ariannus. But after the Enterprise's mission there is concluded, Bele again forcibly sets course to Cheron (instead of Starbase 4) while making self-destruct impossible. Lokai is incensed, claiming a mockery of justice and denial of his right of political sanctuary. His people have been oppressed and kept as slaves for thousands of years by Bele's race. In response, Bele calls Lokai an inferior breed and a criminal. The two aliens fight hand to hand on the bridge in uncontrolled fury. As above on the Enterprise, so below on Cheron: the planet comes into view devastated after a final, apocalyptic war. The entire population, both Bele's and Lokai's races, have annihilated themselves. Though shocked, the two bitter enemies like manic automatons continue to fight. Pursuing each other around the ship they individually beam down to their desecrated, burning planet. Nothing will be left for them down there, Kirk observes, except their hate.

CARD/EPISODE AND MATRIX TAKEDOWN

Energy vampirism fostered by the old Matrix, seen in Episode 61, reaches its apogee here with the warring Bele and Lokai. Belonging to two races, one oppressing the other, the men allow rage and hatred to take them over, fueling bitter conflict. Like warring races throughout Earth history during the Matrix era, they are pawns of a dark force that feeds on nothing but 'fear, anxiety, hate and negativity', to repeat the quote by Stewart Swerdlow on page 303. So with any of us when we refuse to give up inner dark essence allowing us to be triggered by parasites and demons. The process can be complex, with historical factors playing their part in such animosity - the **10 of Swords reversed** - as Bele and Lokai's. Oppressed peoples in North America suffered under white races with the colonization and slavery that built the modern day continent. Africans were forcibly brought to the US and enslaved and abused by the white European settlers. Black Africans were seen as primitive and backward. In the same vein, Bele sees Lokai's people as 'an inferior breed'. They were 'savages', he says, prior to being freed from slavery. In a reminder of blacks being corralled into fighting America's war in Vietnam, Lokai asks Kirk to imagine the fate of being 'dragged out of your hovel to serve in a war on another planet.' Until the civil war of 1861-65, black slavery blighted the whole of the south of the US, enforced by criminal violence. Planet Cheron appropriately lies according to Kirk in uncharted space 'in the southernmost part of the galaxy.'

Subsequent racial tensions caused one of the great American crises of the 20th century (along with the Depression and Vietnam). Civil and racial unrest broke out into protests and riots during the 1950s and 60s as black Americans demanded equality with whites. Denial of decent jobs, homes and inner city development shamefully kept the blacks of the south in the designated role of 'an inferior breed'. Inspirational black leaders like Martin Luther King and Malcom X coordinated protests and legal action that eventually led to significant strides in breaking down racial barriers. As of the 2020s, a degree of tension and inequality remains. Racism still simmers with blacks in the US nervous of targeting by police and of vindictive treatment under the American judicial system. The segregation, discrimination and prejudice experienced by black Americans reflects itself in Lokai's grievances against Bele. The Europeans who annexed the Americas showed the worst kind of arrogance towards native peoples and the abducted Africans. So too Bele who shows nothing but contempt for Lokai based on identity politics. The oppressed in circumstances such as these have every cause and justification to struggle to free themselves from poverty and victimhood. Nevertheless, entrenched and opposed viewpoints represented by the **10 of**

Swords reversed must be overcome. If not resolved, racial struggle threatens to mutate into insane mutual hatred as seen with Bele and Lokai.

Both men reveal themselves locked in the mentality of all-out war, the **10 of Swords reversed** at its most extreme. Kirk pleads with them to give up a hate that will kill them both. Spock concurs: their irrational, emotional viewpoints can only lead to death and destruction. Howsoever, the enemies can neither stop hurling bitter accusations at each other nor manically fighting. They refuse all appeals to cooperate and resolve their differences. Both remain completely and defiantly attached to their labels and issues, their Body Mind self-identities. This was not the way of the American Civil Rights movement under Martin Luther King or of other such movements in recent history. Oppressed peoples in India under the British Raj, South Africa under the Boers, and Palestine under the Israeli apartheid regime sought to arrive at the **10 of Swords upright** - peace and mutual tolerance through non-violent resistance. Where destructive anger or hatred erupted on the side of the oppressed there usually lurked 3rd party interference, namely the incitement of conflict by corporate or government manipulators. We see this lately with covertly funded movements like Black Lives Matter and Antifa, minorities with a grievance organized and paid to fight in street protests with minimal police interference. Society thereby remains divided, diverting attention from government oppression applied across the board.

As Bele and Lokai brainlessly and savagely fight each other, so do their planet's populations. The result is the end of Cheron, a planet burnt to a crisp. Who gains? No one. But on Earth when wars break out, hidden, unscrupulous forces triggering and financing both sides do gain and have a feast. The current war between Russia and the Ukraine isn't a war of political polarization. It's a war manipulated into being by instigators who plan themselves to be the beneficiaries. With this conflict, the remaining Deep State oligarchs intent on their New World Order hope to use Divide and Rule to prolong their defunct Matrix. *Ordo ab chao* runs their motto, 'order out of chaos'. This is why the Cabal always wanted war and thrived on the low vibrational energy of oppositional hate, the **10 of Swords reversed**.

AFTER THE TAKEDOWN

By falling for bait or propaganda and taking sides in any conflict, we play into the hands of the globalists. We need to give up once and for all attaching ourselves to conflictual identities and differences. Our spiritual nature transcends all labels, races, religions and differences. We need to come together once and for all in unity and diversity. As we do so, we will finish off the old pyramid of control built on the illusion of duality and separation.

70. DEPOPULATION

Lies, deception and attempted genocide will no longer fly in the new energy of light and truth

Episode 70 '**The Mark of Gideon**' correlates with the **9 of Coins**; both are themed around transition in physical or material conditions as in childbirth, healing, disease or population change.

THE CARD
All the Minor Arcana 9s represent some sort of transition heralding a radical shift in circumstances. Perfection has already been attained at the previous 8th level. Further improvement or development will be impossible without a restructuring taking place. The 9th Major, The Hermit, withdraws from society for a period of stringent self-examination. His period of transition will enable him to re-emerge wiser and more self-aware, ready for embarking on a new cycle of experience. This idea of something 'in the works', something ending in order that something new and long-lasting be subsequently born is suggested by the cosseted central Coin in the **9 of Coins**. This can represent any type of material transition such as an imminent birth, closing down a business, having a clutter clearout, going through puberty, recovering from illness, an extensive refurbishment or moving house.

When the **9 of Coins** is **reversed**, there is a serious crisis on, possibly life-threatening. Poverty or homelessness may be involved, or heavy financial loss. There may be environmental degradation, problems with ageing, a chronic illness or as on Gideon, a population crisis.

'THE MARK OF GIDEON' PREMISE
Kirk is seduced by a beautiful woman on a replica of the Enterprise. She wants a 'virus' he carries to help quell a population crisis on her planet.

CONTEXT
Deception, Slaughter.

DEPOPULATION
'Something is happening to me. I never felt like this before', says the beautiful blonde Odona swooning into Kirk's arms. The pair are standing on the bridge of a deserted Enterprise. All 430 crew are missing after Kirk went through the transporter and found himself still on the ship, alone except for Odona. But this is not actually the Enterprise. Spock, McCoy and the rest of the crew remain aboard the real vessel. They are swapping diplomacy by monitor with Hodin, the governor of Gideon, the planet below. Hodin denies knowledge of Kirk's whereabouts but has actually taken him captive, holding him unawares in a mock-up of the starship on Gideon. As Odona sickens in front of Kirk she smiles with joy. Having caught a disease from him as planned, she will die as a symbolic martyr. Earlier in his life, Kirk had caught Vegan Choriomeningitis, one of the few diseases fatal to the almost immortal people of Gideon. Being the governor's daughter, Odona's death is intended to inspire a spirit of self-sacrifice. The people will queue up to be likewise infected, thus solving the planet's chronic overpopulation problem. The governor turns up and explains all this. But Spock arrives too. He takes Kirk and Odona with him back up to the Enterprise. After being cured in the real sick bay by McCoy, Odona asks to be returned to her planet to carry on the plan of disease transmission and depopulation - in her father's words, 'to adjust the life cycle of an entire generation.'

CARD/EPISODE AND MATRIX TAKEDOWN
Gideon's problem and Hodin's artificial, genocidal solution both bespeak a major population crisis, as per the **reversed 9 of Coins**. His ruthless strategy would receive a big thumbs up from vaccine promoter Bill Gates. Gates' famous quote on the subject goes: 'The world today has 6.8 billion people. That's headed up to about 9 billion. Now, if we do a really great job on new vaccines, health care, reproductive health services, we could lower that by perhaps 10 to 15%.' Gates is admitting that instead of saving lives

with his vaccines he would either be sterilizing people or terminating them. Earth is nowhere near as heavily over-populated as Gideon. On Gideon we see hordes of citizens milling around bumping into each other for lack of space. They crowd outside the window of the mock starship observing Kirk and Odona interacting. Cities on Earth may be over-crowded but none so much that standing room only remains. And of course large swathes of our planet remain barely populated or deserted. Nevertheless the Georgia Guidestones in the US, before their destruction in 2022, spoke of bringing down the world population to '500 million in perpetual balance with nature.' A drastically reduced population would of course be more easily managed, governed and controlled by those who want to rule the world using the dark AI Matrix - except that that Matrix is now gone.

A great many Cabal members too are gone, removed from this world for attempted coups on humanity similar to Hodin's on his people. However, the situation on Earth is effectively the reverse of Gideon's. On Gideon, depopulation is the end in itself, whereas on Earth depopulation was intended as a means to an end. On Gideon, Hodin seeks to use infected blood to create a serum to enable people to die naturally through disease. He would still be killing them. But Odona's sacrificial death would inspire willing volunteers to come forth and follow her example in likewise sacrificing themselves. Hodin's cull is at least honest, and motivated by a desire to curb a genuine problem. He wants his people to reduce their number by their own choice and action. In the case of the crimes against humanity perpetrated via laboratory manufactured AIDS, Ebola or Covid, the Cabal's aim in reducing the population had the ulterior motive of making it more easily controllable as Matrix slaves. The Cabal planned to arrange the spread of fatal diseases concocted in secret biolabs. Populations would then be deceived or coerced into taking injections called 'vaccinations' purportedly to cure the disease but intended to kill even more people, quickly or slowly.

Added to this, the Covid injections touted by Bill Gates and Antoni Fauci were planned to hijack humanity's consciousness. The sociopaths wanted a digitally mind-controlled population and a transition to a partially cyborg society, again as per the **reversed 9 of Coins**. Covid injections laced with nanotechnology followed decades of preparation through other measures. The skies have been daily sprayed with nanotechnology in chemtrails, food has been adulterated, flu shots mass marketed and babies given dozens of spurious, unnecessary vaccines. Populations loaded with this toxic cocktail were intended to facilitate the merger with AI. The Cabal wanted people acting as terminals in an Internet of Bodies responsive to frequencies transmitted by 5G towers and satellites. With people becoming genetically and cybernetically modified they would be rendered half-human, half-machine. This movement towards 'the singularity', formerly ridiculed for decades as a 'conspiracy theory' now occupies pages on the UK government's own website lauding a phenomenon referred to as 'Human Augmentation'. The end result of society following such a path is vividly portrayed in AI episodes such as No. 20 The Return of The Archons and No. 33 The Apple.

In an individual manifestation of the **9 of Coins reversed**, Odona sickens, apparently from contact with a carrier of a disease to which she and her people are partial. But Kirk is asymptomatic and therefore unable to transmit the disease through normal contact. This explains why none of his colleagues or others encountered are at risk. So how does Odona become infected? The mystery is unsolved but Hodin's plan is clear. Kirk is to stay behind to assist in infecting the citizens inspired by Odona's martyrdom. All very ghoulish and irrational considering other options available such as requesting Federation help for interplanetary migration. Hodin's depopulation plan at least appears to be above board. Participants on Gideon would be aware of it and consciously sacrificing themselves. No government on Earth asked its people to sacrifice themselves. Governments covertly engineered the outbreak of viruses using bioweapons. But their plan went awry. In the case of Covid, its survival rate was 99.7%. Massive worldwide fear was generated but the truth has dawned that nothing made sense - not the lockdowns and other social measures used to supposedly contain it, not the suppression of safe cures such as Ivermectin, and not the large numbers of deaths from blood clots and heart attacks caused by the so-called 'vaccine'. When the total number of deaths in Covid's first year remained normal the 'pandemic' was diagnosed by independent observers as a giant hoax. This was a **9 of Coins reversed** fake population crisis on all levels.

AFTER THE TAKEDOWN
The Cabal's deceitful attempts to cull the population always depended on the herd mentality of a people hypnotizable en masse by false claims, relentless propaganda and fear-mongering. The mainstream media (MSM) has been the Cabal's lie machine. But lies of course do not become true because they come from newsreaders and government or are believed by a majority. The incoming Key Integrated Media System will overhaul the MSM. Corrupt leaders attempting a number on humanity will be swiftly exposed. People may still choose to take injurious injections touted as vaccines believing they may protect them against something. But the numbers of those deceived will diminish as the truth inevitably comes out.

71. SECURITY

Our security depends on not putting our trust in mendacious government and inorganic AI

Episode 71 'That Which Survives' correlates with the **4 of Coins**; both are themed around structural integrity, security and methods of defence especially relating to survival of the body or home.

THE CARD
With the **4 of Coins** we have to be aware of the illusion of solid thingness, of physical reality dependent on how the brain decodes it. Four Coins surround a tulip head contained in a blue and red square. Fourness strongly suggests stable and solid grounding with the square associated with balance, firmness and good order. Burgeoning plant life festoons the Coins, suggesting ideal conditions for health, growth, protection and survival. With Coins standing for body and home this could mean a strong human energy field, a protective immune system, a well-defended installation, a secure residence, a balanced ecological environment. Yet the flat tulip head bears no stem or depth, it is merely the idea of a healthy organism. This is consistent with quantum physics demonstrating physical reality to be but a simulation of the physical, an illusory hologram at least partially created in our minds. Ultimately a tulip or anything that appears to be solid is an electromagnetic field of information and beyond

this, in its foundation state, waveform energy. The consciousness of the observer decodes this information into the perception of a tulip. As philosopher Bishop Berkley maintained, what we perceive, no matter how solid it appears to be, are not things in themselves but our perceptions.

Reversed, the **4 of Coins** symbolizes problems with stability, balance, protection or survival. There could be holes or fissures in a person's energy field. Property foundations may be weak or internal security may have been breached with an intruder or invader present. Hoarding or panic buying and stockpiling could be taking place. Or there may be some kind of imprisonment or a disabling health condition.

'THAT WHICH SURVIVES' PREMISE
A strange, vindictive planetary defence system tries to repel the Enterprise and a landing party. The humans must struggle to protect themselves.

CONTEXT
AI Takedown, Illusion.

SECURITY
A party beam down to a stark, uninhabited planet, arid, rocky, bathed in purple twilight. Investigating, they become stranded when some kind of power surge hurls the Enterprise far away and out of contact leaving the four men without communication, food or water. Their survival is further threatened when a mysterious woman appears and seeks to kill each of them one by one. D'Amato dies, Sulu is wounded. The beautiful woman identifies each victim by name, stating 'I am for you' before reaching out with a touch that causes instant cellular destruction. The same woman is responsible for two on-ship deaths but a security alert finds no intruder aboard. With the engines sabotaged, Spock and Scotty struggle to return the ship 990 light years back to its original orbit. On the planet, Kirk is the woman's next target. She accuses him in stilted speech of being an invader. Her job she says is to defend the planet even though painfully admitting killing is wrong. Sulu and McCoy protect Kirk causing the hologram that is the woman to disappear. The party find its source to be a computer located in a nearby cave but are attacked by more projections of the same woman called Losira. Spock and co appear just in time to rescue the three from destruction. A video of Losira now informs them that the real Losira was the last survivor of her disease-ravaged planet, Kalanda. While maintaining its security she was awaiting an antidote from off-planet Kalandans not knowing they had died out. After her death the computer continued selectively defending against invaders. But by using the image and personality of Losira it also registered

her remorse at killing, reducing its protective and murderous capability.

CARD/EPISODE AND MATRIX TAKEDOWN

Security, the **4 of Coins**, or national security, has always been ever so responsibly looked after by our leaders the Matrix controllers. For their protection, not the people's. How often have we suffered infringement or destruction of our freedoms because of their great concern for our well being? With one hand they generate fear and concern through their own contrived terrorism (false flag attacks) or biolab-created contagions. With the other hand they offer reassuring remedies in the form of increased surveillance, supposedly safe 'vaccines' or restrictions such as mask-wearing or lockdowns. 'I Wear This Mask To Protect You' announced the masked face on street posters disingenuously and deceitfully during the Covid psyop. Tracing the deception to its origins we arrive at government and AI combined as on Kalanda. At the top of the Earth Matrix are, or were, Archon-controlled elites, both human and non-human, using black magic and AI technology aimed at turning the population into a hive-minded race under full spectrum Matrix domination. Clown show government leaders, ego-driven corporate and banking chiefs, disingenuous educational authorities and fantasy land MSM all played a part in programming and manipulating the people toward this end. They actually made no secret of their power grab - touted as 'The Great Reset' - being designed to instal an AI-run cyber grid society. The danger thus proceeds from the very ones claiming to protect us. Our free range imprisonment was wanted for their security.

Likewise, the one pretending to befriend the party on Kalanda poses the greatest threat. Approaching each intended victim, the lovely Losira's 'I am for you' sounds spooky but almost reassuring. This and her seductive beauty lull the crew members into dropping their guard. She further claims that she and the person touched 'will live as one'. A morbid fate befalls the crew members who trust this message, the **4 of Coins reversed**, just as it did those of us on Earth believing in our governments' caring intent. With our leaders' AI Matrix gone and so many of their lies exposed, it is now their survival that hangs in the balance, not ours. The survival of the landing party on Kalanda is an issue because the AI there remains a danger despite the planet's near destruction. The population along with most of the vegetation has been finished off by a virus-like parasite. The message relayed by the computer tells of the destruction of the Kalandans due to their botched work creating a rogue bioagent. Shades of the man-made AIDS virus or the Covid bioagent created in the Wuhan lab in China. The AI caretaker on Kalanda lives on, a fallible computer operating on automatic. With its devastated ecology, the planet is insupportive of humanoid life. For the marooned landing party it is a lonely, bleak environment. **Reversed 4 of Coins** survival is at stake, they must forage for food and water.

Added to this, the **reversed 4 of Coins** very much symbolizes Kalanda's hostile security system. Non-Kalandans are identified as invaders regardless of their nature or motives. To prevent them from accessing the planet the AI guardian catapults the starship far away. If an intruder does breach this defence the computer confronts them on the planet surface, treating them as antibodies to be destroyed. The projected image of the beautiful Losira serves to either welcome Kalandans or eliminate non-Kalandans. Her holographic form reminds us of the holographic illusion ultimately constituting all physical reality. The projected Losira reaches out to touch an intruder, just as an antibody in an immune system responds to a specific antigen (disease agent). To keep a body well protected an antibody binds to a particular germ and destroys it. Likewise Losira acts against each individual intruder by name and specifically destroys that person. Each intruder is treated as a unique kind of antigen requiring a separate and distinct projection of Losira acting as the specific antibody. Several times Losira is thwarted from killing a crew member by one or more of his colleagues interposing himself between him and her. As bodyguards they are another representation of the **4 of Coins**. With digital AI on the ascendant, our fate on Earth as free and biologically sound beings was similarly precarious. The AI Matrix infesting us from the lower astral plane had to be abolished and it has been, at the behest of forces of light. On Kalanda, the party are saved by the original Losira's compassionate instincts causing a computer glitch that enables them to evade her projection and terminate the AI. The beauty of Losira survived, notes Kirk on leaving. Her beauty survived in her human qualities of compassion and harmlessness, divine instincts that only ensouled beings or organic AI possess. It was this that made the soulless AI system fallible.

CARD/EPISODE AND MATRIX TAKEDOWN

Prior to the takedown, organic life on Earth was heading towards contrived extinction. As on Kalanda, only inorganic AI and sparse life would remain, allowing Negative Alien Elites to use the planet to access nearby inter-galactic stargates and wormholes enabling conquest of the entire multiverse. Far from protecting inorganic life à la **4 of Coins**, our insane leaders were rushing to instal AI's complete takeover. This can no longer happen, but the need remains to drop the belief in the moral legitimacy of authority and government. We need to overhaul our concept of government and develop our cosmic awareness to eschew any form of AI capable of controlling us.

72. RECEPTIVE MIND

Realizing our infinite mental potential will open up new possibilities for communication with the multiverse

Episode 72 '**The Lights of Zetar**' correlates with the **8 of Swords**; both are themed around a meditative or receptive mind conducive to higher knowing, intuition and channelling.

THE CARD
Degree 8 in the Major Arcana manifests as the perfect balance aimed at by Justice and the receptivenes of The Moon. Receptive and perfect balance therefore characterizes the Minor Arcana at this Degree. The Coins and Cups cards are accordingly full of healthy, abundant vegetation. By contrast, the Wands and Swords cards have minimal flowers and no plants or foliage. This is because at their zenith, Wands represent action that is pure and streamlined and Swords represents mind that is pure and transparent. At the centre of the **8 of Swords** card is an eight-petalled flower head representing receptiveness and perfection in emptiness of mind - the Buddhist ideal of *shunyatta*. The mind is quiescent, empty of distracting chatter and obsession. This is the state of no-mind or meditation, or intuition or psychic sensitivity involving higher consciousness and receptiveness to channeling.

Reversed, the **8 of Swords** can indicate too much complacency in attitude or an apathetic mind when knowledge or discernment are needed. Another danger is poor concentration or a non-functioning memory. Moreover, if mental defences are weak, thoughtforms and negative entities can invade. Trance states entered into may be detrimental; channeling or mediumship that is done may attract beings of selfish or dubious intent.

'THE LIGHTS OF ZETAR' PREMISE
A female crew member is targeted by disembodied aliens. With her clear, receptive mind they intend to use her as their future physical vehicle.

CONTEXT
Sensitivity, Multi-Dimensionality, The Adversary.

RECEPTIVE MIND
The Enterprise is en route to the Federation's library base on the planetoid Memory Alpha when the starship is attacked by a cloud of coloured lights. The swirling lights resemble a brain in space. Crew members each find a different part of their brains most affected. In the case of Lt. Mira Romaine, she goes into trance and starts garbling strange noises. The storm moves on to the library, ravaging it and killing the staff. While Romaine recovers in sick bay she has a vision of this. Subsequently visiting the library, an investigating party finds the corpses of her vision. Romaine accompanying the party has another accurate vision - of the storm returning. The party get safely back to the Enterprise where as she foresaw, the lights swarm back in on them. The ship's sensors are disturbed and again so is Romaine. Kirk tries firing phasers into the colourful space cloud but this seems to cause Romaine injury. The reason seems to be her brain waves now entrained to those of the coloured light beings. Kirk encourages her to allow them to function through her receptive mind. His plan is to then exorcize them through placing Romaine in a pressure chamber. Before doing so and as planned, the lights come again. This time they completely take Romaine over and with her exceptional channelling ability they start speaking with her vocal chords. They identify themselves as the mental energies of the last 100 survivors of Zetar, a destroyed planet. They desire to continue living through a physical body and find Romaine ideal for this purpose. But both she and Kirk refuse permission. Kirk goes ahead with his plan and the pressurizing process repels the entities. Scotty, having fallen deeply in love with Romaine, supporting her all along, is elated.

CARD/EPISODE AND MATRIX TAKEDOWN
For all their experience of space travel, of alien worlds and phenomena, the

crew of the Enterprise seem to find it puzzlingly difficult to accept the unlimited potential of our multi-dimensional consciousness. Likewise, Matrix-trained scientists remain slow or unwilling to accept the existence of astral planes, telepathy, dream visitations or higher faculties. And yet such abilities are our natural birthright, often requiring only a calm receptive mind, the **8 of Swords**, to access. Children may remember past lives or be able to commune with fairies or elves in the garden. But as they pass through school, most become attached to the five senses and to scientific dogma that dismisses these and other aspects of higher realms. Parents, educators and peers will usually discourage credence in experiences that seem to them weird, unscientific or delusional. Lt Mira Romaine, psychically talented though she is, even worries that her encounter with the unseen Zetarians will disqualify her for her new librarian post on Memory Alpha.

Through cultivating the clear, empty mind of the **8 of Swords** we can go into psychic states of great knowing and potential. Different people discover different strengths. Some excel in teleportation, some in out-of-the-body travel, others in telepathy, clairvoyance or mediumship. Such sensitivities continue to be ignored, derided or ridiculed by mainstream sources such as school textbooks, television or Wikipedia. The Matrix control system has nothing to gain from educating children in the potential of their unlimited consciousness. The System would rather have an obedient and compliant population trained not to think outside the box and not connecting to higher sources of truth and knowing. Curiously, crew of the limitlessly exploring Enterprise express plain disbelief in visions of the future. They are, says Scotty, 'pure bunk'. He puts Romaine's psychic encounter down to space sickness. 'A space trip', he says, 'can play strange tricks on your mind.' Spock, Kirk and McCoy show incomprehension at the sight of shapeshifting. And until confirmed by radar, they dismiss Romaine's premonition of the storm returning. It takes a series of visceral encounters with the alien lights to force the crew into an arduous rethink of the powers of the mind and Romaine's predicament. They experience the phenomena of physical shapeshifting and voiceshifting in the fate of a dying scientist at the library. She utters strange guttural sounds while her face twists and contorts into something reminiscent of demonic possession. The same twisted functioning will later befall Romaine after her subjugation by the Zetarians. The turning point in understanding comes when the Enterprise's phaser fire threatens to kill her. Bewildered but erring on caution, Kirk stops and pauses before wisely cancelling another attack. It takes an official investigation conducted by the senior crew with computer back-up and examination of brainwave patterns to convince them of the psychic reality of Romaine's situation: possession by - or attachment of - the spirits of alien entities.

The vulnerability of a pure and clear mind to invasion by other-dimensional beings, particularly those with negative intent, is the **8 of Swords reversed**. Trance mediums are accustomed to emptying their minds in order to put their faculties at the service of a communicating spirit. But this should only ever be done with the medium's permission and for a known benign purpose. Famous spirit channels in the past have included the Oracle at Delphi, Joan of Arc, Nostradamus, Edgar Cayce and in our own time the spiritual teacher Ramtha channeled by J.Z. Knight. But with or without permission being given, a communicating entity may be covertly taking advantage of 'an unusually pliant and flexible mind'. These are McCoy's words for Romaine. Spock agrees, concluding that it is her pliancy of mind that has enabled the Zetarians to make their thoughts hers. She later goes into full and involuntary trance channeling mode during the final attack. But Kirk and co know what they're dealing with by now and act successfully to free Romaine from her attached entities.

AFTER THE TAKEDOWN

The thoughts of those around us, including deceased relatives or discarnate beings such as the Zetarians have the same basis in waveform information as 'physical' reality, yet can travel anywhere in the universe. There are no boundaries to mental communication despite what we are taught at school. We all have the potential for higher sense perception represented by the **8 of Swords**. Using this natural gift we can access untold beings and Über-Matrix realities and perpetually evolve our intelligence. Just as the Enterprise crew were each variously affected by the Zetarians, each of us may tap into different types of knowing through methods such as channeling, remote viewing and mediumship. The danger lies in attracting and communicating with, nefarious or impostor entities. As Romaine became a voice for the dubious Zetarians, so in 2022 there was the controversy over alien contactee Elena Danaan communicating with Enki. Danaan was announcing the supposed return of this highly suspect Anunnaki being who was claiming to help humanity - a dangerous situation according to knowledgeable authors with receptive minds *and* the benefit of prior research, such as Ashayana Deane, Lisa Renee and Ileana Kapulnik. Post-Matrix, the Elemental AI on the 5th level of the astral will no longer disrupt our natural state of being. And societal controls on education and mass media will be lifted, encouraging people to more openly communicate with higher beings and realities. But as with Romaine and Danaan, caution will be necessary.

73. MATERIAL ATTACHMENT

We grow not through holding on to what we create or receive but through flow and release

Episode 73 '**Requiem for Methuselah**' correlates with the **King of Coins**; both are themed around a mature man creating, releasing or holding on to material wealth or objects of desire.

THE CARD
Like all the Kings, this is a mature man of accomplishment, confidence and vision. The Kings all clasp the symbol of their suit lightly, almost casually, while looking into the distance to our right. Lightly touching a Coin in his lap, the **King of Coins** has attained effortless mastery of the business of wealth accumulation, physical manifestation and material creativity. Although the material master he's free from material obsession, from clinging. Unattached to what he possesses, he looks instead to the direction representing future expansion through improved stewardship or further growing and sharing. Instead of a throne, this King rests on a makeshift-looking chair that requires his own legs to ensure stability. Practicality, flow and adaptability are suggested rather than luxury and stagnation. Alone among the Kings he sits outside in nature. He's respectful and understanding of biological processes, organic growth, our place in the natural world and his contribution to it. He could be a bio-dynamic gardener, a

quantum physicist, a concert musician, a painter, a cobbler, a dealer in fine fabrics and textiles, a sole trader, a builder, a financier or a CEO.

Reversed, the **King of Coins** grasps at material advancement or clings to and hoards existing profits or possessions. He scorns the natural flow of energies, living on dubious wealth creation, ill-gotten gains or corrupt business practices in fulfillment of personal desires.

'REQUIEM FOR METHUSELAH' PREMISE
An immortal wizard of unparalleled accomplishment and acquisition seeks the culmination of his material projects, a female android lover created by himself.

CONTEXT
Power, Relationship, Taking Stock, Transhumanism

MATERIAL ATTACHMENT
Flint is a recluse blessed with his own planet - one that harbours a rare mineral that can cure a fatal fever threatening the crew of the Enterprise. Flint at first miserly refuses to allow Kirk, Spock and McCoy to gather supplies of the much needed Ryetalyn. But when told about the epidemic his manner changes as memories return to him of the bubonic plague of 14th century Europe. He seems to have actually been there. Not only that but in his byzantine palace are to be found priceless originals of a Shakespeare folio and the Gutenberg bible. On the walls are paintings by Leonardo da Vinci and on his piano a waltz by Brahms. Even more incredibly, these treasures of art and music are newly created. While Flint's robot servant gathers and processes the Ryetalyn, the shore party make the acquaintance of Flint's ward and companion, the introverted, beautiful blonde, Rayna. Kirk almost immediately falls in love with her but after their sharing a dance together, Flint takes her away. The two jealous men both want the same woman. Kirk's feelings don't change even when Rayna turns out to be Flint's android creation. Flint confesses that he is an immortal, 6000 years old, and that he is Leonardo and Brahms as well as many other great figures known to history. In his material attachment and having designed Rayna with his deep desire for a lover he intends to keep her for himself. Kirk is furious since it was he and his loving kisses that completed Flint's creation by bringing Rayna's emotions to life. The two men come to blows watched by the distraught woman. Her barely formed emotional capacity cannot handle the strain and overwhelmed, she collapses and dies. Both men succumb to tears with Kirk needing a memory wipe from Spock to help him in his distress.

CARD/EPISODE AND MATRIX TAKEDOWN

Religion, science and education during the Matrix era propagated many distortions of truth and spiritual reality. Staying connected to the soul took a special kind of effort. One way that will always help is maintaining balance, between giving and taking. By helping others on their path we help ourselves. By only taking, our Body Mind loses connection to the soul and loses its balance in relation to the rest of existence. Thus excessive clinging to possessions restricts and distorts our growth. Material attachment, that of the **King of Coins reversed**, produces a greedy and selfish ego, forcing it to repeatedly experience situations in which it will lose what is most meaningful to it, as Flint eventually loses Rayna. The isolated, melancholy Flint fits the stereotype of the man of prodigious accomplishment who has everything yet remains both attached to his possessions and unfulfilled by them. For Flint these include his own planet selfishly cloaked to hide the existence of biological life, his beautiful young ward Rayna and his servant robot who sees to all their material needs. As with Earth's insatiably selfish ruling Cabal now being phased out, he has attained his goal of massive material wealth. Yet like them, he remains in want of more.

Flint's personality and situation bear much in common with other **Kings of Coins** in myth and fable. We may recall the wizard Prospero from Shakespeare's The Tempest and the reference to him in the proprietorial Morbius from the movie Forbidden Planet. There is the voracious press baron Charles Foster Kane from the movie Citizen Kane, Dickens' miserly Scrooge and Baron Frankenstein. All these formidable men exemplify an eccentric and at least partially **reversed King of Coins**, each a wealthy and capable but lonely self-made man troubled with controlling desires or demons. Never mind that Flint has gained physical immortality, material prosperity and stupendous creative mastery. Flint was after all Merlin, Solomon, Alexander, Leonardo and Brahms among other icons of history during his 6,000 year long life. The fact remains that he still yearns to perfect the android he has created and turn her into his loving wife. Not content with Rayna's current devoted state, Flint wants her to express her love sexually and passionately. He has so far been unable to bestow her with these qualities. She remains slightly undercooked, torpid, frigid. We see this when Flint tries to kiss her. She holds her head stiffly, keeps her lips closed, seems uncomprehending of his desire. Yet she speaks of the 'exciting opportunity' of being able to meet the three male guests. Flint now sees a heaven-sent way to ignite Rayna's dormant emotionality. Manipulating the situation, he successfully contrives to have her share intimate moments with Kirk. Flint, nervously watching on CCTV, sees her come alive with Kirk in a rhapsody of embracing and kissing. Flint now wants her back. And having outlived their usefulness, the three visitors must be done away with or they may reveal the existence of his planet. But Flint falls prey to his own jealousy, attachment and possessiveness. He brawls with Kirk and both lovestruck men lose the object of their desire when the upset Rayna drops dead.

Living 6,000 years in one Body Mind (dimensions 1 to 3 in the 15-dimensional model of personal identity) seems to have loosened not strengthened Flint's connection with his soul (dimensions 4 to 6). As explained in Voyagers 1 by Ashayana Deane, it is the soul that guides the Body Mind in terms of biological manifestation, life purpose and experiential drama. With his extraordinary long tenure in a single Body Mind, Flint has become intoxicated by the power accruing to a material master, the **King of Coins**. Having experienced multiple personas over eons of time, he has become distanced from his soul and over-attached to physical states and the apparent form of his material creations. The Matrix illusion of an exclusive material existence now has him as it has his female parallel, Sylvia the Queen of Coins in Episode 35. Memories of his various alter-egos such as Solomon, Leonardo and Brahms conceal from him his soul's blueprint for his current life. Instead of maintaining a bridge between his lower self and his soul and yet higher selves, his ego has closed itself in on his dazzling achievements and possessions. He lives in and for selfish endeavours, isolating himself on his own planet, attempting to create and possess the perfect lover - even briefly, arrogantly miniaturizing the Enterprise. Living only for himself, Flint distorts his energies in relation to universal energy. Inevitably and ironically, he comes to grief losing the very thing that was dearest to him.

AFTER THE TAKEDOWN

Nothing created from waveform reality can be truly possessed and separated from the rest of existence. No person can possess another person and override their free will without negative energies eventually wreaking internal havoc. A person by only taking, or by clinging, projects a detrimental ego, or power-consciousness. The ego develops an emotional wall around it - symbolized by Flint's cloaked planet - and loses connection to its higher levels of identity. And yet all is one and one is all. We can realize this by going within and expanding our consciousness to include soul awareness. By tuning deeper into ourselves, the defunct Matrix and material obsessions will no longer have us. Attachment to what we manifest physically will give way to the process itself, to using our mind as a reality creation machine. For material mastery in line with the **King of Coins**, this means staying in touch with our soul and with the field of infinite potential.

74. NAÏVE IDEALISM

We should beware extreme or naïve idealism in the return to a balanced and natural way of life

Episode 74 'The Way To Eden' correlates with **The Star**; both are themed around finding our place in the world where we are guided by inspiration and idealism to live in harmony with land and nature.

THE CARD
The Star appears to show a wide discrepancy between the starry heavens above, occupying more than half the card, and the earthy, lumpen reality below. The soft flesh of a naked woman kneeling by a river seems far from ethereal and pristine. Her belly is rounded, a knee is misshapen, while water suggestive of menstrual fluid flows from a jug near her sexual region. She seems at one however with the rugged hills and river as she lovingly exchanges waters between them and the two red jugs. Living systems, natural processes, biological reality and a utopian Edenic existence are suggested. She plainly eschews any sort of affectation or technology, instead nakedly caring for and nourishing her place in the world with simplicity and sincerity. In so doing she radiates a pure and humble contentment as beautiful as the sky above. The multi-coloured, twinkling stars, the singing bird and the fertile trees and river suggest inspiration that is both heavenly and grounded. Idealism coexists in harmony with earthiness; art,

music and cosmic awareess coexist with gardening and farming. The card implies that a service-oriented and receptive attitude enables one to shine one's inner cosmic light. As a result one lives in a state of grace alongside nature in harmony and peace.

Reversed, the starry sky appears where the stabilizing ground should be. Attitudes are over-idealistic and ungrounded, faith and optimism are misplaced or taken to extreme levels. With the earthy land hanging overhead, nature threatens us or is itself threatened. Idealism that is either unreal or demolished contaminates inspiration or optimism.

'THE WAY TO EDEN' PREMISE
Six colourful 'space hippies' musically entertain the crew. They ask, then compel by hijack, to be taken to their idealized natural paradise, planet Eden.

CONTEXT
Perverted Paradise, Coercion.

NAÏVE IDEALISM
A group of hippy-like humanoids come aboard the Enterprise and immediately stage a sit-down protest. They refuse to recognize Federation rules and regulations including Kirk's charges of traffic violations aboard their stolen vessel, the Aurora. They go about bare-foot wearing colourful decorative garb, singing songs and espousing freedom from authority. Kirk finds them too rebellious to deal with but Spock, a half-Vulcan, establishes a rapport based on their common outsider status. The group's leader Dr Severin, demands the group be taken to the planet Eden, there to actualize their 'back to nature' ideals in an idyllic setting away from planned communities, programming and technology. One of the group's beautiful females, Irina, was a lover of Chekov at Starship Academy. The two step aside for an uneasy heart-to-heart. Irina urges the uptight and recalcitrant Chekov to be true to himself and to relax his disapproval of the free-living outsiders. Severin has a sterner confrontation with McCoy who insists on innoculating him against a virus he carries. Severin who seems asymptomatic, refuses, citing the fact that modern civilization which he rejects would have given him the virus in the first place. Severin in his extreme idealism decides on a ruthless hijack of the Enterprise to redirect it to Eden. His fellow hippies naïvely follow his lead. The planet turns out to be a false paradise. Though gorgeously beautiful and fertile, its vegetation proves dangerous to walk on and deadly to consume. Two of the group die from its effects. The rest are retrieved by Enterprise crew for ferrying to a local Starbase.

CARD/EPISODE AND MATRIX TAKDOWN

Going back to nature or 'back to the garden' was a blissful ideal of Western fringe culture of the 1960s. Hippies were encouraged by Timothy Leary to 'turn on, tune in and drop out'. They turned on to Eastern religion and drugs and embraced **The Star** card in potent ways: environmentalism, ecology, yoga, shamanism, peace in Vietnam, 'flower power' and following nature's way in line with E.F.Schumarcher's dictum 'small is beautiful'. As symbolized in the 7th degree of the Tarot decads, these gentle values of No 17 **The Star** complement those of No. 7 The Chariot: technology, materialism, militarism, urban development, capitalism and corporate power. Indeed, the hippies on the starship as on Earth actively rebel against those mechanistic values. Chariot action is masculine, outgoing, goal-oriented and technology-driven. **Star** action is feminine, settled, nurturing and natural. In recent history, the ethos of The Chariot, as opposed to **The Star**, has markedly gained the upper hand. The Industrial Revolution of the 1700s accentuated them, followed by computerization 200 years later. With the Matrix gathering steam, a cyber grid empire threatened, constructed by an arrogant Deep State, powered by AI systems and EMFs. The WEF's Agenda 2030 would have finished off the balance between nature and technology. Technocracy and totalitarian world government were the goals aided by 5G, DNA-altering mandatory vaccinations, abolition of private property, ubiquitous clones and drones and state management of ecosystems. The ethos of **The Star** - rewilding, ethnic culture, cottage industries, simple rural living - would have been thrown under the bus (Chariot) were it not for the takedown.

With the Aurora group coming on board the Enterprise, representatives of **Star** and Chariot cultures clash head on. Or do they? The free-living, back-to-nature group of social rebels and the mission-oriented, technologically enabled crew of the Enterprise certainly ruffle each other's feathers. But in some respects the two groups representing opposed lifestyles and values respond to each other in mutually beneficial ways. The hippy group learn about the dangers and delusions of naïve and wayward idealism; the starship crew learn about the limitations of 'Herbert' style conformity and denial of inner truth. Both groups have to get over resistance to each other's contrasting mindsets and learn to recognize and respect the oneness of all life. With a joyful, spontaneous ability to live in the moment, the alien group alternately confound and delight the crew. Kirk finds himself initially standing for Federation authority in opposition to the hippy group who explicitly reject such authority. But the talented Adam's infectious singing and guitar-playing brings his group an appreciative audience. Spock adopts the middle ground as symbolized by his joining with Adam in a musical jam session. Spock is the only senior crew member to see reason in the hippies' rejection of technology. He sympathizes with their search for the idyllic simple life as represented pictorially in **The Star** card. Aided by Chekov he cooperates with the rebels by actively helping them with a literal aspect of **The Star**, perusing star maps to physically locate their dreamed of Eden. At this point some kind of mutual acceptance and agreement seems to have been reached.

The sticking point remains that of Severin allegedly carrying a dangerous virus. Whatever his medical condition, Severin claims it was caused by technology. He believes that primitive (shamanic) medicine will cure him. McCoy and Spock disagree. Who is right? At any rate, Spock, believing him to be infectious, sees Severin as insane for attempting to settle a new planet. With this impasse reached, the group take the matter into their own hands. Whether their idealistic search for a planetary Eden can be called healthy or naïve, it truly becomes insane with their next move. At Severin's lead they sabotage the ventilation system and recklessly, desperately, heartlessly, take over the ship. They act in complete defiance of the peaceful, accepting principles of **The Star**, their avowed lifestyle. More like in fact, the reversal of The Chariot, the complementary card. The poisoned paradise they find on their idealistically cherished planet only confirms the message that idealism when it becomes ruthless leads to disaster.

AFTER THE TAKEDOWN

Matrix operatives promoting Agenda 2030 bandy buzzwords about like 'sustainable development', the 'Green Deal', 'environmentalism' and 'saving the planet'. This the language of the nurturing **Star** card deceitfully applied to policies of the Chariot reversed that destroy health and the environment. All the environment needs is the cessation of toxic, barbaric polices pursued by Elite psychopaths. This will happen as the Global Peace and Restoration Project initiated by Kim Goguen takes effect. The Project will restore our balance with nature as advocated by the 60s generation and Star Trek's 'space hippies'. Ecosystems will be rebuilt free from Matrix manipulation and control. This must of course be done in the spirit of humility with respect for people's values and new technologies - those that do no harm. Recreating our 'Eden' on Earth will depend on rejecting weaponized tech without succumbing to naïve idealism or fanaticism. Not everyone will acknowledge the shackles of the Matrix or want to escape them. This means adopting a Third Way that harmonizes the values of **The Star** and The Chariot - idealism and realism, nature and technology.

75. THE SAVIOUR

Learning to live truly from the heart will free us from self-perpetuated slavery

Episode 75 '**The Cloud Minders**' correlates with the **Knight of Cups**; both are themed around a person on a humanitarian mission to help, save or support those in trouble.

THE CARD
Both the Kings and Knights are masters of their suits. But whereas the Kings are builders and maintainers of the established order, the Knights are catalysts, trouble-shooters and agents of change. They instigate change by coming from outside and acting rapidly or dramatically. With Cups symbolizing kind or compassionate action with humanitarian or romantic intent, how does a crusading **Knight of Cups** operate? Looking to the card we find this Knight riding to the left, showing he comes to a status quo from outside, from another reality. The Cup is open, representing flowing and empathic feeling. We can infer a charming and likeable person not given to shows of strength or grandiosity but to sincere, heartfelt action. The Cup seems to float mirage-like in front of him, suggesting an idealistic mission motivated by kindness or inspiration. The horse is small, of humble size for the rider, and like the Cup seems to float in the air as if magically or spiritually empowered. Whatever the mission it will embody compassion and the desire

to help through channelling higher powers of healing or benevolence. This is a kind-hearted person, male or female, entering the scene as a saviour or rescuer, a good samaritan who goes out of his way to assist the downtrodden or fallen. He provides practical help with sensitivity and understanding. He or she is something of an adventurer but chivalrous, tactful and peace-loving. Positive transformation will attend his interventions.

A **reversed Knight of Cups** provides help ineffectively or unnecessarily. If romantically inclined he or she doesn't know when he's not wanted; or he has impure motives. If on a humanitarian mission he needs to reassess his goals or methods and ensure he is taking sufficient care of himself.

'THE CLOUD-MINDERS' PREMISE
On a mercy mission for a life-saving mineral, Kirk opens the way for opposing leaders on the divided planet Ardana to negotiate greater social equality.

CONTEXT
Third Force, Power, Awakening.

THE SAVIOUR
Kirk visits planet Ardana on an urgent mission of humanitarian action to obtain supplies of Zenite, a mineral needed to halt a botanical plague on another planet. He and Spock soon find themselves drawn into a situation of racial segregation and conflict. Rebellious 'Disruptors', freedom fighters representing Troglytes, the oppressed miners of Zenite, interfere with their mission. Their rebel leader, a feisty woman called Vanna complains bitterly to Kirk and Spock who learn that a two-tier social system prevails on Ardana. The Troglytes labour in the mines and fields suffering living conditions of poverty and hardship. High above the planet surface, the sky-dwelling people of Stratos live leisurely in luxury. Their High Advisor Plasus lords it over both peoples with stern and implacable authority. He takes Vanna captive and in efforts to confirm her theft of a missing consignment of Zenite tortures her in front of Kirk and Spock. Even Plasus' waif-like, sensitive, beautiful daughter Droxine seems to condone this treatment. But Kirk the saviour, assisted by Spock, intervenes pleading moral entitlement of the Troglytes to 'kindness, justice, equality.' After rescuing Vanna, Kirk discovers that the miners are kept mentally subdued and belligerent due to a gas given off by zenite in its raw state. He promises Vanna to provide the miners with a supply of filter masks in exchange for the mineral. The masks will help them restore their level of evolution to that of the sky-dwellers. Plasus vehemently rejects the idea of an awakened majority but Kirk transports the

dictator down to the mines so he can personally experience the effect of the gas. Kirk goes on to secure Vanna's approval of the masks and her delivery of the zenite. The way is open now for Vanna to negotiate new civil rights with the bitterly reluctant Plasus.

CARD/EPISODE AND MATRIX TAKEDOWN

Wars and injustice down throughout Earth history show abundant need for the transformative work of humanitarians. Famous examples of the **Knight of Cups** in action include Abraham Lincoln whose American presidency in the 1880s oversaw the abolition of slavery; Gandhi who advocated non-violent resistance in order to overthrow British occupation of India; Nelson Mandela who campaigned against apartheid in South Africa before dismantling it as the country's first black head of state; Archbishop Desmond Tutu who furthered Mandela's anti-apartheid and human rights activism; and Martin Luther King, the black pastor who championed civil rights during the racial turmoil in the USA of the 50s and 60s. These afflicted nations and societies have their parallel in the plight of the oppressed miners on Ardana. Kirk's intervention in their struggle for civil rights and social equality typifies the efforts of a saviour **Knight of Cups** to act as a catalyst for change, in this case against the wishes of the planet's single authoritarian ruler. While Plasus' fellow sky-dwellers enjoy the fruits of the Troglytes' labours the latter work like slaves in the dark, dirty, oppressive conditions of the caves. Most are resigned to their life of toil and misery but a few hardy Disruptors among them vigorously resist and fight against the Stratos regime. Plasus stands in equally stubborn resistance against their demands. Both parties occupy opposite ends of a polarized stand-off with no end in sight. Underground freedom fighters using knives and guerrilla tactics struggle ad infinitum against the sky-dwelling leadership armed with phasers and electronic torture machines.

There are many parallels on present day Earth. We have seen the Matrix controllers step up their Orwellian One World Order plan with ever-increasing surveillance, censorship and legislation. The Covid false flag saw politicians revert to 20th century dictatorial ways in so-called democracies like Canada, USA and Australia. Even with the Matrix fatally scuppered, the surviving elites remain determined to try to keep the 99% functioning according to social programming, expanding government powers and shrinking freedoms. The opposite of freedom is control that eclipses values of the heart and ignores respect for personal sovereignty. The public are kept ignorant or dismissive of their innate freedoms under Natural Law by a continuing hush hush policy on this vital aspect of life. Another area of cover up and secrecy is the dual-use capability of modern technologies. Street-lighting, 5G, smart meters and mRNA 'vaccines' can double up as frequency and biological weapons with the potential to dumb down, maim or kill. Meanwhile, technologies that include med beds, replicator machines and hyper fast transport are denied to all on Earth while used as standard fare on the Moon and Mars in the Secret Space Program. With the brain drain of the 1950s/60s, tens of millions of scientists and those with desired skills were taken into space to form an advanced breakaway civilization. This two-tier situation parallels that on Ardana with the Troglytes in their poverty contrasting with the technologically advanced sky-dwellers. As on Ardana, qualities of freedom and citizen care on Earth have, up till the 2020s been tightly constrained within a Matrix society headed by a Service To Self minority of super-rich elites dictating to the impoverished majority.

A humanitarian **Knight of Cups** raising awareness and living standards on a prison planet such as Ardana or on corrupt Earth has his work cut out for him. On both planets, the oppressed peoples need to relearn how each of us is a sovereign free being. The gas given off by the zenite blocks the full range of consciousness on the surface of Ardana, just as ubiquitous Matrix-ordained censorship and propaganda does on Earth. It might be thought that the solution on both Ardana and Earth is to fight for Natural Law and equality, exposing the evil actions of psychopaths running the show. But what mentality would violent struggle come from? It would come from the same fearful mentality that gave rise to the problem and so would only perpetuate it one way or another. A different level of consciousness is required if either Troglytes or humans are to cease manifesting their own enslavement. Kirk's expedient is to raise awareness of the zenite gas that keeps the miners living in a low frequency mindset. His initiative with the masks will help them return to living in their own true vibrations.

AFTER THE TAKEDOWN
The solution on Earth runs parallel to that on Ardana. The control grid of Matrix AIs has come down as have many hidden weapons threatening humanity with global disaster. The clean-up operation continues, coordinated by Earth Guardian Kim Goguen. At the same time all of us need to be our own **Knight of Cups** strengthening community life and heart-centred ways. Returning to living in the pure energies of compassion, kindness and empathy will enable us to come from a higher consciousness in all we perceive and do. This will consolidate the new energy and further reconnect us with the soul. The result will be ceasing to cooperate with our own enslavement, using our energies in more harmonious ways for the good of all.

76. IGNORANCE

Raising our vibration will help disperse ignorance instilled in us by the system

Episode 76 'The Savage Curtain' correlates with the **2 of Swords**; both are themed around observation and data-gathering to dispel lack of knowledge; or negatively, lazy ignorance.

THE CARD
At the centre of an empty oval created by two curved swords is a resplendent, idealized image of a flower. The large luxuriant head with its eight petals and eight burgeoning leaves (eight in the Tarot standing for perfection) seems more an icon of a flower than a realistic object painted from life. The dreamlike, florid, exaggerating tendency of the imagination is suggested. 2 in Tarot numerology is the degree of gestation and accumulation due to its alignment with Arcanum No. 2, The Popess who incubates spiritual purity. Swords means the mind. The **2 of Swords** therefore denotes a mind or intelligence in a stage of development, one that is incubating or accumulating information or understanding. This may come through reading, study or contemplation. Another aspect is the ability to entertain an idea or theory without either accepting or denying it. Whatever is or is not in mind is allowed to simply gestate. Being essentially passive, the **2 of Swords** is about observing or recording mental phenomena

in all their variety, whether passing thoughts, conjectures, ideas, theories, fantasies, reveries or verbalizations.

Reversed, the mind is over-receptive to impressions or to one's own imagination. Lazy forming of opinions or assumptions may be replacing bona fide research. The mind may be overly distracted by a hectic lifestyle, intrusive thoughts, daydreams, unruly imagination or random guessing. Or there may be troubling bewilderment or lack of knowledge, or ignorance borne of arrogance. Poor mental preparation or difficulty concentrating are also indicated.

'THE SAVAGE CURTAIN' PREMISE
Trial by combat is forced upon Kirk and Spock by a powerful but ignorant alien who believes this will prove which of good or evil is the stronger.

CONTEXT
Coercion, War.

IGNORANCE
Enterprise crew are mystified by an apparition of Abraham Lincoln appearing out in space. Whatever it is comes aboard in physical form and incredibly seems to be the real Lincoln. He invites the baffled and uncomprehending Kirk and Spock down to the unknown planet below. There they find waiting for them Yarnek, a rock-like creature . Yarnek wants to learn from humans from Earth and from other planets about human concepts of good and evil and which is stronger in reality and practice. To this end Yarnek forces Kirk and Spock to partake in a trial by combat between two sides of four humanoids each. The absurd contest only proves the alien's ignorance of sovereignty and Natural Law. The good side, including Kirk and Spock, after mind games and physical combat, prevail over the bad side. Yarnek allows Kirk and Spock to return to the Enterprise, although confessing he has learnt little from the experiment.

CARD/EPISODE AND MATRIX TAKEDOWN
As multi-dimensional beings we exist at multiple levels, from Body Mind up to non-dimensionalized Infinite Awareness. To ignore the levels of our identity above Body Mind would keep us limited to mere cogs as we were in the former Matrix era. At the Body Mind level we experience thoughts, feelings and decodings of the five senses. By contrast, higher levels of our identity give us access to the unbounded multi-dimensional universe. All of us are capable of perceptions far transcending the restrictive Matrix mindset. Some achieve states of samadhi or undergo mind expansion through drug

or ayahuasca experiences, or meet with discarnate beings, or travel out of the body cosmically or inter-dimensionally. Near Death Experiences and Remote Viewing further enable the discovery of new vistas of knowing. But without experiencing such things ourselves, how do we relate to them? The matter becomes one of uncertainty or incomprehension, sometimes called nescience, till we have learnt to transcend merely rational thought.

The **2 of Swords** represents this restricted state of 3D knowing and of patiently accumulating information. Social conditioning being all-pervasive in a 3D world, many people simply dismiss higher or expanded states of awareness and so remain stuck in **2 of Swords reversed** states of crass denial or ignorance. Educational curicula that still follow the defunct Matrix model take no account of the ability of the young to function above the Body Mind level. To escape the control narrative may necessitate home schooling or special independent education known as micro-schooling. Children taught to integrate higher levels of their identity could open the way to universal telepathy - interacting with each other purely mentally. That ways lies mental release and freedom for the incarnated soul. More and more scientists validate abilities such as telepathy, so to confine our awareness to the Body Mind represents an abdication of our multi-dimensional nature. And until we make the leap as a species to thinking and operating multi-dimensionally we will continue to limit our perceptual abilities and remain pawns of the system. The landing party suffers likewise at the hands of the Excalbians. This rock-like race seems not only ugly but particularly lacking in knowledge and understanding, confined mentally to a mixture of the **2 of Swords upright** - nescience - and **reversed**, ignorance.

The crew experience bafflement right at the outset. Abraham Lincoln floating in space? Incredible. But Yarnek's bafflement is more philosophical. He feels a lack of knowledge and understanding of the nature of good and evil among worlds of the humans. So he effectively kidnaps Kirk and Spock to observe them in a confrontation between humans from different planets and times in history. By having them combat each other he hopes to learn which of good or evil is the stronger quality. His lack of knowledge may be one of nescience, but the design of his test shows total disdain for universal personal sovereignty under Natural Law. His test, like that of the Vians utilizing torture in Episode 66, can only cause the participants gross physical harm. Added to this is more **reversed 2 of Swords** ignorance - that of the most basic principles of scientific method.

Scientists would want to carry out dozens of such experiments before drawing conclusions by induction. The data Yarnek stands to gather from just one test can only be woefully inadequate. He tests the humans by forcing them to engage in a crude war game. But why should goodness have anything to do with superiority at physical combat? Would not Kirk and Spock be more likely to demonstrate qualities of goodness by peaceful rather than aggresive means? The 'good' beings joining with Kirk and Spock are Excalbians shapeshifted, or holographically projected, into Lincoln and the renowned Vulcan peacemaker, Surak. True to form, Surak advocates adopting a strategy of peace. As he observes: 'Perhaps it's our belief in peace that is actually being tested.' As Gandhi said, a good person will resist an evil system with his or her soul. Although non-compliant, Gandhi advocated peaceful non-cooperation not conflict or war as sought by Yarnek.

The 'bad' side play a game of hide and seek and deception. They capture peace envoy Surak and use him to lure the good side into the open. 'Help me, Spock!' goes up the repeated cry of anguish, apparently from Surak. Kirk and Spock hiding among the rocks are faced by painful uncertainty, the **reversed 2 of Swords**. Is it Surak? Should they try to rescue him? But Surak has been killed, his voice impersonated. In the end, the evil side succumb or run off. Kirk and Spock end up lone survivors while Yarnek professes to have learnt little. He acknowledges that while the evil ones fought for power, Kirk fought for the lives of his crew, and that evil withdraws when forcibly confronted. The two humans are released and leave the planet. The Excalbians meanwhile are no wiser than before, still mired in the **2 of Swords** - nescience and lack of understanding.

AFTER THE TAKEDOWN

It's no accident that children's education, TV, mainstream media and mass entertainment operate at levels not much higher than Yarnek's. Such limits on intelligence keep the population unaware of knowledge that would otherwise enable us to leap forward in our evolution as a race. It will happen, the question is, how quickly. Meanwhile, a little research using books or on-line resources exposes the nature of false flags and deceptions like the triggerings of revolutions and world wars, Aids, 9/11, the Covid fraud or toxic vaccines. The numbers of people waking up to these travesties are multiplying. The MSM and the official narrative will increasingly give way to the truth. People freeing themselves from a lifetime of induced ignorance - the **reversed 2 of Coins** - are gaining from the courage to take the red pill, diving down a rabbit hole that plunges very deep. Even if we disdain to do any independent research, at higher levels of consciousness we know the truth. But few know that they know. As we raise our vibration, this will change. The inner knowing of truth and goodness will lead the way.

77. CLOSURE

Heart and mind operating in a new harmony will restore peace to emotional endings

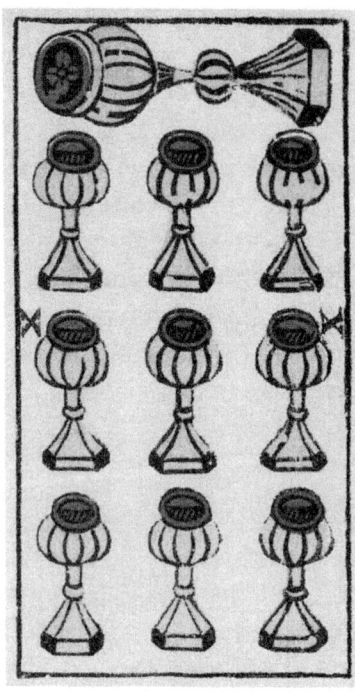

Episode 77 '**All Our Yesterdays**' correlates with the **10 of Cups**; both are themed around closure or lack of it following the ending of relational or emotional experience.

THE CARD
The emotional or relational journey is over at the stage of the **10 of Cups**. Nine Cups are neatly, uniformly arranged, all poured full. Satisfaction or satiety has been reached, no further need or desire remains for emotional involvement or for a relationship to continue. Neither is there the impulse at this juncture to start on the road of a new such venture. A large 10th Cup lies across the nine others as if emphatically closing a chapter and preventing further emotional involvement for the time being. This 10th Cup is sealed and facing left, the past. Peace has been made with pre-existing friends, acquaintances or loved ones. They can be happily forgotten and no longer desired or worried over in any way. Nostalgia is absent. Instead there is a sense of contentment and freedom from emotional ties. Or there is the sense of needing to be alone or out of relationship for a while.

When **reversed**, the small Cups are detrimentally downturned, pouring out energy variously experienced as sorrow, regret, remorse, unfulfilled desire, unfinished business, loneliness or obsession. The sealed 10th Cup now faces the future. Being sealed, it represents resistance or inability to move on to fresh experience. Emotions to do with an ending are running too high. Or emotions are there to give but there is no one to share them with; only the pain and waste of loneliness is felt.

'ALL OUR YESTERDAYS' PREMISE
Spock emotionally regressed, and a beautiful young woman exiled to solitude, fall deeply in love before having to be prematurely, devastatingly separated.

CONTEXT
Relationship, Multi-Dimensionality.

CLOSURE
Kirk, Spock and McCoy beam down to a planet about to perish in a solar explosion. They find no one in need of rescue, only Mr Atoz the warden of a portal to other space-times in the planet's history where its inhabitants have taken refuge. The trio, while perusing his index system of these other times and places, accidentally stumble into two different realities. Kirk goes to one, similar to 17th century Britain, and Spock and McCoy to another, a 5,000 year old frozen wasteland. All feel marooned and anxious to return. But with the throwback in time Spock has himself regressed to more primitive Vulcan ways of being. A beautiful, sympathetic woman appears in Spock and McCoy's cave. Spock, now with the instincts of a primitive Vulcan, falls in love with her. She too came through the portal but long before, having been exiled by a cruel dictator to this arctic wilderness, effectively solitary confinement. Now having found each other, Spock and Zarabeth desire to stay together as lovers. The dilemma facing everyone is that this method of time travel requires previous 'preparation'. Without it, Spock and McCoy unknowingly have only hours to return before they die in that wilderness. With 'preparation', in the case of Zarabeth, she will die if she returns to the future. Kirk manages to return with the help of another exile he met who had incarcerated him for witchcraft. Atoz helps Kirk to set about bringing back the other two, but the currently more atavistic Spock feels torn between returning without closure or staying by Zarabeth's side. McCoy cannot return without Spock and badgers him. Spock becomes aggressive but finally abandons the lovely, lonely Zarabeth. The two rejoin Kirk and beam back up to the Enterprise to just barely escape the nova.

CARD/EPISODE AND MATRIX TAKEDOWN

The landing party's experiences here reaffirm the message of the very first episode - the vulnerability the Matrix instilled in us that can be called the Emotional Matrix. Strong desire, worry, indignation, nostalgia, regret, sorrow ... such mixtures of feeling and mind can wreak havoc and cause unending suffering. When mind or emotions overly predominate we lose connection with our heart. We fall into the kind of trance state in which we are most enslaved. We lose multi-dimensional consciousness of ourselves and identify completely with a limited, suffering, transient Body Mind. Emotions that can upset us intensely and prolongedly often link with the **10 of Cups** - states such as separation, abandonment and the pain of loneliness. But Tarot Cups do not stand only for emotions and relationships. They also stand for the heart itself, our unconditionally loving real self that exists beyond personality and duality. But rarely do relationships emanate exclusively from feelings of the heart such as kindness, empathy, compassion, joy or generosity. Relationships usually involve a lot more than just the heart. People often find their supposedly most loving relationships tainted by attitudes of the mind including projections, desires, fears, and shoulds and shouldn'ts. The principle of 'I will love you if ...' sets conditions. Moreover, transitory physical attraction and declining levels of sexual desire set us up for disaffection. And fear of loss, abandonment or betrayal can provoke controlling behaviour, suspicion, anger or resistance. Such is the case with Spock and Zarabeth.

Like any romantic attachment, theirs is heavily influenced by desires of mind and body. Would Spock have fallen so deeply and suddenly in love with Zarabeth were it not for her beauty, the first thing he exclaims about her? Such vulnerability to the Emotional Matrix is heightened by his reversion to the instinctive ways of a 5000 years less evolved Vulcan. On Zarabeth's side, how influenced is she by the need to unite with a partner to stave off loneliness? When a relationship bases itself too much on needs or desires of the Body Mind as opposed to the heart we can be certain that some degree of emotional pain will attend its dissolution. This will almost certainly present a separating couple with emotional difficulties during the subsequent period of readjustment to single living. Spock and Zarabeth therefore both undergo trials in line with the **10 of Cups reversed** but both come through with honour.

The challenge of the **10 of Cups**, of emotional transcendence, is shown in one of the most heartbreaking, despairing moments in all of Star Trek. Spock must give up Zarabeth in order to leave the planet as McCoy insists. Spock's painful emotional struggle rises to a peak causing him to push

McCoy into the portal near the mountain while holding himself back with Zarabeth. But the portal fails to work for McCoy alone since he and Spock had come through together. Spock finally relents and re-enters the portal with McCoy, leaving behind the sad, lonely Zarabeth who trudges back through the snow to her cave of exile. We can all too easily imagine her **reversed 10 of Cups** sorrow in the aftermath of her passionate affair. How does Spock feel after returning to his normal time and sanguine, rational self? On emerging from the portal he stays in a brood. He asks to be relieved of the weight of McCoy's stare, reassuring the doctor that he has returned to himself. 'Yes, it happened,' Spock admits unsentimentally. 'But that was 5000 years ago. She's dead now, dead and buried long ago.'

Does Spock truly feel closure? During his time in the cave, a regressed Spock provoked by an insult from McCoy leaps at the doctor to grip him savagely by the neck. 'I don't like that,' says Spock in fury, 'I don't believe I ever did. Now I'm sure!' Spock was acting as his ancestors would but there is the implication that Vulcan though he is, he feels past emotional experiences just as we all do. Unhealed emotional traumas suffered in childhood or in past lives leave their mark on us. McCoy and Kirk also have their own issues with the emotional hold of the past, the **10 of Cups**. Neither feels peaceful or resigned in the timeframe of exile. Both resist the change and make efforts to return to the life they always had. In such an extraordinary situation it is of course right and natural to resist change and seek a return to the usual life. Spiritual gurus with a superior mindset like to advocate living by unconditional acceptance. They advise us to warmly allow whatever happens to us. But this is misguidance. A sincere 'No' when in the best interests of the one being threatened far outweighs an insincere and holier than thou 'Yes' or saying nothing. Ultimately both ourselves and the situation itself will decide, as we saw with The Lover Episode, No. 29 Amok Time, and as we see here.

AFTER THE TAKEDOWN
It was the Capernaum AI on the 3rd level of the astral that maintained a dark overlay around everyone's aura, preventing a full 1-to-1 natural connection with each other. With this AI removed along with the rest of the AI Matrix, the exaggerated pain of forced connection, separation and loneliness will leave us. We will connect out of heart to heart resonance, no longer suffering the kind of trauma at separation afflicting Spock and Zarabeth. We will relate out of a sense of peace and mutual acceptance, freedom and spontaneity, without fear of consequences. Coming from the heart, we will always know the right thing to do and in the most compassionate way.

78. INTEGRATED MIND

An integrated mind combines logic with feeling, imagination, intuition and other higher senses

Episode 78 **'Turnabout Intruder'** correlates with the **Queen of Swords**; both are themed around the ability to organise and integrate all components of Mind without distortion or attachment.

THE CARD
A sensitive-looking woman facing left holds aloft a slightly tilted, red sword like an antenna. The sword symbolizes her focus of attention, a kind of receiver-transmitter of information. Its red colour denotes the passionate nature of her perceptions and beliefs. This Queen caresses a swollen or scarred abdomen. She looks thoughtful, as if deploying several components of the mind at the same time. We can infer a sound reasoning ability attentive to explanations and understandings. She can translate and synthesize data from multiple components of the mind and clearly, passionately communicate her observations. These other components, explored in such Episodes as 5, 28 and 40 include according to Ashayana Deane in the Voyagers books, the 'dream self', the 'astral self' and the 'intuitive self'. Thus, with her ego functioning healthily, the **Queen of Swords** creates a lively picture out of perceptual data from all components of the mind, lower and higher. Her ego takes responsibility for being the

conscious director of energy, thus allowing her to think and express herself with multi-dimensional awareness and balanced functioning.

A **reversed Queen of Swords** implies a mind operating in an unbalanced, isolated or distorted manner. The intellect may be limiting itself to the five senses of Body Mind as scientists are wont to do. Thus it views data from the intuitive, emotional or astral selves as unreliable and suspicious causing it to cut itself off from these other aspects of awareness. Mental attachment then sets in. Outwardly this may cause the person to appear ignorant, stubborn or narrow minded to the point of wilfulness, ruthlessness or vindictiveness. Or the intellect may be jumbling up impressions causing a chaotic and disturbed gestalt. The person may then appear to others as hysterical, neurotic, duplicitous or capricious. Their reasoning mind or ego personality may not recover its balance until emotional aspects of the being are healed and cleared including past hurts and traumas such as hinted at with this Queen nursing her belly.

'TURNABOUT INTRUDER' PREMISE
An ex-lover of Kirk resents both him and her thwarted career as a starship captain. As an imposter, she takes over his body and captain's position.

CONTEXT
Femininity, The Adversary, Deception, Justice.

INTEGRATED MIND
Kirk and McCoy answering a distress call from Camus II find a colony of scientists killed by radiation. One of only two survivors, Janice Lester, was a lover of, and fellow trainee with Kirk at Starship Academy. As Kirk attends to her, she reminds him of her thwarted ambition to be a starship captain, feeling resentful that only men could qualify. While off-guard, Kirk is immobilized by her and subjected to a mind transfer technology. Having taken over Kirk's body, the mentally deranged Janice can now fulfil her ambition. She has only to get rid of Kirk who remains alive in her old body, albeit semi-conscious. Kirk (J) tries to kill Janice (K) but circumstances won't allow it. He resolves to have Janice (K) removed to another planet ostensibly for treatment but becomes over-wrought on the issue, showing outward signs of impetuousness, faulty leadership and suspect decision-making. McCoy can find nothing wrong with Kirk (J) but Spock through a mind meld with Janice (K) confirms to his own satisfaction that a mind transfer has taken place. Before Spock can help further, Kirk (J) accuses Spock and McCoy of mutiny. Kirk (J) convenes a hearing at which Janice (K) speaks of Kirk (J)'s temperamental unsuitability for captaincy and Kirk (J)'s hatred of having

been a woman. Kirk (J) declares Spock and McCoy guilty of mutiny and hysterically passes the death sentence. The mind transfer starts to weaken and in desperation Kirk (J) arranges with his accomplice, the other surviving scientist Dr Coleman, to immediately kill Janice (K) by lethal injection. But the conspirators are overpowered by their captives and in the frenzy the mind transfer breaks down completely. Back in her own body, Janice Lester devastated and tearful, is led away for mental and emotional reintegration.

CARD/EPISODE AND MATRIX TAKEDOWN

The Matrix thrived on individuals operating exclusively out of the Lower Self: the ego or dualistic Body Mind cut off from Higher Self. As seen in Episode 5, the Body Mind swings between docilely conforming or hatefully fighting, rendering it easy prey to Matrix manipulation. If confined to this level we live indulgently and decadently in attachment and perilously in reactiveness. Like Janice Lester we become spiritually locked in unconsciously changing 'I's (or self-identities) based on attachment to any of a patchwork of 5-sense based beliefs, desires, values, fears or memories of past experience. Brooding on her perceived victimhood and emotional hurts turns Janice into a bitter and vengeful **Queen of Swords reversed**. Feeling herself a woman wronged - ostracized and under-valued - she develops an intense mental and emotional attachment to this wounded self-identity. 'Your world of starship captains doesn't admit women,' she tells Kirk. A function of the Matrix, now disabled, was to subjugate women. One as intelligent as her and with the necessary training would have every right to feel frustrated by Matrix influence and traditional values propagating women as breeders and men as workers. For Janice is still the beautiful and all-creative Sacred Feminine but, like Queen Elaan in Episode 67, blocked and disempowered. But this is not her only grudge. After starting a relationship with Kirk that slid into stress and conflict, Kirk left her. For this she has never forgiven him. She acquires an even more maladjusted self-identity that feels impelled to murder her colleagues. She then engenders a full body swap with the man who was her lover and is the holder of the job she craves. Stealing into Kirk's body and captain's chair, she hijacks the Enterprise having lost herself completely in dominant and uncontrollable self-identities based on desire, perceived victimhood and vengeance.

Janice's inner chaos and imbalance, her disturbed sub-conscious mind, made for the kind of traumatized state specifically sought by Matrix mind controllers. Handlers of MK Ultra victims know we are not one but many, and that by manipulating a traumatized mind it can be subsequently reorganized in a plethora of ways. CIA mind controllers employed within secret government projects like MK Ultra, Kruger and Monarch knew that the mind can be split into as many as 2,197 separate compartments or 'alters' (13x13x13). Subjects could then be triggered by code words and other signals to carry out hostile assignments, message-carrying, sexual services or drug smuggling with no conscious knowledge of what they are doing. At a collective level, populations can be and are mass mind-controlled using a range of techniques. The infamous Tavistock Institute helped to develop programming by television, MSM propaganda, cumulative fear mongering, EMF frequencies and subliminal advertising. All depends on the level of conscious awareness of the victim, whether an individual or a population. An awareness traumatized or limited to the 5-sense-only worldview becomes prime fodder for Deep State handling, easily conditioned or triggered by false flags and other Illuminati psyops. Such an awareness is Janice's, attached to scientific materialism and her disappointments in career and love. This all breaks her sanity leaving her a **Queen of Swords** pitifully **reversed**.

Kirk by contrast remains conscious and perceptually clear even when mentally transferred into Janice's body. He/she shows the qualities of an impeccable **Queen of Swords** as Witness for The Defence during Spock's court martial. Kirk as Janice cooly tells the court of the motives and psychology of Janice driving her vindictive and desperate actions. Displaying a fully conscious, integrated mind he/she uses logic alongside emotional and intuitive faculties coordinated under soul level guidance - compassion. Janice in Kirk's body by contrast acts increasingly frenetically, becoming in Scotty's words 'red-faced with hysteria'. Living in hatred, and in her shame of victimhood, she becomes victim of her own narrowed perceptions and obsessions. She breaks down completely, sobbingly muttering 'kill him!' A loving hug and sympathy from Dr Coleman augurs good care to come for this very distraught and traumatized **Queen of Swords reversed**.

AFTER THE TAKEDOWN
Freed from AI manipulation and Deep State exploitation, individuals and populations will reconnect safely with all aspects of Mind. The reasoning mind will no longer be so prone to negative attitudes, rigid, dualistic thinking and congealed self-identities. According to Voyagers I[1], the reasoning mind or ego has the function of directing and integrating all aspects of Mind including the knowing of the heart and the awareness of the soul. The Matrix takedown will enhance our ability to integrate the rational mind with the other levels of our identity. The kind of drama created by Janice Lester acting out of her wounded shadow side will dissipate, as we learn to function with all of our Mind integrated.

[1] Deane, A., (2002) *Voyagers Vol. I*. Columbus, NC: Granite Publishing, p. 140-1

7

CONCLUSION

The conclusion is Star Trek told from beginning to end as a single prophetic story. With the story refracted through the Tarot we gain a magical perspective on the epochal changes currently dawning on Earth. Star Trek is a prophecy like the quatrains of Nostradamus or the parchments of the gypsy Melquiades in which he foretold the town of Macondo living 100 Years of Solitude. The Star Trek prophecy tells of the liberation of humanity from an encroaching global tyranny that has been in the works for thousands of years. Bringing this right up to date, we have been brought to the edge of the abyss by a Deep State gunning for nuclear war, viral plague, fake vaccines, economic ruin, EMF attacks and artificially triggered earthquakes and tsunamis, all planned for 2023-24. Another prophecy, the Four Horsemen of the Apocalypse from Revelations was the playbook of the Deep State occultists: War, Pestilence, Famine and Death. The resulting chaos and devastation was intended to clear the ground for Agenda 2030 and the AI-powered dystopian Great Reset. Man would be turned into machine and Earth eventually connected by wormhole into the anti-matter dark universe. The solar system, the galaxy, then the entire light side of the multiverse would follow, sucked into a black hole as food for the Archons. Ashayana Deane in Voyagers 2 calls them the Fallen Angels of the Phantom Matrix.

It was an all or nothing game plan with the Deep State acting as puppets of the Fallen Angels - demons and negative aliens made up of competing factions of Anunnaki, Zeta and Draconian races from many different star systems. As Kim Goguen reported on February 3rd, 2023, the denizens of the Dark Side had rejected the agreement in the Law of One to maintain balance between the Dark and the Light. It wanted it all. Source had no alternative therefore but to extinguish the Dark Side itself. A zero tolerance policy has since been implemented allowing for termination of all individuals and forces making war on humanity. The non-repairable humans staffing the political Matrix have been sent back to Source plus any and all remaining Deep State insiders who might still plot terrorism. Goguen has halted any funding from the Global Repository managed by her going to Illuminati globalists for their projected Third World War. The Omega Matrix has been wholesale taken down and as she said: 'not just in AI systems ... but also in the multiverse. He (Source Consciousness) decided because the Dark Side was unable to create balance anywhere, they must all die, it must go ... so we are going to experience what everybody calls the Golden Age.'

The story of this epic transition is told as encoded prophecy in Star Trek's three seasons from 1966 to 1969. The encoding makes the prophecy both open and hidden. To decode it here in this book I have related the 78 episodes to the mystical images of the 500 year old Tarot, specifically the anonymous Tarot de Marseille. The precise match in number between the images and the episodes is the signifier of the correlation and the key to its interpretation. The episodes show the wondrous voyages of a ship and its crew across the far reaches of space. Decoded by their correlation with the cards, they tell of the trends, events and challenges fated to befall us on Earth before, during and after the dismantling of the Matrix. A curse on our species lasting 300,000 years has been lifted. We are transitioning to an incredible new Earth, inaugurating a glorious Age of Light.

Star Trek prophesied this in many ways - allegorically, literally, allusively, fragmentarily. The 78 episodes consisted of adventures that are fictional and unworldly. They nevertheless tell of the very real and literally down to earth drama now propelling us into a new Dawn of Man. It will not be the reawakened Dawn of Man eulogized in Kubrick's 2001 A Space Odyssey, with an astronaut representing the human race transformed by an AI monolith into a sinister threat to the planet. The course of the Star Trek prophecy bears out not the triumph of inorganic AI but the end of its attempted coup. Time and again, dictatorial, malign and soulless forces are encountered, confronted and reasoned with or terminated. The prophecy begins right inside us with the Emotional Matrix flaring up in our sexual passions and desires (Eps. 1 and 2). As well as healing the traumas involved we must deal with uncontrolled ego and desires for power (3). Emotional and mental healing will come, not by repressing our unresolved issues but by allowing and understanding them (4). Thus we will integrate the lower and higher aspects of our psyche (5) for example in always doing business ethically and honestly (6).

The threat, continues the prophecy, of a transhumanist dystopia will recede (7). The AI systems making a fearfully obedient, mind-controlled herd out of humanity will be shut down *(8 and 9)*. This came true with the 2023 shutdown of the Omega Matrix. This will quicken our destiny to become a space-faring civilization *(10)*. Those who blocked or sabotaged our development will face justice *(11)* regardless of the usual defence of following orders *(12)*. Humanity's disempowerment *(13)* will inevitably continue for a few years longer. For how long will depend on our self-belief as master creators of our reality *(14)* allied to our willingness to drop mistaken ideas *(15)* about the fallen Matrix and false perceptions of our ego-driven elites *(16)*. This is our initiatory test *(17)*, a rite of passage for mankind that will synchronize us with the new positive timeline *(18)* for the entire multiverse. Our Matrix leaders will be exposed as the morally bereft parasites they are. We are the leaders now *(19)*, no longer herded zombies *(20)* drifting along at the beck and call of power-crazed, unscrupulous narcissists *(21)*. Our weakness historically was the dark essence installed in us by an AI system keeping us at odds with each other *(22)* and within ourselves, addicted to the highs of emotional fixes *(23)* and the lows of death and destruction wrought by wars, conquest and revolution *(24)*. We would support wars against invaders and tyrants to supposedly end war *(25)*, having no true peace within, nor any sense of our multi-dimensionally connected selves and universe *(26)*. And yet loving goodness has, and always will, remain in the human heart. The ideals of peace, freedom and humanitarian service *(27)* will live on and they will blossom as we transcend Matrix darkness. As in the heart, so in the mind, with the information age and new contact with superconsciousness inspiring in us higher solutions and perceptions of freedom *(28)*.

The prophecy continues in Star Trek's second season, addressing cultural strictures governing love and marriage *(29)* and religion and worship *(30)*. Restrictions will come down as we take back our power. New challenges will then come into view, first and foremost with AI systems *(31)* continuing to be propagated despite the demise of the Omega AI. An AI-run world would enable would-be tyrants *(32)* to take full control of humanity. Digital, inorganic AI is the problem, an Archonic, soul-less technology that seeks to parasitically dominate, control and regulate all forms of life *(33)*, failing which it will seek to destroy and consume it *(34)*. Subscribing to an exclusively materialistic worldview and lifestyle *(35)* downgrades consciousness of our spiritual nature. It's then a short step to accepting inorganic technologies such as brain-computer interface that can turn us into controllable AI-human hybrids *(36)*. It's essential then to forego excessive material acquisitiveness and, as in relationship, to restore love as the basis of our being *(37)*. As we ascend in consciousness we will rid our relationships of fear of loss, gaining the ability to radiate and be love without needing others to love us back *(38)*.

With the halfway point reached in the Tarot-Star Trek correlation, the prophecy enters some of the darkest areas of our former Matrix condition. Crises whether accidental or engineered will need us to first ask far-reaching questions (39) about our systems and leaders. A calm but courageous approach will work best to ensure we stay out of Lower Self traps such as despair, apathy or obsession (40). This will help us deal with the dark demonic spirit of Wetiko (41). Murderous impulses and violence manifesting in dominating, parasitical behaviour will have to be tackled. They can emerge anywhere as in the sabotage of ecosystems (eg with GMOs) in the cause of competition or profit (42). At its worst, Wetiko becomes a system itself - inhuman, exploitative, all-encompassing - as in the global and interplanetary trade in humans for beastly purposes (43). The exploitative financial system too will have to be reformed (44). AI's involvement in this as in all human life will increasingly resemble an invasion. Represented by the giant amoeba in space eventually eliminated (45), malign AI too will be eliminated implies the prophecy. Yet another threat will have to be dealt with - international tension, war and chaos covertly fomented by outside parties using superior weaponry for bribery or conquest (46). In the field of medicine too, selfish interests, lies and deception, as with Big Pharma will come up for overhaul. Treachery here, manifesting in profiteering, corruption and cheating (47) will be rooted out. Most infiltrated and debased of all will be government (48). The prophecy points to deceitful and totalitarian governance masquerading as benevolent rule and this too will be addressed and reformed.

The correlation goes on to predict what we would become like if separated from our divine Source. This of course was the goal of the Omega AI and is shown by the Kelvan men (49) who despise nature and sensual life yet paradoxically cannot resist losing themselves in it. Selfish desire overcomes another spiritually lost man (50) who incites whole races to trample on each other's freedoms and mutual rights. Such regressiveness is the result of people inhabited and overrun by the Omega system now shut down. This shutdown is again prophesied in Kirk pulling the plug on the AI system installed on his starship (51). The termination is shown as absolutely imperative. With this now accomplished on Earth a mass awakening can at last proceed. People will see our Deep State oligarchs as every bit as immoral, arrogant and elitist as the rulers of the Roman Empire (52). Or they will see the taboos, restrictions and misunderstandings of their hidebound cultures as similarly repressive (53). Nobody is to be humanity's sole rescuer, this has been much voiced in disclosure circles. But two catalyzing Knights will coordinate forces of positive change. The correlation predicts a Knight of Swords (Ground Command Kim Goguen in our real world) using knowledge and expertise to prevent nuclear war (54) and to help avert a crippling reset for humanity as a dumbed down, farmed race (55). Quite the contrary, we are all of us destined for intelligence increase (56) as the lifting of the Omega system takes effect. Our best attributes will be needed to cleanse our world of corruption and restore the ecosystem starting at community level (57). With Omega no longer provoking inner demons (58) that blocked connection to our true, divine selves (59) we will see the former Matrix dreamworld (60) for what it was - a feeding pool for energy parasites and vampires from the darkest astral realms possessing our human elites (61).

With freedom from mind control, global restoration will involve us coming more from the heart (62). Equally importantly, we must patiently work to free ourselves from a tholian web (63) of dictates, mandates and security states. The psychopathic and patriarchal plutocracy (64 and 65) masquerading as democracy will collapse and with it the victimhood (66) of the people propping up the pyramid of control. New systems will be put in place that respect the Empress-friendly holistic, natural and organic fabric of life (67). This is predicted to provoke a last stand by the residual demonically possessed and crazed oligarchs (68). In their insane desperation they will resort to blatant fearmongering, deceit and legislation in attempts to forestall their own demise. They will fan the flames of war (Russia v Ukraine etc) in hopes of bringing on Armageddon (69). They may attempt to raise again the spectre of pandemic plague in last ditch efforts at global panic and genocide (70). All such abuses will fail along with their ultimate hope, digital AI dictatorship

Conquest by AI will backfire as organic AI instead comes to the fore, a benign technology with divine attributes of compassion and respect for biological life (71). We had all been invaded mentally and astrally (72) by an inorganic network of etherical implants, overlays, pheromones and dark essence. The most invaded and dehumanized of all were our ruling elites addicted to power and obscene wealth (73). They are bankrupt now in every way. There will be no more need for idealistic and escapist cults and movements (74) that were doomed to failure while the Matrix lasted. In its wake we will henceforth develop the vision and the will to be our own saviours as per the second heroic Knight, the Knight of Cups (75). Freely sharing uncensored information and truthful reporting, people en masse will grow out of the ignorance (76) cultivated by the mainstream media's lies, distractions and propaganda. People will come together shaking off their induced sense of separation, isolation and vulnerability (77). The prophecy ends as it began, with inner trauma coming up to be healed. Thus we will integrate heart and mind (78) for rebuilding our world in a healthy, balanced consciousness.

RESOURCES

I hope you have enjoyed reading about the amazing correspondences between the Tarot, Star Trek and the Matrix. I apologise for the lack of references, footnotes and index. In their place here are the main sources of information, knowledge and wisdom underpinning my findings presented in *Tarot Trek*. They will provide in-depth explanations where I have been remiss in doing so.

BOOKS

THE TAROT

The Way of The Tarot Alejandro Jodorowsky, Destiny Books, 2004. Jodorowsky has done brilliant, ground-breaking, in-depth research into the reconstruction and meanings of the Tarot de Marseille. *Tarot Trek* follows Jodorowsky's rationale for interpreting the Major and Minor Arcana.

The Marseille Tarot Revealed Yoav Ben-Dov, Llewellyn Publications, 2017. Another wise and comprehensive guide available in English. Some meanings attributed to the cards may differ from Jodorowsy's and mine. Each to their own. Written in English by a one-time student of Jodorowsky.

STAR TREK

The Encyclopedia Shatnerica Robert Schnakenberg, 2008. I use Schnakenberg's listed order for the 78 episodes. His book provides an entertaining, witty guide to the life and work of the charismatic William Shatner, including of course his Captain's contribution to Star Trek.

The Star Trek Compendium Star Books, Allan A. Sherman, 1983. An early and thoroughly reliable episode guide with plenty of background information on the cast and production.

THE MATRIX

CONSPIRACY

Everything You Need To Know But Have Never Been Told David Icke, David Icke Books, 2017. One of Icke's essential, all-inclusive guides to the inner and outer workings of the whole Matrix. All his books are recommended. They provide a prescient and painstakingly researched analysis of the duping of humanity and the path back to sanity.

Beyond Esoteric Brad Olsen, CCC Publishing, 2021. In the wake of Icke comes Brad Olsen, equally as pithy and even more wide-ranging in his analysis. A cornucopia of hard-edged truth and research lifting the lid off a Pandora's Box of occult, ET, Illuminati, cosmic, quantum, mind-bending conspiracies. Includes the American Nazis, the DUMBS, the reptilian control of Earth, and the SSP with its colonizing of the moon and Mars and beyond.

TranceFormation of America Cathy O' Brien, Reality Marketing, 1995. Cathy along with the man who rescued her, Mark Phillips, tell the story of her appalling experiences in MK Ultra mind control programs and covert service as a White House sex slave and message carrier. Exposes first hand the shams we call politics, government and justice as never before or since. One of the greatest, most important books of the 20th century.

Geoengineered Transhumanism Elana Freeland, independently published, 2021. A comprehensive and vastly informative yet lucid account of, as its sub-title proclaims, 'how the environment has been weaponized by chemicals, electromagnetism and nanotechnology for synthetic biology.' If you ever doubted the evil intent of the Matrix architects and the necessity to overhaul the whole anti-freedom system, this book will replace your doubts with conviction.

180° Feargus O'Connor Greenwood, ind. publ., 2021. A comprehensive guide to the topsy turvy world of the malign Matrix with truth everywhere inverted and the people disempowered. This book incisively shows, as the subtitle goes, how to 'unlearn the lies you've been taught to believe'.

COSMIC AWARENESS

Voyagers 1 & 2 Ashayana Deane, Granite Publishing (Vol.1) and Arhayas Productions (Vol.2), 2002. Probably the most authoritative of all accounts detailing humanity's true cosmic origins, evolutionary progress and labyrinthine involvement with ET and higher dimensional guardians and intruders. Volume 1 sets out the structure of the 15-dimensional universe and our own corresponding 15 levels of multi-dimensional identity - these in addition to the non-dimensionalized level of Infinite Self or Unity Consciousness spoken of by spiritual gurus. Volume 2 addresses in great depth galactic history, multi-dimensional physics and ascension mechanics.

Defending Sacred Ground Alex Collier, 1996, available as a free download at alexcollier.org. Alex tells of his contact experiences with Andromedans and their perspectives on cosmic history, human consciousness and Draconian and other ET involvement in Earth affairs. Much of this information has helped provide a foundation for study of these subjects right up to the present day.

A Gift From The Stars Elena Danaan, 2020, independently published. Elena's wonderful books and YouTube channel cover metaphysical, cosmic, ET and spiritual topics relevant to raising human consciousness. Here in this remarkable guide to over 100 ET civilizations she reveals how they look, behave and interact with Earthlings. Her main source of information is the Pleiadian human Thor Han based on Venus. He makes no secret of the reptilian-built Matrix on Earth and the scuppering by the Cabal of diplomatic efforts by the Galactic Federation to free our planet during the 1950s.

We Will Never Let You Down Elena Danaan, 2021, independently published. Elena recounts her experiences off-planet with emissaries of the Galactic Federation of Worlds. They take her to an Ashtar Command base on Jupiter, to Ganymede and to Venus. We learn of humanity's enemy the Deep State in league with malevolent reptilian and grey races from the Orion system and Andromeda such as the Ciakkhars (Draco reptilians), the Nebu and the vicious Maytrei. On humanity's side are extremely powerful, benevolent forces. 'We will never let you down' is their message.

Ceres Colony Cavalier Tony Rodrigues, 2021, independently published. Tony served in the Dark Fleet from 1988 to 2001. Tony lived on the moon, Mars and Ceres and worked as a cargo handler delivering supplies all over the solar system and beyond. His knowledge of inter-galactic human trafficking and SSP slavery is 1st hand, making his trail-blazing testimony one of historic importance.

Rebel Gene Kerry Cassidy, independently published, 2020. Subtitled Secret Space and the Future of Humanity, Kerry distils her decades of research into the Secret Space Program, ETs, UFOs and cosmic conspiracies into one probing, provocative book. She draws on interviews with an amazing number of cosmic experiencers, insiders and whistleblowers, disseminated through her website projectcamelotportal.com

Insiders Reveal Secret Space Programs & Extraterrestrial Alliances and **Galactic Federations Councils & Secret Space Programs** Dr. Michael Salla, 2015 and 2022, Exopolitics Institute and Consultants. Michael Salla's many books are a lucid and readable guide to the formation and development of the SSP and other ET/human programs on and off planet. 'Insiders Reveal' compares the testimonies of three authoritative whistleblowers including Corey Goode and Randy Cramer. Salla's books, podcasts, exopolitics website and internet seminars provide detailed and lucid reporting of humanity's emergence into the cosmic community ongoing since the early 20th century.

The Ascension Mysteries and **Awakening In The Dream** David Wilcock, 2016 and 2020, Dutton. Wilcock has been a popular teacher and presenter of cosmic and SSP info through his talks and interviews on Gaia TV and YouTube and in books such as these two. He elicits and distills the testimonies of insiders and whistleblowers on Matrix topics ranging from ancient mysteries to time travel, stargates, advanced technology, the Cabal and the Draco. He comments extensively on Law of One channelings.

Alien World Order and **Dark Fleet**, Len Kasten, 2017 and 2020, Bear & Company. Kasten presents the facts missing or glossed over in conventional histories of the world. The story of mankind's experience under Matrix control comes across loud and clear. Kasten illuminates the part played by off-planet races referred to in our mythologies and ancient religious texts but covered up or ignored by historians conforming to the official narrative. He thus follows in the tracks of William Bramley's groundbreaking book The Gods of Eden, with special focus on intrusive Draco reptilians and their recent prime collaborators, the German Nazis.

PSYCHOLOGY & SPIRITUALITY

In Search of The Miraculous P.D. Ouspensky, 1950, Routledge & Kegan Paul. The definitive exposition of the teachings of Greek-Armenian mystic G.I. Gurdjieff. *Tarot Trek* owes a debt to Ouspensky's book for its revealing of Third Force as the hidden pre-requisite in the manifestation of any phenomenon. Another of Gurdjieff's crucial teachings included in *Tarot Trek* is the multiplicity of small 'I's (and indeed 'alters') existing in us at Body Mind level. This lack of a permanent and unchangeable 'I' at the basic level of 3D accounts for the fragmented identity of our Body Mind and our vulnerability to Matrix programming and mind control.

Columbus and other Cannibals Jack D. Forbes Seven Stories Press, 1979. A brilliant book, short, easy to read, yet devastating in its analysis of the human psyche vis-à-vis the impulse to do evil, known to the Native Americans as Wetiko. Forbes decries the European conquest of the Americas with its imposition of empires and authoritarian societies on pain of depravity, barbarity, slaughter and slavery in the cause of Matrix expansion. This quest to make Satan the God of humanity makes shocking, shame-inducing reading. And yet Forbes shows us a positive path out of this sickness of the human spirit, a path of beauty, love, peace and wisdom.

OTHER MEDIA

unitednetwork.tv Kimberly Ann Goguen is Earth's ambassador to the Universal Council, Guardian of the planet and Ground Command. She took over from the corrupt Marduk in the 2010s, a fact confirmed (without actually naming her) by Penny Bradley. Claiming the highest security clearance on the planet, Goguen coordinates the clean-up, restoration and rebalancing of global finance and politics. She works with higher dimensional assistance to end abuses of power by the Deep State. United Network News presents thrice weekly updates of her progress together with uncensored news from around the world particularly that gathered impartially by Field Messengers. Anyone is invited to participate as a Field Messenger, offsetting the propaganda, distractions and censorship endemic of the mainstream media.

energeticsynthesis.com and **ascensionglossary.com** Lisa Renee disseminates a wealth of spiritual and cosmic knowledge in these gigantic websites. Detailed analyses emphasize our multi-dimensionality including the functioning of our soul and related higher levels of our being.

davidicke.com The website for David Icke reports assiduously on global Deep State activity and mankind's quest for freedom.

whatonearthishappening.com The website of Mark Passion contains hard-hitting video presentations that break down to their fundamentals such subjects as Natural Law, Good and Evil, Truth and Deception. He examines the Dark Occult having once been a Satanist himself and its manipulations including psy-ops, corrupt institutions and psychological warfare.

Penny Bradley Nacht Waffen Pilot This is the YouTube channel for Penny Bradley a former fighter pilot for the Draco in the SSP. Her information is lucid, authoritative, crucial and often unsettling in its honesty.

Awakening Cosmic Reality Show This is Ileana Kapulnik's YouTube channel. A veteran of the SSP, she has done three 20-year terms of service, much of it in biological labs on Mars. Her presentations and interviews on spiritual, scientific and metaphysical subjects are incisive, sincere and lucid.

ACKNOWLEDGEMENTS

I would like to thank Maria my late mother for her constant, loving encouragement to finish this book. And for their generous support my late father Patrick and stepmother Rosy, and in the Netherlands my cousin Liena. Others who gave invaluable help when needed were Désirée Ickerodt who selflessly created the beautiful cover and Lydia and Francis who added expert assistance. Antoinette and Joana did very kind secretarial work and Kevin contributed conversations and book gifts that helped extend my research far and wide. Numerous other friends also helped or encouraged me including Nick K, Jane, Charlotte and Kate. To all, my heartfelt thanks.

Printed in Great Britain
by Amazon

Notes from higher grounds

An altitude training guide for endurance athletes

Dr Elizabeth Egan